The Brass Band of the King

Armenians in the Modern and Early Modern World

Recent decades have seen the expansion of Armenian Studies from insular history to a broader, more interactive field within an inter-regional and global context. This series, Armenians in the Modern and Early Modern World, responds to this growth by promoting innovative and interdisciplinary approaches to Armenian history, politics, and culture in the period between 1500 and 2000. Focusing on the geographies of the Mediterranean, Middle East, and Contemporary Russia [Eastern Armenia], it directs specific attention to imperial and post-imperial frameworks: from the Ottoman Empire to Modern Turkey/Arab Middle East; the Safavid/Qajar Empires to Iran; and the Russian Empire to Soviet Union/Post-Soviet territories.

Series Editor
Bedross Der Matossian, *University of Nebraska, Lincoln, USA*

Advisory Board
Levon Abrahamian, *Yerevan State University, Armenia*
Sylvie Alajaji, *Franklin & Marshal College, USA*
Sebouh Aslanian, *University of California, Los Angeles, USA*
Stephan Astourian, *University of California, Berkley, USA*
Houri Berberian, *University of California, Irvine, USA*
Talar Chahinian, *University of California, Irvine, USA*
Rachel Goshgarian, *Lafayette College, USA*
Ronald Grigor Suny, *University of Michigan, USA*
Sossie Kasbarian, *University of Stirling, UK*
Christina Maranci, *Tufts University, USA*
Tsolin Nalbantian, *Leiden University, the Netherlands*
Anna Ohanyan, *Stonehill College, USA*
Hratch Tchilingirian, *University of Oxford, UK*

Also Published
The Politics of Naming the Armenian Genocide: Language, History and 'Medz Yeghern', Vartan Matiossian
Picturing the Ottoman Armenian World: Photography in Erzerum, Kharpert, Van and Beyond, David Low

Ararat in America: Armenian-American Culture and Politics in the Twentieth Century, Benjamin F. Alexander

The Armenian Diaspora and Stateless Power: Collective Identity in the Transnational 20th Century, Talar Chahinian, Sossie Kasbarian, Tsolin Nalbantian

The Armenian Social Democrat Hnchakian Party: Politics, Ideology and Transnational History, Bedross Der Matossian

The Brass Band of the King

Armenians in Ethiopia

Boris Adjemian
Translated by G. M. Goshgarian
With a foreword by Khachig Tölölyan

I.B. TAURIS
LONDON • NEW YORK • OXFORD • NEW DELHI • SYDNEY

I.B. TAURIS
Bloomsbury Publishing Plc, 50 Bedford Square, London, WC1B 3DP, UK
Bloomsbury Publishing Inc, 1359 Broadway, 12th Floor, New York, NY 10018, USA
Bloomsbury Publishing Ireland, 29 Earlsfort Terrace, Dublin 2, D02 AY28, Ireland

BLOOMSBURY, I.B. TAURIS and the I.B. Tauris logo are trademarks of Bloomsbury Publishing Plc

First published in 2013 in France as *La fanfare du négus: Les Arméniens en Éthiopie (xixe–xxe siècles)* by Boris Adjemian

First published in the UK, 2024
Paperback edition published 2026

Copyright © Boris Adjemian, 2024
English translation © G. M. Goshgarian, 2024
Foreword © Khachig Tölölyan, 2024

Boris Adjemian has asserted his rights under the Copyright, Designs and Patents Act, 1988, to be identified as Author of this work.

G. M. Goshgarian has asserted his right under the Copyright, Designs and Patents Act, 1988, to be identified as Translator of this Work.

The English translation of this book has been made possible by a grant from the Armenian General Benevolent Union (AGBU), and by a grant from the National Association for Armenian Studies and Research (NAASR) and the Knights of Vartan Fund.

Cover design: Adriana Brioso
Cover image: The Royal Brass Band of Ethiopia and Negus Täfäri, 1929.
(© Bibliothèque Nubar de l'UGAB, Paris)

All rights reserved. No part of this publication may be: i) reproduced or transmitted in any form, electronic or mechanical, including photocopying, recording or by means of any information storage or retrieval system without prior permission in writing from the publishers; or ii) used or reproduced in any way for the training, development or operation of artificial intelligence (AI) technologies, including generative AI technologies. The rights holders expressly reserve this publication from the text and data mining exception as per Article 4(3) of the Digital Single Market Directive (EU) 2019/790.

Bloomsbury Publishing Plc does not have any control over, or responsibility for, any third-party websites referred to or in this book. All internet addresses given in this book were correct at the time of going to press. The author and publisher regret any inconvenience caused if addresses have changed or sites have ceased to exist, but can accept no responsibility for any such changes.

A catalogue record for this book is available from the British Library.

Library of Congress Cataloging-in-Publication Data
Names: Adjemian, Boris, author.
Title: The brass band of the king : Armenians in Ethiopia / Boris Adjemian.
Other titles: Fanfare du Négus. English | Armenians in Ethiopia
Description: London ; New York : I.B. Tauris, 2024. | Series: Armenians in the modern and early modern world | Includes bibliographical references and index.
Identifiers: LCCN 2024006271 (print) | LCCN 2024006272 (ebook) |
ISBN 9780755648412 (hardback) | ISBN 9780755648450 (paperback) |
ISBN 9780755648436 (epub) | ISBN 9780755648429 (ebook)
Subjects: LCSH: Armenians–Ethiopia–History–20th century. |
Armenians–Ethiopia–History–19th century.
Classification: LCC DT380.4.A7 A3413 2024 (print) | LCC DT380.4.A7 (ebook) | DDC 963.2/00491992–dc23/eng/20240329
LC record available at https://lccn.loc.gov/2024006271
LC ebook record available at https://lccn.loc.gov/2024006272

ISBN: HB: 978-0-7556-4841-2
PB: 978-0-7556-4845-0
ePDF: 978-0-7556-4842-9
eBook: 978-0-7556-4843-6

Series: Armenians in the Modern and Early Modern World

Typeset by Newgen KnowledgeWorks Pvt. Ltd., Chennai, India

For product safety related questions contact productsafety@bloomsbury.com.

To find out more about our authors and books visit www.bloomsbury.com and sign up for our newsletters.

Contents

List of Maps	viii
List of Figures	ix
Foreword	xi
Preface to the Second Edition	xiv
Introduction: From the Sedentary Logic of Diasporas to the History of the Nation-State	1

Part 1 The Genesis of an Ethiopian Political Tradition

1	Wax and Gold: The Royal Brass Band's Unsuspected Political Role	11
2	The Long Time of an Event: From Jerusalem to Jerusalem	23
3	Of Immigrants and Kings: Toward a Symbolic Nationalization	39

Part 2 The Friendship of Kings

	Prelude to the History of a Collective Memory	73
4	A Past that Engages the Present: The Social Stakes of the Making of Heroes	91
5	Menelik's Armenians: From the Welcome as Experienced to the Sedentarization of an Imaginary	121
6	*Arba Lejoch*: The Logical Apotheosis of a Collective Destiny	155

Part 3 The Sedimentation of the Ungraspable

7	From Threshold to Interstice: A Space of Decompartmentalized Sociabilities	173
8	Between Stateless Person and Citizen: The Belle Époque of a Legal Gray Zone	185
9	Between *Färänj* and *Habäsha*: Representations and Social Practices of Hybridity	199

Conclusion	213
Notes	217
Unpublished Materials	247
Bibliography	251
Index	265

Maps

0.1 Main places of origin of Armenian emigrants to Ethiopia　　　xvii
0.2 Main places of Modern Ethiopia and neighboring countries mentioned in this book　　　xviii

Figures

3.1 Khosrov and Aghassi Boghossian with a portrait of their godfather, *Däjazmach* Balcha, around 1907 — 58
3.2 Laying the first stone of the new Basilica of Saint George in Addis Abeba, 1905 — 61
3.3 Laying the first stone of the Menelik II Hospital in Addis Abeba in 1909 — 62
3.4 Letterhead of Krikorios Boghossian — 63
3.5 Mass celebrated in 1928 in *Ras* Täfäri's and Empress Zäwditu's presence by Archbishop Kevork Arslanian, come from Istanbul to attend the foundation ceremony of the Surp Kevork Armenian church in Addis Abeba — 67
3.6 Colonel Khosrov Boghossian's funeral — 68
3.7 Burial of Colonel Khosrov Boghossian in the Surp Hagop Armenian cemetery in Addis Abeba — 68
4.1 Boghos Markarian, known as "Hayrig" — 93
4.2 Dikran Ebeyan, Menelik's goldsmith — 97
4.3 "Serkis Terzian, Abyssinian grandee, former governor of Geldeissa" — 104
4.4 "First locomobile in Ethiopia" — 110
4.5 Abraham Terzian receiving the title of *azaj* conferred by Emperor Menelik — 111
5.1 Sarkis Terzian and his wife Vartuhi, née Yazedjian — 122
5.2 Krikorios Boghossian, Dikran Ebeyan, Sarkis Terzian, and Gron Khachadurian, photographed in Djibouti in 1903 — 127
5.3 Sarkis Terzian's "passport," issued by Menelik — 131
5.4 Signature accompanying the dedication of a portrait of the emperor — 133
5.5 Reproduction of the "handwritten signature of Negus Menelik II" — 134
5.6 Sarkis Terzian, his wife Vartuhi, and their two children, Yervant and Avedis, welcomed by the Armenian community — 136
5.7 On the porch of the Boghossian family's house in Aqaqi, around 1908 — 138
5.8 Picnic with *Nägädras* Haylä Giyorgis — 138
5.9 Picnic with Dikran Ebeyan — 139
5.10 "Matheos Karamanian 1912 [*sic*], Joiner" — 145
5.11 Portrait of Levon Yazedjian in the uniform of Addis Abeba's "police chief" — 153

5.12	The royal brass band at the head of Levon Yazedjian's funeral procession	154
6.1	The brass band of the Araradian Orphanage in Jerusalem	158
6.2	The forty children before their departure for Ethiopia	161
6.3	Crown Princess Mänän visiting Patriarch Yeghishe Tourian in Saint James Armenian Monastery in Jerusalem	162
6.4	Crown Princess Mänän and Archbishop Papken Guleserian in Jerusalem, accompanied by Araxi Yazedjian	163
6.5	The brass band of the *arada zäbäñña* and its conductor Garabed Hakalmazian	164
6.6	Photomontage commemorating the royal brass band, 1929	167

Foreword

When Boris asked me to write a Foreword for the English translation of his wonderful book, I was flattered but also faced a predicament. I assumed he asked me because I have some expertise in the study of the Armenian diaspora, and this book does contain, among other things, a history of diasporic Armenians in Ethiopia. It begins by offering a fascinating account of pre-diasporic travel by Armenian clergy on religious missions, and by merchants and artisans seeking economic opportunity. It then traces an increase in the number of migrants due to a variety of factors, followed by an account of the arrival of survivors of the Armenian genocide. The major actors of the emerging community include businessmen, artisans, clergymen, and, notably, similar figures who also function as state officials and as intermediaries between Ethiopia, the Ottoman Empire, and the West. Between the second and third quarters of the twentieth century, the population rises to around 1,200; eventual decline led to its current near-disappearance, reportedly with fewer than seventy-five people. All these matters I could discuss competently.

But the book offers much more. In episodic fashion, Boris narrates how he carried out his research, which extended far beyond the archive and the library: "The bulk of my research took place far from any academic framework," he writes. Living near and in Ethiopia, he interviewed at great length the oldest surviving members of the community, one of whom died three weeks after his last conversation with Boris. This required him to work as an anthropologist as well as a historian. For me, one of the most engaging features of the book is its account of detective work conducted in old homes, teacup in hand, eliciting the memories of communal elders. Research is rarely so dependent on timeliness—archives wait patiently; the old Armenians of Ethiopia were dying as Boris was saving the past they had lived and built.

Of course these accounts of the past needed to be recorded, reported, and interpreted. Boris tells us that "the history of the Armenians in Ethiopia" as narrated by the elders "fascinated me from the first work I did on it, for it had an epic dimension, was peopled with heroes and heroines, was woven of delightful anecdotes sometimes bordering on the fantastic, between the memorable exploits of pioneers with long white beards, the bon mots become proverbial, of an ancestor, and the bedroom secrets of Menelik's palace." As he listened, he realized it was not merely anecdotal memory that he was encountering. He was hearing repeated versions of the "grand narrative" of the community, a collective story.

So this marvelously rich book weaves together three strands: the history of the enterprise and agency of various Armenians who also became Ethiopians; a suspenseful account of how the scholar and researcher carried out his work, talking a little and listening a lot to the elderly who recounted a particularly potent but quite partial narrative of intimate relations between three generations of Ethiopian emperors and empresses and their Armenian subjects; and finally a thoughtful and astute analysis of the making of Ethiopia as a nation-state by a dynasty of African Christians whose clerical elite had maintained respectful relationships with the Armenian Church and the Patriarch of Jerusalem from the late Middle Ages on—a state that needed and could accommodate a small number of Armenians who were not just middlemen but also intermediaries in a larger diplomatic and political field.

Never slackening the pace of his analytical narrative, Boris weaves these three elements together, creating a vivid, intricate account that is as complex as it needs to be but never confused or confusing. The book is not the customary account of a diasporic community, with the usual exhaustive itemization and enumeration of public institutions (churches, schools, political factions, charitable foundations, cultural organizations). It is instead the exemplary reconstruction of how "the social formation of communities and the fabrication of collective identities" happened in the Abyssinian/Ethiopian context. Setting out from a seemingly limited and special case, Boris does not permit the specificity of the case to limit his analytic reach. He depicts the making of an Armenian community in the context of a far larger, simultaneous enterprise, that of the making of the Ethiopian nation and state. He then ventures the possibility that he is "considering the possibility of generalizing the results."

This aspect of the book is a revelation in its handling of both matter and method. The reader is strongly engaged by the account of an emerging Christian African indigenous "empire," first beset and threatened at every step by Muslim rulers at the periphery of emerging Ethiopia, then by Italian colonizers and West European diplomats and entrepreneurs, whose deeply prejudicial Orientalism is captured brilliantly as they condescend to and dismiss both Ethiopian nobles and Armenian intermediaries. His demonstration of the ways in which European condescension deployed the term "Levantine" (used for Armenians and Greek merchants above all, but also Arabs) both to misperceive and misrepresent the role of non-European whites like the Armenians in the service of Ethiopia's new state both taught me and elicited my admiration. I knew Edward Said well for decades (we attended the same school in Egypt, at different times, and for a semester shared an office); I won't hesitate to say that he would have particularly applauded the exploration of Orientalism in Boris's book.

This narrative of the interwoven trajectories of the making of the Ethiopian imperial state and nation, alongside the construction of the community of diasporic Armenians in Ethiopia, successfully combines sympathy for Armenians and Ethiopians with detached, dispassionate analysis. The episode that gives the book its title refers to the future Ethiopian Emperor's decision to bring a band of forty Armenian orphans of the genocide from Jerusalem to Ethiopia at his own expense, along with a conductor. The exploration of the not at all glamorous role of that band/orchestra in the next five years is by turns delightful and sobering. Boris lays bare the future emperor's ambition to equip Ethiopia, the first and only African entity to become a member of the League of Nations in 1923, with features of Occidental statehood, including a national anthem composed by the conductor of that band.

Here and elsewhere, diasporic Armenians play a key though always subordinate role. When *Ras* Täfäri Mäkonnen was crowned Emperor Haile Selassie of Ethiopia in 1930, prominent Armenians were everywhere in his retinue, as Boris documents. It was an event that resonated in the Black Atlantic, above all Jamaica, leading to the Rastafarian movement; in a grudging Europe; and among the Armenian community favored by the emperor, one of whose subjects I came close to becoming; when I was a child, my father was offered an enticingly remunerative contract to become principal of the Armenian school of Addis Ababa, the capital. I would then have become a later elder informant for Boris to embed in this splendid book, which manages the nearly impossible, developing a warm and humane narrative that is nevertheless astutely analytical and skeptical when it must be, weaving out of anecdotal specificity a potent, exemplary account of the making of one diasporic community and one nation in a still-colonial, oppressive world.

Khachig Tölölyan (Emeritus Professor, 2021)
College of Letters, Wesleyan University, Middletown CT 06459
Cofounder and coeditor, *Pynchon Notes* (1979–2009)
Founder and editor, *Diaspora: A Journal of Transnational Studies* (1991–2020)

Preface to the Second Edition

It has been about ten years since the first French edition of La fanfare du négus was published. On the occasion of this new English edition, appearing more than twenty-five years after I began, in 1997, to do fieldwork in Ethiopia, I feel the need to say, in a few words, what this book is and what it is not.

I am often asked what led me to study the Armenian presence in Ethiopia. The question is usually tinged with astonishment, so improbable does the subject seem to those who ask it. The courses I took at university were initially oriented toward history and what goes by the name of "African Studies"; as I went along, I decided to specialize in Ethiopian history. At the time, like others studying under Bertrand Hirsch's guidance at the Centre de recherches africaines in the Rue Malher in Paris, I was attracted by the Ethiopia of monks, manuscripts, and churches built in caves, at a time when the histories of the Middle Ages and, a fortiori, the Ancient world seemed to me to be the most beautiful, because they were the hardest to decrypt. It was almost by proceeding backwards, and yielding to the friendly insistence of several colleagues working on Ethiopia, that I took up the study of the history of the Armenians in Ethiopia in the framework of a master's thesis that was supposed to lead on to graduate studies and the preparation of a doctoral dissertation. In the end, I did not embark on a Ph.D thesis—at least not right away.

I was afraid of wandering too far from the terrain of the Ethiopian high plateaus that had fired my imagination, afraid of finding myself marginalized in a restricted academic environment in which this subject could only seem peripheral. And I was right. Yet I have never regretted setting off on this Armenian tangent. The history of the Armenians in Ethiopia fascinated me from the first work I did on it, for it had an epic dimension, was peopled with heroes and heroines, was woven of delightful anecdotes sometimes bordering on the fantastic, between the memorable exploits of pioneers with long white beards, the bon mots, become proverbial, of an ancestor, and the bedroom secrets of Menelik's palace. The bulk of my research took place far from any academic framework, during the free time of the amateur historian I was on the way to becoming. Nevertheless, many years after conducting my research in the field, I finally prepared and defended the doctoral thesis that I had long put aside. My dissertation was jointly directed by Gérard Noiriel, of the Paris École des Haute Études en Sciences Sociales, a pioneer of the historiography of immigration to France, and Alessandro Triulzi of the University L'Orientale in Naples, an outstanding connoisseur of the historiography of the societies of the Horn of Africa. The intellectual rigor of these two dissertation directors, together with their considerable open-mindedness—one has to have an open mind not to be frightened off by a subject as strange as the history of a brass band made up of Armenian orphans in Ethiopia—made me aware of the interest that the subject held for people other than myself, or, in other words, of its heuristic value. It was as if the Armenians of Ethiopia had suddenly burst into the academic lecture hall. This doctoral work allowed me to refine my way of perceiving the subject: a singular case, and a limit case at that, of the integration of a diasporan community into its host society. At the juncture of historical anthropology and *socio-histoire*—attentive to the relations that are constantly being woven between the individual and the collective—my work allowed me to rethink, in a decentered fashion, the construction of the foreign and the national in Ethiopia, from the nineteenth to the mid-twentieth century.

Ever since I was charged with directing one of the Armenian diaspora's richest libraries, the AGBU's Bibliothèque Nubar in Paris, I have been well aware that many other sources—drawn, for the most part, from the inexhaustible reservoir of the Armenian press—could have enriched the course of this narrative. What is more, the bifurcation of my different fields of study has distanced me for good and all from Ethiopia's languages, and when I was doing my field work, I had neither access to Ethiopian archives nor the time to conduct oral interviews outside Addis Abeba's small Armenian community. Yet, despite all, my initial fieldwork proved fundamental, because the interrogations that served as the guiding thread for the present study derived from the field, not from a corpus of archives ready and waiting to be exploited, as is often the case where the work of historians is concerned. The conditions under which this research was carried out led me to privilege certain witnesses at the expense of others, to attach more importance to such and such, when an investigation with pretensions to objectivity should, in theory, have multiplied standpoints, interlocutors, and sources, the number of which, here, was fairly limited. Thus it was the circumstances and time of the investigation, not just my methodological choices, which led me to attach such importance to the work that I carried out in collaboration with Avedis Terzian, who is cited at great length in the following pages. It is, in other words, obvious that other people, at other times, and with other abilities would have proceeded differently than I did.

For the reasons I have just laid out, this book is not the history of a community. Readers will not find in it all the names and events that fashioned that history. This is because it was not written by a son of the community, because I had a different perspective. Nor have I sought to cover the whole of the period that runs from 1945 to the present, and, in particular, the evolution of the community after the 1974 Ethiopian revolution.[1] My research is nevertheless based on interrogations that emerged from the field at the very end of the 1990s. It is sustained by testimony that was itself shaped by the historical transformations of the latter half of the twentieth century. It sets out from the present in order to interrogate the past and, in this sense, it covers, in my view, a long historical period running down to the moment I carried out my work.

Thus the present book intends to go well beyond the bounds of a monograph in the classic sense of the term. The critical gaze that I bring to bear in these pages on the historiography of the foreign presences in Ethiopia still seems valid to me today, even if a number of studies have renewed that historiography in the past few years.[2] The critical gaze I mean also applies to Armenian historiography and the scholarly literature on diasporas. In the one case as in the other, my ambition has been, via the decentering provided by the Armenian case in Ethiopia and setting out from an apparently insignificant case study, to pose transversal questions about the construction of collective identities and nation-states in the contemporary period by way of a problem-history (*histoire-problème*) that goes beyond the narrow framework of specific cultural domains, be they Ethiopian or Armenian.

All research in the social sciences is a form of militancy, a colleague once told me. This militancy answers to both scientific and social stakes. For me, it was first of all a matter of saving a history from oblivion, of managing to gain a hearing for the anecdotes and hearsay that constitute its charm yet do not ordinarily have the good fortune to find a place in the history books ("because they are outside history," as Avedis Terzian would put it). Because my research is based on fieldwork, it also implies a form of commitment to the object it studies. My work connected me to the Armenian community in Ethiopia, from whose active support I benefited, and to several of its members, in Addis Abeba or that other diaspora formed by the Armenians of Ethiopia in exile in Europe, the United States, Canada, or elsewhere. The period in which I began and carried out my initial fieldwork in Addis Abeba, between 1997 and 2000, allowed me to collect, *in extremis*, testimony which is essential to grasping the lived experience of the descendants of the Armenian immigration in Ethiopia, but which has long since disappeared. In this sense, I was very lucky to arrive in time. I think, nonetheless, that luck was not just on *my* side: for Avedis Terzian, who was to die three weeks after our last interview, at the age of ninety-seven, officially (perhaps over one hundred, in reality), the transmission of this past murmured on the edge of oblivion and its inclusion in a written history were so essential that our collaboration represented an unhoped-for opportunity. This book is greatly beholden to him.

I am happy that it can now live a second life thanks to its translation into English by G. M. Goshgarian. I am immensely honored by the foreword Khachig Tölölyan has generously accepted to write for this edition. I thank Bedross Der Matossian for inviting me to publish this work in the series that he founded, and the Armenian General Benevolent Union (AGBU) as well as the National Association for Armenian Studies and Research (NAASR) and the Knights of Vartan Fund for Armenian Studies for the generous support that made it possible to finance the work of translation. My particular gratitude goes to Anita Anserian (AGBU) and Marc Mamigonian (NAASR) for their personal involvement in this project. I also thank the Armenian Community in Ethiopia and the people who counted along this road, some of whom are no longer with us: the Nalbandian family, especially Mary, Vartkes, Salpi and Elise; Francis Falceto; Anna, Robert and Alain Marcerou; Mikael "Mike" Melake; Jacques Bureau; Mihreteab Tsighe; Antranig Agopian; Marie and Mesrob Sarkissian; Gennet Boghossian; the Kherbekian Family; Kevork Hintlian; Father Hovsep Behesnilian; Michel Aghassian; Agnès Ouzounian; Berhanou Abebe; Elsa Ferrari; Éric Van Lauwe; Denis Gérard; Anne Bolay; Estelle Sohier; Antonio Fiorente; Bertrand Hirsch, Gérard Noiriel, Alessandro Triulzi, Alban Bensa, and Michel Bruneau; and Raymond Kévorkian and Vahé Tachjian.

I dedicate this book to the memory of my father and his family.

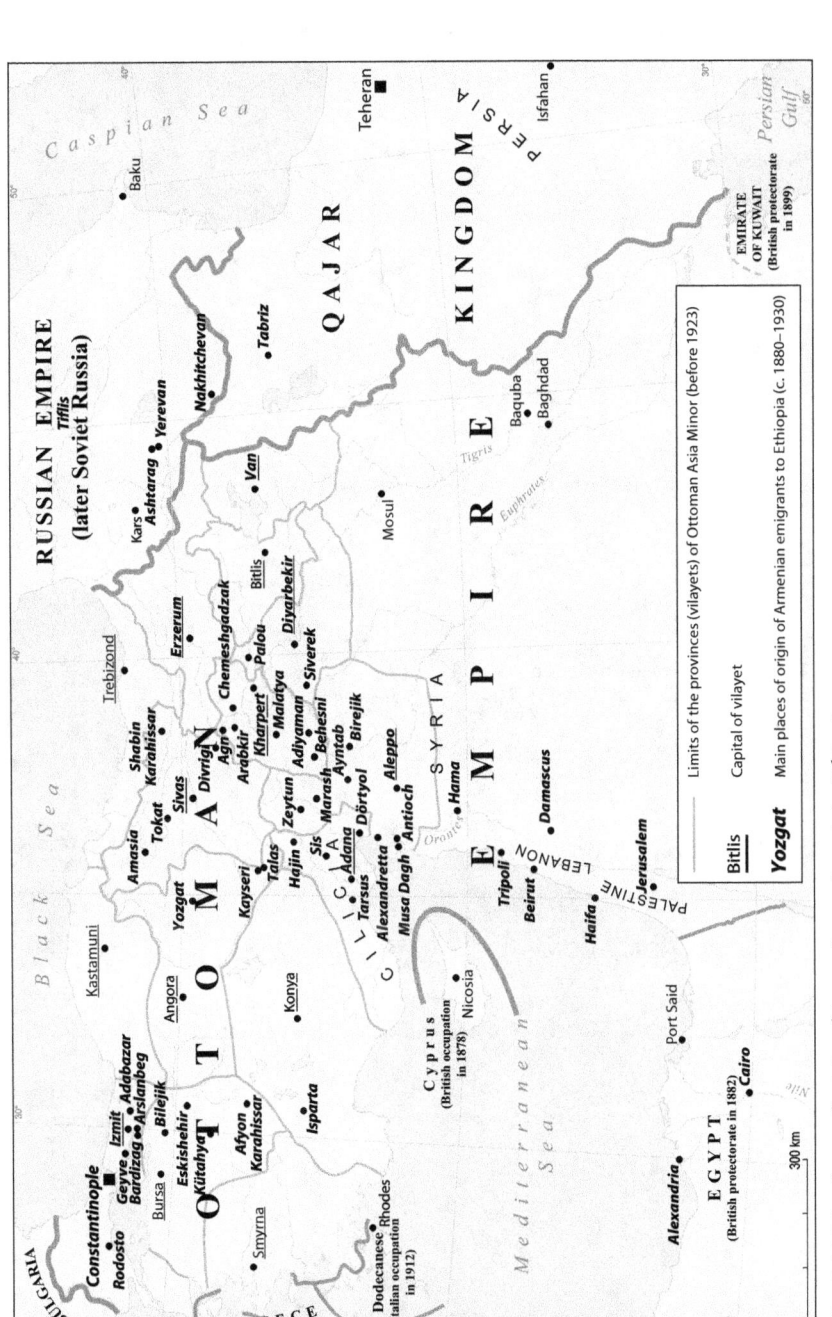

Map 0.1 Main places of origin of Armenian emigrants to Ethiopia

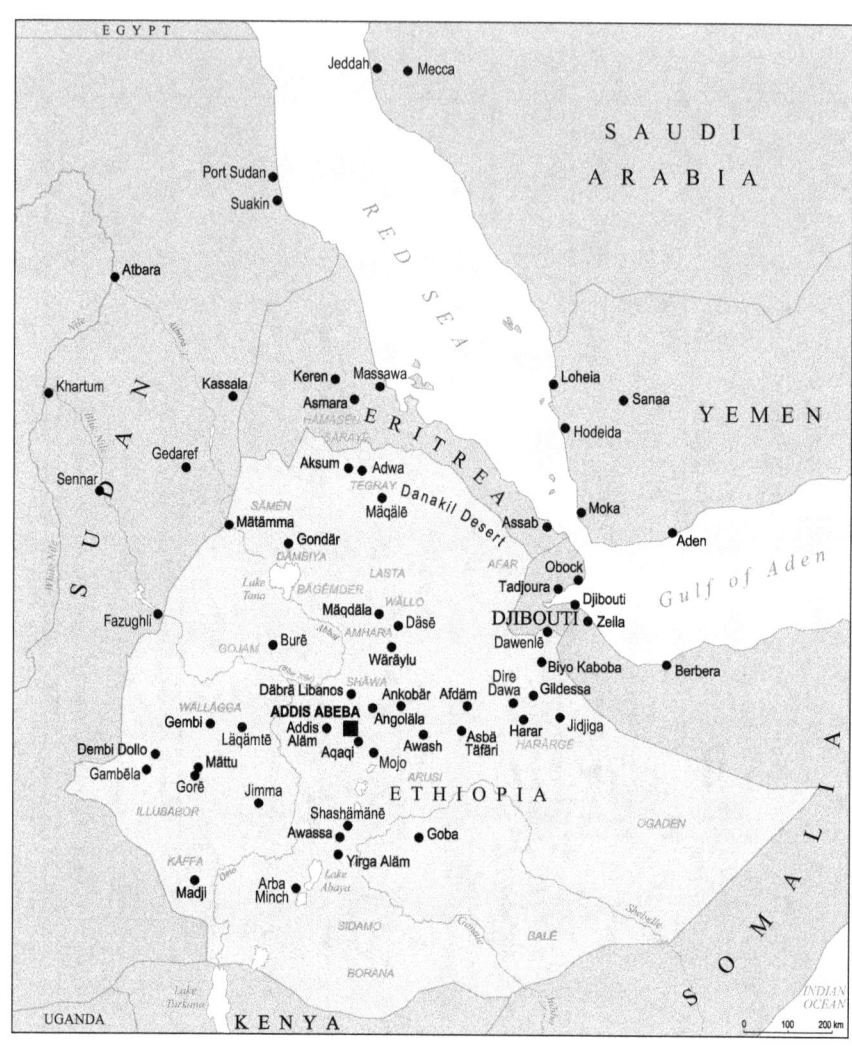

Map 0.2 Main places of Modern Ethiopia and neighboring countries mentioned in this book

Introduction: From the Sedentary Logic of Diasporas to the History of the Nation-State

To produce a mighty book, you must chose a mighty theme.
No great and enduring volume can ever be written on the flea, though many there be who have tried it.

—Herman Melville, *Moby Dick*

"We, the Ethiopians, are a nation made up of eighty ethnic groups, and the Armenians are the eighty-first," a friend told me on my first visit to Addis Abeba. There were, at the time, fewer than one hundred descendants of the Armenian immigration in Ethiopia. In their little church, the Sunday mass now attracted only a sparse handful of the faithful, and were it not for the beauty of the admirable choir, the church would have seemed quite empty. Only the graveyard, with its five hundred gravestones, still created the illusion of numbers. Thus it was some time before I could believe in the truth of my friend's affirmation—the time it took to see that these men, women, and children, who seemed perfectly at ease in their social environment, unquestionably comported themselves like people from here, although they obviously were not *just* that. They were, in other words, both inside and also outside. How often did I hear, later on, that "the Armenians were the closest to the Ethiopians"; that, unlike most whites in Ethiopia, they were not *färänji*,[1] were not, that is, considered "foreigners" (the meaning of the word "*färanj*" is open to discussion). Among the descendants of this immigration, there was manifest idealization of a supposedly unique collective tie to Ethiopia and "the Ethiopians." It was embodied in a host of anecdotes, of which the most revelatory, sometimes shading off into legend, were also the least susceptible of verification. The most astonishing of all, the history of the Negus's brass band—this orchestra made up of forty Armenian orphans that was founded in 1924 by *Ras* Täfäri, Ethiopia's crown prince and the future Emperor Haile Selassie I—seemed to embody, as in a parable, a claim to a sort of indefinable Armenian exception. The feeling that this specificity existed was very pronounced in the small circle of descendants of the Armenian immigration but not easily observable outside it. For this reason, it was relegated to a kind of assumed confidentiality. The aim of the present book is to shed light on the construction of this symbolic gray zone, the silent labor of a paradoxical implantation that puts individuals halfway between the national and the foreign.

I make the wager that a tangible phenomenon which strikes visitors like something obvious, yet remains hard to grasp, can be objectivized.

Before proceeding, it seems advisable to provide a few elements of the context here, and a few statistics. The Armenians of Ethiopia represent no more than a grain of sand in the archipelago of the diaspora, far less significant than the much bigger communities that have long found homes in certain Middle Eastern countries, such as Lebanon, Syria, Jordan, Iraq, Iran, or Egypt, or the heavyweights of the diaspora—in Europe, the community of France, and, in the Americas, those of Argentina, the United States, and Canada—to say nothing of the many communities scattered through former republics of the Soviet Union, from Ukraine through Russia and Georgia to Kazakhstan. Without a doubt, its small numbers make Ethiopia's Armenian community seem more like the minuscule, and equally unknown, Armenian communities of Sudan, Albania, and Malaysia. In addition to its numerical and geographical marginality, the Armenian immigration in Ethiopia is, in the diaspora, historically distinguished (although it is of course not unique in this regard) by the fact that it is not a direct consequence of the 1915 genocide. It had already begun in the nineteenth century, during the reign of Menelik II (1889–1913). Still earlier, between 1840 and 1860, Armenians were present in the cities of Northern Abyssinia,[2] such as Adwa or Mäqälē,[3] or, again, in the port of Massawa, on the shores of the Red Sea. From the sixteenth to the eighteenth century, the long-standing ties between the Ethiopian and Armenian Churches in Jerusalem had encouraged Armenian merchants and clergymen to travel to this part of the world, which was little known to Europeans at the time. The existence of big Armenian communities in Egypt's major cities, such as Alexandria, Cairo, or, later, Suez, doubtless goes a long way toward explaining the resurgence in Armenian migration to Ethiopia in the nineteenth century. Thus several Armenians settled in Harar when the Egyptians occupied this old Muslim city between 1875 and 1885. Arthur Rimbaud knew some of them. They brought their families here after the Armenian massacres perpetrated in the Empire of Sultan Abdülhamid II between 1894 and 1897. That is why the small Armenian community in Ethiopia boasted women and children among its members from a very early date. On the eve of the Great War, it could not have counted more than 150 to 200 people, yet it figured as one of the most dynamic immigrant communities in this sovereign African state, suddenly opened up to a significant foreign presence, in which many Armenian families cultivated close ties with the imperial court. The Armenian population grew, however, after the genocide, in the 1920s and down to the early 1930s, when it leveled off at around, probably, 1,200. It remained at this level through the 1960s, shortly before the Ethiopian monarchy was overthrown by the 1974 revolution.

The Armenian presence in Ethiopia is ancient and indubitably constitutes part of contemporary Ethiopia's history. Yet it remains all but invisible. There is almost nothing to be gained by rushing off to a library. Painstaking readers will find no more there, initially, than a handful of allusions in books on Ethiopian history, encountered haphazardly in footnotes or drab indexes of proper names. We would do better to begin by taking the physical measure of the object we propose to study.

Attentive observers who tour, on foot, the part of Addis Abeba's historical center that used to be called Arada and is, in our day, more commonly known as Piazza, cannot help but stumble upon traces of the Armenian presence, or, still more often, of this presence's past. In an avenue just around the corner, for example, it is thinly veiled beneath the family name, or the pun addressed to the happy few, that adorns a shop sign; on the chipped marble of a commemorative plaque that no one has yet seen fit to remove; beneath the name of a venerable Armenian restaurant, the Omar Khayyam, which, today, serves its Ethiopian patrons raw meat—one wonders whether its current owner even knows who Omar Khayyam was. More affluent patrons, diplomats, and tourists who wish to set themselves apart from the crowd while varying their everyday fare can also dine at the Ararat Club with a rather good reputation, where the Armenian cuisine is prepared and served by Ethiopians. Finally, it is impossible to miss the Armenian church that stands close to the Ras Mäkonnen Bridge on the road to Arat Kilo, at the foot of the stairway of seventy steps leading up to the former Armenian quarter, with its many Indian-style wooden chalets.

On the other side of the torrent that separates it from the Greek church opposite, one glimpses the steeple of the Armenian church, which, at this distance, looks as if it had surged up out of a thick jungle. Like the traces that a painting leaves on a wall when it is removed after hanging there for years, the Armenian presence in Addis Abeba stubbornly refuses to disappear. Thus the children of a big Armenian merchant who settled in Ethiopia late in the nineteenth century were still there. Three sisters and their niece, as well as two brothers, all of a very respectable age, all of them now gone. The misses—for they never married—were very fond of talking, and although their testimony was never very precise, I always delighted in listening to them. They lived in one of the most beautiful houses in Addis Abeba and, no doubt, one of the oldest. Made of wood and mud brick, it was crowned with an imposing thatched roof and stood side by side with a second house that was quite curiously constructed in the form of a spiral: one went from one room to another as if one were wending one's way through a snail shell. To the extent that I can recall the afternoons that I spent with the three misses during the usual five o'clock downpour, chatting and sipping tea in their living room decorated with photographs and hunting trophies 100 years old, they were still living in much the same way that they had in the Ethiopian empire of their childhood, still accompanied by the handful of servants that the Ethiopian revolution had left them, as well as by an enormous turtle, perhaps even older than the house, who had his haunt in the garden. All three misses passed away the same year, more than twenty years ago now, but I like to visit their house whenever I return to Addis Abeba. The turtle is still there.

Once in a while doesn't hurt, as the saying goes: the historian's questions followed, this time, from his initial reconnaissance of this terrain—from the present of these descendants of the Armenian immigration in Ethiopia. Thus a degree of chance was involved here, bound up with the random choice of a terrain. It finds its reflection in the singularity, the non-representativity of the case studied, an atypical, limit case—by no means exemplary and even less generalizable—of the amalgamation of a population of foreign origin with the society in which it resided. We are, moreover, incapable of giving it a precise name. This investigation, however, invites us to reflect more broadly on the genesis of collective representations of the foreigner, the effects such representations have on the fabrication of a national "we," their appropriation, and their translation into the forms of individuals' material life and also their dream life. Conversely, the Ethiopian example offers an occasion to take up again, on new bases, a discussion of the Armenian diaspora that began long ago.

Essential at the heuristic level,[4] comparison is inevitable in the field of Diaspora Studies, in which the Armenians have become, together with other "migratory peoples" (the Jewish, Greek, Indian, Chinese, etc. diasporas), a veritable textbook case.[5] The interest taken here in individuals' implantation or taking-root (*enracinement*), their moorings in the society in which they reside—in a word, in the sedentary logic of diaspora[6]—lead us to envision the diasporan condition in a new light. For whether it is in Alfortville and Issy-les-Moulineaux (in the suburbs of Paris), in London, New York, or Nicosia, the Armenian diaspora is often associated with the wrenching effects of exile and genocide, whose transmission seems to play the role of catalyst of a distinct identity among the members of the community in their society of residence, a reaction to the processes of acculturation. The "communal bond" (*lien communautaire*) accordingly figures as the condition sine qua non for attaining the goal of "non-dilution" of an identity; it favors the reemergence of a "unity of place" in the "non-place" of exile, a unity imagined or re-created by a series of territorial markers and practices of appropriation.[7] In Addis Abeba, however, where the last descendants of the Armenian immigration now live, there is no obsessive fear of assimilation in sight. Ties to the original fatherland have, by and large, been physically cut off for a long time now, and this distanciation does not seem to have engendered a void or an absence. Investment in the country of residence, which has become a homeland, is virtually total and is reflected in a perception of the ancestors' arrival embellished to the point that it does not appear exaggerated to speak of a *host*land. This is diaspora, to be sure, but without exile or the feelings that go to make up exile. The discourses of memory by no means refer to a lost, regretted elsewhere, to the suffering of being uprooted, or to other traumatic ruptures that might have left indelible traces. The relationship with the host, which has been idealized, occupies a central, structuring place in those discourses. Far from perpetuating an unsatisfied tie with an elsewhere, the common Grand Narrative of the past is firmly and, it seems, unreservedly rooted in the host society. For better and for worse, we might say.

Much has already been written about the Armenians in diaspora, so that this book might seem to be an umpteenth contribution to the inventory of Armenian communities in the world. That, however, is not at all what it is. Moreover, the reader will not find in it all the facts and details about the Armenian presence in Ethiopia that he would have had the right to expect of a monograph worthy of that name. For the goal of my approach to the material was never to produce a learned history of a community for its own sake. My project, which attempts to shed light on the construction of the foreign and the national in the imperial Ethiopia of the nineteenth and twentieth centuries by examining the case of the history of the Armenian presence in this African country that was never subject to colonization, is much more closely related to the problem-history advocated by the founders of the *Annales*. The stakes, here, is to explain the genesis of a configuration, in the sense Norbert Elias gives the word,[8] which placed individuals in a situation allowing them to move from one network to the other, one sphere to the other, at every rung of the society of which they were an integral part, by highlighting, as their needs, circumstances, and choices dictated, this or that form of belonging, this or that facet of themselves. Rather than try to redefine the identity of a group or the individuals who issued from it, the aim is to grasp how this space of sociabilities, of interstitial dimensions, was opened up to the Armenian immigrants and their descendants in Ethiopia and to map the effects it had on individuals' choices, margins of maneuver, or practices and life trajectories. One of the hypotheses advanced in this book is that study of the immigrants', and their descendants', past and present situation should make possible a better understanding of the society in which they lived or still live.

Stated that way, this project may seem presumptuous, given the sparsity of the available documentation. An "interstitial" reality, by definition, does not leave many traces, and this is a fortiori the case when it bears on such a small number of individuals. In the field, one has a presentiment of this "interstitial" reality, but it remains hard to pin down, because it is indefinable and does not fit into the usual categories. One cannot rely on official documentation alone to study it, for it is largely invisible and eludes institutions', diplomats', and most travelers' and authors' gaze. In the period in which the bulk of foreign immigration to Ethiopia occurred, the Ethiopian state had only a rudimentary governmental and administrative apparatus at its disposal. The first Ethiopian cabinet was put in place by Emperor Menelik II only in 1907. Modern means of communication (the post, a written press, the railroad) were still in their infancy in the country. The historian is also faced with the problem that the Ethiopian monarchy's archives remain largely inaccessible to the present day. Finally, while there has been no lack, since the 1960s, of studies of the history of the foreign presence in Ethiopia, those that have seriously posed the question of the fabrication of foreignness or otherness in this country are rare, although that question is closely tied to that of the emergence of the nation-state. It is in this perspective that study of the Armenian presence in Ethiopia turns out to be the most fruitful.

It would of course be illusory to claim to comprehend, setting out from a case as limited as that of the Armenians in Ethiopia, problems as vast as the construction of a nation-state in Africa or the construction of the Armenian diaspora in the world of the twentieth century. This should, however, not dissuade us from considering the possibility of generalizing the results of even a localized study based on fieldwork. As Clifford Geertz emphasizes, "Anthropologists don't study villages (tribes, towns, neighborhoods…); they study *in* villages."[9] The case of the Armenians is, to be honest, not at all "typical" of the situation of foreigners in Ethiopia. More, it would be hard to find its equivalent there. It makes it possible to understand, however, as a "particular case of the possible,"[10] the social arrangements that favor the emergence of interstitial and plural sociabilities. The attention lavished on what seems to be an invisible or insignificant detail is of interest here only to the extent that "traces that may be infinitesimal make it possible to understand a deeper reality than would otherwise be attainable,"[11] thus helping us "move from one history to another."[12] It is in this sense that the Negus's brass band appears, to borrow a felicitous expression of Marc Bloch's, as a "little-trodden track"[13] that lends itself to an attempt to grasp the original character of the Armenian presence in Ethiopia in the twentieth century: "I found that what had so far been merely anecdotal could be turned into history."[14]

Absent from the history books, but actively reinvested in memory in our day, the creation of Ethiopia's royal brass band by forty Armenian orphans is surprising, for it does not square with the received notions about merchant diasporas or middlemen minorities that are classically applied to Armenians, and also to Greeks, Lebanese, and Indians, in Africa and elsewhere. In place of the conventional description of the Middle Eastern shopkeeper, predestined from all time to engage in trade, an auxiliary to European colonization locked into subaltern roles, we witness, here, an encounter between music and politics, monarchs and artists. Apparently nothing more than a curious chapter in the history of music that can only interest music lovers, fans of ethio-jazz and Afrobeat, and also, of course, devotees of military music, the creation of this brass band can also be understood as a political phenomenon in the full sense of the word. *Ras* Täfäri, then crown prince and regent (from 1916 to 1930) of the Empire of Ethiopia, was not just content to found, with these forty waifs who survived the 1915 genocide, his country's first official brass band; he also entrusted its conductor, the Armenian Kevork Nalbandian, with the task of composing the first Ethiopian national anthem. One has to know something about the uses to which music and national anthems were put in Europe in the nineteenth and the first half of the twentieth century, the age of nations, to measure the symbolic importance of an event of this kind. Choosing Armenian musicians to play and compose this official music seems to confuse the issue, as if, suddenly, the "foreign" and the "national" were no longer necessarily antithetical. This should be viewed in conjunction with the use that Ethiopian sovereigns made of Armenians and foreigners in general, from the reign of Menelik II (1889–1913) to that of Haile Selassie (1930–74), in such a way as to dismantle, to the extent it can be, "the combination of factors that make up the non-evental of the event."[15] One is, however, well advised to exercise caution in advancing this interpretation, which seems to offer a shortcut leading from the Negus's brass band to the foreign policy of the kings of Ethiopia and the sedentarization of a diaspora; one must beware of the "narrative leap"[16] represented by a labor of writing that is never innocent, without pretending not to know that the historians' "long term" (*longue durée*), like the anthropologists' "tradition," is readily transformed into "retrospective or self-creating prophecies."[17] The study of the memory of the Armenian presence in Ethiopia, which comprises the heart of the present book, responds to this call for a reflexive analysis.

When I began my research, it would have been a vain endeavor to attempt, in order to reveal the collective representations of the descendants of this immigration, a study of different perspectives on it, for the man in the street—above all the young man, I am tempted to say—was quite simply ignorant of the existence of those representations. The Armenian presence in Ethiopia had all but disappeared, even in Addis Abeba, because its vital forces had left for Europe, North America, and Australia: this exodus represented more than nine-tenths of the total Armenian population after the 1974 revolution that brought the regime of the *Därg* (the "committee") to power and led to the rule, until 1991, of a military junta of Marxist inspiration. I therefore set myself the task of bringing together as many indications and testimonies as possible, without a preestablished plan and without really knowing the uses to which it would be given to me to put them later. It was a question of attending to the most urgent task first, to beat, by a nose—somewhat like an archaeologist making a salvage excavation—the inevitable, all too rapid disappearance of the testimonies and the old people who were passing on. Much later, after taking a step back and examining the material I had in hand, I decided to use it in a study of memory which would, I believed, in the tradition initiated by Maurice Halbwachs, make it possible to test a hypothesis about the immigrants' and their descendants' sedentarization in a sort of symbolic gray zone. To make a success of this procedure, it was necessary to historicize what I here call "memory," which is, properly speaking, nothing other than a product of the conditions under which the investigation was carried out, of the choices that shaped it, and of the social stakes of the testimony collected during it. For testimony never revives the past; it constantly reconstructs it in the present, by responding to the "demands that impose themselves on a society's memory."[18] It is precisely by attending to these deformations that we can attempt to transform the subjectivity inherent in the recomposed nature of memory into an object of historical investigation.

The first chapters of this book propose, by way of a rereading of the "classic" sources, an alternative to the usual historiographical treatment of the foreign presence in Ethiopia. I then show, thanks to the original materials just mentioned, that the symbolic gray zone in question here was, until the most recent generations, a reality experienced by the descendants of the Armenian immigration in this country. To put these conclusions to the test, the book's final chapters attempt to bring out the social effects this gray zone had on practices and life experiences. At the end of this trajectory, I also attempt to show how this particular chapter in the history of migrations, apparently sui generis, invites us to consider, more generally, the problem of the construction of "communities" and the ties that are eventually established between the foreign and the national.

Part 1

The Genesis of an Ethiopian Political Tradition

1

Wax and Gold: The Royal Brass Band's Unsuspected Political Role

Ras Täfäri's 1924 decision to create an official brass band was made in a pivotal period in the foreign policy of his country, which had just been admitted to the League of Nations. The reign of Menelik II (1889–1913) and the regency of Täfäri (1916–30), followed by the first years of his reign as emperor under the name Haile Selassie I (1930–6), profoundly modified Ethiopia's relations with foreign powers. Profiting from the transformation of the Ethiopian Empire's image in the international arena, Ethiopian leaders affirmed their sovereignty in the heart of an Africa under colonial domination. The creation of the royal brass band, however anecdotal it may seem, was integrated into this policy that sought to project the image of an independent state. The wax-and-gold metaphor, which figures prominently in Ethiopian poetry and political life, nicely expresses the play between form and meaning to which the invention of an official form of music lent itself.

The Political Virtues of an Invented Tradition

Early twentieth-century Ethiopia, especially under Täfäri's regency, seems to have been highly productive of invented traditions, which, in the contemporary period, are creations characteristic of societies intent upon establishing or symbolizing social cohesion or bringing together individuals in communities, real or artificial.[1] The creation of the royal brass band and the public uses of music took their place in this new monarchic "language of symbols."[2]

My Life and Ethiopia's Progress

The official chronicle of the regency, a veritable panegyric to Täfäri's policies, first evokes the royal brass band in connection with the January 1925 Ethiopian Christmas festivities:

> The foreign notables and their ladies and the children were invited to the house of His Highness the Crown Prince in honour of the Feast of the birth of Christ, and a big feast was held. And after the feast meal, forty Armenian orphans who had lost

their father and mother and whom His Highness the Crown Prince had brought from Jerusalem played on trumpets and made music.[3]

The fact that the orphans are mentioned on the day of Christ's birth, the allusion to Jerusalem, and the fact that the concert was given before European merchants and their families seem to inscribe this performance in a logic demonstrating the royal family's charity and generosity. The fact that the orphans taken in hand were white could only reinforce the European audience's favorable impression of the crown prince at a time when memory of the massacres that had occurred during the Great War was still fresh and the need to rescue of thousands of Greek and Armenian orphan refugees was still a burning question. The image of the very Christian king here takes priority over that of the reforming monarch. The creation of this brass band, however, also takes its place in the ideology of Ethiopia's progress.

With its gleaming musical instruments and resonant music, the royal brass band brought a significant element of modernity to the regularly organized parades celebrating the Ethiopian monarchy. *Ras* Täfäri, who, if we credit the chronicle's insistent evocation of this subject, appreciated the musical pomp accompanying the ceremonies organized during his journey through Europe, seemed to pay particular attention to the musical presentation of his regime. In his autobiography, the Amharic edition of which displays a picture of the prince surrounded by his "forty Armenian child musicians" (*yä40 lejoch yäarmän muziqäñoch*), Haile Selassie notes the contribution music made to his effort to introduce "European civilization" into his country:

> At any time foreign national anthems could be heard in Ethiopia on a gramophone, but there was nothing that might be called Ethiopia's national anthem. But now, since 1920 [1927 or 1928],[4] there has appeared a distinct Ethiopian national anthem and march Tafari, a military march; it is to be heard at the Palace and any other appropriate place, when Ethiopian envoys go abroad and a reception or banquet is given in their honour.[5]

The evocation of an official Ethiopian music (the two pieces cited were composed by Kevork Nalbandian) purports to show, as does the whole of this text written during the emperor's exile in England in 1937, during the Italian occupation of his country, that Ethiopia is not the backward, savage land depicted by partisans of the Italian conquest. A modernizing ambition runs from one end of this autobiography to the other, and the creation of the royal brass band should be understood in this context.

Music and Political Cohesion

Properly to assess the interest the crown prince took in music, we have to examine the political uses to which national anthems were put in post-1870 Europe, a period in which Giuseppe Verdi was described as "a kind of musical Garibaldi."[6] There could be nothing like national feeling in the Ethiopian Empire, with its great linguistic and religious diversity. It was an empire whose land area Menelik's conquests had, very recently, suddenly tripled, one in which regional powers still resisted the central authority then under construction. The Ethiopian national anthem's Amharic lyrics show, moreover, that what this anthem celebrates is the king's person, not the nation or an allegory of it, unlike the *Marseillaise*, the first modern national anthem.[7] Yet this identification of the "nation" with the sovereign's person is comparable to the "nationalization of monarchs" that occurred in Europe before 1914, where it shored up dynastic legitimacies in decline.[8]

The advantage that anthems have over other national symbols stems from the fact that music is a universal language. Its immediacy works miracles at big civic or patriotic meetings, for songs are recalled more easily than long speeches and make it easier to propagate slogans. In Risorgimento Italy, in the France of the Third Republic or of Maréchal Pétain, anthems, as "ideological shortcuts," played an effective role in showing political regimes off to advantage.[9] In the years following the brass band's creation, Täfäri seemed to lavish special attention on the development of music and orchestras in his country. Kevork Nalbandian taught at the Lycée Täfäri Mäkonnen, which was supposed to train the country's enlightened elite. Garabed Hakalmazian, once an orphan in the royal brass band, himself conducted the policemen's brass band of the municipality of Addis Abeba (*Arada zäbäña*).[10] Every evening at the stroke of eight, a contemporary noted, the police force's trumpets enjoined the capital's inhabitants to go home, as required by the curfew prohibiting Abyssinians from circulating at night.[11] Other Ethiopian brass bands, made up of young men in uniform who were either orphans themselves or hailed from the empire's southern provinces, were conducted by the Swiss André Nicod, who taught at the Lycée Impérial after 1928. Thus there were almost 250 Ethiopian performing musicians in the empire's garrisons by 1935, in orchestras that crisscrossed the country.[12] The potential political uses of this musical development did not escape observers. Acknowledging the impact, in this domain, of the "forty Armenian orphans who ceased their activity in 1930, while their conductor undertook to organize the brass band of the three big lycées taken together," the Swiss teacher foresaw that "the Italians will easily be able to find all the equipment they need when the fancy of reconstituting a propagandistic brass band to meet the needs of Ethiopian *ballilas* takes them." Since the green, yellow, and red Ethiopian flag was quite similar to the Italian, "the yellow band on the heads of the drums need only be replaced by a thin white line, and the switch in national colors will be complete."[13] In Ethiopia, however, the strange harmonies of the military marches and modern musical instruments, as well as the very idea of national anthems, were all almost entirely unknown. This new ceremonial arsenal was used to appeal to people's emotions and surround the state with the necessary pomp in the presence of foreign countries' representatives, rather than to display and inculcate a specific ideology. The musical works that Täfäri commissioned Kevork Nalbandian to compose, a set of marches honoring the crown prince, his wife Mänän, his eldest son Asfa Wäsän, and his youngest child, Mäkonnen, were ideally suited to accompanying military parades or other processions.

Setting a Modern Ethiopia to Music and Putting It on Display

From the 1920s on, the army and brass band worked hand in hand to put Täfäri's regime on show. The chronicle of the years of his regency systematically presents the brass band's creation and the use of music on major occasions as signs that Ethiopia was striding down "the road to civilization"[14] opened up by the regent's renowned predecessor Menelik. Thus the chronicler heavily emphasizes this claim when he describes the big military parade organized for October 10, 1925, on the plain of Fell Woha in Addis Abeba. "After this, the troops of His Highness—*while music was being played*—marched *in rhythm with the music* in front of the parade and thus showing the progress of civilization [i.e. the modern, 'civilized' style of marching in orderly fashion in parade], and they passed on," saluting the crown prince as they marched by. "Next came *Armenian children, singing a beautiful song accompanied by music*[al instruments] and escorted by machine gunners in front of cavalry soldiers; and the machine gunners and the cavalry soldiers adorned the parade by dressing in blue coats and making their horses march *in rhythm with the music*."[15] The introduction of the brass band, brought into relation with the acquisition of new weapons, is closely associated with things military and ideas of order, efficiency, and modernism: "Behold, all who saw that the guards [troops] of the Municipality had progressed with respect to skill ['civilization'] compared to the previous year were very pleased."[16] In this parade, which was followed by the distribution of gold medals stamped with the figure of a lion, the symbol of the Ethiopian monarchy, we have an exemplary case of the invention of tradition. The blue uniforms of the troops of the imperial bodyguard, who wore impressive caps decorated with lions' manes, replaced the white togas once worn by Abyssinian warriors, even if the army continued to march barefoot. The forty children in the brass band wore the same uniform themselves, "the costume of navy blue wool cloth" provided courtesy of the crown prince.[17] Such public performances were occasions for demonstrating that Ethiopia was now part of the modern civilized world. It could speak the same language of national anthems used in Europe and at big international meetings, as it did when the first airplane landed in the country and the *March Täfäri* and *Marseillaise* were played in Täfäri's and the French plenipotentiary's presence.[18] Music and the royal brass band became integral parts of every event that the Ethiopian monarchy wished to turn into an important occasion.

Concerts were given during the horse shows organized by the Imperial Club under the aegis of foreign diplomatic legations; annually on November 2, to mark the anniversary of the 1930 imperial coronation; and on European Christmas, Ethiopian Christmas, European-style New Year's Day, Abyssinian-style New Year's Day, the Festival of *Temqät* (commemorating Christ's baptism in the Jordan), the blessing of the Tablets of the Law, and so on.[19] The brass band now accompanied the very devout Empress Zäwditu when she went to church in Addis Abeba four or five times a week on muleback, behind Kevork Nalbandian on horseback and the forty children on foot at the head of the procession.[20] Music was played at the October 13, 1927, funeral service of *Wäyzäro*[21] Sehin, the crown prince's mother-in-law, and at that of Emperor Haile Selassie's second daughter. Musicians were present—this time without performing—when the mortal remains of *Ras* Gugsa Wälē, Empress Zäwditu's former husband, who was killed in combat after rebelling against the regent in April 1930, were brought back to the capital.[22] The official receptions of foreign dignitaries thus combined reinvented Ethiopian traditions with new, imported practices. A colorful example is provided by the June 28, 1929, reception for the Ethiopian Church's new *abun*,[23] the Egyptian archbishop Qērelos (Cyril), and five Ethiopian bishops freshly ordained by the Coptic patriarch of Alexandria. The prelates' arrival by train at Addis Abeba's spanking new train station represented a sharp departure from the traditional mule trains that had come from Egypt since time immemorial. Täfäri, with his soldiers, waited for the churchmen at the station. His guests were conducted to the palace in convertibles moving at a walking pace, while "the official 'government' trumpeters and flautists and drummers together with many soldiers" marched out ahead of them to various airs. A few months later, when, observing the same protocol, Täfäri received the Coptic patriarch of Alexandria at the Addis Abeba train station, the Armenian brass band was once again on hand to add to the pomp and circumstance of the event.[24] This quest for form peaked with the 1928 and 1930 coronation ceremonies that, respectively, bestowed the titles of *negus* and *negusä nägäst* ("king of kings" or emperor) on Täfäri. Attended by a throng of diplomats and journalists, they constituted two great moments in the display of the Ethiopian monarchy on the international stage. The place given to the brass band in the ceremony—drums mounted on mules, flute players and trumpet players, and "those who played [in] the King's fanfare"—amid ceremonial shields and umbrellas, lions' manes and prancing horses, was once again of the first importance.[25] This evolution in ceremonial forms reflected the change in the meaning of these great events, which now aspired to put Ethiopia on an equal footing with the great powers. Setting the imperial Ethiopian regime to music and putting it on display thus echoed *Ras* Täfäri's foreign policy.

The Royal Brass Band as an Instrument of Täfäri's Foreign Policy

The year 1924, which saw the creation of the royal brass band, consecrated Ethiopia's entry into the concert of nations. It was ratified by the country's September 1923 admission to the League of Nations and the crown prince's first voyage abroad. At the level of foreign relations, the main stakes of Täfäri's diplomatic tour was to obtain guarantees that Ethiopian sovereignty would be respected, notably by an Italy led since 1922 by Mussolini, which had been frustrated by its "mutilated victory" of 1919 and was still traumatized by the disaster of Adwa, inflicted on Italy by Menelik's armies in 1896. At the level of domestic politics, the voyage was intended to heighten Täfäri's influence in the empress's entourage, where his decisions were still being submitted to the council of ministers for approval. The disagreements agitating the government at this time came to a head, in particular, over the scope to be given to relations with foreign powers. In this controversy, Täfäri emerged very early as a champion of the idea that Ethiopia should open itself up to foreigners and Western modernity by adopting an energetic foreign policy. Just as, in the executive couple, Zäwditu incarnated the tradition of attachment to the Ethiopian Church, so Täfäri personified an opening to Europe for which the conservative wing of the aristocracy criticized him. Thus he was accused of wanting to sell the country to foreigners, a suspicion that his Francophone education and friendships with Catholics did not fail to fuel.[26] It is in this context that the royal brass band's creation can be read as an integral component of a foreign policy strategy, even if it is hard to affirm this categorically because of the silence surrounding the Armenian musicians.

False Notes and Bad Taste? Or True Political Messages?

Let us be frank: their contemporaries' testimony about these musicians is as rare as it is disobliging. When, in Addis Abeba on September 26, 1925, Jean d'Esme, an author whose writing was typical of the interwar colonial novel, attended the ceremony of the Festival of the Invention of the Cross (*Mäsqäl*) in the presence of *Ras* Täfäri, diplomatic delegations, and a huge crowd, he seemed less than convinced of the quality of the royal brass band's performance:

> An orchestra comprising Armenians under the baton of a conductor whose mercilessly tight uniform fails to hide his imposing belly strikes up the national anthems, hailing each minister's arrival […] The royal bodyguard marches by, impeccably attired in khaki from cap to garters, with the band in the lead—that horrible brass band whose rehearsals we had occasion to savor—while, under the green-yellow-and-red flag, the branches pile up.

Then, once the ceremony had come to an end with the lighting of a blazing bonfire, as is customary on the Festival of the Cross,

> the foreign ministers depart one by one, saluted by the cacophonous blaring of the Armenian orchestra pitching in on, one after the other, the *Marseillaise*, *Gode* [sic] *Save the King*, *Deutschland* [sic] *über alles*, *La Brabançonne*, and the bouncy, perky measures of the Italian national anthem.[27]

The rare authors to mention the brass band have mocked its grotesque attire—behind its conductor's corpulence, the reader will have no trouble imagining the musicians' poorly fitting uniforms—but also the false notes that punctuated its concerts and offended music lovers' ears. The situation was the more comic in that, by common consent, the musical tastes of the Ethiopians, who "did not appreciate the polyphonic style, which, moreover, did not exist in their impoverished music," were quite dubious: "The bigshots loved to parade through the streets at the head of a throng of their servants, to the sound of brass, more piercing and more martial than the reed flutes. It did not matter whether the music was in tune or in good taste, as long as it raised a racket, for the essential thing was to attract attention."[28] This might lead one to suppose that the Armenian brass band's performances had no real effect on their audiences. The narrative of the Festival of the Cross creates the impression that the brass band, with its slovenly dress and pretentious airs, had no place in a traditional Ethiopian ceremony full of religious fervor. To say so, however, is to forget that there exists a liturgical Abyssinian music which is customarily performed by priests at events of this kind, with chanting and dances. The royal brass band's participation here, as well as the playing of several national anthems, is explained only by the presence of foreign delegations.

In the denigration of imperial Ethiopia, the symbol of a backward Africa that continues to reject the benefits of colonization, the Armenian band is an appropriate narrative element. A master of the genre, the writer André Armandy, insists heavily on this exotic brass band in describing the 1929 reception, mentioned earlier, that Täfäri gave the Coptic patriarch of Alexandria:

> The Negus went over to him and kissed his hand. I listened, attentive and wide-eyed. Then the fanfares rang out, celebrating this solemn act with their brass… I felt slightly nauseous… I listened to more… Either I was mistaken, or this was an enormity! Yet no one anywhere near me batted an eyelid. No one?… Not quite: through a space between two heads, I recognized the mocking face of my old travel companion, who seemed to be asking me, at a distance, "Well then, how do you like this story?" Refusing to let me entertain the least doubt, the Armenian brass band attacked the finale, so that this liturgical hymn echoed through the train station: Ta-ta-ta… ta taire / Ta-ta-ta… ta taire / We give him… a *"pouet-pouet"* / Yes, that's the way!

After which, Armandy adds, "I do not think it superfluous to affirm that I have invented nothing in the course of this narrative."[29] In mocking the brass band, he targets Ethiopia's regent and, through him, a sovereignly ridiculous African state. What is more, he makes no attempt to hide his profound contempt for the Armenians, who, in his view, are nothing but fakes and parasites. The performance, at an official reception, marked, in theory, by the greatest possible solemnity, of a French air in vogue—the unforgettable *Pouet! Pouet!*, a fairly saucy tune drawn from an operetta produced by Georges Milton that very year, *Elle est à vous* [She's yours], which invites motorists to engage in a little hanky-panky without undue regard for the marital niceties—heavily underscores the Negro king's naiveté. Incapable of appreciating the difference between a national anthem and an operetta, he wishes to afford himself a European-style brass band. The Armenians whom he has hired in lieu of authentic musicians, however, offer him nothing but a cheap tinsel modernity.

To be honest, these violations of good taste seem to have been the rule with the brass band. Its repertory also included *Ne pleure pas Jeannette* [Don't cry, Jeannette], *Auprès de ma blonde* [With my blondie], and *Viens, Poupoule!* [Come, chickadee!].[30] The story goes that the Duke of Abruzzo, an Italian government envoy received with great pomp in Addis Abeba in May 1927, was surprised to hear the royal brass band perform Chopin's *Funeral March* in his honor: "'But what in the world is that?' Later, he learned that 'it was the whole repertory: they finished with that, and they're going to start up again.'"[31] The suggestion is that this was an incongruity in the repertory, explicable, quite simply, by the brass band's amateurishness and the need to pad out a ceremony that was too long. The parade of Ethiopian troops staged for the Italian delegation's benefit that day had indeed lasted longer than planned. According to the irritated Italian representatives who had had no choice but to sit out the ceremony to the end, the military parade, which had begun around eight in the morning, did not wind up until late in the afternoon.[32] Moreover, the Armenian musicians' tendency to repeat certain numbers—"that horrible brass band whose rehearsals we had occasion to savor"—has been noted by several auditors.³³ It is not, however, impossible that the seemingly incongruous choice of pieces in its repertory had real significance. An anecdote famous among Addis Abeba's Armenians affirms that the municipal brass band, made up of young Ethiopians and conducted by a former member of the royal brass band, Garabed Hakalmazian, had struck up an Armenian revolutionary march during the visit that the Republic of Turkey's representative, Muhettin Pasha, paid the city on the occasion of the 1930 coronation. For a Turkish official, the message was clear. And hearing young Ethiopians obediently performing subversive scores in the middle of an imperial coronation ceremony is not devoid of a certain drollery. Yet to what extent were the Ethiopian participants aware, or unaware, of the significance of these musical choices? All things considered, it is by no means certain that Täfäri and the Ethiopians responsible for the diplomatic protocol were fooled by caprices of this kind.

I am indebted to the historian Jean Doresse for the idea that these seeming incongruities in the brass band's repertory are comparable to the art of producing verse with two meanings, one ordinary, the other allegorical. Such verse, still very popular today in Abyssinian proverbs and songs, traditionally authorizes criticism (even political criticism), as long as it is not direct. It was on this condition of knowing how to make the listener smile that the *azmari*, wandering musicians who were long compared to medieval European troubadours, could, in the past, take the liberty of making fun of the sovereign and his courtiers, as they continue, today, to tease the clientele of the bars and the *tädj bēt*, consenting victims of their irreverent lyrical improvisations:

> We shall never know whether the brass band that, in 1930, welcomed Maréchal Franchet d'Espèrey by playing *Viens poupoule, viens!* instead of the *Marseillaise* for him, or the one that, much later, welcomed the Japanese Crown Prince to the tune of the *Bridge over the River Kwai*, did not do so deliberately, to please the Ethiopian officials. The mastery of sentences with a double meaning, one ceremonious, the other insulting, manifested itself even in remarks made to the Emperor by his subjects.³⁴

The conceptual association between wax and gold (in Amharic, the *sämennä wärq*) allows us to interpret the formal innovations in the great political liturgies of the regency as authentic messages. The account that the Ethiopian chronicle gives of the Duke of Abruzzo's visit is edifying in this regard. Received by the crown prince as he stepped out of his train on March 18, 1927, "while the musicians were playing music of salutation," the emissary of King Victor-Emmanuel II of Italy was treated to a veritable orgy of invented traditions during the parade staged by the whole army. The public speech of friendship that the Italian emissary delivered was, however, deemed hypocritical by the chronicler, who had, in the immediately preceding chapters of his chronicle, underscored the difficulties that the Ethiopian government had had to put up with while negotiating with Mussolini. He assures us that, on the day of the parade, no one—beginning with Täfäri—was fooled by the hypocritical marks of Italian friendship.³⁵ In this light, the *Funeral March* played during the Duke of Abruzzo's visit takes on a new meaning. What was in question was not necessarily a faux pas due to the amateurishness of Ethiopia's royal brass band; it may have been—why not?—a veritable warning issued to Italy's representative. The Duke was at the head of an important diplomatic mission, dispatched at a moment when border disputes in the Somalian frontier region were exacerbating tensions between Italy and Ethiopia. The question of the embargo on importing firearms that the powers had imposed on Ethiopia at the beginning of Menelik's reign continued to envenom relations between the two states, at a time when the long-standing negotiations over granting Ethiopia access to the sea via the port of Assab in the Italian colony of Eritrea were dragging on. The fascist government, which thinly veiled its expansionist ambitions and desire to avenge, in a new war, the affront that Italy had suffered with the defeat of Adwa, was thus discretely but firmly warned by the Ethiopian government that it was venturing down a dangerous path and that the Ethiopians were ready and waiting for the Italian battalions.

Choosing Foreigners to Play the "Nation's" Music

Once music is instrumentalized to accommodate foreign policy needs, the choice of foreign musicians to transmit messages of this type is not without symbolic implications. It also raises political questions.

Before the creation of the royal brass band, secular music in Ethiopia had been left to indigenous performers fitted out with their traditional instruments. These musicians were not highly regarded.[36] Only liturgical music was deemed sufficiently respectable to merit being written down or formally taught.[37] Creating a brass band thus necessarily implied, initially, paying foreign musicians for their services. There had already been a few attempts to do so, such as that of the Marquis de La Guibourgère early in the twentieth century. Under Menelik, there had been several Russian, Italian, French, and Swiss attempts to develop an embryonic European music in the country; all, however, had been short-lived.[38] A Russian brass band dispatched by Czar Nicholas II was briefly active in Ethiopia. An ephemeral Ethiopian orchestra was conducted by the Italian Salvadei, with tubas, horns, cornets, and trumpets.[39] Täfäri's attempt stood out from those that preceded it in that it lasted. Once Armenian musicians arrived in Addis Abeba in 1924, the development of a Western form of music was never again interrupted in the country.[40] In this context, the choice of Armenian musicians could hardly have been a matter of indifference. The question had been posed in the same terms in the wake of the 1896 battle of Adwa, when "none other than Menelik II, letting himself be persuaded, accepted the offers of the all-powerful imperial Russian diplomatic legation, *because Russia appeared to have no territorial ambitions in the region*; it provided him with the instructor and the instruments of the first Ethiopian brass band early in the century."[41] In the mid 1920s, it would doubtless have been impolitic to employ Italian musicians to this end, when the regime celebrated its victory at Adwa year in year out. Because of complicated relations with France and the United Kingdom, other states that were neighbors of an Ethiopia hemmed in by colonies of these three powers, hiring French or English musicians would have sown discord of the same kind.

From Menelik's reign onward, the creation of national symbols was bound up with the assertion of independence and Ethiopia's quest for international recognition. For example, the commemoration of the battle of Adwa instituted by Menelik made it possible to repeat symbolically, every year, the victory over the Italians, who personified the foreign threat. The perpetuation of this celebration during Täfäri's regency seems to have stood in for a national holiday in a period marked by flagrant imitation of European models.[42] Thus the idea of the nation was constructed in opposition to that of an external danger. The choice of other national symbols met the same imperatives. The tricolored Ethiopian flag gradually took final form between 1891 and 1897. The minting of Ethiopian coinage in 1894, an essential element in the affirmation of a state, constituted a way of denouncing the treaty of Ucciali, one of the clauses of which stipulated that minting money would be left to Italy.[43] Menelik insisted that, like his new coins, the first Ethiopian stamps, printed that same year, bear his likeness as well as that of the Lion of Juda, the emblem of the Solomonid monarchy; but, above all, that their legends appear only in Amharic, not in any European language, something that, by the same stroke, made them useless as international postage. Similarly, Menelik's equestrian statue, inaugurated in 1930 in the capital on the site formerly occupied by the "hanged men's tree" (before being transferred to its current site opposite Saint George's Church), was deliberately oriented toward the northeast, that is, toward Adwa, at a time when the sound of boots could again be heard on the borders with the Italian colonies.[44]

The choice of artisans to produce national symbols is, apparently, never innocent. Evoking the many gifts that Täfäri and Empress Zäwditu earmarked for heads of state whom the crown prince would encounter in Europe, the chronicle spells out that "these gifts were only made by Ethiopian skilled craftsmen, but no imported gifts were included ['mixed in']."[45] The same holds for the insignia worn to symbolize the exercise of imperial authority. When the British government acceded in 1924 to *Ras* Täfäri's demand that it return Tewodros's crown to Ethiopia—it had been spirited away when Lord Napier's expeditionary corps looted the royal fortress of Mäqdäla in 1868[46]—it aroused an unexpected reaction of mistrust that the French plenipotentiary in Ethiopia described as follows:

> It seems that the middle-level and the petty chiefs have categorically ruled out the possibility of restitution. They have declared that this was a trick of the English, who wished to "give the crown to their next emperor themselves," and that they felt obliged to protest against so humiliating an eventuality for their country. Their protest was, moreover, so vigorous that it was decided not to fire the canon in honor of the new announcement by *Ras* Täfäri. If an important personage should come from London to return the crown, as rumor has it he will, I wonder whether the reception accorded him would be the one he would—it must be said—have every right to count on receiving.[47]

The wearing of a crown can conceal an assumed political allegiance. The chronicle of Menelik's reign emphasizes that he refused to don the crown of his predecessor Emperor Yohannes, who was long his political rival and from whom he wished to mark himself off. With the repatriation of Tewodros's crown, an object delegitimated because it had passed through a foreign government's hands, Täfäri apparently made a political blunder that the chronicle of his regency opportunely glosses over by taking no notice of the grandees' objections. On the other hand, the chronicle prudently evokes the October 10, 1925, arrival of a royal throne made in England and offered as a gift by the British government, while clearly spelling out that Empress Zäwditu would continue to sit "on the throne of her father" Menelik, and that accepting the English throne, which bore engravings of the roses of England and the lion of Ethiopia, could in no way be interpreted as a token of submission to a foreign power, but was, rather, a mark of the friendship and equality between the two states.[48] Yet while Menelik and Haile Selassie refused to don a "foreign" crown, they did not seem troubled by the fact that their personal goldsmiths were Armenian artisans, as we shall see. The same remark holds as far as the treatment of the emperor's image is concerned, an eminently political and eminently sensitive question, with Menelik's choice of an Armenian immigrant as official Ethiopian court photographer. As appears in the case of the musicians and the royal brass band, indications are that preference was repeatedly given to employing Armenian immigrants rather than citizens of European states at court, especially when those states were colonial powers. To develop this reflection, we must now consider the circumstances under which the brass band came into existence during Täfäri's visit to the patriarch of the Armenians of Jerusalem.

2

The Long Time of an Event: From Jerusalem to Jerusalem

The April 29, 1924, meeting between *Ras* Täfäri and Patriarch Yeghishe Tourian in Jerusalem merits consideration, however poorly documented it may be. This event, at the origins of the creation of the royal brass band, gives us reason to think that, contrary to what has been written about the ostensible "tolerance and indifference" shown to foreigners in Ethiopia,[1] the religious question made a difference in the kings' attitude toward the Armenians.

Two Sister Churches

Because the crown prince had been brought up by Catholics under the supervision of the vicar apostolic of the Galla, Monseigneur André Jarosseau, rumors about his alleged sympathies for Catholicism or indifference to religious matters made the rounds. These were grave suspicions which, in the Ethiopian Church's view, were all but equivalent to the damning accusation of apostasy. Täfäri's political adversaries often resorted to this accusation to check his rise. In 1914, while still *däjazmach* of Harar, Täfäri was charged by the head of the Ethiopian Church, *Abunä* Matēwos, with having converted to Catholicism.[2] In the context of the internal struggles that divided Empress Zäwditu's entourage and the government into "conservatives" and "reformers," it was politic for *Ras* Täfäri to make a display of his religious orthodoxy by piously visiting the holy places before leaving on his journey to Europe.

Täfäri's journey to Jerusalem, the preliminary stage of his diplomatic tour, had all the features of an authentic pilgrimage. The visit to the Armenian patriarchate took place against the current, as it were, of a voyage geared to a quest for European-style modernity. The Ethiopian and Armenian Churches, with Egypt's Coptic Church, Syria's Jacobite Church, and the Indian Church of Malabar, are non-Uniate Eastern Churches, often improperly called "monophysitic" because of their refusal to accept the conclusions of the 451 Council of Chalcedon. Their mutual ties, of which many traces have come down to us from the Middle Ages, endure to the present day. Thus the priest Mgrdich Chelghadian was received in 1905 at the imperial court of Menelik II, whom he presented with a vial of holy chrism and a fragment of Christ's tomb set in mother-of-pearl. More recently, we may note the meeting of the patriarchs of the five non-Chalcedonian Eastern Churches held in Addis Abeba in 1964 under Emperor Haile Selassie's patronage.

The presence of an Ethiopian monastic community in Jerusalem, attested since the thirteenth century, has conferred a certain regularity on these exchanges. In contrast, Ethiopia, whose religious culture and literature were initially elaborated in the context of the Christian Near East, had only sporadic contacts with Roman Catholicism before the mid-fifteenth century.[3] Material traces of these Armenian-Ethiopian exchanges can be found in ancient manuscript collections.[4] Literary traditions, too, bear witness to them. Thus the greater part of the *Käbrä Nägäst* or *Glory of Kings*, a "*chef-d'oeuvre* of Ethiopian literature" written down in the fourteenth century, was composed setting out from words attributed to Saint Gregory the Illuminator, who evangelized Armenia early in the fourth century.[5] Together with his contemporaries, the martyred Saint Hripsime and King Tiridates, the first Christian king of Armenia, Saint Gregory has been adopted by the Ethiopian Church.[6] It was in Armenia that one of the best known Ethiopian saints, Ewostatēwos, ended his days in 1352, after fleeing Ethiopia in the wake of grave disputes dividing the monastic world there. According to his hagiography (the *Gädlä Ewostatēwos*), as I was reminded some twenty years ago by a young Eritrean priest who naively considered this story to be true, Ewostatēwos is supposed to have crossed the sea by sailing across it on his own coat, when the Virgin Mary informed him in a vision that Armenia was to be his final destination.[7] Father Dimotheos Saprichian's narrative, which recounts a mid-nineteenth-century voyage by two Armenian churchmen, shows that these religious ties remained sufficiently strong to influence the way Armenians were received in Ethiopia in periods closer to our own.

Dimotheos's Travels

The story goes that Patriarch Yesayi Garabedian (1865–85), when he received a visitor of standing in Jerusalem, never failed, after favoring him with the seven ritual gifts—a little arak, a little rose water, bread and salt, and so on—to summon the archimandrite (*vartabed*) Dimotheos, who would hand the visitor a copy of his book, printed at the Armenian monastery's press. Involved here, no doubt, was a touch of pride at being able to show that the radius of action of the Armenian patriarchate in the Holy Land extended as far as distant Ethiopia, which, at the time, was reputed to be hostile and dangerous. Father Dimotheos's travel narrative is indeed exceptional testimony to the institutional and spiritual bonds between Armenian and Ethiopian Christians in the mid-nineteenth century.

Armenians and Ethiopians in the Holy Land

The voyage of Archbishop Sahak Kharpertsi (Isaac of Kharpert) and Father Dimotheos Saprichian to Ethiopia, between 1867 and 1869, was linked to the diplomatic crisis that broke out between Emperor Tewodros II (1865–8) and the United Kingdom in the mid-1860s. It led to the seizure of European hostages, among them the British consul Charles Cameron and, subsequently, a special envoy of the British government, Hormuzd Rassam. In 1867, the United Kingdom's ambassador to the Sublime Porte, arguing that "the Abyssinians of Jerusalem were under the jurisdiction of the Armenian Patriarch of the Holy City," requested that the patriarch send emissaries to Tewodros to urge him to intercede to free the hostages.[8] Contacts between Armenian and Ethiopian monks of the Holy Land were, indeed, not just customary but even inscribed in a form of relation of dependency. As Dimotheos reminds his readers, "Before our stay in Abyssinia, we were already somewhat familiar with its inhabitants, since a colony of monks of this nation is found in the holy city; the monks have been living there for several centuries under the patronage of the Armenian monastery, whose Patriarch they recognize as their spiritual head."[9]

One has doubtless to go back to 1517, when Palestine came under Ottoman rule at about the same time as Imam Ahmad Grañ's campaigns and the destabilization of Christian Ethiopia began,[10] to explain why the position of the Ethiopian monks of Jerusalem had grown weaker and why the Armenian patriarchate had begun to extend its patronage to them. Until this time, the Ethiopians had rights of access to the Holy Sepulcher (where they kept the Holy Flame burning), comparable to those of other Churches, and were the proprietors of a number of clearly identified holy places.[11] The Ottoman authorities converted the prerogatives that they confirmed or conceded to the various Churches present in Jerusalem into a source of revenue. From this point on, possession of chapels and other parts of the Holy Sepulcher was conditioned on the payment of sums that the smallest religious communities, such as the Ethiopians', could not afford. It was thanks to this policy that the Greek, Roman Catholic, and Armenian communities were able to expand their real-estate holdings in Palestine, gradually establishing themselves as the main guardians of the holy places. This preeminence, already firmly in place by the early eighteenth century, was fixed in its existing form by a firman of Sultan Abdülmejid's (1852) that gave rise to the Status Quo of the Holy Places, internationally recognized by the Treaties of Paris (1856), Berlin (1878), and Versailles (1919).[12]

By taking up their quarters in the Dayr al-Sultan monastery, on the roof of the Holy Sepulcher just above the chapel of Saint Helena that had fallen to the Armenians inside the basilica, the Ethiopian monks had found a way of continuing to live in the greatest possible proximity to the holy places to which they had lost their rights. Clientelist relations were gradually instituted between the Ethiopians and the Armenians, who posed as protectors of the other Eastern Christian communities vis-à-vis the sultan's representative. From the 1640s on, the Ethiopian monks were considered to be bound to the Armenian patriarchate, like the Jacobite Syrians whom official Ottoman documents designated as the Armenians' *yamak*.[13] We can hear, perhaps, an echo of this ancient terminology in the strange charge leveled by the Anglican bishop Samuel Gobat and relayed by the British consul James Finn in 1850, according to which the Armenians had, two years earlier, beaten the Abyssinians of the city and chained "an iron collar round their necks, with a screw to tighten the collar."[14] The same source accuses them of inciting the Turks to burn the Ethiopian monks' precious manuscripts in the days of the plague that, twelve years earlier, had swept the Ethiopians off. It is in these troubled circumstances that the deeds according to the Ethiopian monks possession of the Dayr al-Sultan monastery are likewise supposed to have disappeared. These are, however, isolated accusations.[15]

At all events, it is clear that the Ethiopian monks were in a position of weakness vis-à-vis the other religious communities, the Armenian community not excepted. A firman issued by Sultan Mehmed IV in 1654 shows that the Armenians had taken possession of several places in Jerusalem that had once been Ethiopian. The following year, a judgment by the kadi of the city ratified this state of affairs, alluding to a certain "Sarkis al-Armanī al-Habašī," whose two surnames (meaning "the Armenian" and "the Abyssinian") are revealing; he passed for the Armenian patriarchate's man in charge of Abyssinian affairs in his capacity as Armenian cosignatory for Ethiopian properties before the court. The controversy of Dayr al-Sultan, which precipitated an extraordinary imbroglio between 1820 and 1863, reveals that this relation of subordination had crystallized and been institutionalized. It long pitted the Ethiopian monks against their Coptic counterparts over the issue of possession and retention of the keys to this monastery. The Armenian patriarchs, who presented themselves as the Ethiopians', Copts', and Syriacs' patrons, seized on the question and posed as arbiters, taking care not to infringe the interests of any of the parties so as to maintain the fidelity of all of them to the Armenians. This episode highlights the great precariousness of Jerusalem's Ethiopian monks, who, since the Copts had evicted them from Dayr al-Sultan, no longer disposed of a place where they could celebrate the Eucharist. The Armenian patriarchate procured their daily sustenance for them. According to a Protestant minister's 1860 testimony, this assistance in the form of foodstuffs consisted of two big kettles of soup accompanied by seventy-five little loaves of bread. Indications are that it was first provided early in the eighteenth century "when the Abyssinians were starving," after which this practice was perpetuated and institutionalized. In 1841, the head of an Ethiopian mission to Jerusalem, Aläqa Häbtä Sellasē, implored the Armenian patriarch to see to augmenting the quantities of food that were thus doled out to the Ethiopian monks. Seven years later, Emperor Sahlä Dengel sent a letter to Patriarch Giragos Mnatseganian and his treasurer, Boghos Krikorian, protesting against the suspension of this aid, which had become indispensable.[16]

These gifts of foodstuffs are still fresh in people's minds in Jerusalem, where the Armenian patriarchate, from which the Ethiopians obtain their holy chrism, conspicuously continues to extend its protection to them. Until 1948, the Ethiopian monks were allowed to celebrate Pentecost in the churchyard of the Armenian church of the Holy Savior—a favor that the patriarchate persisted in not granting the Syriacs and the Copts, for fear that they might someday make territorial claims. Similarly, although the burial of Ethiopians, Syriacs, and Copts in the Armenian cemetery adjacent to the church near the Zion gate was only allowed on a case-by-case basis, on condition that the gravestones not bear inscriptions—in order to avoid, once again, future imbroglios and disputes over real estate—an exception was made, it seems, for two Ethiopian "princes" who had died in exile in Jerusalem after Italy conquered their country. Kevork Hintlian, Patriarch Yeghishe Derderian's (1960–90) former secretary, to whom I owe this information, has told me that he had for his part put the sum of 5,000 dollars in the hands of the impoverished Ethiopian monks in the 1970s (doubtless after the collapse of Ethiopia's imperial regime). Even if the gifts in foodstuffs had long since ceased, the patron-client relations between the Armenian patriarchate and the Ethiopian monks had apparently endured.

Dimotheos and Sahak set out for Ethiopia at a time when the Armenian patriarchate was clearly profiting from the strengthening of its position and the impoverishment of the Ethiopian monks in the Holy Land in order to pose as their benefactor, while letting it be known that it had assumed that role. In his March 30, 1867, letter to Emperor Tewodros, Patriarch Yesayi took care to remind him of "the charitable affection that we show in a material fashion to the pious Ethiopian monks living in Jerusalem who, from time immemorial, have stood under the protection of our Apostolic See,"[17] as if to put the emperor in a better disposition to give his two emissaries a warm reception. The patriarch was also at pains to point out that his predecessor, Hovhannes Smiurnatsi (John of Smyrna), had in 1858 been happy to receive one of Tewodros's representatives during his pilgrimage to Jerusalem.[18] It was, moreover, well known in Ethiopia that the situation left the Ethiopian monks and, consequently, their sovereigns, beholden to the Armenian patriarchate. The chronicle of the reign of Yohannes IV (1872–89), in whom Sahak and Dimotheos found a benevolent protector at the end of their stay in Ethiopia, cites a letter from the emperor to the Ethiopian monks of Jerusalem in which he takes umbrage because he has heard it said that "the people of Ethiopia have no King, that they were beggars and lived by begging from the Armenians and other countries."[19]

The Vicissitudes of the Voyage: From Suspicion to Recognition

The two Armenian churchmen, who set out from Jerusalem on April, 1867, would not return until June 1869, after a long, arduous journey that culminated in the utter failure of their bid to act as mediators.[20] The problems began as soon as they left the banks of the Red Sea in the Sudan and plunged into the African land mass, heading for northern Ethiopia. As Dimotheos tells it, their lives were repeatedly threatened and they nearly lost the precious gifts, among them a fragment of the True Cross, that they had been charged with taking to Emperor Tewodros. The two men failed, in fact, to reach the emperor's court, because a spate of rebellions had thrown the area they were traveling through into turmoil. The greatest of their misfortunes was a forced stay of several months' duration near Gondär, where they were held captive by a rebel leader, Teso Gobäzē, and subjected to a trying itinerant captivity in the Bägēmder and Lasta regions, as well as endless attempts on the part of the inhabitants of the poverty-stricken villages in which they stopped to divest them of their possessions. Dimotheos bitterly insists on the fact that these villagers and their leaders gave him very little to eat:

> I was constantly flying into a rage at those who approached us, asking them for bread and calling them heartless, cruel creatures. One of them once told me, "We are aware of your plight and are touched by it, but we can do nothing for you nor meet any of your needs before learning your Haïmanote (religion)."[21]

Somewhat earlier, Teso Gobäzē had demanded that the two captives wear their ceremonial dress in public. According to Dimotheos, the Ethiopians were "breathless with admiration" for the embroideries of silk and gold thread in which the Armenian bishop was arrayed, and for the gems adorning his cowl; they said that even their own bishop who had come from Egypt had never worn such beautiful things. The two Armenians, of course, deemed this obligatory display "an insult to the veneration due the Church and its sacred objects," yet could not but acknowledge that it did not leave its spectators indifferent. "And those who had looked at us askance now started to alter their behavior toward us and fear us, as if they had beheld some heavenly vision."

The sequel is still more interesting. The two men's situation changed radically after "Abyssinian learned men" (i.e., priests) were sent out to meet them and question them about their faith: "When they learned that we were Armenian Orthodox, they were overcome with joy, respectfully kissed the cross that we were wearing, and promised, after asking us for our benediction, to intercede with the sovereign in order to incline him in our favor." The treatment meted out to the two Armenians did in fact improve considerably once they were no longer assimilated to foreign peoples, for whom, according to Dimotheos himself, the Ethiopians harbored the greatest imaginable mistrust:

> Learned and well-read men are very rare in Abyssinia, where the whole people is awash in the crassest ignorance, so that some took us for Turks, others for Europeans or Englishmen, while a few even thought we were Copts. However, once our religion and nation became known thanks to learned men, they gradually came to hold us in high esteem, paying us the same respect that they showed their clergy and ecclesiastical dignitaries.[22]

The similarity between the Ethiopian and Armenian churches was, then, a major asset. After this episode, Dimotheos and Sahak were never again harassed during their stay in Ethiopia and had no occasion to complain about a single act of negligence. Having fallen, now, into the hands of *Wagshum* Gobäzē, one of Tewodros' rivals (he would have proclaimed himself emperor under the name of Täklä Giyorgis at Tewodros's death in 1868), the two men gained the confidence of the population of the regions in which they sojourned, even distributing amulets "which sick people carried around with them like relics," something that the Ethiopian clergy noted with equanimity. If Dimotheos is to be believed, their prestige in the region in which they were held captive was such that it was only reluctantly that they were allowed to leave when the order to free them, issued by the United Kingdom's consul general in Egypt, finally reached *Wagshum* Gobäzē, enjoining him to arrange for the clergymen to be handed over to his rival, *Däjazmach* Kasa of Tigré, who had promised to grant them safe passage to the port of Massawa. In Adwa, Tigré's biggest city, Sahak and Dimotheos were received with multiple marks of consideration. They encountered an Ethiopian monk there whom they knew from Jerusalem, "the doctor Mikayel the Abyssinian, who had been brought up in our Saint James's Armenian monastery, where he had once enjoyed the favors and friendship of several members of the same congregation."[23] The fact that he was part of *Däjazmach* Kasa's entourage seems to have facilitated things for the two Armenians. Dimotheos writes that they were paid the signal honor of being allowed to enter the sanctum sanctorum of the church Maryam Tseyon (Maria of Zion) in Aksum in order to contemplate the most precious of the Ethiopian Church's treasures, the Ark of the Covenant, which was supposed to contain the Tablets of the Law that Moses received on Mount Sinai—it had reputedly been pilfered from the Temple in Jerusalem by King Solomon's and the Queen of Sheba's natural son, Menelik. Dimotheos and Sahak rejoiced in anticipation of the opportunity that they had thus been offered to expose the contradictions in this legend by demonstrating that the ostensible Tablets were nothing but crude counterfeits. Convinced, after the fact, that what was involved was well and truly a hoax, they were nevertheless polite—or prudent—enough not to reveal what they thought to the Ethiopian priests accompanying them. However that might be, the fact that they were allowed to contemplate the Ark of the Covenant speaks volumes about the prestige that the Armenian Church enjoyed in Ethiopia in this period.[24] The only reasons for satisfaction that Dimotheos mentions in his book, in the course of a narrative about the vicissitudes of a voyage that he seems to have otherwise recalled as calamitous and all but traumatic, were the numerous honors shown him as an Armenian monk; they inspired Archbishop Sahak to write in a letter addressed to the British vice-consul general in Egypt a few months later: "We have received many […] marks of kindness and favor from Dédjadjmatch-Kassa [*Däjazmach* Kasa], prince of Thègri [Tigré], who received us as if we had been his co-religionists."[25] Therein resides the interest of Dimotheos's book: it shows that in the mid-nineteenth century, at the heart of the Ethiopian political and ecclesiastical elites, a sharp distinction, based on religious ties, could still be drawn between Armenian visitors and other foreigners.[26]

The Question of the *Abun*: two Armenian Monks in the Labyrinth of Ethiopian Politics

According to Dimotheos, Kasa was aware of the preeminent status of the Armenian Church in Jerusalem. It was thus in full awareness of the facts that he proposed the office of *abun* (or metropolitan) to Archbishop Sahak:

> He had been informed of the great difference between the Armenian and Coptic communities, between the spiritual prerogatives of one and the other with regard to jurisdiction and hierarchy; he had been told about the jurisdiction that His Grace the Armenian Patriarch of Jerusalem had over the three communities residing in the Holy Land, the Copts, the Abyssinians, and the Syrians; mention had also been made to him of the daily nourishment and benefits that the Abyssinian colony of Jerusalem received from the Armenian monastery. After the Great Prince had learned all these details, he spoke to them, it is said, as follows: "These are signs of the true Christian religion. I had already been apprised of everything that you have just told me, especially the food that has been given to the Abyssinian monks of Jerusalem from time immemorial." From that day on, Prince Kasa showed us the most gracious attentions and paid us the greatest honors. One day, during one of his visits, he said to us: "I would like to acquaint all my subjects with the Armenian Abuna [bishop] in order to plant the seed of sympathetic consideration in the hearts of them all; they will soon see with their own eyes the difference in

morality and manners between you and the Coptic Bishop, and how much more magnificent your Church is in its rite and offices."[27]

In the Ethiopian Church, the *abun* was the supreme authority, the only person empowered to ordain priests and deacons and bless altars, the people, and the chrism of the imperial unction. This also gave him a position of the first importance on the Ethiopian political scene. It was customary to summon an Egyptian bishop delegated by the Coptic patriarch of Alexandria to exercise the office of *abun*, for the Ethiopian Church was not yet autocephalous. Relations with Egypt were complicated by the dangerous nature of the roads, but also by Muslim domination of Egypt, with which both the Coptic Church and the Ethiopian monarchy had had to come to terms. The Ethiopian Christian community had therefore gone through several periods in which its only episcopal see was vacant. For centuries, the difficult negotiations connected with the dispatch of a new *abun* had comprised a major stake of Ethiopian sovereigns' foreign policy, and this continued to be the case during Täfäri's regency and thereafter, until the first Ethiopian *abun* was enthroned in January 1951 under Haile Selassie.[28] The proposal made to Archbishop Sahak thus bears witness, in its turn, to the Armenian Church's prestige in Ethiopia in the nineteenth century. It was not an isolated proposal, since, according to Dimotheos, Menelik himself, "prince of Shoa [Shäwa], when he was informed that we had left for Thegri [Tigré], immediately sent a messenger to ask us to govern his country's Church." As Dimotheos tells it, only the opposition of the "partisans of the Coptic prelate, who had the support of Dédjadjmatch-Kassa's enemies," prevented him "from making this change of prelates and bringing his peoples to accept, without disposing them to do so in advance, the Bishop of what was, for them, a foreign Church."[29] Moreover, the imperial chronicle of Yohannes IV (the name that Kasa, who was crowned *negusä nägäst* in 1872, took upon becoming emperor), mentions this proposal in terms that corroborate Dimotheos's account, while ascribing rejection of the proposal to the unwillingness of "a Metropolitan whose name was Abuna Yeshaq [Archbishop Sahak] from Armenia" to remain in Ethiopia.[30]

Not long before, several Ethiopian political leaders had made a bid to appeal to the Armenian rather than the Coptic Church to exercise the office of *abun*. Although such a proposal represented a departure from the practice of bringing a bishop from Egypt to Ethiopia, it did not violate any religious principle, as a French traveler remarked in the 1840s: "The Ethiopians cannot choose an aboune [*abun*] from among the people of their nation," but they can "bring him from Cairo or anywhere else, as long as he is white," even if "the custom is to ask that he be sent by the Patriarch of Alexandria, who grants this request in exchange for the sum of 5,000 thalers."[31] Dimotheos maintains that a request had been addressed "to our Patriarch fifteen years ago," that is, around 1855, by Emperor Tewodros himself, who renewed it three years later, unsuccessfully, "because of the dangers of the journey and the constant turmoil reigning in the country," but also because

> our Patriarch did not want to seem to be usurping the spiritual power and infringing upon the jurisdiction of the Abyssinian Church, which belongs to the Patriarch of the Copts. The latter needs the resources represented by the 10,000

thalers that he is paid as a fee for delegating a prelate, since the time when Abuna-Selami [*Abunä* Sälama, who died in 1867] breathed his last.³²

Other Ethiopian potentates made similar attempts, sending a mission to the archbishop of the Armenians of Egypt in 1826–7 or directly addressing letters to the same effect to the Armenian patriarchate of Jerusalem in 1850. An Armenian priest named Hovhannes, a native of Isfahan, is said to have boasted that he held the title of *abun* at the court of the King of Shäwa, Sahlä Sellasē, in the 1820s and 1830s.³³ While the two Armenian clergymen were held prisoner in Ethiopia, *Wagshum* Gobäzē is also supposed to have nursed a plan to make Sahak the new *abun*, upon the announcement of Tewodros's death, as a replacement for the deceased *Abunä* Sälama, so that Gobäzē might be proclaimed emperor with Sahak's benediction. A few weeks earlier, the rebel leader who had taken the two Armenians captive on their arrival in Ethiopia, Teso Gobäzē, is said to have contemplated establishing Sahak as "Grand Prelate of Abyssinia" in Gondär.³⁴ Not all these attempts were motivated by religious considerations; some stemmed from a strategy to conquer political power, or to legitimize a power obtained in bitter struggle. Such attempts are reminiscent of the instrumentalization of the institutional ties between the Armenian and the Ethiopian Church, to which many Ethiopian sovereigns and political leaders seem to have had recourse from the beginnings of the modern period on.

The Kings of Ethiopia, the Armenians, and the Outside World

To understand the creation of the royal brass band, the identification of Armenians as coreligionists by Ethiopia's Christians must be taken into account. This identification invites us to reflect upon the genesis of a political culture over the *longue durée*.

Politics of the Past, Politics of the Present

Cultural anthropology takes up a very similar problematic when it seeks to elucidate "one of the deepest mysteries confronting the human sciences," namely, "the kind of thing that binds the England of Elizabeth I to that of Elizabeth II, Tokugawa's Japan to modern Japan, the Russia of the Czars to the Russia of party secretaries," and so on. This problematic can be summed up in the following formula: "Everything changes, except for what remains the same." In this perspective, "the mixed voices [of the past and the present] must be distinguished so that we can hear what each of them says,"³⁵ in order to determine "the ideological contribution of politics past to politics present."³⁶ Similarly, when we try to set the 1924 creation of the royal brass band in relation to certain episodes of Dimotheos's journey, the connections we think we can discern between present and past suggest the existence of a kind of ideological continuity in the Ethiopian sovereigns' policies. This is, however, a far cry from invoking the static, immutable existence of representations of the other and the outside world in order to explain the original features of the Armenian immigration in the twentieth century. The criticism that one can make of Geertz's culturalist theory, the interest of his interpretive approach notwithstanding, is that it ends up reifying the subject under observation. This behaviorist premise, which claims that a theory of culture remains possible "by building up from directly observable modes of thought,"[37] also marks the work of Donald Levine, who claims to reveal the mentality of entire peoples without being aware, it seems, that he reasons on the basis of collective entities without drawing finer distinctions.[38] The problem of the construction of representations is more complex than the definition of a "mentality" would suggest, because, like any other social phenomenon, it indiscriminately combines individual and collective factors, present considerations and traces of experiences of the past. It would be unwarranted and illusory to claim to discern a hypothetical Ethiopian mentality or collective imaginary capable of explaining Täfäri's decision to create a royal brass band with Armenian musicians, for such an interpretation would come down to conceiving, in a direct line of descent from Fernand Braudel, "mental frameworks" as "long-term prisons [*prisons de longue durée*]" endowed with the same permanence that Braudel attributed to the "geographic frameworks of civilizations," hence as limits "from which man and his experiences can hardly free themselves."[39] Taking our distance from this conception of the *longue durée*, influenced by structuralism, we shall consider representations as the fruit of constant negotiation and reflect upon their political uses, rather than assuming their hypothetical permanence.

Religion, Diplomacy, and the Differentiation of Attitudes vis-à-vis Foreigners

In Ethiopia, the question of religion seems to have helped differentiate both the Armenians and the Greeks from the "Franks." The recrudescence of European voyages to Ethiopia beginning in the second quarter of the nineteenth century, the favorable reception often given to travelers by political leaders—for example, Tewodros II and Yohannes IV, although they were reputed to be intransigent in this domain—who wished to better their armies, the education or "industry" of their subjects, or, again, their relations with the foreign governments from which they could reasonably expect support, clearly show that the image of a generalized hostility toward foreigners must be relativized, even where Catholic or Protestant missionaries were concerned.[40] The missionaries, to be sure, could be tolerated only to the extent that they did not interfere with the Ethiopian clergy, as is shown by the case of the Lazarist mission established in Tigré in the 1840s by Justin de Jacobis with *Däjazmach* Webē's support, in the face, it is true, of a certain hostility from the head of the Ethiopian Church, *Abunä* Sälama. Thus, despite a manifest relaxation of the extreme tensions typical of the seventeenth century, the religious question remained a ticklish one in the mid-nineteenth century, continuing to exercise an influence on the reception accorded to foreigners.[41] A French government envoy could, consequently, still explain the negative reception that the *negus* of Shäwa, Sahlä Sellasē, gave an English diplomatic mission by invoking "the suspicious jealousy with which Abyssinians regard foreigners who, when they arrive in the country, display a political character; this is an uneasy prejudice bequeathed them by the Muslim invasions that swept down on them in the sixteenth century, and by the civil unrest stirred up among them in this period by the presence of Portuguese and Catholic missionaries."[42]

It is true that, under Emperor Gälawdēwos (1541–59), in the early stages of the *rapprochement* with the kingdom of Portugal inspired by the prospect of an anti-Muslim alliance, differences in rite and doctrine had sown discord, making the Portuguese, initially regarded as saviors in the confrontation with Imam Ahmad Grañ,[43] seem like a new source of danger. In 1632, in reaction to the early seventeenth-century attempt to unite the Ethiopian Church with Rome,[44] the Jesuit mission was expelled after Emperor Susenyos abdicated in favor of his son Fasilädäs and European clergymen were prohibited from entering the kingdom.[45] Not until the 1769–72 stay of the Scotsman James Bruce in Gondär and the 1790 publication of his *Travels to Discover the Source of the Nile* did Europeans once again have access to a recent description of Ethiopia.

Some European voyages to Ethiopia did take place in this long interval, but they were rare and closely monitored. Among them were voyages by the German Lutheran minister Peter Heyling during the reign of Emperor Fasilädäs (the mystery of Heyling's disappearance has yet to be solved), the French physician Charles Jacques Poncet in 1699, and the 1751–2 mission led by the Franciscan monk of Czech extraction Remedius Prutky. The Catholic missionaries did not abandon all effort to bring the Ethiopian Church from "heresy" to the "true faith." Several of their number were, however, decapitated on their way to Ethiopia, or stoned to death upon their arrival in Gondär, during the reign of Fasilädäs and also thereafter, in 1714 or 1716. According to Prutky, the kings of Ethiopia had acquired the habit of putting these clergymen, who disguised themselves by dressing as laymen, to the test "by offering a woman to the first foreigner who happened along."[46] Thus Poncet wrote to Maillet, the French consul in Cairo, upon learning that two Jesuits named Grenier and Paulet had left for Ethiopia in November 1700: "Sir, where are they going? The country I have just left nurses so fierce a hatred of the name Frank that they do not eat white grapes; I leave the rest to your imagination."[47] These two Jesuits were finally held up at Sennar in the Sudan in the middle of the rainy season, where they died one after the other in December 1701. As for the 1705 mission led, after Poncet's return to Versailles, by Lenoir du Roule, Louis XIV's ambassador and French vice-consul in Damiette, it was massacred to a man in Sennar before it could reach Ethiopia, although this did not prevent its guide, an Armenian named Elias, from turning up in Gondär a few months later.[48]

The Armenians at the Court in Gondär

Despite the relative impenetrability of Christian Ethiopia, Armenian and Greek travelers continued to be accepted there without major problems after 1632. Some have even left us manuscript notes on their travels, or true travel narratives, of which one of the best known is Bishop Hovhannes Tutunji's. It has been repeatedly published, translated, and commented on.[49] Tutunji set out from Cairo in September 1678. In 1679, he reached the imperial capital city of Gondär, where he spent four months. He was aware of the privilege that this represented, for he notes in his travel narrative that foreigners were not allowed to sojourn in Abyssinia. The chronicle of Emperor Yohannes I's reign

(1667–82) confirms that "a bishop named Yohannes [Hovhannes] came from Armenia and entered the city, carrying a priceless, very precious object in his hand, a bone from the hand of the renowned ecumenic doctor Ewostatēwos, and bearing a letter from the patriarch of Alexandria," who asked that Hovhannes be well received. According to the chronicle, the emperor convoked an assembly of the highest clerical dignitaries, among them the metropolitan Sinoda and eminent members of the monastic order founded by disciples of Ewostatēwos, the Ethiopian saint who had died in Armenia three hundred years earlier, before proceeding to question "this bishop on the subject of the faith" "through the intermediary of an interpreter for the language named Murad." The very closely conducted theological examination to which Hovhannes was subjected—the chronicle provides a detailed account of the questions and answers—prefigures the one that Archbishop Sahak and Father Dimotheos would undergo some two centuries later. The bishop's answers were deemed satisfactory: "Because the faith and the precepts that he follows are in accord with ours, we should receive this venerated bone with hymns and canticles."[50] Accepting the relic was tantamount to acknowledging the visitor's doctrinal respectability. Tutunji nevertheless writes that he requested that his visit be cut short because of the priests' searching investigations of his faith. This request may have its explanation in the opposition to the return of a relic of Ewostatēwos expressed by a fraction of the Ethiopian clergy and echoed in the imperial chronicle. Certain authors, such as the German orientalist Job Ludolf, have also claimed that Emperor Yohannes wished to make Bishop Hovhannes Tutunji the new *abun*, at a time when *Abunä* Sinoda was still in office, a hypothesis that is rendered credible, if one trusts the Armenian sources, by the Armenian's tumultuous ecclesiastical career. It may explain the Ethiopian clergy's eagerness to see him leave Gondär.[51]

European scholars as well as travelers curious about things Ethiopian regarded this as the consequence of a religious proximity that was there for all to see in the Church of the Holy Sepulcher, but also of the complementarity between the Armenian merchants' savoir-faire and the well-known distaste of the kings of Gondär for extended voyages. Long-distance Ethiopian trade was accordingly entrusted to Arab or Armenian merchants; the latter, "not much differing in their form of worship, from the Abessines [Abyssinians], carry the greatest Trade, as being great Dealers in all part of the World."[52] James Bruce, the first European to make an extended stay in Ethiopia after the break of 1632, notes that, late in the eighteenth century, Abyssinia's grandees were still accustomed to employing foreigners as agents to conduct commerce on their behalf: "These men are chiefly Greeks, or Armenians, but the preference is always given to the latter," since, as Ottoman subjects, they had the advantage that came with being able to trade from the Levant to the shores of the Red Sea "without being liable to those insults and extortions from the Turkish officers that other strangers are." To explain this preference, the Scotsman invokes the good reputation of the network created by Armenian merchants from the Persian city of New Julfa, which stretched from the Baltic Sea to the Indian Ocean. He does not hesitate to make use of the stereotypes of his day in the process: "The Armenians, of all the people in the East, are those most remarkable for their patience and sobriety. They are generally masters of most of the eastern languages; are of strong, robust constitutions; of all people, the most attentive to the beasts and merchandise they have in charge; exceedingly faithful, and content with little."⁵³ This "preference" is reminiscent of the privileges that Ottoman Empire's Armenian merchants had over their European counterparts. It contrasts with the treatment reserved for "schismatics" in European ports such as Livorno or Venice, where the Armenian merchant communities were, like the Jews, ordered to keep a low profile.⁵⁴

The 1802 publication, in the Armenian monastery in Venice, of an original description of "Habesh" (or Abyssinia), coming only a few years after Bruce's, shows that the Armenian presence in Ethiopia was quite stable. The author of this text, the abbot Sdepannos Agonts, knew that certain non-European sources at his disposal could provide fresh, previously unpublished information in a day and age in which few Europeans ventured into this part of the world. He relied in particular on the manuscript narrative of the jeweler Hovhannes Thovmajian, whom Empress Mentewwab had employed as her treasurer in Gondär between 1764 and 1766; he did not expressly cite it yet very faithfully reproduced it. On the basis of these unpublished sources, Agonts affirms that "the bulk of the country's trade was in the hands of Jews and Arabs," adding that "it is also said to be in the hands of Armenians, but this was the case a long time ago, because, in our era, few Armenians have gone there." Like European authors before him, Agonts notes that the Armenian presence in Ethiopia benefited its inhabitants, who were "eager for knowledge, but wholly deprived of all the sciences of the trades." Taking his inspiration from Thovmajian's caustic, voluntarily sardonic text, he declares:

> They perform their calculations with beans and chick peas, for they have no knowledge of arithmetic. Yet it is said that, today, at the court, people have taken lessons in the use of written numbers from the Armenians [...]. In recent times, the title of guardian of the treasury has been given to two men of the Armenian nation in succession. There may have been others, but these two are the only ones known.⁵⁵

Employing Armenian auxiliaries in commerce, but also in the administration of the empire's properties, became a rather frequent practice in the modern period. Many of these Armenians have doubtless slipped through the gaps in the sources, such as the young man by the name of Stepan whom he had seen, Thovmajian writes, dazzling the court at Gondär with his bravery by wrestling bare handed with one of the emperor's lions. There was also the unnamed thirty-year-old Armenian who knew Turkish, Arabic, Malayalam, and *Tegreñña*, and had a perfect command of Amharic to boot; Bruce crossed his path in a port in southern Arabia. The Scottish traveler reports that the man "spoke with tears in his eyes of Abyssinia," from which he had been banned after having been one of the young Emperor Iyoas's favorites.⁵⁶ This may have been Boghos, Thovmajian's son, although this is uncertain.

We are, in contrast, remarkably well informed about the activities of a certain Murad, or Khodja Murad, the interpreter mentioned in the imperial chronicle of the Armenian bishop Tutunji's 1679 visit to Gondär. Born in Aleppo around 1619, Khodja Murad probably lived in Ethiopia from 1653 on. For some fifty years, he was also the commercial agent of three successive Ethiopian emperors, Fasilädäs (1632–67), Yohannes I (1667–82), and Iyasu I (1682–1706). It was on their behalf that he traveled to Yemen, the Indies (Surat, and then to the court of the Great Mogul Aurangzeb in Delhi in 1663–64), and, on three occasions, to Batavia (Insulindia): in 1674–5, 1689–91, and 1694–7. Countless traces of his peregrinations survive in the Dutch archives of the United Company of the East Indies (*Verenigde Oost Indische Compagnie*, or VOC), the travel narratives of voyagers such as François Bernier and Jean-Baptiste Tavernier, and the correspondence between the German Orientalist Job Ludolf and the VOC's agents in Batavia. Intrigued by this personage who invariably presented himself as the emperor of Ethiopia's envoy and was reputed to speak Arabic, Turkish, Farsi, Hindi, and Amharic, although he could neither read nor write, his interlocutors hesitated. Was he well and truly an ambassador or was he just an impostor? In a 1699 letter, Ludolf tried to explain the man's contradictions in these terms: "To send such an inept ambassador is truly unbecoming to such a great king. However, the Abyssinians, being totally ignorant of lands, journeys, and travelling, are accustomed to send foreigners, mostly Armenians, who know several languages."[57]

As early as the beginning of the sixteenth century, Queen Eleni, acting as regent for her son Lebnä Dengel (1508–40), had dispatched "an Armenian merchant named Matthew"[58] or Matēwos, "skilful in Foraign Affairs, and one that understood the Arabic language,"[59] to King João of Portugal with a letter. Matēwos lived in Ethiopia, spoke several languages, like Khodja Murad, and had traveled extensively in the Near East. His mission was of the highest importance, since the queen was offering one-third of her domains in exchange for military assistance against the Muslims, who were threatening Christian Ethiopia ever more seriously.[60] As with the Dutch in Murad's case, the Portuguese were hard put to decide whether Matēwos the Armenian really was an Ethiopian court envoy. Suspected of being a Turkish spy, he was imprisoned for several years in Goa on orders from the viceroy of the Indies, Albuquerque. He was finally received in Portugal by João's successor, King Manoel, and sent back to Ethiopia together with the famous Portuguese mission in which Father Alvares also took part. He died at the end of his return voyage in 1520.[61]

In the same line of descent as these missed diplomatic meetings is the astonishing imbroglio that occurred in 1701 when the French physician Poncet, who said he was on the way back from Gondär, presented himself to Consul Benoist de Maillet in Cairo in the company of a certain Murad. The latter, a nephew of the famous Khodja Murad just mentioned, introduced himself as the envoy of the emperor of Ethiopia, Iyasu I, to King Louis XIV of France. It seems that this Murad the Younger, who was supposed to be a former cook from Aleppo and was said to be illiterate, had only been chosen to accompany Poncet to France on the recommendation of his uncle, who had grown too old to undertake a voyage of the sort, and also because he knew Turkish and Arabic. The consul suspected him of being an impostor, and this, by ricochet, sowed the first doubts as to whether Poncet had really traveled to Ethiopia; his voyage was regarded as imaginary until James Bruce attested its authenticity almost a century later. On Minister Pontchartrain's instructions, the consul saw to it that Murad could not pursue his journey further than Cairo.[62]

These oddities should not prevent us from reading the fact that the kings of Ethiopia employed Armenians as ambassadors from the seventeenth century on as a carefully thought out policy or practice. As Thévenot was told by a Syrian merchant traveling in the Negus's service,

> This king is utterly hostile to the Franks, whom he accuses of being heretics and of wanting to give the crown to an enemy of his, so that, if a Frank wished to enter this country, he would have to pass for an Armenian or a Coft [Copt]; for the King and his whole people are of the same religion as the Copts.[63]

French diplomats were perfectly well informed of this situation in the period in which Lenoir du Roule's hapless delegation was massacred in Sennar. Consul Maillet described the dangers of such an undertaking as follows: "It is certain that the Ethiopian language and an olive-skinned complexion are the minimum requirements for this purpose [...]. It would suffice not to be known as Franks, since the Coptic clergy who govern there have taken extremely good care to render the name of Frank hateful."[64] Certain Catholic missionaries even disguised themselves as Armenian merchants in order to make their way into Massawa, the port of access to Ethiopia.[65]

The practice of employing Armenian auxiliaries and brokers was not a matter of indifference for the Ethiopian sovereigns and does not, perhaps, find its only explanation in their linguistic and commercial talents. By preventing new representatives of the Catholic powers of Europe from entering Ethiopia, it foreclosed the risk of new religious unrest. The travel narratives of the Europeans who began crisscrossing Ethiopia again in the nineteenth century often mention the presence of apparently well accepted Armenian artisans.[66] In the 1840s, the Greek architect "Demetrius" and his five Armenian workers were attached to the court of *Negus* Sahlä Sellasē of Shäwa in Angoläla. Some twenty years later, a certain "Gorguos" (doubtless Giyorgis, i.e. George, or Gorgorios, i.e. Gregory), a Constantinople native, figured in Menelik's entourage in Wäräylu as a valued Armenian hat maker. Around 1879, an Armenian cartwright was teaching the art of making wooden wheels in the workshops of the residence of *Ras* Adal of Gojam.[67] Armenians often played a more or less clearly delineated role in the entourage of Ethiopian leaders, serving as interpreters or middlemen and informing travelers of the political situation in the regions they had to cross. The Armenian merchant Bethlehem is an example. A native of Tiflis, Georgia, described by many authors as a credible informant who had a good way with people, he is supposed to have spent time in Java and, later, Palestine and Egypt before heading to Ethiopia to seek his fortune. From there, according to reports, he was sent around 1835 by *Däjazmach* Webē of Tigré on a mission to Cairo in order to negotiate a purchase of firearms with the khedive Mehmet Ali and the British consul. This Armenian, Bethlehem, was working in the service of *Abunä* Sälama when the *abun* came from Egypt as the new metropolitan and was given a reception in Adwa in 1841, and he is supposed to have been personally embroiled in the religious controversies then underway in Ethiopia.[68] Sources from the same period note that a certain Hajji Hovhannes, an Armenian goldsmith and gunsmith who was also reputed to be a former counterfeiter and one of the principal foreign notables in Adwa, Tigré's biggest city, was at ease with *Däjazmach* Webē and had influence over him.⁶⁹ Together with Turks, Syrians, Egyptians, Greeks, and Albanians, a handful of Armenian merchants also resided in northern Ethiopia cities such as Adwa or Massawa and the border towns of Mätämma or Kassala in Sudan; in the period in which the clergymen Sahak and Dimotheos traveled to Ethiopia, they offered their services for hire to both Europeans passing through the area and also Abyssinian leaders. A few years earlier, Arnauld d'Abbadie reported the presence, in Gondär, of Greeks, Armenians, and Turks "who had committed misdeeds" and were fugitives from the justice of Egypt's viceroy, Mehmet Ali. The viceroy's dragoman in Ethiopia was an Armenian who had been born in Baghdad. The Frenchman also noted that he had encountered, in Tajura, an Armenian named "Hajitor" who had "a perfect command of English, Hindi, Farsi and Arabic" and was working in Ethiopia for the English East India Company. The man in question was doubtless "M. Hatchatoor [Khachadur], an English agent in Toujourra [Tajura]," who accompanied Captain William Cornwallis Harris's mission to Sahlä Sellasē in Angoläla and crossed paths with Rochet d'Héricourt in 1842.⁷⁰ The Ethiopian diplomats who play the most conspicuous role in the European sources of the day were themselves descendants of an Armenian caravaneer known for having long engaged in trade between Constantinople and Abyssinia, earning himself the moniker Habeşlı Karapet (Karapet or Garabed the Abyssinian). Father Sahak and Father Dimotheos encountered one of his sons, who had settled in Adwa as a goldsmith. Born in Tigré of an Ethiopian mother, this Wärqē Karapet is supposed to have followed in his father's footsteps as a caravaneer between Ethiopia and the Ottoman Empire. He is mentioned in the travel narratives of many English, French, Swiss, and German travelers and missionaries between 1820 and 1860. He was, notably, *Däjazmach* Wäldu's envoy to Egypt in 1822–3. In the 1850s, he is also reported to have interceded, together with Adwa's other Armenian goldsmith, Hajji Hovhannes, with the Lazarist missionary Justin de Jacobis, with a view to reconciling him with the Coptic metropolitan, *Abunä* Sälama.⁷¹ His children were educated in Bombay's Scotland Mission School and repeatedly served as interpreters for, and emissaries to, the British consul Cameron during his difficult negotiations with Tewodros, or, at the time of the British expedition against Tewodros, in the discussions between *Ras* Kasa of Tigré and Lord Napier. Wärqē Karapet and Hajji Hovhannes were also sent to England as Ethiopian envoys to Queen Victoria.⁷² Let us note, finally, that the merchant Boghos Markarian, whom we shall have occasion to discuss at length, was sent first by Emperor Yohannes IV and then by his rival, Menelik, to the khedive of Egypt, Ismail, in quest of rifles and political support.⁷³ Of course, it may seem artificial to draw parallels between men as different as Murad and Markarian simply because both played the role of emissary for various Ethiopian sovereigns. The comparison is not unjustified, however, from the standpoint of Ethiopia's political and religious elites, whose foreign policy strategies were necessarily inscribed in a temporality longer than that of individuals.

3

Of Immigrants and Kings: Toward a Symbolic Nationalization

Explaining the creation of the Negus's royal brass band by citing earlier facts of the same kind comes down to drawing a connection between past and present policies. The question of this connection is essential. It suggests the hypothesis that, in the late nineteenth and early twentieth centuries, reliance on Armenian auxiliaries was inscribed in a kind of governmental culture of the ruling circles in Ethiopia. It is not a matter of lapsing into a culturalist or behaviorist reading of such political choices here but, on the contrary, of demonstrating the active part that these leaders took in mobilizing the past to meet the imperatives of the present. The way Ethiopian sovereigns from Menelik on employed Armenian immigrants suggests that a strategy was at work here. To defend this hypothesis, we must first deconstruct the view of the Armenians that the European sources on the historiography of Ethiopia usually take.

The Missing Brass Band: Explaining Armenian Invisibility

The Armenian presence in Ethiopia is generally viewed through the grid implicitly provided by the concept of a commercial diaspora. This reading is not specific to Ethiopian studies, nor does it concern the Armenians alone. The theoretical model of commercial diasporas affirms that they do not participate in the political affairs of their countries of residence, or even that they are apolitical. A certain scholarly literature then happily uses the terms "intermediary" or "middlemen minorities" to designate "groups" supposedly fated to engage in commerce, so that they are inevitably cast in the role of scapegoats in the societies they live in whenever those societies undergo crises.[1] This concept is commonly applied to Lebanese or Indians in Africa, to cite just two examples. It is not, however, always borne out by the findings of empirical studies,[2] nor is it certain that it takes us beyond a rather simplistic level of understanding of social and political relations. This is clearly shown by the example of Iranian reliance on the Armenian merchants of New Julfa, a suburb of Isfahan settled by Armenians at the initiative of Shah Abbas I early in the seventeenth century. The fact that they were Christians long led historians of international trade to consider them as foreigners in Iran and to take an interest only in their role as transmission belts in the export of silk to Europe in the modern era. This was to forget their direct involvement in the construction of the Safavid state and the extraordinary solicitude with which the kings, in turn, rewarded them for it. This solicitude found symbolic expression in visits to the Armenian merchants' provosts at Epiphany to attend the christenings celebrated on this day of Armenian Christmas. New Julfa, which enjoyed autonomy, was regarded as the Queen Mother's appanage, something that conferred considerable prestige on it in Iran, all economic considerations aside.[3] In much the same way, although, of course, on a more modest scale, personal ties and the signs of good will that the Ethiopian sovereigns showed certain families of Armenian immigrants, with whom they maintained permanent, privileged relations, relativize the pertinence of the notions of "commercial diaspora" and "middlemen minority." Before putting such analytical categories to work, we should determine whether their utilization in the case before us is not an echo chamber for stereotypes.

To understand the dead end to which reliance on this type of pre-notion leads, it is instructive to consider the way the historiography of Ethiopia has tended to analyze the presence of each "national group" with reference to its exercise of a particular economic activity. Richard Pankhurst's works have long served as a model for this reading of the foreign presence in Ethiopia. This holds, more particularly, for the Armenian presence there,[4] the recent history of which is reduced to a list of trades and commercial enterprises.[5] The stereotyped vision of Armenian immigration makes a politicized interpretation of its history hard to conceive: "The Armenians were engaged in small-scale trade and handicrafts, the word Armenian, says Mérab, being synonymous with that of trader. Armenians were to be found as ironmongers, goldsmiths, saddlers, tailors, embroiders, upholsterers and photographers and were, according to De Castro, generally intelligent and industrious."[6] This caricatural vision is directly patterned on one that finds expression in most European sources of the period—diplomatic archives, travel narratives, articles in the press, general works on Ethiopia, colonial novels, and so on—and rarely goes beyond a superficial, conventional description of the Armenian presence. It has, however, powerfully influenced the way the history of foreigners in Ethiopia is written.[7] Under these conditions, it is hardly surprising that the original characteristics of the Armenian immigration, to which the Negus's brass band has, so far, simply drawn our attention, remain perfectly invisible in the history books.

Armenians, Greeks, Syrians, and other "Levantines": Stereotypes and Historiographical Conformism

Contemporary written sources evoke the Armenian presence without assigning it any particular profile. Because Menelik's reign served as the stage for an unprecedented increase in the number of foreigners in Ethiopia, Armenian immigration was simply perceived as one aspect of a phenomenon the magnitude of which transcended it. A Georgian physician likened it to the proliferation of a species of tree recently imported into Addis Abeba, the eucalyptus: "A sad picture of what is taking place, ethnologically speaking, with the growing immigration of foreigners to this country!"[8] After the resounding victory over the Italian general Baratieri's army at Adwa (1896), most European governments had official legations in Addis Abeba, a city founded a decade earlier by Menelik and his wife Taytu. The construction of the Franco-Ethiopian railway, which reached Dire Dawa in 1902 and Addis Abeba in 1917, as well as the development of traffic in the port of Djibouti, where 300 Europeans were already living by the turn of the century, facilitated the arrival of new immigrants by sparing them a month of travel in caravans on camelback or muleback. Beside the Armenians, Indian merchants and workers accompanied by their families settled in large numbers in the capital, encouraged by the British legation, which guaranteed them protection in hopes of thereby increasing its influence in Ethiopia. It also protected the many Greeks who had come to the country since 1905 in order to take part in the ongoing work on the railroad. Thus the Greek population is supposed to have risen from some 100 for the whole province of Harar (including Dire Dawa) in 1908 to around 600 in 1911. As for the Armenians, if we lend credence to the rare breakdowns available, their number, women and children included, was 150 to 200 by the latter date, before increasing appreciably in the interwar period. At the end of Menelik's reign, the Armenian, Greek, Arab, and Indian "colonies" (as they were then called) were by far the biggest in the foreign population, of which, the commentators agree, they formed the "great mass." The proof is that the desire to keep French consular affairs running smoothly justified nominating an agent of this nationality who knew the Ethiopian languages as well as Arabic and Greek, "something that is highly necessary in this country peopled by Indians and Levantines."[9]

The idea that there was massive immigration to Ethiopia should be modified in view of the fact that the capital, which in certain areas still looked more like a big camp than a city, counted barely 1,000 foreigners in a total population of 50,000 around 1910.[10] Similarly, the number of foreigners living in Harar was estimated at a scant 100, in a total population of 40,000: some fifteen French people, six Italians, three English people, and a dozen Greeks. "The rest," that is, nearly seventy individuals, were said to be "Armenians, Turks, and Syrians, who, with the Greeks, have, as always, a monopoly on petty trade"—this in a city that passed, late in the nineteenth century, for the gateway to Ethiopia and the city of foreigners.[11] The foreigners' numbers are hard to determine, for there were no official statistics on them before the Immigration Office began keeping "Ethiopian records of resident permits" between 1944 and 1949.[12] It is true that historians have no choice but to rely on the diplomatic legations' archives or the rare indications figuring in travel literature or the press; the fact is, however, that they often use them uncritically. The ostensible precision of these figures is deceptive; often contradictory, they are based on impressions rather than real population breakdowns.[13] The terminology employed is an additional source of confusion. It is not always easy to determine what "European population" or "white population" means in the sources, for certain groups are sometimes included in these categories and at other times are not. Greeks, for example, are clearly distinct from Europeans for Henri d'Orléans, who counts around fifteen Europeans in Addis Abeba in 1897, of whom a majority, he says, were French, whereas other sources show that Greeks and Armenians were a clear majority. Another author, in contrast, will treat Greeks as Europeans, while classifying Armenians as Asians. The language barrier complicates identification of the numerically biggest fringe of foreigners, made up of people "of doubtful nationality," among whom one hesitates to recognize Armenians or Greeks, when authors do not hastily lump the "notable Greco-Armeno-Syro-Hindu merchants" together. Armenians and Greeks are conflated because they belong to the "purely mercantile races that are European by birth and Oriental by temperament— the only ones, moreover, to succeed in this country"; they are also likened to Syrians, Turks, and "other Asians" such as Indians.[14] Lumping together all the "Levantines" reduces perception of the Armenian presence to a series of stereotypes applicable to Greeks, Arabs, and Indians as well. With that, literary and academic cliches dovetail, in a way described by Edward Said in his discussion of the genesis of an Orientalist tradition.[15]

The Thaler-Men and the Mean-Spirited

> In the Ethiopia of our day, Europeans are put, whether by the country's leaders or the poorest native, in one of only two possible, clearly distinct social categories: the thaler-men and the mean-spirited. And the mean-spirited can never be Europeans, unless they are Greeks, Armenians, or Syrians, who are considered inferior, decadent races.[16]

The expose provided by a correspondent of the Italian Geographical Society early in the twentieth century, which presented commercial opportunities as well as the difficulties that "the scientist, the politician, or the voyager and explorer" might encounter in their future commercial or colonial undertakings, distills the essence of the stereotypes shaping European sources' vision of Armenian migrants to Ethiopia. The Europeans, who travel for noble reasons, have nothing in common with "the Greek, Armenian, or Syrian merchants, who are compared, and are comparable, to the natives for their utter lack of dignity and concern for the amenities, as well as for their nations' weakness." These characteristics ascribed to the "mean-spirited," perceived as parasites, stand opposed to those of the "thaler-man," supposedly personified by the European travelers who, exceptions aside, arrive "followed by a train well furnished with supplies, as well as a solid escort of servants and freeloaders, even when they have no official mission"; they often find themselves victimized by unscrupulous intermediaries who are after their money."[17] The parable of the thaler-men and the mean-spirited nicely sums up the problem posed by the utilization of European sources as the primary, and often the only, material for a history of foreigners in Ethiopia. The perception of the most disparaged segment of the foreign population (Armenians, Greeks, Syrians, and other "Levantines"), characterized by its commercial function alone and viewed through the lens reserved for sordid matters, as if it were an epiphenomenon of European expansion and the kind of necessary evil that expansion trails in its wake, blacks out the Armenian immigration's original features and the links that the Armenians forged with the Ethiopian sovereigns.

A long-standing stereotype, the vision of the Armenian as eternal merchant, continues to make itself felt in most European sources. Their authors, who, for the most part, frequent the same places (palaces, embassies, hotels, markets), never fail to include a description of the main cities and their foreign population in their narratives.

The visit to Addis Abeba's market becomes a standby in the accounts published between the two world wars, like, from the late nineteenth century on, the depiction of the narrow lanes of the "half-oriental, half-Abyssinian city"[18] of Harar, with its bazaar, run by Indians, but also by "a good many Greeks and Armenians, who seem to have the power of flourishing in strange places."[19] The Armenians' shops, better stocked than the natives', specialize, like the Greeks', in the sale of staples, manufactured goods, hardware, canned food, tobacco, alcoholic drinks, soap, and other imported products sought primarily by a European clientele. The sources note the same situation in Dire Dawa, where Greeks and Armenians dominate the retail trade.[20] Obligatory chapters of this kind become a staple of the travel narratives, intended to seduce readers fond of the picturesque and Orientalizing touches.

Observed "en passant" in the cities and markets, these immigrants are essentially perceived as characterized by their commercial functions: "Eight-tenths or nine-tenths of the Armenians are merchants; that activity, more than any other, is the one in which they excel [...], so that Armenian is a synonym for merchant."[21] The correspondence of diplomats posted in Addis Abeba is likewise permeated by these stereotypes. A report by the French ambassador on "the Ottoman colony, made up for the most part of Syrians and Armenians," essentially contents itself with observing that the Armenians "generally have underfilled purses" and "are merchants or low-level government employees." The ambassador, unaware that Armenians families had settled in Harar in the 1880s and 1890s, affirms that this colony "has been in existence in Abyssinia only since 1905" and that it "arrived in the country after the railroad went into operation." The fact that the Ethiopian government employed many Armenians, whom he treats merely as service providers, does not inspire him to ask about their possible ties to the emperor:

> In the Palace they are engineers, clockmakers, blacksmiths, mechanics, and embroiderers. Thanks to their numbers and ingenuity, they enjoy relatively high turnovers and are the leaders in the field of retail sales. Because they have a knack for commerce and a capacity for endurance that is equal to any ordeal, they survive and make money where Europeans would starve to death or go bankrupt.[22]

Unsurprisingly, it was the Armenians' hammerlock on commerce that aroused the diplomat's interest. We find this *topos* in all the categories of personal testimony mentioned earlier. Conjoined with accounts of the dire poverty and the unscrupulousness supposedly characteristic of "Levantines" and "Indians," it leaves no room for observations of any other kind.

Like Indians, Syrians, and Greeks, Armenians, too, are described as people who accept abject living conditions. They seem to be reduced to working in professions, commerce, and the crafts, that Ethiopians supposedly despise. "People without the slightest importance,"[23] they barely scrape by, rather than enriching themselves, and "have lost all prospect of being able to leave the country any time soon."[24] The description of the Armenian colony provided by the Swiss Alfred Ilg, one of Menelik's state advisors, at a reception for the diplomatic legations and the whole group of foreigners, testifies to this degeneration:

All were thin, with greenish complexions and a sickly look. They presented themselves in extraordinary outfits and seemed to have collected all of a European ragman's bricabrac. Some of them, without detachable collars, had tied a black necktie around their necks, while others wore a cyclist's jersey over their skinny torsos. They went their way in a long, pitiful procession.[25]

Paradoxically, these individuals' lack of resources and ambition—"for they content themselves with the most meager rewards and are almost all dependent on Menelik"[26]—is grounds for gratuitous complaints about their propensity to monopolize retail trade in the early twentieth century, especially trade in staple commodities. The names of Armenian retail firms recur regularly in the many lists of businesses drawn up in Harar, Dire Dawa, or Addis Abeba (the Kevorkoff, Ebeyan, Terzian, Melik, and Hachadurian companies, among others), alongside those of Greek firms. In the list produced in connection with a collection taken up among European and foreign merchants in Djibouti for the victims of a catastrophe caused by a volcanic eruption in Saint-Pierre, in Martinique, there are no fewer than sixteen Greeks and Armenians among the seventy-five contributors. In Dire Dawa and Harar, Greeks were far more active than Italians or Frenchmen. Together with Armenians, they served as middlemen for wholesale businesses in Aden and played an important role in importing goods from Europe and Egypt. Thus Greeks were the leading distributors of Italian foodstuffs in Ethiopia. As for Indians and Armenians, they had even milk, canned butter, and conserves of fruit brought to the country by caravans to meet the needs of a European clientele made up of travelers, railroad employees, and the personnel of foreign legations.[27] In the 1920s, the most prosperous merchants in Addis Abeba's market were still "Asiatics, greasy fat men from India, Syrians, Arabs, Armenians, and so forth."[28]

With rare exceptions, the sources convey a negative image of this fringe of the foreign population. When Rimbaud compares his paltry commissions with those received by "a dirty Greek," a chargé d'affaires working for the Frenchman Brémond in Harar, the remarks he makes are by no means extravagant in a day and age in which Pierre Loti could denounce the "Greek scum" that marred the beauty of the shores of the Bosporus, or affirm, citing a member of the French Academy, Edmont About, that "there is only one thing that the Greeks haven't stolen: their reputation."[29] The view generally taken of the Armenians now diverged appreciably from that of travelers of the modern period. Until the period 1830–50, those who encountered Armenians or Greeks on their travels, such as Théophile Lefebvre, Arnaud d'Abbadie, or Edmond Combes and Maurice Tamisier, rarely failed to note their ties to the Abyssinian grandees. In this out-of-the-way country, the figure of the Armenian whom one happened across while visiting the courts of Ethiopian princes still evoked the remote, astonishing East of a Chardin or a Tavernier. The Armenians' skills in dealing with people and their knowledge of the country's customs seemed to be valuable assets. In the 1900–20 period, in contrast, when travel from Europe to Ethiopia was freer and much easier, the negative figure of the "Levantine," the European entrepreneur's dishonest competitor, came to predominate, making it imperative to combat the "noxious, pernicious, poisonous Greek and Armenian competition."[30] The British and French legations were alarmed by the negative side effects they might suffer because of the bad reputation of their protégés from the Greek colony, "made up of the worst sorts," and from the Armenian colony as well.[31] Denunciation of "Levantine meddling" in the country's affairs became an effective rhetorical device for denigrating the Ethiopian government and its administration.[32] Many people seemed to rally to the view that "about the bulk of the Armenian, Syrian and Greek traders the less said the better."[33] After the Great War, the Armenians, classified among the "Mediterranean or exotic races [...] because of their common preferences for trade," were perceived in Europe and the countries that took in the most immigrants as refugees, parasites, or even undesirables.[34] To understand the particular uses to which the kings of Ethiopia put the Armenians, we must read these sources differently.

Armenians in Ethiopian Sovereigns' Foreign Policy

Under the reign of Menelik II (1889–1913) and in the interwar period, employment of Armenians by the kings of Ethiopia seems to have taken its place in a veritable political strategy intended to maintain the country's independence.

Setting Foreign Interests in Competition with Each Other as a Line of Conduct

Early in the twentieth century, the reception that Ethiopia reserved for foreigners often seems to have depended on their national origin. This is why the Russians comprised, after their legation in Ethiopia was closed in the wake of the 1917 Bolshevik revolution, "the most interesting community in Addis Abeba." Accompanied by their wives in many cases, and sharing a rather modest standard of living with the indigenous Ethiopians, the Russians were, an observer reported, viewed with sympathy by the local population, because they were now stateless and no longer represented any imperialist power. For this reason, he went on, the Russians were given responsible posts in the Ethiopian administration more readily than other Europeans, such as Italians, Englishmen, or Frenchmen, who were suspected of harboring annexationist designs.[35] Under Menelik's reign, the imperial Russian government's envoys seemed to have been aware of this distinction and willing to take advantage of it at the diplomatic level. Lieutenant Vikentii Mashkov, extraordinary representative of Czar Nicholas II in Ethiopia, likewise claimed that Russians were given privileged treatment of a sort by the imperial Ethiopian authorities. During his second, 1891–2, voyage, he was, he wrote, received in Harar with great pomp by "six or seven thousand Abyssinian soldiers in their fantastic parade uniforms, under their superiors' command, accompanied by almost all the Greeks living here," on orders from *Däjazmach* Mäkonnen. When he protested that this was doing him too much honor, he was told "that the honors were being paid not to his person, but to the great nation of the same religion as the Abyssinians, whose sole representative they took [him] to be."[36] The idea that there was a religious affinity between Russian orthodoxy and the Orthodox Ethiopian Church was then invoked by both parties, even if, as the Italian Nerazzini, present at the imperial court in Entotto at the time, explained, the Russians used the argument of their religious affinity with Ethiopia to mask the reality of their political and economic ambitions, feigning ignorance of important doctrinal differences between the two Churches in order to foreground this supposed affinity.[37] Such attempts at rapprochement echoed the Ethiopian sovereigns' instrumentalization of their ties to the Armenian Church.

Comparisons in this domain are highly instructive. Thus the example of the Swedish missions and the cooperation established between Ethiopia and the Kingdom of Sweden clearly bring out the political dimension of Haile Selassie's utilization of a foreign workforce or foreign advisors, in conformity with a practice that Menelik had adopted before him. Pitting the colonial powers against each other and playing "little" states off against "big" ones, the employment of foreigners constantly accompanied the affirmation and consolidation of Ethiopian independence.[38] The particular use to which the Armenian immigrants were put may be regarded as one instrument of this political strategy among others—with the nuance that, because of the long-standing existence of distinct representations of the Armenians in Ethiopia, the Ethiopian sovereigns who employed them in the late nineteenth or early twentieth century could appear to be following a kind of political "tradition."

The Armenian Immigrants' Personal Ties to Menelik

How the interests of foreign powers were played off against each other is illustrated by Menelik's attitude toward the arms trade and the attribution of concessions or trade monopolies. Gun smuggling was of critical importance for Ethiopia, which was under a European embargo at this time. Several Armenians were involved in it, including the Terzian brothers, Sarkis and Ohannes. On his letterhead, Sarkis Terzian presented himself as Menelik's "official purveyor" of arms and munitions. An Italian author was doubtless referring to Terzian when he wrote that "an old merchant, a refugee from lands dominated by the Turks, had, with the war, acquired a certain popularity with the Ethiopian authorities by selling arms without end and proffering advice that was hardly favorable to us Italians," or when he evoked, elsewhere, secondhand dealers trading in old blunderbusses who had, in a few years, been metamorphosed into merchants of modern rifles, gold, and ivory, and "woken up, one fine day, transformed into politicians."[39] In several different narratives by European authors, Terzian is presented as a servant closely associated with the imperial court who enjoyed *Ras* Mäkonnen's and Emperor Menelik's favor. He was in the service of *Ras* Mäkonnen of Harar in the early 1890s, standing guard on his behalf over the Ethiopian border post of Biyo Kaboba, where, in 1892, he forced Italian and English diplomats to wait for authorization before continuing their journey to Ethiopia.[40] Halfway between Zeila and Harar, Biyo Kaboba was just a small post defended by a squad of Ethiopian soldiers. An obligatory way station thanks to its wells (Biyo Kaboba means "big water"), it amounted to nothing more than a big stone shack perched on a hill and surrounded by a few huts.[41] Although the post attributed to this Armenian, a recent immigrant, was not an important command post, it seems to have comprised the first stage of a long "career" in Menelik's service, in a period in which posts of command were very rarely entrusted to Europeans. In the following years, Terzian made many voyages abroad on the emperor's behalf, most probably for commercial purposes—among other things, in order to purchase arms in Europe—but it seems that he often boasted, rightly or wrongly, that he was also acting as a diplomatic representative, inspiring Rimbaud to write, in one of the many letters that he sent Alfred Ilg from Harar, "Serquis [sic] is leaving tomorrow on a diplomatic tour of Obock, Djibouti, Zeilah, Aden, etc., etc.; what the devil are they sending him to look for in those parts."[42] These voyages made on the emperor's behalf also took him to Paris, Liège, London, Vienna, Berlin, New York, and Washington.[43] Sarkis Terzian's "career" is not entirely unlike Boghos Markarian's, mentioned in the previous chapter: Markarian served as Menelik's emissary in his difficult negotiations with the Egyptian khedive in the 1870s. He, too, saw to the transportation of cargoes of rifles to Shäwa.

The presence of Greek or Armenian immigrants, it will be recalled, is usually described from a purely mercantile angle, or with reference to the crafts that the immigrants exercised in the workshops of the *gebbi*, the imperial palace. A few commentators, however, acknowledge that they had a certain influence in the emperor's entourage, a noxious influence, the commentators hasten to affirm. Thus Montandon, who can hardly be suspected of sympathy for the "Greek rabble" or the "wogs" in general (a disciple of Vacher de Lapouge, the founder of racial anthropology, he was close to the extreme right in the 1930s and participated in the General Commissariat for Jewish Questions during the German occupation of France), explained that the 1908 disgrace of the state counselor Alfred Ilg was the fault of "new arrivals, Greeks, Armenians, Levantines in general," who "present themselves with a veneer of our civilization" and "claim to know as much about it as the Europeans, while the natives cannot judge the matter."[44] What we know from other sources about Menelik's employment of foreigners undermines this judgment, which is based on the typical colonialist premise that "natives" are naive. The oft bewailed grip that the "Levantines" are supposed to have maintained on the country's economy was in fact clearly analyzed by many observers as stemming from the emperor's desire to counter Italian and British influence in the country. The idea, very common in this period, that the Ethiopians were suspicious of Europeans led many to conclude that the "Levantine beggars" and other "low-class Europeans" who gravitated around the palace were hostile to the big powers' influence in Ethiopia, such as the Armenian interpreter "Surin" [Suren] Chakerian, whom Mérab vilified.[45] Thus Menelik's denunciation of the Italian-Ethiopian Treaty of Wechalē (Ucciali), drawn up by Count Pietro Antonelli in 1889, and of its famous Article 17, the Italian translation of which made Ethiopia a semi protectorate, was quietly prompted, according to a rumor circulating in Italy, by an influential handful of Frenchmen, Swiss, Greeks, and Armenians, "so that, practically speaking, no economic or commercial advantage could put Antonelli and the Italians in a position more favorable than theirs."[46]

In the same period, the Armenians, who had now become expressive figures in colonial novels, are alleged to have close ties to *Ras* Mäkonnen and Menelik.[47] These ties are supposed to have taken concrete form in the attribution of concessions and monopolies to these entrepreneurs close to the palace, although they very often had only modest functions as servants or craftsmen:

Not a day goes by on which Menelick [*sic*] does not mull over some project of selling or franchising a monopoly [...]. The beggars are usually Asian whites, Turks, Armenians, etc., or Hindus and Arabs, in the service of the negus's workshops, for, as people who happily grovel, they are usually preferred to the citizens of European powers by the Abyssinian grandees, who are proud to see whites or half-whites at their feet."[48]

This holds, for example, for the abortive project of opening a cartridge factory in Addis Abeba, in which the emperor and Sarkis Terzian, "who has a rather bad business reputation in Addis Abeba," seemed to have colluded in order to give competing Franco-Swiss and British companies simultaneously the impression that they could obtain a concession by paying out tidy commissions: "It's the usual game in Abyssinia. [...] The Emperor and Sarkis are hesitating, since they're waiting to find out which side the biggest profits will come down on."[49] In the same vein, we may cite the monopoly granted in 1906 to two Armenian goldsmiths in the palace, Dikran Ebeyan and Hagop Baghdassarian, a decision that provoked French merchants' ire. The privilege that the emperor accorded them bore on the production and import of alcoholic beverages of all kinds and gave the two men the right to apply a surcharge—with the help of another Armenian appointed to do so at the customs office—on all imported wine, beer, and champagne.[50]

How are we to explain the fact that these relations between emperors and humble immigrants went beyond the simple exchange of orders and services between masters and servants? In fact, in Menelik's day, foreigners of all stations in life still had relatively easy access to the emperor: "An insignificant individual, the hero of a day, could be given preference over court dignitaries and bask in ephemeral favor."[51] As Count Pietro Antonelli wrote at the time, evoking the anti-Italian propaganda put out by the Greeks, "it thus happens that even a joiner can make policy at Menelik's court, and if it happens that the king pays him no mind, he often manages to interest the king's grandees, especially those whom the king never invites to counsel him on such matters." That is why, Antonelli argues, "the person charged with defending the Italian government's interests" in Ethiopia "must, above all, be aware of what both the natives and the Europeans are saying and doing, must know how to address himself directly to the sovereign in order to acquire influence with his grandees, and must be familiar with Ethiopian customs."[52] Menelik, after his victory at Adwa, which helped make his image as a sovereign known abroad, personally received many diplomats, merchants, journalists, and adventurers, who never failed to report on their audience with the emperor in their accounts. It seems that Menelik was willing to be disturbed by his servants. He could interrupt a conversation with any visitor, even an ambassador, at the slightest alert about an incident that had occurred in his workshops or stables.[53] The fact that the emperor was so easily accessible, like the apparent simplicity of prevailing protocol, stemmed from the absence of an Ethiopian government worthy of the name, in a period in which "Foreign affairs" came down, in reality, to the emperor's business affairs with foreigners. The *gebbi* was the imperial couple's private residence and, at the same time, the chief political decision-making center. Subsequently, until the first segment of Haile Selassie's reign, personal relations often continued to determine political choices, even if access to the emperor was increasingly restricted in the interwar period. Witness, for example, the appointment of the Swede Johannes Kolmodin as the emperor's advisor on foreign affairs, or, again, the influence attributed at the time to the emperor's Greek physician, Yakobos Zervos.[54]

The way Dikran Ebeyan used his contacts to mix with the small world of foreign diplomats gravitating around Menelik's court in Entotto in 1890 provides a good illustration of the originality of the ties forged between the emperor and part of the Armenian immigrant community. Salimbeni, the Italian government's emissary, observed that this artisan was a useful person to know at the court, because he cultivated relations with both the Ethiopian grandees and foreign citizens. He provided Salimbeni with food when he first arrived, perhaps on Menelik's orders, and sold him a carpet that the Italian, bent on currying the emperor's favor, planned to give him on Ethiopian New Year's. On one occasion, Salimbeni even noted that Dikran had been informed before he himself was about important political news with a bearing on Italian-Ethiopian relations. Yet Dikran had no claim to any official title. The sole explanation for his presence at the court seemed to be that he was the emperor's goldsmith.[55] Remarkably, Dikran was, according to the man who published the chronicle of Menelik's reign, former French ambassador Maurice de Coppet, "the only foreign resident who, a few Italian officers and diplomats aside, was identified by name." The text points out that "an Armenian goldsmith by the name of Dicran who knew how to make crowns" was present at Empress Taytu's coronation in Entotto. Later in the same text, we read that "an Armenian merchant named Dicran had come from abroad, bringing many objects with him" to the imperial residence in Ankobär in 1892, among them, doubtless, arms and ammunition.[56] According to the testimony of Dikran's daughter Arusiag Ebeyan, Menelik borrowed the considerable sum of 5,000 thalers from him before setting out on his campaign in the Wälamo region in 1894. Two years later, the emperor is supposed to have charged him with guarding and feeding some 20 of the 1,800 Italian prisoners captured at Adwa, since he could not afford to feed them all at his own expense and had accordingly undertaken to divide up the responsibility for them with his grandees.[57] This information is unverifiable, but it suggests the nature of the relationship between the Ethiopian master and his Armenian servant, for Menelik held up his good treatment of his Italian captives as proof of his magnanimity and an argument in favor of his foreign policy.[58] The place Dikran Ebeyan held with the emperor thus probably did not stem from his profession as a goldsmith alone.

Armenian Artisans and the Staging of Ethiopian Power

Relations between the Ethiopian sovereigns and their Armenian servants certainly went further than the European sources' near-total silence suggests. The function of the goldsmith in the imperial workshops was hardly insignificant, for fabricating a royal or an imperial crown had a political dimension. One can say the same thing about the many other Armenians who worked in the palace on staging and representing imperial power and the people who held it. Over and above technical savoir-faire, the concrete realization of these attributes of monarchical authority required that these servants have sufficiently detailed knowledge of Ethiopian customs and political symbols. In this colonial context, the decision to appeal to Armenian artisans was also guided by a concern not to give foreign powers signs of allegiance in any way, shape, or form. We saw, in Chapter 1, the trouble that could be caused by importing objects connected with the throne or regalia manufactured and stamped with the seal of a foreign power, or even objects that had simply passed through foreign hands on their way back to Ethiopia. In contrast, the fact that Armenian goldsmiths had produced Menelik's, Taytu's, Mäkonnen's, Zäwditu's, and Täfäri's crowns, and, later, Haile Selassie's and Empress Mänän's, does not seem to have posed a problem at the level of political symbolism. Thus Count Salimbeni reports that Menelik, a year after being crowned emperor, had two crowns in his *gebbi*, "the one made by Dicraèn [Dikran Ebeyan] and the one made in Italy" by the Milanese jeweler Confalonieri, doubtless offered him as a gift by the Italian government as a token of friendship after the Treaty of Ucciali was signed. The Italian diplomat observes, however, obviously without understanding what motivated Menelik's preferences in the matter, that "the latter did not please the king and he wished to send it back," although the Milanese goldsmith's work was "more regular and refined that Dicraèn's."[59] Menelik's attitude is no doubt not explained solely by aesthetic considerations. His plan to send the crown he did not like back to Italy also harbors an obvious political message: to wear it would be to acknowledge an Italian protectorate over Ethiopia; returning it clearly signified refusal of any form of subordination to a European state, even if it was merely symbolic. Under Menelik's reign, as also under Haile Selassie's, the choice of Armenian artisans could surely be justified by their ability to respect a style or aesthetic canons appreciated at the imperial court. It also shows us, however, that the Armenian immigrants of this period were not associated with a colonial power, nor even unequivocally regarded as foreigners.

Thus a traveler recounts the public punishment, in the emperor's presence, of a sentence pronounced against an old Ethiopian grandee around 1901–3. On this day, the grandee, initially condemned to death, saw his sentenced commuted into amputation of both hands, and ultimately reduced, magnanimously, to the amputation of just one foot. The fact that Greeks and Armenians were in the crowd that witnessed this corporal punishment does not seem to have troubled anyone, although Menelik, who, abroad, cultivated his image as the respectable sovereign of a forward-looking empire, saw to it, in the same period, that European visitors whom such scenes might disturb not witness them.[60] Generally speaking, the presence of Armenians in Menelik's entourage was not easy to explain for visitors passing through the country, who often even explained one and the same event in completely opposed ways. Thus an Austrian engineer presented the 1903 importation of a land-based locomotive, a traction engine, as proof of the dishonesty of Armenian servants who were trying to put one over on Menelik, whereas a French journalist interpreted it as an attempt on the emperor's part to circumvent the delays occasioned by rival French, Italian, and English interests in building the first Ethiopian railway. For one of these observers, the imperial palace's Armenian servant was simply a parasite making unwarranted use of his situation as the holder of a monopoly to sell shoddy technologies, while the other saw in him a true éminence grise behind the emperor.[61] What little we can glean from the sources of the day does not unambiguously confirm either of these visions but does seem to indicate that Menelik and his successors used the Armenian servants in a particular way.

The majority of Armenians present in the *gebbi* were employed in domains that contributed to representing or staging imperial power, especially on occasions when those who held it found themselves in the presence of foreign visitors. In the same way that, as we have seen, *Ras* Täfäri's brass band did, Menelik's Armenian servants contributed to modernizing the image that the court presented to foreigners who were passing through. The European visitors received at the *geber*, the banquet the emperor gave under the royal *addarash*, an immense canopy that could shelter several thousand guests at the same time, rarely failed to note that, in this environment and this décor that seemed so exotic to them, the emperor called on the services of an Armenian chef to make sure that the meal served the Europeans accommodated their culinary habits. *Ras* Mäkonnen paid the same sort of attention to the table presented to the distinguished European guests he received in Harar, which had been the Ethiopian Empire's gateway to the east since 1887, before they pursued their journey to Menelik's *gebbi*. Here, too, the European meals were prepared by an Armenian couple, the *Ras's* "majordomo" and "wine waiter" and his wife, whose savoir-faire came in for high praise from the British mission to Ethiopia in 1897.[62] In the imperial *gebbi*, Menelik's chef, Avedis Yamalian, was also his gardener. He was given the task of creating and then tending a small European garden planted with fruit trees and vegetables from foreign habitats, to which, it seems, Empress Taytu herself lavished personal attention. Europeans who had been granted an audience with Menelik or Taytu were often asked to wait there.[63] The functions of gardener and chef, however modest they may have been, helped give foreign visitors a favorable impression of the refinement displayed by the imperial couple. The procedure was not without effect, because, frequently, details of this sort garnered some attention from the press or the European books that set out to regale the broad public with travel narratives. According to an anecdote reported later by a ferociously anti-Ethiopian author, Menelik one day made fun of the horticultural science of a French agronomist and two of his colleagues while praising the empirical savoir-faire of a "palace gardener, an Armenian by the name of Amadis [*sic*]," who worked "as Abyssinian custom dictated." The emperor urged the European specialist to go "plant potatoes in some other continent."[64]

Thus, as was the case with the subject of the crowns, we find here, too, a political discourse that sets acceptable foreigners in competition with others about whom mistrust is very openly expressed. Although offers of favors or gifts from citizens of foreign states are turned down with alacrity, employment of Armenian servants in areas that have directly to do with the sovereign's image, in professions involving the dress and the decoration of the court, or, again, that give them access to the royal family's private life, seemingly pose no problem. Armenian leather workers, carpet makers, and tailors worked in the *gebbi* in the same period as Dikran Ebeyan did. Mihran Hazarian, a carpet maker, and Vahram Kharibian, an embroiderer, were introduced into the court in 1903 by *Däjazmach* Mäshäsha, who had returned from an official mission to Sultan Abdülhamid in Constantinople. They were still working there in 1930, at a time when Krikor Chorbajian, a tailor who made Abyssinian-style ceremonial costumes (notably the black *kabba* embroidered with gold thread that court dignitaries wore) and engaged in leather-working and harness-making, too, was also employed in the palace. Even Emperor Haile Selassie's and Empress Mänän's boot maker was an Armenian in this period. From the turn of the century on, several Armenian women were likewise employed in the palace by Empress Taytu, who had placed the daughter of one of her nieces in an Armenian nanny's care, thus showing "that she understood just how much poor hygiene had to do with infantile mortality."[65] Early in the 1930s, Empress Mänän's midwife was also an Armenian by the name of Helen Hatzakordzian. Araxi Yazedjian, who had arrived in Ethiopia in 1908, became the head of the palace's carpet workshop at the end of Menelik's reign, a post that she continued to hold under Täfäri and Mänän, with whom she was eventually closely associated, as we shall see later. While the intention behind the use of Armenian servants seemed to be to make the imperial court appear as presentable as possible, the affirmation that Ethiopia would not subordinate itself to any outside influence remained a constant preoccupation. In this perspective, the employment of an Armenian and, later, his children to produce official portraits of the monarchs inevitably raises questions.

It has often been pointed out that Armenians made a significant contribution to the development of photography and the art of the portrait in the countries of the Middle East, especially the Ottoman Empire and the Egypt of the khedives. From the 1850s on, the leading photography studios in Istanbul were Greek or Armenian. One of the most famous belonged to the Abdullah brothers, Vigen, Kevork, and Hovsep. It was patronized for decades by Istanbul's most influential politicians, and both Sultan Abdülaziz and Sultan Abdülhamid honored the three brothers, who enjoyed international fame until the 1890s, with the title of official photographers. Again, one of the pioneers of photography in Palestine was the Armenian patriarch of Jerusalem, Yesayi Garabedian (1865–85),[66] who had learned the art in the Abdullah brothers' workshop in Istanbul[67] and himself initiated Garabed Krikorian into it. Krikorian opened one of the first photography studios in Jerusalem in 1884 and handed his technique down to many young Armenian and Palestinian photographers. Armenian photographers opened studios in all of Turkey's other big cities beginning in the late nineteenth century. They dominated the Near Eastern market for the production of photographic images until the mid-twentieth century, in Egypt (Cairo, Alexandria), Lebanon (Beirut, Tripoli, Zahleh), Syria (Aleppo, Damascus), Irak (Baghdad), Iran (Tabriz, Teheran), and Palestine (especially in Jerusalem and Haifa). Their studios had a decisive influence on the development of photography and the art of the portrait in the urban societies of these various countries: the Boyadjian brothers, Angelo and Levon (known as Van Léo), active in Egypt in the mid-twentieth century, are examples. Finally, it should be pointed out that Armenian photographers, like the Abdullah brothers in the Ottoman Empire, were often granted the privilege of producing the sovereigns' official portraits: among them were G. Lekegian of Cairo, who produced Khedive Ismail's portrait, or Boghos Tarkulian in Istanbul (who was Sultan Abdülhamid's official photographer from 1905 on and who also made, in 1926, the portrait of Mustafa Kemal that was to adorn the young Republic of Turkey's bank notes).[68]

In Ethiopia, photography was doubtless the field in which the use of Armenian labor was the most conspicuous, if only by virtue of the number of official portraits of emperors or other leading political personalities bearing an Armenian photographer's signature.[69] This was a delicate subject from a political standpoint, for photography truly appeared as a new political instrument in Ethiopia in the early twentieth century, playing a role in both the seizure of power and the enthronement of pretenders to power, and also serving as a vehicle for an imperial ideology that was then being elaborated. As with other objects mobilized to represent royal power, Ethiopian sovereigns seem to have carefully avoided entrusting the treatment of their images to photographers who could be all too easily associated with one or another foreign power. Under Menelik's reign, control over the emperor's image was strict enough that foreign visitors passing through the country were not authorized to photograph him themselves.[70] The bulk of the portraits of this period were the work of the Armenian photographer Bedros Boyadjian, who was given the official title of photographer of the court of Ethiopia by imperial decree on February 16, 1906.[71]

Menelik did not choose his accredited photographer for his professional abilities alone, no more than Täfäri did the musicians of his royal brass band. Other concerns were doubtless taken into account. The fact that Boyadjian held the rank of a deacon of the Armenian Church and that he had earlier served as secretary to the Armenian archbishop of Cairo but also his arrival in Ethiopia in the Armenian priest Mgrdich Chelghadian's company in 1905 may have influenced Menelik's choice. For, in principle, only painters chosen from among the Ethiopian clergy had the right to paint kings' portraits. Choosing an active member of a sister Church to photograph Menelik would thus have made it possible to avoid purely and simply disregarding this rule, since it allowed the emperor to preserve the "very deep connection between images and Christian culture in Ethiopia."[72] After his death, *Negus* Mikaēl is supposed to have conferred the privilege of serving as chief photographer on Boyadjian, a privilege that Prince Täfäri Mäkonnen is said to have confirmed on December 17, 1917, shortly after *Lej* Iyasu was dethroned. Boyadjian was also the photographer at Empress Zäwditu's February 11, 1917 coronation. Finally, when Menelik's ashes were transferred to his mausoleum, Bedros Boyadjian's portrait of him was chosen to adorn one of the mausoleum's walls. The Armenian continued to exercise his office until his death in 1928,[73] that is, throughout a period in which abundant use was made of photography as an instrument of political legitimation and propaganda in Ethiopia. Another Armenian immigrant, Levon Yazedjian, who had come to Ethiopia around 1905 and whose wife Araxi, as we have seen, directed the imperial palace's carpet workshops, also exercised the profession of photographer in *Ras* Mikaēl's service in this period, claiming the title of "photographer of the court of Wollo [Wällo]" on his business cards and letterhead.

Early in the twentieth century, the function of photographer often had a political dimension. When, in 1907, Menelik asked Bedros Boyadjian to make a portrait of his grandson Iyasu, then a child, and, later, sent it to Emperor Wilhelm II, his intention was to reassure the governments of foreign powers as to the existence of a designated heir to the Ethiopian throne. The role of photography acquired particular importance in the portraiture of Menelik's successors between 1909 and 1917, as is shown by the affair of *Negus* Mikaēl's crown, which involved both the palace's Armenian goldsmiths and also its Armenian photographers. *Ras* Mikaēl created a scandal when, in 1914, he had himself crowned as *negus* by arranging for the deceased Menelik's crown to be brought to his provincial court in Däsē, an act interpreted by the imperial court dignitaries as an illegitimate attempt to transfer power from Shäwa to Wällo. Mikaēl also took care to summon Bedros Boyadjian to his court; Boyadjian immortalized him wearing the imperial crown, or, in another photograph, seated beside his son Iyasu, who is on his knees to Mikaēl's left, with the famous crown in reach of his right hand.[74] The purpose of this use of the crown produced by Dikran Ebeyan was clearly to remind those who might dispute Mikaēl's legitimacy that Menelik himself had designated his grandson *Lej* Iyasu as heir to the throne. In the same spirit, the "cooptation" of the imperial court's official photographer, Boyadjian, although *Ras* Mikaēl had for several years had a personal photographer of his own, Levon Yazedjian, was another way of underscoring this transfer of supreme authority to the court in Wällo. This political instrumentalization of the Armenian photographers has left many different traces in the memory of the descendants of the immigration.

It demonstrates these photographers' ability to mobilize the grammar governing the use of Ethiopian political symbols, thus legitimizing the transmission of authority while also publicly sealing a pact concluded between former political foes.[75] A photograph published in the chronicle of the reign of Menelik II, said to have been taken by Bedros Boyadjian in Däsē in 1914, shows, side by side, Iyasu, his father, *Negus* Mikaēl, and *Ras* Wäldä Giyorgis. Its objective was probably to seal the agreement concluded in April 1914 between two former enemies, Mikaēl and Wäldä Giyorgis, about leadership of the province of Tigré. The fact that the three men, who pose standing upright, are all wearing the same outfit—the black cape and felt hat that, as it happens, the late Emperor Menelik ordinarily wore—may have been intended to show that they were assuming the succession as equals. Appealing to the photographer Bedros Boyadjian seems to have served as a way of ratifying this political accord, with the photograph acting as a signature. Estelle Sohier sets this interpretation in relation to the use of religious painting in Ethiopia as a means of attesting oaths taken by exalted figures. This political utilization of photography might also be compared to the many examples of portraits retouched by the same artists to signal, via a new sovereign's face and pose, a new departure in the conduct of the empire's affairs. Thus the official portrait that Bedros Boyadjian produced after Empress Zäwditu's coronation in 1917 is marked by a slight turn of her head, which serves to display, head-on, the cross on the crown that dominates this three-quarters portrait. It is possible to discern, in this manipulation of the image, a desire to justify *Lej* Iyasu's dethronement by valorizing a return to the Christian faith that the dethroned emperor was accused of having abandoned in favor of Islam. Haygaz Boyadjian, Bedros's son made a montage of the same kind in a portrait of Haile Selassie, who was crowned emperor in 1930.[76] The photographers were perfectly well aware of the uses to which their work could be put for propaganda purposes. It would therefore be unreasonable to assume that they were simple artisans who were happy to provide certain services to their clients in all neutrality.

Armenian Dynasties in the *Gebbi*

For the Ethiopian sovereigns of this period, choosing Armenians as servants was a way to avoid too conspicuously turning to foreigners. The perennity of the Armenian presence in the palace seems to confirm that this practice had a political dimension. In this connection, it is perhaps worth recalling the parallel that can be established with the Egypt of Khedive Mehmet Ali (1805–49), whose policy of modernizing while maintaining independence of the Ottoman Empire was bolstered by the services of a great many Armenian agents who belonged to a small circle of families descended of the big bourgeoisie of Smyrna and Constantinople and were, by turns, the viceroy's, and, later, his successor's, interpreters, secretaries, counselors, administrators, diplomats, and ministers.[77] We find an example in Boghos Yusufian, chief interpreter and, beginning in 1826, director of Trade and Foreign Affairs under Mehmet Ali. Yusufian's nephew by marriage, Nubar Pasha, also pursued a successful career in the service of the government of the khedives from 1842 to 1895, when he was repeatedly named minister and, on three different occasions, in 1878–9, 1884–8, and 1894–5, entrusted with the office of prime minister of Egypt. We might mention, as well, the careers of certain members of the Cherakian family, which settled in Egypt in 1812, notably that of Artin, Mehmet Ali's chief interpreter from 1839 on, who succeeded his compatriot Boghos Yusufian in the post of director of Trade and Foreign Affairs, an office he held from 1844 to 1850.[78] Artin's son, Yakub Artin, was named tutor to Khedive Ismail's children in 1873, and served, in 1878–9, as European secretary in the viceroy's private cabinet, after which he pursued a brilliant career as a high-ranking Egyptian civil servant until his death in 1919.[79]

The profile of these state servants in the Egypt of the khedives, who belonged to a financial and industrial bourgeois elite the members of which had often received their higher educations in European *grandes écoles*, is not, to be sure, readily comparable to the much more modest profile of the Armenians in Ethiopia who worked for the *gebbi* from Menelik's reign to that of Haile Selassie. Both countries nevertheless witnessed the emergence of veritable dynasties of Armenians employed in the local political authorities' service. Most of the Armenian servants of Menelik's *gebbi* remained there after their master died and were still there during Täfäri's regency. From 1908 on, Emperor Menelik, beset by a series of strokes, had gradually to relinquish oversight of the kingdom's affairs to Empress Taytu, but also to members of his court who were preparing his succession.[80] Indications are that Dikran Ebeyan left the court around 1908, for no contemporary account mentions his presence there after this date, although he died much later, in 1926.[81] Another Armenian goldsmith, his former partner in the monopoly on wine and alcoholic beverages, Hagop Baghdassarian, succeeded him in the palace. Menelik had already put the workshop of the *gebbi's* mint under his supervision and had entrusted him with the task of striking a thaler bearing his likeness; this, the first Ethiopian coinage, was intended to replace Maria Theresa's old thaler, which had until then been imported from Trieste.[82] Baghdassarian, who created Empress Zäwditu's crown, according to Armenian oral sources, worked in the palace alongside another Armenian goldsmith, Panos Vartanian, to the end of her reign. At the same time, the goldsmiths Nigoghos Jidedjian and Krikor Chalgjian were working for Täfäri, who was crowned *negus* in 1928.[83] According to Avedis Terzian, Jidejian served the crown prince's wife Mänän as her personal goldsmith. Finally, Hagop Baghdassarian is also supposed to have made the crown that Haile Selassie wore during his coronation as emperor. At the end of the monarchical regime in

Ethiopia, the emperor's goldsmith was still an Armenian, Bedros Sevadjian, the son of Armenian immigrants. This situation was somewhat reminiscent of that of Armenian goldsmiths in Egypt, of whom there were a great many in the khedive's court from the mid-nineteenth century on. Let us also note that the first Egyptian bank was created in 1837 by Armenian *sarraf* ("moneychangers") from Constantinople who became, like their counterparts working for the Sultan in the Ottoman Empire, the financiers of the khedive's court, and saw to minting coinage in Egypt.[84]

In the same perspective, it may be observed that the Boyadjian family formed a veritable dynasty of photographers at the imperial court in the twentieth century. Bedros Boyadjian and his eldest son Haygaz had been working together in the 1920s. After Bedros's death in 1928, *Negus* Täfäri appointed Haygaz to take his place, with the same official title, which he held until the 1936 Italian invasion. It was Haygaz who provided the photographic service at the emperor's November 1930 coronation. After his death in 1941, Haile Selassie, who had just made a triumphant return from England, designated Haygaz's younger brother Torkom (known as Tony), born in Addis Abeba in 1920, to succeed him. Tony Boyadjian accompanied the emperor on his many foreign journeys after the war and remained court photographer until the imperial regime was overthrown in 1974. By producing, in that year, the portrait of the president of the provisional military government, Täfäri Benti, Tony also ensured the transition between the two regimes: thus the Boyadjian dynasty covered the whole period during which photographic portraits were put to official use, from Menelik's reign to the establishment of the Marxist military junta of the *Därg*.[85]

Among the *gebbi*'s Armenian craftsmen, it was not rare to see a post in the service of the emperor and his entourage transmitted from parent to child, sibling to sibling, or, in a broad sense, one member of a family to another. The goldsmith Hagop Baghdassarian's brothers, Ghevont and Hrant, had been employed in the imperial palace's workshops in the late 1920s, as had Hagop's brother-in-law, Ardashes Karaseferian, and his brother Hrant, who were, like him, natives of Van.[86] Armenag Baghdassarian, Hagop's mixed-race son, was the head of Zäwditu's palace workshops, where he was known by the Ethiopian title of *lej*. With no particular skills, *Lej* Armenag, who cultivated solid friendships at the highest state levels, continued working in Haile Selassie's service after his father's death in 1932. Robert Yazedjian, one of the sons of the photographer Levon Yazedjian and his wife Araxi Yazedjian, who directed the imperial palace's carpets workshops, was himself employed as a carpet maker in *Negus* Täfäri's *gebbi*. His brother Paylag Yazedjian held various high-ranking posts in the Ethiopian administration and was mentioned as being the government's chief accountant and inspector-general of trade in the Finance Ministry early in the 1930s. He pursued his career after the war, becoming vice-governor of the municipality of Addis Abeba in 1956.[87] These dynasties of Armenians in the authorities' service generally emerged from families that had settled in Ethiopia quite early, the oldest members of which had been servants of Menelik's. This did not hold for Abraham Koeurhadjian, who nevertheless performed multiple functions of some importance, such as administrator of customs for forests and hot springs in Addis Abeba, as well as government accountant and commissioner, or, again, general administrator of the royal estate (i.e., "treasurer"). Koeurhadjian became a servant of Täfäri's and remained a close associate of his even after Täfäri was crowned emperor, acting as his private secretary.[88] He had arrived in Ethiopia in 1908 and was not a former servant of Menelik's. We would, however, do well to recall that he was the son-in-law of one of the oldest and most famous of the former emperor's servants, Boghos Markarian.

The perpetuation of personal ties to the Ethiopian sovereigns is particularly striking in the oldest Armenian immigrant families, especially when employment in Menelik's service went hand in hand with marriage to an Ethiopian aristocrat. The children of these families, born in Ethiopia, were often godchildren of Ethiopian grandees or even of the emperor himself. Thus Khachig and Aghassi Boghossian were godchildren of the very famous *Däjach* Balcha, as is attested by a photograph that shows the two little boys posing in front of a portrait of their illustrious godfather (Figure 3.1). Hagop Baghdassarian provides another example. *Ras* Täfäri, the son of *Ras* Mäkonnen, who had been Hagop Baghdassarian's protector before Baghdassarian came to work in Menelik's *gebbi*, had been the godfather of one of his sons who had died in infancy, Anushavan Baghdassarian. We can further cite the example of *Negus* Mikaël's daughter Sehin, *Lej* Iyasu's sister, and the wife of Regent Täfäri's Minister of Justice. She stood godmother to Araxi and Levon Yazedjian's daughter Anna, who was born in Addis Abeba in 1914. Anna Yazedjian's own daughter (who married a French soldier, Robert Marcerou, during the war) became, in her turn, the goddaughter of Empress Mänän, who was herself Sehin's daughter. When these children grew up, they often took posts in the service of the government or the court, in one sense or another of the term. Khachig Boghossian worked in the Ethiopian Ministry of Agriculture after the Second World War, supervising, notably, the profitable business of exporting khat to Aden, a British protectorate. One of his brothers, Khosrov Boghossian, a close associate of Haile Selassie's since the 1930s, retained his post of head of the imperial stables after the war, with the rank of colonel in the Ethiopian army. Thus the relations that the sovereigns established with their Armenian servants often involved more, for the Armenians, than the simple exercise of their function.

The Invention of an Armenian "Loyal Nation" in Ethiopia

The special relation between Ethiopia's sovereigns and their Armenian servants is a reality that contemporary sources fail to reveal, although it found expression for several decades in a "social discourse" of the Ethiopian monarchy about the Armenians.

The "Symbolic Nationalization" of the Armenians in Ethiopia: A Hypothesis

In his thank-you letter of March 19, 1929, to the author of the Armenian book *Modern Ethiopia and the Armenian Colony*, *Negus* Täfäri affirms that

> there is no one who does not know how much the Armenians who have been living in Addis Abeba for such a long time love our country and religion. [...] Some of them work as employees in our government affairs: consequently, we can

Figure 3.1 Khosrov and Aghassi Boghossian with a portrait of their godfather, *Däjazmach* Balcha, around 1907.

Source: Boghossian collection.

say that the Armenian children who have been educated and who have grown up here also love Ethiopia as their fatherland, and that they will serve it in future.[89]

The idea that the Armenians were loyal, which the Ethiopian monarchy seems to have played on in the early twentieth century, is somewhat reminiscent of that of the "loyal nation" in the Ottoman Empire. In the highly codified *millet* system that predominated there until the early twentieth century, the conspicuous concession, to the Armenian patriarch of Constantinople, of formal privileges and marks of attention was an assertion of the existence of a privileged, almost emotional, relationship between a non-Muslim minority and its sovereign. Formal, above all—it by no means prevented the 1894–7 massacres of Armenians under the reign of Sultan Abdülhamid II—this terminology formed an integral part of the political discourse that the sultan addressed to all his subjects. The "symbolic nationalization of the Armenians," realized one small touch at a time from Menelik's reign through Täfäri's regency, entered into the logic of the construction of an Ethiopian nation-state in an imperial context that was, however, far from displaying the homogeneity that this concept implies.

It is clear that early twentieth-century Ethiopia did not comprise a nation-state, at least not in the sense in which we understand the term when we consider the problem of nationalities in Europe in the same period. The thesis that "Greater Ethiopia" is "an ingathering of peoples with deep historical affinities"[90] is very much open to question because of its culturalist and political presuppositions and, no less, the conclusions it sustains. As soon as we abandon the classic state-centered, historiographical grand narrative, we have no trouble detecting signs of hostility to the domination imposed on what is today southern Ethiopia by Menelik's military conquests from 1880 to 1904. At a time when this country's past is increasingly being written along ethno-national lines, what was long presented as an Ethiopian *Reconquista*, the *aqänna*, is decried on all sides as an enterprise of colonization pure and simple.[91] The empire that emerged from Menelik's conquests covered a territory that had suddenly become three or four times bigger than the one that the Ethiopia's "king of kings" had ruled over until then. Its heterogeneity was still very pronounced in the 1930s, when Emperor Haile Selassie, like his predecessors, had to come to terms with an aristocracy that withdrew to the provinces, where communications with the capital were unreliable, the better to free itself of the monarchy's vague desires to centralize the country. Haile Selassie repeatedly had to confront secessionist temptations and revolts in Tigré. The Italians, after conquering Ethiopia in 1936, took care to exploit this heterogeneity by promoting expressions of linguistic, religious, and ethnic difference and creating or reinforcing administrative divisions in the provinces in order to aggravate preexisting centrifugal tendencies—in short, by sapping the efforts to unify the country that the emperors had undertaken since the mid-nineteenth century. In the same period, however, the Ethiopian monarchs had begun to elaborate a political discourse of a national cast, and it had begun to find its uses. Far from being a mere rhetorical device, this discourse answered, rather, to "the objective need for homogeneity" that Ernest Gellner invokes when he explains the emergence of nationalism in changing societies.[92] For very real transformations were distancing the empire of Ethiopia of the years 1920–30 from the classical model of a segmented agrarian society: sudden territorial expansion, a redefinition of its geopolitical surroundings, a new flowering of the cities, and the unprecedented development of a foreign immigrant presence. Like the invention of traditions—a phenomenon that is, moreover, closely bound up with the phenomenon of nationalism—the nascent discourse about the Ethiopian nation was a surface manifestation of these underlying transformations. The sense of belonging to an Ethiopian "nation" was basically founded on the idea of loyalty to the emperor, who was presented as a descendant of Solomon and the chief defender of the Ethiopian Church. There were not, properly speaking, Ethiopian citizens, but only subjects. The millions of individuals who peopled the empire were not united by a common set of equal rights and duties but by their theoretical submission to one and the same supreme authority. Thus the Armenians' "symbolic nationalization" constituted a form of political integration only in the sense that they were accepted in the royal house, in the circle of the emperor's faithful followers and servants.

Snapshots and Show: How Are We to Understand the Imperial Discourse on Loyalty?

It goes without saying that the written sources sustaining this thesis are rare. Several photographs of the period, however, offer visible evidence of the lowly immigrants' political integration into Ethiopia's royal house. Taking into account what we know about the Ethiopian sovereigns' control over images, and their political use of them, it seems reasonable to suppose that the presence of Armenian servants in these official photographs, when it is conspicuous, provides a public reflection of the emperor's trust in his loyal followers, as if they were being awarded an official decoration.[93] Those whom written European sources describe, invariably, as people relegated to the shadows, are, for the space of an instant—but an immortalized instant—bathed in light. In two photographs taken by Bedros Boyadjian, Menelik's official photographer, we see the emperor posing in the company of these loyal followers, whom written accounts ordinarily consign to anonymity, at a foundation ceremony for a new building in the capital. One of the photos (Figure 3.2) was taken as Menelik laid the first stone, blazoned with a protective cross, of Saint George's Basilica in 1905. To the best of my knowledge, it has never been published, although it answers perfectly to Mérab's description of the photographs taken at this event:

> Old photographs show *Abuna* Matheos blessing the first stone, while Menelik holds a roll of gold rings, weighing three kilos in all, that was supposed to be buried beneath the foundations. In fact, only thalers bearing Menelik's likeness, struck especially for this occasion in gold and silver, were buried, along with an account of the foundation enclosed in a bottle.[94]

What this description does not say, but what the photograph shows, is that Sarkis Terzian, wearing his eternal cap, is posing just behind the emperor and *Abunä* Matēwos. Nonchalantly seated, he has not been relegated to the background occupied by an indistinct multitude thronging the edges of the excavation where the emperor, *Abunä* Matēwos; the Italian engineer Castagna, with a hammer in his hand; and,

Figure 3.2 Laying the first stone of the new Basilica of Saint George in Addis Abeba, 1905, in the presence of Emperor Menelik, *Abunä* Matēwos, and Sarkis Terzian (behind them, seated). Photograph by Bedros Boyadjian, official photographer of Ethiopia's imperial court.

Source: Avedis Terzian papers, collection of the Armenian Community in Ethiopia.

perhaps, the Greek architect Orphanides, holding the ceremonial umbrella that serves as a parasol, are all standing. The presence of the faithful Armenian servant—by the time this photo was taken, he had served Menelik for seventeen years—does not find its only possible explanation in the idea, of which we find no evidence whatsoever elsewhere, that he helped build the church. His privileged position in the photograph is not insignificant, given the importance the emperor attached to the production and composition of these official images of his power. Indeed, the pose struck by many of the participants in this ceremony, at least those who are in the foreground and center of the composition, does not create the impression that it was improvised, but, on the contrary, suggests that it was carefully arranged.

This type of document has inestimable social value for descendants of Armenian immigrants, who construe it as proof that their ancestors had their place in the *gebbi*, that they were indeed part "of the house" of the king. Thus this photograph was transmitted to me by Sarkis Terzian's son Avedis, who had an original print of it. Motivated by much the same desire to corroborate stories about their father's role at the court early in the century, Krikorios Boghossian's daughters showed me a photograph taken by Bedros Boyadjian at the 1909 laying of the first stone of the Menelik II Hospital, "the walls of which collapsed even before it was inaugurated (1910)"[95] (Figure 3.3). The composition is centered on Menelik, his health already more than shaky, leaning

Figure 3.3 Laying the first stone of the Menelik II Hospital in Addis Abeba in 1909, in the presence of Emperor Menelik and Krikorios Boghossian (on the left).

Source: Boghossian collection.

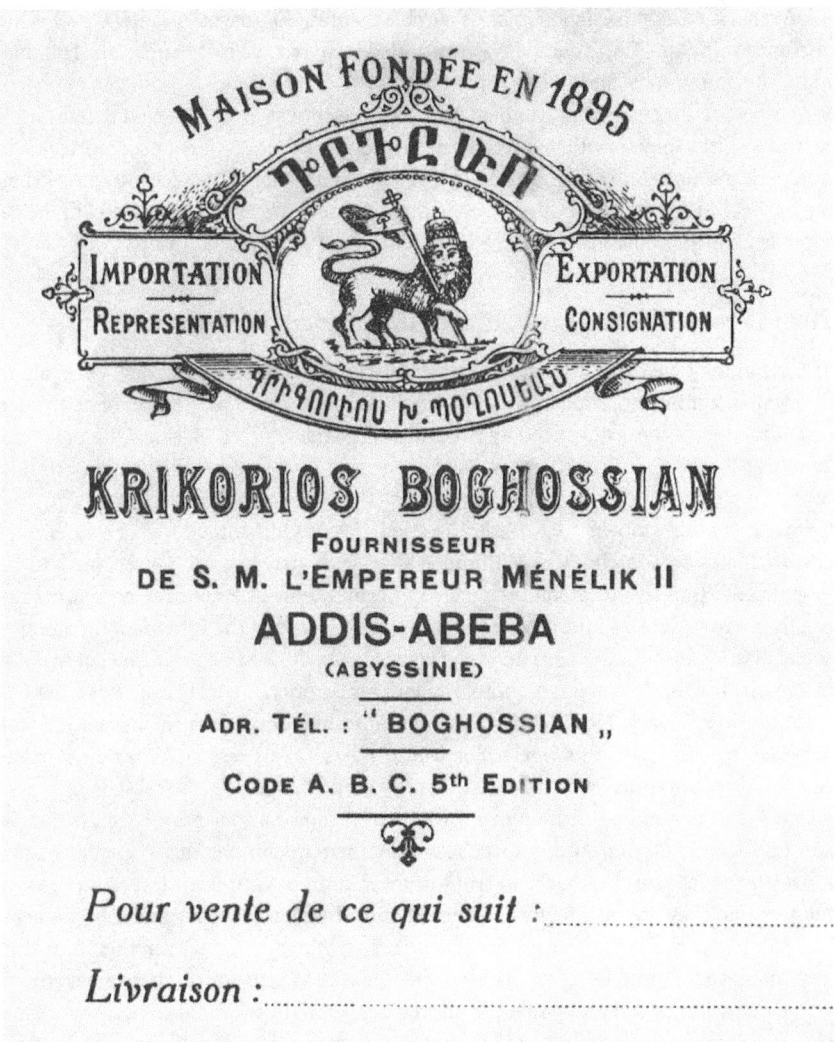

Figure 3.4 Letterhead of Krikorios Boghossian, known as Gorgoryos, purveyor of Ethiopia's imperial court.

Source: Boghossian collection.

on a cane and accompanied by his new private doctor of Guadeloupean extraction (Dr. Vitalien, wearing a suit and a bow tie), who was to head the future hospital. The emperor seems to be looking toward Krikorios, "Gorgoryos" for the Ethiopians, who is standing bare headed on the left. The fact that he has been placed in the foreground, a few meters from Menelik, is a sign of his close association with the imperial court, whose "official purveyor" he was, according to his letterhead (Figure 3.4), but also a sign of his personal ties to the sovereign. In a more recent photograph that was published in the Amharic edition of Haile Selassie's autobiography, Gorgoryos and his son Khachig also appear in *Ras* Täfäri's company, surrounded by his royal brass band.[96] The fact that, in these photographs, Sarkis Terzian and Krikorios "Gorgoryos" Boghossian appear at the emperor's side was, plainly, not at all fortuitous; it was even expected that, as loyal servants of his, they should be present on such occasions. Yet these posed portraits do not, perhaps, stage only the monarch's personal relationship to his servant(s). As I shall try to show in the following analysis of a document, it seems that they also officialize, more generally, monarchical acknowledgment of the Armenians' loyalty.

From a Short to the *Longue Durée*: A "Thick Description" of the Event

The symbolic density that I am tempted to attribute to facts which may seem slight, or even insignificant, suggests that there is something to be gained here from a consideration of ideas advanced by the anthropologist Clifford Geertz, who pleads in favor of a "thick description" of social acts, one that goes beyond the thin description of the conventional ethnographic approach.[97] The sociological treatment of symbolic forms thus comes down to considering them "as 'saying something of something,' and saying it to somebody."[98] Without claiming to detect in acts presumed to be "significant" the keys to a comprehensive interpretation of a cultural system, I shall briefly borrow Geertz's interpretive theory to make sense of the Ethiopian monarchy's social discourse about the Armenians by way of an analysis of a short film shot in color in 1962 by the third Armenian photographer at the imperial court, Tony Boyadjian.[99]

Shot on February 15, 1962, that is, a month after the funeral of Emperor Haile Selassie's wife Mänän, this one-reeler immortalizes a procession of Addis Abeba's Armenian community, which placed a spray of flowers on the deceased Empress's grave.[100] The beginning of the film shows men in their Sunday best, both Armenian and Ethiopian, entering Addis Abeba's small Armenian church. The Armenians seem especially at ease on the square in front of their church, an impression reinforced by the fact that they are personally acquainted with the director. They are at home here. The dignitaries of the Ethiopian Church who are walking up the stairs in their liturgical costumes are followed by a few distinguished men in elegant suits. There are so many participants in the ceremony that the church cannot hold them all, so that some have to watch it from the church door. Then, the procession forms again and sets out for the Ethiopian church of the Trinity, where the empress's remains are lying in state. Archbishop Mampre Sirunian, who has come from Cairo for the occasion, walks at the head of the procession, draped in a beautiful robe of red silk richly embroidered with gold thread, wearing the usual conical miter, covered, now, with a black veil, and carrying a processional staff. The choristers, in white and blue tunics, march out ahead of him, carrying banners held high. The procession ripples through the street, bringing hundreds of people together under the gaze of the many onlookers whose respectful presence on both sides of the cortege makes the procession seem even bigger. The members of the *kaghoutayin*, as Armenian community's leaders are collectively called, take part in the procession in their dark suits. The Armenian and Ethiopian schoolchildren of the national Armenian Kevorkoff school—which had a student body of about 200 in this period—are easy to make out in the crowd, thanks to their white tunics and the narrow black bands they wear on their arms as a sign of mourning. They, too, join the procession, swelling its ranks. It finally makes its way through the gate of the Ethiopian church of the Trinity.[101] Preceded by the choristers' red and golden banners, the Armenian archbishop, received by Ethiopian clergymen, is the first to enter the sanctuary. When he leaves it, he lingers on the church steps to hold a long conversation, hand in hand, with one of the participants in the ceremony, perhaps a member of the imperial family. Then the Armenian procession leaves the churchyard of the Ethiopian church and scatters in the streets.

Now that we have described the document, let us read it. Despite appearances, the Armenian procession does not just wend its way through the capital's streets. In view of the size of the cortege, the image of a prosperous community emanating from it, the manifest dignity of the archbishop and the *kaghoutayin* marching in it, the sumptuous colors and embroideries of gold thread, and the solemnity of the banners and liturgical chasubles, it is easy to guess that this procession makes a certain impression on the public. This solemnity notwithstanding, a feeling of normality exudes from the whole, almost a sense of déjà vu. The Ethiopian churchmen we see walking up the steps of the Armenian church seem completely at ease as they stride briskly into the building, leaving the impression that this is not their first visit. The same impression flows from the apparently spontaneous conversations struck up between Armenians and Ethiopians on the square in front of the church, probably in Amharic. There is a kind of familiarity and everyday simplicity in the unfolding of this ceremony whose outward appearances, albeit highly ritualized, are not particularly formal. A procession of Catholics or Protestants of this kind, even Ethiopian Catholics or Protestants, would have been unimaginable, when the political legitimacy of the dynasty in power largely depended on the close alliance it took pains to maintain with the Ethiopian Church. For the other Christian Churches, albeit tolerated, by no means enjoyed the same status as the Ethiopian Church. The images of Tony Boyadjian's film, which show us a solemn procession led through the streets of the city by the Armenian archbishop, not furtively, but conspicuously and in obvious concord with the dignitaries of the Ethiopian clergy invited to join the procession, are thrown into even starker relief as a result.

This simple, apparently banal, document is thus much more eloquent than it seems. Beyond a literal reading, there is, in this one-reeler, eloquent testimony to the normality of a manifestly long-standing and relatively close relationship between the members of the Ethiopian clergy and the imperial family on the one hand and the Armenian clergy and community on the other. We can discern a very concrete illustration of a social discourse that made the Armenians a "privileged minority" in Ethiopia, a discourse that is especially manifest in ceremonies of a religious nature. The inhabitants of Addis Abeba had, in the past, repeatedly had occasion to attend similar events: the 1928 benediction of the first stone of the Armenian church of Surp Kevork, for example, in the presence of Archbishop Kevork Arslanian, come from Istanbul expressly for this purpose,[102] surrounded by community leaders and the twenty sponsors of the church in their white tunics embroidered with gold thread. *Negus* Täfäri and Empress Zäwditu were present that day, accompanied by Ethiopian Church dignitaries, at the mass celebrated under a canopy by the Armenian archbishop. A photograph bears witness to this moment of communion, even if, unlike the photographs on which I have commented so far, it is not posed, and almost seems to have been taken surreptitiously (Figure 3.5). This is not, then, a photograph that delivers an official message, but the event itself, insofar as it seems to participate in the institutionalization of the "loyal nation" of the Armenians in Ethiopia. Among the members of the public, their gazes converging on the altar and the bishop's miter, the ambassadors and the other guests are confined to the background. We recognize, standing and facing the camera, Hovhannes Semerjibashian, the German legation's interpreter and a personal friend of *Negus* Täfäri's. In the quadrangular central area, the church dignitaries occupy the places of honor. In front of Semerjibashian, near the column on the right, sit two prelates of the Greek Orthodox Church. An individual draped in white, who may be the *echägē*, the head of the Ethiopian regular clergy,[103] sits imposingly near the column opposite the Greek archbishop's. Between the two columns, finally, directly aligned with the altar, we can discern the silhouette of Empress Zäwditu, wearing a felt hat and a veil, as well as the profile of *Negus* Täfari, both of them seated. The handwritten inscription on the back of the original print of this photograph, which is, let us note, unsigned, adds that the mass by the Armenian composer Yekmalian was sung by four voices under the baton of Maestro Kevork Nalbandian, who was the empress's and the crown prince's musical director in this period. Religious reasons, to begin with, explain the presence of the empress and crown prince at a ceremony of such great importance for the small Armenian population, which had, by this time, been established in Ethiopia for a generation; it may, however, also be interpreted as a conspicuous mark of good will and an assurance of political protection.

The funeral of "Colonel Khosroff" (Khosrov Boghossian), the last example I shall comment on here, provides an eloquent illustration of this collective symbolic status of the "loyal nation." Born in Addis Abeba in 1904 of an Ethiopian mother and an Armenian father (Krikorios Boghossian, a former servant of Menelik II and a man who cultivated many friendships with the country's leading aristocrats), godson of the famous *Däjazmach* Balcha, the deceased, who held Ethiopian nationality, was a member of the Imperial Guard and director of the palace stables. Close to Emperor Haile Selassie, he had stood by his side down to the days just before the emperor went into exile in England in the wake of the May 1936 Italian conquest of Addis Abeba.[104] He continued to serve Haile Selassie after he was restored to the throne in 1941. The photographs taken at his funeral (Figures 3.6 and 3.7) on September 8, 1970, show an impressive array of Ethiopian soldiers standing at attention in Addis Abeba's little Armenian cemetery. The ceremony attests the emperor's desire to reserve for this faithful servant of the throne, heir to one of the Ethiopian-Armenian "dynasties" close to the imperial palace, a treatment worthy of a high-ranking member of the Ethiopian army. It also resonates with the social discourse that, from the early twentieth century on, tended to present the Armenians as a privileged minority that was consciously set apart from all the other "foreigners" and considered to be "at home" in Ethiopia.

***

At the end of this retrospective approach, we may interpret the 1924 creation of *Ras* Täfäri's royal brass band as a political act in the full sense of the word. It seems to form

Figure 3.5 Mass celebrated in 1928 in *Ras* Täfäri's and Empress Zäwditu's presence by Archbishop Kevork Arslanian, come from Istanbul to attend the foundation ceremony of the Surp Kevork Armenian church in Addis Abeba.

Source: Bibliothèque Nubar de l'UGAB, Paris.

Figure 3.6 Colonel Khosrov Boghossian's funeral procession, Addis Abeba, September 8, 1970.

Source: Boghossian collection.

Figure 3.7 Burial of Colonel Khosrov Boghossian in the Surp Hagop Armenian cemetery in Addis Abeba, September 8, 1970.

Source: Boghossian collection.

an integral part, in this pivotal period in the affirmation of Ethiopian sovereignty, of a social discourse that assigned the Armenians a specific symbolic place in Ethiopia. The genesis of this specificity, the result of which we see at work here, runs counter to the usual view of the Armenians in Ethiopia. By the same token, it invites us to revise certain judgments on the history of the foreigners in this country and to refine certain conclusions by asking about what the sources do not say or, in the case of most of them, say only involuntarily. The "symbolic nationalization" involved here, however, if it is not mere speculation, will have found its reflection in individuals' lived experience. We have therefore to appeal to other types of testimony, derived from work carried out in the field, to discern the echoes of this historical construct in the memory of the Armenian immigration in Ethiopia.

Part 2

The Friendship of Kings

Prelude to the History of a Collective Memory

This investigation began with fieldwork. It soon led me to perceive Armenian immigration to Ethiopia from the angle of memory. The chapters that follow attempt to give objective expression to the lived experience of an Armenian exception in Ethiopia, legible in the memory of the descendants of immigrants. The period covered by the memory of the Armenian presence in Ethiopia does not exceed two or three generations. It does not coincide with the long course of the Ethiopian monarchy's political strategies, which make use of collective representations with roots reaching back as far as the seventeenth and eighteenth centuries. Beyond the plurality of historical times and the divergences that follow from them, however, this contradiction is only apparent. The widely shared feeling of the descendants of Armenian immigrants that their parents benefited from an exceptionally close relation to the Ethiopian monarchs and their entourage forms the very basis of a collective memory. It is a memory that postulates and affirms the unique nature of the Armenian immigrant experience in Ethiopia.

It is not a question of finding, in these "alternative" testimonies, "information" passed over in silence by written history. The rather naive idea that the spoken discourse of the person who recounts a narrative is "true" and needs no analysis, like the idea that one can more effectively account for a social reality by letting this supposedly "raw" discourse express itself, tape recorder in hand, has occasionally been taken to justify the researcher's total self-effacement before life narratives that are, at best, transcribed.[1] It is, however, crucial to go beyond a purely descriptive reading of testimony, whether it is written, oral, or iconographic, in order to constitute collective memory as a true object of historical investigation and thus to historicize the lived experience of a political and symbolic condition of the Armenians in Ethiopia.

Avedis Terzian's Narratives: An Aperçu of an Original Source

Because of its importance to what follows, I here present an extract from the oral text produced in the course of the several interviews that I conducted with Avedis Terzian, the son of Armenian immigrants. Terzian was born in Harar in 1904 and died in Addis Abeba on July 25, 2000. The interviews were conducted in French in his home, with no others present, in August and September 1997, December 1999, and May–June 2000. They comprise a group of narratives that I have numbered from 1 to 33. I shall be citing many extracts from these narratives, in addition to the one found further on.[2]

In the following pages, I present, virtually *in extenso*, what Avedis Terzian said during our first, August 14, 1997 interview, which was also our first encounter. He spoke at one go, almost without interruption or questions from me. In transcribing his discourse, I have tried to introduce as few alterations as possible. I have held annotations and commentary to a minimum for now in order to make the text easier to read. The following signs indicate:

[-/-] a question of mine;
[...] omission of a few words or sentences that contributed nothing to the text's overall meaning; and
[?] a word uttered by Avedis Terzian that I was not able to transcribe; [...?], similarly, a string of inaudible words.

The punctuation added to the oral texts aims to restore its spoken rhythms while paying due attention to the need to produce a readable text. The indentations and paragraphing by means of which I have subdivided the text and numbered its successive parts are, obviously, subjective demarcations: based on my understanding of the text, they are intended to facilitate the commentary that follows.

Narrative 1

§ 1. They are traders, adventurers.

The first one arrives in Massawa in 1865. This was Mr. Boghos Markarian… He's practically the first Armenian to find himself in a community: Boghos Markarian, 1865. He travels to Adwa and Mäqälē; it was under the kingdom of Tigré [Tegray], under Emperor Yohannes. So there we have this first contact, Boghos Markarian who contacts Emperor Yohannes, and he becomes Yohannes' employee, his treasurer. As you can see, it's not the people: the sovereign first. You know, in all these countries, there are problems: movements are prohibited by the sovereigns.

§ 2. The second one is a certain Dikran Ebeyan, a prosperous merchant who comes to Tadjoura. Tadjoura is located—it's a port—in French Somalia, just outside Djibouti. France, at this time, had occupied Obock [...]. So there we have Dikran's arrival… Dikran, too, arrives for two reasons: he had already had to do with Emperor Yohannes; Emperor Yohannes had sent a messenger to Egypt looking for a goldsmith who was capable of making a crown. So the Armenians proposed Dikran. Dikran comes to Ethiopia, he makes Emperor Yohannes's crown. So there we have a second Armenian who approaches the sovereign, very important, with [the] crown, etc. On a second trip, Dikran leaves him; he leaves for Egypt; he makes a second trip with merchandise, he comes to Tadjoura in order to enter by way of Shoa [Shäwa], where Menelik is. He arrives in Entotto. But there was no Addis Abeba [yet]. He settles in Entotto, he does his trading, he leaves for Egypt again, he makes a second trip later.

§ 3. Thirdly, the Egyptians occupy Zeila. Armenians, my father's uncle, whose name is Kevork Terzian, is in Harar—I don't know how, I think he followed the Egyptian army, he was a contractor and a baker there. So there we have a third arrival. My father leaves Egypt, he had left his native city—he comes from the city of Arabkir. [-/-] They're from Arabkir [?]. So he comes to live with his uncle. The Egyptians occupy [Zeila] in [18]75. My father arrives in [18]82. Seven years later, in [Zeila]. [-/-] Yes, from Zeila. From Zeila to Harar, there was no other port. It was the Egyptian line. So there you see a third arrival. I don't know, maybe there were one or two Armenians besides that: it was my uncle and my father, they were the founders of the colony in Harar.

§ 4. Afterwards, in 1898, the French government was transferred to Djibouti... From Obock to Djibouti [?] and created another city in Djibouti. Afterwards, things develop, Djibouti becomes a fourth place of entry... Becomes a fourth gateway for Armenians, but later, by rail, because from Djibouti, they build the railroad to [as far as] Dire Dawa, which is very close to Harar. So there we have the four arrivals.

§ 5. Meanwhile, Italy appears in Africa in 1875. Supported by the English who had a war against the Mahdi of Sudan—there was a revolt. The English, looking for support in Ethiopia, they encourage the Italians to settle here. So there we see Ethiopia's big problem: the Italians who start to make their way in and the Italians, with colonial intentions, also intend to contact Menelik. Menelik, at this time, was king of Shoa [Shäwa], under Emperor Yohannes. So the Italians cultivate Menelik and give him encouragement against the Emperor. Ethiopia found itself in a special situation; it was an empire born of a mirage. Yohannes, basically, called himself the first among the grandees... It wasn't a strong empire, so the Italians who were advancing toward Tigré, northern Ethiopia, gave Menelik encouragement against the Emperor. So you see that there was an Italian intrigue in the south and the north: political in the south, military in the north. But!... It was still vague. Now, Menelik, profiting from his geographical situation, started to expand toward the south: he couldn't expand toward the north, so he started to push toward the south. All these regions of subject peoples... The Ethiopians said it was a reconquest but it was a sort of colonization toward the south. So you see the kingdom of Shoa [Shäwa] that becomes a colonizer. The Italians, in giving Menelik encouragement, encouraged him to go toward Harar. The Egyptians, after a ten-year stay, leave Harar in 1885. They hand power over to the local chieftain. Now, Menelik, encouraged, starts a campaign in the direction of Harar. The petty Muslim chieftain [of Harar] was very fanatical and the Armenians, above all my father and my uncle, found life very unpleasant. He was very fanatical. So my father, who was young, starts to take an interest in Menelik, starts to send messages to Ankobär, before the arrival [of Menelik] in Addis Abeba, and starts to cultivate Ethiopian elements. So when Menelik sets out, near Harar, there's a small village. There, there's a battle. When the Egyptians leave, they hand all the ammunition over [to the emir]. The petty chieftain would like to fight Menelik, he is beaten. He escapes from Harar. Menelik starts to approach. My father, seeing that the Ethiopians were advancing, disarms all the artillery that the Egyptians had left behind. He captures the five gates, because Harar is a city with the wall [a walled city]... Seeing this situation, the last of the [Muslim] chieftains leans in front of the wall [leans out over the city wall], but afterwards he is terrified, he leaves, he flees for the Somali region. Menelik approaches the city, he camps outside it and he's afraid to enter the city: he thinks that the Harari have buried explosives, so he's afraid for a moment. My father leaves the city, he says: "The city is in my hands, there aren't any explosives." So the Emperor sends someone, he runs a check, everything's fine. He [Menelik] enters the town. So this is [in] 1877 [sic]. The Italians [sic] start their move toward the north in [18]75 [sic]. Menelik conquers Harar in [18]77[3] and starts to collaborate with Italy—he sees that it is certainly very useful—and he sees two problems. He says, "First, transport the Egyptian ammunition and artillery." So my father takes on the task of transporting all the artillery and ammunition to Entotto. Secondly, there are the conditions of contact with the sea. To go to Zeila from Harar, you have to go through Somali territory. He appoints, uh... My father is appointed governor of this region. First time a white man is appointed governor... There's a photograph that someone found in an Italian illustrated newspaper, maybe you've seen it? Yes, my father in Ethiopian dress. So there you see that the Armenian contact is becoming profitable. He's no longer a merchant or a goldsmith, he becomes a soldier and an administrator. Meanwhile, Haile Selassie's future father, *Ras* Mäkonnen, was a low-ranking officer, Emperor Menelik's nephew, he's appointed *däjazmach* and my father as governor. He [Mäkonnen] is appointed governor of Harar. So Menelik's nephew becomes governor of Harar, Sarkis Terzian becomes governor of the gateway of Gildessa.

§ 6. Gildessa and Biyo Kaboba. Take a look, what you're seeing are the Gildessa and Biyo Kaboba events. Now certain Armenians who found themselves in Harar start to go from there to Shoa [Shäwa]. To Entotto. [...] Meanwhile, in 1879, Yohannes dies. There's a battle against the Sudanese, he's slain in the battle. So Menelik proclaims himself emperor: he was king of Shoa [Shäwa], he proclaims himself emperor. After that, in this period, the Italians who were cultivating Menelik make [him] sign a treaty in a village called Wechalē [Ucciali]; outside Addis Abeba, in the countryside. It was a treaty of friendship, but, underhandedly, it was a protectorate, because they had put in an article that said that Ethiopia, where its contacts with foreign countries were concerned[, had to submit them to Italy for approval]. The Italians proclaim this in Europe and all the governments accept the fact that Ethiopia has become a protectorate. Only Russia and another country didn't accept it. Menelik heard this. At that time, the Armenians or the foreigners, above all the French, begin to contact Menelik. He's informed [by them] that he had become a protectorate. Menelik proclaims: "It's not true! The text [stipulates that this article] is optional." But the Italians insist, and it was a five-year treaty. [18]79 [sic].[4]

§ 7. Meanwhile, Menelik has become emperor, and he had to do a coronation. Who was to do this coronation? It was Dikran Ebeyan who makes the crown, organizes the celebrations. His wife organizes the receptions and all that. So, you see, another contact with Menelik.

§ 8. Her name is Serpig.[5] Madam Serpig.

[She was] Armenian... And the day of the coronation, she faints. It was a big affair, thousands of soldiers, drinks [for everyone]... She faints. The soldiers say: "The white woman is dead," because they don't know what fainting is. So the Emperor had a bottle of eau de Cologne. He poured [some on] Serpig. And there, you see, the contact become closer. [...] So Dikran, on the one hand, becomes very close [to Menelik]. Madam Serpig makes Menelik's clothes, Dikran makes the grandees' crowns, and all that. So you see what contact there is, friendlier.

§ 9. Now Sarkis contacts the Emperor, he says: "We've brought ammunition, weapons, but these are very primitive things, so [more modern] arms are needed, and also cooperating with Italy is inevitable." "But Sarkis, how can we procure arms [for ourselves]?" Meanwhile, in Berlin, the Europeans have signed a treaty by which they took it upon themselves to prevent weapons from being brought into Ethiopia. It was France, Italy, England. They had unsuspected colonial ambitions; impossible to bring in arms. My father says: "I'll bring you arms." "And how?" He travels to Marseilles. To Marseilles. Because Djibouti [the French Somali Coast] was almost starting to develop with Obock, and my father often made trips to Belgium... I think he had a Belgian mistress. So he travels to Marseilles. In Marseilles, he contacts Frenchmen and he says: "Do you have arms?" He [purchases] large quantities of scrapped arms: France had changed its armaments, from the Gras to the Lebel rifle. They say: "You can buy these Gras rifles, but we can't put them on board for you." What was to be done? They say: "Go to Belgium, you have contacts, you can buy these weapons in Liège and transport them in Belgium." He travels to Belgium, he thinks it would be possible to smuggle these weapons into Ethiopia. He makes zinc-covered crates. Thirteen million... It was eighty thousand rifles bought at a good price with money the Emperor had given him: ivory and gold. Naturally, I even think that France gave [them] to him for free... Because France wasn't in agreement with Italian expansion. Even while acting [taking measures] against smuggling, Djibouti's governor, Mr. Lagarde, was for Ethiopia. Naturally, out of politics [political interest]. So you see that this blockade was probably not very honest. So, thirteen million cartridges [?], all that in Belgium. [...] The transfer was made in Amsterdam. There was a ship leaving for Indonesia and they were loaded at the port [...]. There are also thirty-three French canons... Thirty-three French canons, a machine-gun, and, afterwards, five hundred thousand rounds, manufactured in Solingen, in Germany. [...] So all that was loaded onto the ship, it came by the Red Sea. My father knows Tadjoura very well. In Tadjoura and in Djibouti, there's a low tide. Every night, the sea recedes five kilometers. So my father organizes the unloading of this equipment at sea... [In the] zinc-covered [crates of rifles]. The ship leaves. Naturally, I think that there was... French knowledge [connivance]. Very possible. But the matériel is at sea. At night, the water recedes five kilometers. My father, who is in contact with these small desert peoples—they are Danakils—organizes the transport. These crates are transported to the land. So they're there, on land, they begin the transport with this word: "to Ankobär." So you see that Ethiopia is immediately supplied with a lot of matériel. Italy didn't know that and the Ethiopians, of course, only had spears but… So Menelik provided them with matériel. Now, in 1895, war breaks out. The Italians advance. Menelik advances toward the north and, in 1896, there's the battle of Adwa. In this battle the Italians were seventeen thousand, and there were some ten [thousand] natives, native soldiers; there was a lot of artillery, sixty-two canons and all that, well organized and Ethiopia only had soldiers. They arrived at nearly 120,000, and a lot of soldiers had spears and sabers. In 1896, Italy attacks the Ethiopian encampment… On 2 March 1896, they attack, thinking they could win a battle. They lose the battle. Ethiopia had naturally been provided with weapons, it's true that it wasn't the equal of the Italian armament, but, despite that, there were many of them and… They had an advantage, they approached the enemy before firing. Until one meter [away], they didn't fire. So all this matériel, this old matériel becomes very useful. And, lo and behold, the Italians lose the battle. The Emperor returns to Addis Abeba. He has 1,800 terrified prisoners, the Italians. And now, what interests me is that the contact with Menelik becomes closer. When the soldiers go back to Addis Abeba, they sang: "Call Sarkis, call Sarkis, with whom we destroy everything and give it to the sparrowhawks." They're very enthusiastic, and my father's name becomes… general [famous?]. You see that the contact… The [Armenians] become the Ethiopians' saviors. Naturally, these things aren't repeated, they're all lost. But the Italians know that the Armenians had contributed to their defeat. This is applauded by France, because France supported Menelik and the whole situation changes, Menelik becomes emperor and is recognized by a lot of states. [With] Italy, there were negotiations, the 1,800 prisoners are turned over, etc. So another life begins. Now the Armenians' numbers start to increase.

§ 10. That's how, all of a sudden, with two or three people, a goldsmith, a young man, another who comes from the north, Boghos Markarian, who becomes a kind of advisor to Menelik, a delegate, etc. So you see that three persons surround Menelik; since Menelik was in need of everything: shoes, hats, figuring out how to eat. So the Armenians start to surround the palace and make it thrive. That way, the contact became friendlier and friendlier and the number of Armenians grows. We're coming to the year 1908. The Turkish revolution. And a lot of Armenians find ways to leave Turkey. Then the community starts to grow. And we're coming now to a period of Menelik, who begins creating Addis Abeba. The Armenians and all that, and Mr. Boghos Markarian, contribute to Addis Abeba's [urban] plan, and all that. Meanwhile, the Ethiopians' relations with the Armenians change. The Ethiopians see all these countries have colonial designs. The only people they could be sincere with were the Armenians. So we remain their advisors, etc. That way, we also move on directly to politics, to government. We have a facility for languages: we speak *Amhareñña*, of all the foreign peoples, we're the best [at speaking this language]. I, for my part, am an expert. So our facility for languages gives us [an additional] facility. The fact that the Emperor is a friend of the Armenians, of the leading grandees, too; so you see the Armenians also making their way into the [entourage of the] leading grandees; you see how things are developing.

§ 11. Meanwhile, in 1915 [sic],[6] you see what changes everything: when the massacre happened, our whole family was massacred in Arabkir. So my father and our uncle say: "At all costs, we have to bring what's left of my family [to safety]." So all of what's left of my family was brought to Harar: women, widows, children… Harar becomes a little Arabkir city [a Little Arabkir]. One brings in [the next]… the community grows and, gradually, Harar is transferred to Addis Abeba. Addis Abeba is a forest. Harar is transferred to Addis Abeba now. Harar is [no] longer important because, in 1902, the railroad reached Dire Dawa, so it [Addis Abeba] becomes next door. Now we start up a community with a lot of relations with Menelik. Factories are created by Armenians, mills and all that… The contact becomes more profitable. They [the Armenians] start to become part of Ethiopia and we have two or three interesting cases… The Ethiopians have a monastery in Jerusalem. Jerusalem was under the Ottoman Empire. The Egyptians[7] had cast an eye on it and the Ethiopian government sent a grandee[8] to Abdülhamid[9] to help him turn this monastery over to the Ethiopians. In a conversation, Abdülhamid says: "Are there Armenians in your country?" The general says: "Yes, there are." "Tell Menelik: one is enough to destroy your country. Drive them out!" The general comes, says: "Majesty, the Sultan tells us […] that." He says: "Answer him that he should send us all those whom he doesn't like!" So you see that the Emperor becomes a protector [of the Armenians], even with Abdülhamid.

§ 12. Maybe Anna[10] has told you how?… Anna's father was a revolutionary. He was exiled in Turkey, out of Arabkir. He escapes, comes to Addis Abeba. My father introduces him into the Emperor's entourage, because my father was married to… [this man's] sister. Anna's aunt. […] He [Menelik] says: "What does he know how to do?" He [Sarkis] says: "He's a painter." So the Empress—you know, you may have learned, that the Emperor was greatly supported by the Empress, very energetic—she was building a church in Entotto. They needed a painter. "So Léon," says the Empress—he was called Monsieur Léon—"you'll have a room here in the palace, you're leaving tomorrow." Léon says, "Fine." The next day, early in the morning, he goes up to Entotto. He begins painting. The Empress visits [him] almost every day, she's very satisfied… There's the question of the devil. Because there are the Ethiopians, there's the Emperor, there's [the Empress], there's also the devil [all are painted on the wall of the church]. So my uncle says, asking my father the question: "What color should I paint the devil? If it's black, they're black! How should I paint him?" He tells him: "Wait." My father goes to the palace, he says: "Mr. Léon wants to know how he should paint the devil." The Emperor understands and says: "Give me five days." They hold a conference, afterwards they tell him to paint him indigo blue. So the devil becomes blue! So as not to be black!

§ 13. All of this [? shows?] you this closeness and this development: the Church, the army, [the] contacts. Armenian women began to have servants, but not white women, and life begins. The Emperor… Madam Serpig was very friendly with the leading grandees' wives. She was the only white woman to whom they could go. So they went to get advice. And since they knew that the Emperor was very friendly with Tigran [Dikran], all the leading grandees came with a lot of [?]. So Madam Serpig says, "Madam, how do you sleep at night?" Because the Ethiopians slept naked at night. Men and women, naked. She says, "but we have nightgowns." That great lady says, "What is a nightgown?" So she sews her a nightgown. She's very happy. Two days after that, Serpig is summoned to the palace. The Emperor sends her a note, he says, "Serpig, come quickly." He says, "Madam, one of our leading grandees has come to complain that his wife has been buried in a winding sheet." He said, "my wife is wearing a winding sheet, she says that Madam Serpig provided [her] with this winding sheet." Then a priest says, "Why did you do that?" But she says: "She wanted it!"

§ 14. So you see how, this closeness… little by little, the Armenians became advisors of a kind… And then the Ethiopians had deposits of money. They left [their money] with an Armenian, that's what they did, since there were no banks. You see how things are developing.

§ 15. Now, the number of Armenians is growing. Menelik proclaims that all the Europeans in Addis Abeba have to register with their embassy. So the Europeans go to their consulates. The Armenians have no embassy. They go tell the Emperor, "Where should we go to register?" "I'm your consul." There you have a step forward. They become the Emperor's subjects.

§ 16. I have my father's passport in my possession; in 1903, I believe, or 1904. Menelik… My father had to travel. How was he to travel? He didn't have a passport. They're refugees from Turkey. Menelik gives him a passport on a parchment. He says, "Sarkis Terzian was my soldier for so-and-so-many years; from now on, he's an Ethiopian. An Ethiopian… A native of Arabkir!" on the parchment. And he signs it! As a rule, they didn't sign anything, the Emperors of Ethiopia. There is the imperial seal. He signs it. So we have that, something unique: a passport on parchment from Menelik, in which he says: "From now on, he's Ethiopian." This means that he's reached such a point that he calls him "Ethiopian" on a passport, and he requests that foreign governments [?].[11] This means, you see, the pact that exists, so Menelik declares himself a protector.

§ 17. Now the community is growing, we have started to […] think, to organize. In 1911, the [Armenian] merchants and all that, they come [together]. They say, "let us organize a committee for our community." So they organize themselves in a committee, with seven members, and they take everything there is in hand, since the community doesn't have much of anything, and the committee says to Menelik: "We want to keep our language."[12] In 1913, the question of the graveyard. In the old days, foreigners were buried in an Ethiopian graveyard. So the Armenians were interred in the churches [?]. So the Armenians say, "Emperor, give us a graveyard." So he gives us a graveyard. And when you see the park!… [-/-] Because… It wasn't like the Europeans. The Europeans, too, would have liked all the Europeans to be together. There are the Catholics, and all that. We don't want to be buried in… [Ethiopian graveyards]. Because the Ethiopians have very little respect for the dead. They don't have any… They have graveyards, but there are neither monuments nor… So the Europeans wanted to acquire all that. So they wanted that, they got it. And, next to it, there's the French [graveyard]… Like that… a step forward.

§ 18. 1913, graveyard. 1915, nursery school. In the beginning, there were just Franciscan missionaries… You see, all these Armenian girls went to the [missionaries]... They said, "the girls should learn our language." So, nursery school in [19]15. In [19]18, grade school. You see, little by little, the community is starting to organize.

§ 19. In [19]13, Menelik dies. An extraordinary thing: the night Menelik died, someone knocks on an Armenian's door. He [the visitor] says, "a coffin at all costs." At night, they go looking for an Armenian to make a coffin that goes to the palace. The Armenians understand that Menelik has died. For two years, they hid it... Menelik didn't die, he died [officially] two years afterwards! That means, all that, that means trust. You see: they have to keep the Emperor's death [a secret], and they have to turn to Armenian friends to make a coffin. You see how things are advancing.

§ 20. Now we're coming to the first World War. Meanwhile, Menelik dies, and [*Lej* Iyasu reigns] for three years... Then the Allies, France, Great Britain, and Italy, tried to cultivate [the Emperor] against the Germans, [with whom] they're at war. Something must be done at all costs. *Lej* Iyasu, too, a puppet, he had grand plans, he wanted to scorn the leading grandees, the feudal lords. He wasn't yet aware that he wasn't powerful enough. So the feudal lords, supported by the Allies, decide to dethrone *Lej* Iyasu. In 1916, *Lej* Iyasu is dethroned. He was in Harar, he escaped. They found Menelik's daughter, Zäwditu, they named her Empress, and they named *Ras* Mäkonnen's son, Haile Selassie [*Ras* Täfäri], Crown Prince and Regent. There you have our government. In those days, maybe Anna has told you, there's the question of Addis Abeba's security. There's a battle on Addis Abeba's high plateau. *Lej* Iyasu's father[13] advances on Addis Abeba with 80,000 soldiers in order to put his son back in power, and the Ethiopian government goes out to meet them. There's a battle and the central government wins the battle.[14] But there's tremendous disorder. Then the government says, "We need a police chief." So they appoint... Anna['s father]... Our uncle, police chief! Léon Yazedjian! You see how things... Paylag,[15] second. So now, in difficult periods, they have to organize better security.

§ 21. Onward... I also have to tell you the great story of the Sarkis locomotive. In 1904, when Addis Abeba starts to budge [to grow], Menelik decides to go to another city, to Addis Aläm, fifty kilometers away [from Addis Abeba]. He sees that there isn't enough wood, it's deforested, [there is] no water, so he calls the ambassador of France, the ambassador of Italy [and the ambassador of the United Kingdom]. "Gentlemen," he says, "I am going to have myself transferred to Addis Aläm, fifty kilometers away." The Englishman and Frenchman say, "Why? We've created embassies here, everything's fine, the climate's a good one..." He says, "I don't have any wood, I don't have any water." Then the Englishman says: "One doesn't go to the woods, one fetches wood." He says, "How does one fetch it?" "One makes roads, one makes carts, all that..." "And the water?!" "One makes pipes." That very evening, the Italians agree, [because] they wanted to cultivate Menelik's friendship. The Italians agree to be transferred. Meanwhile, the boss, Menelik, calls and says to Sarkis: "The whites don't want to go; what should I do?" "Majesty, if it's a question of locomotives [...?]. In England, I saw a steam-powered locomotive that runs, that makes traction, too, we can bring it here."

He [Menelik] says, "Is that true? Is there something like that? All right, you're leaving tomorrow!" So my father travels to England. He finds the factory, he finds, buys this steam-powered locomotive, which had two wheels for traction and two carrier wheels with... And all that arrives in Djibouti... Everyone looks down his nose, says: "Who is this lout? He has the steamroller, [but there is] no road and no bridge, either." When my father arrives in Djibouti, he announces to the Emperor that he's there. The steamroller is brought to Dire Dawa. Dire Dawa, easy. But how to leave Dire Dawa for Addis Abeba? They start, they start, the Emperor gives the order to all his leading grandees, he gives the same order. There are three thousand mobilized soldiers then. Every governor [...?]. So they reach Addis Abeba in three months. Pushed, hoisted, all that... The Emperor's very happy, he's going out to meet the engine, forty kilometers from here; the whole court [with him]. The great Mr. Pineau... uh, non, Mr. Roux [Hugues Le Roux], a French journalist, they go out to meet them... The Emperor sees it. He says, "it's quite small, it's not big enough to [...?]." They're very happy, all that... So there you have the first steam engine... And songs are created and all that... And, you see, the affair develops further. The road is built and the engine... So you see what people call the Sarkis locomotive, *Sarkis babur*. So all the roads have become *babur mängäd*, that means "roads of *babur*." So all the roads bear my father's name. There you see how things are developing…

§ 22. The first World War brings the Armenian genocide, in 1915. In 1915, Turkey destroys Turkey's entire Armenian population. Deportations, massacres... The big genocide. The genocide, it was Abdülhamid's dethronement that contributed to the arrival of the young ones [the Young Turks] and then the genocide, and then the genocide... When all these refugees started arriving in large numbers. So, little by little, the community grows, and it reaches as high as 1,200. [-/-] [Earlier] there were very few, maybe fifty, sixty, eighty. Very few. Because there were neither communications—the railroad arrived in [19]17. Earlier, one traveled on muleback. From Harar to here, it took sixteen days... There were caravans.

§ 23. But the Armenian women, above all, showed a lot of courage, to come and create a life, houses, to teach the Ethiopians how to behave. They didn't know how to read, they had neither eiderdown quilts nor soap... They didn't know anything! Now, when we became closer with the palace, my father saw that they needed glasses, cups. Because in the Ethiopian military system, they were big banquets— four or five thousand soldiers eat with the grandees, the Emperor [?]. They want to drink. They brought goblets made of bone, of horn, but it wasn't enough. So my father [?], he goes to Belgium, he orders a little carafe. A little carafe that is a copy of a bottle of Chianti wine, you know? Because during the war, the Ethiopians had taken bottles of Chianti [...?]. So the little carafe was made of glass and it could be put down [unlike the goblets of horn]. And then he'd ordered a big cup almost a liter in size, with rifles [?] from the Emperor of Germany [?]. So they were very happy. Imagine, the Ethiopians, they were drinking out of foreign cups. [...?] You see how the military men, the leading grandees were starting to have friends.

§ 24. You see, a very small community of 1,200 is becoming a force. An extraordinary thing. The government usually received ambassadors on big holidays. All the embassies, the consuls were invited. The Armenians too, on the side. They said, "Armenian community," equal to an ambassador! President of the Armenian community! Naturally, the Europeans were happy to see [that]. "But how did he worm his way in there?" Since the Emperor received them, for them it was a community, his community. But neither Europeans nor Ethiopians. You see, that way too, in the diplomatic corps, we are present.

§ 25. And now, we start to build: in 1923, we build, after the grade school, a little church. A very rich Armenian promises us a big church, which you're going to see on Sunday. [-/-] Yes, something terrific [?]. He says, "if I make a fortune in Ethiopia, I'm going to build you a church." This was a merchant from Istanbul. He builds the [?] churches. [...?][16] comes with Haile Selassie to be present at the foundation. You see... By way of the Church, too, we've arrived. Because, since we're Monophysites, monophysitic doctrine, we're the only ones, together with the Ethiopians. We are: Ethiopia, Egypt, Armenia, and Syria, with a few Indians. So you see that [...?] by way of the Church, too.

§ 26. So we're becoming a community... Ethiopian, European, Armenian, and, little by little, the government gives us nationality cards. We've become Ethiopian citizens. And they gave us the right to own land... Because Europeans don't have the right to have property. So the Armenians have succeeded in having this church, all that was built on Armenian land. You see that we're becoming part of this country.

§ 27. But, naturally, the question of color still exists. Marriages, naturally, the Armenians, the young Armenians who came, found Ethiopian wives. So we started to have mixed-races. Armenian families with an Ethiopian woman. There weren't many of them, but it's a situation that exists. And then the Ethiopians have a question about baptism... Godparents. Ethiopians become godparents of Armenian children: Anna's godmother was the Empress. You see how, that means a part of their family. There are godparents [who are] leading grandees. On all sides... but the question of color has always existed. The question of having [of giving] our women to Ethiopians. Now that, that didn't please people. Armenian women didn't marry Ethiopians. Ethiopian women married, but not vice versa. In sum, all that, that creates a kind of racism... Inevitable.

§ 28. In spite of all that, we were the only ones to be part of Ethiopian life. As I told you: nightgown! And then the question of languages. The ambassadors had contacts with the Ethiopian government. The Ethiopian government had no translators. The Ethiopians insisted that everything had to be done in Amharic. So, an extraordinary thing, in all the big embassies the interpreters were Armenians. We spoke the two languages, and then, a sort of neutrality: for the Ethiopians, we were considered to be sympathizers. As for me, I was [the interpreter] for America. Another Armenian for Germany. Another for... America, France, Germany, England. [...]

§ 29. So there you see how a community was formed. Now, your question about the question Armenians/Ethiopians. Of all the foreign peoples, we're the closest to the Ethiopian people. You've listened to everything that happened: our [?], our honesty, our fatherland. We've had cases where Armenians fought in the Ethiopian army, they died on the battlefield. Armenian military brass band. You know that, in 1924, the Emperor traveled to Jerusalem. He made a voyage to Europe. At that time, he's going to meet our Patriarch, because we have the same doctrine. There was a brass band that played. So Haile Selassie—he was [still] Crown Prince—he says, "Father, who are these children?" He says, "these are children saved from the Turkish genocide. We're educating them, they're happy to meet you." He says, "Would you allow me to take these children to Ethiopia?" He says, "yes." So the Emperor says right away, "organize everything; for my part, I'm going to travel to France; take these children to Ethiopia." So they're the forty children, they're known [by the name of the] forty children. The forty children reach Addis Abeba. They're lodged in a palace where there's a tied-up lion. Poor children! And then they start to organize the military brass band. Their chief, Nalbandian, who is of Ethiopian nationality [?] [composes a march] for the Crown Prince. You see, that way, music, too. And among these children, there were children who fought for Ethiopia. Against the Italians. They died. They did all the military transport and all that. You see how all that ties together.

§ 30. But Ethiopia was changing. Foreign contacts, contact with foreign civilization has destroyed Ethiopian traditions. Lack of respect with the sovereign. [...?] I did the translating for an American delegate saying "Mister." To the Emperor! All these contacts, the Italian occupation, destroyed imperial prestige. The Emperor and the system thought they could continue the feudal system, somewhat civilized [modernized]. But it wasn't possible. On top of everything else, he starts to contact Russia and China, who start to poison the youth. The university was commanded by Americans. So the Ethiopian Empire was destroyed. [...?] It was a country making progress. To know Ethiopia, one has to know... It's an agglomeration of peoples in which there are two nations that are developed and that dominate: the Tigrayans [inhabitants of Tigré] and the Amharas. All the others had to be prepared. No one prepared, they looked for the [...?] the Oromo, all that. That takes times. Now, these two advanced, civilized races, with their alphabet and their religion, are equal to, are in a federation with, semi-savages. [...] On top of everything else, these two great peoples are enemies. So these two great peoples that had created Ethiopia—the Ethiopia that you see was created by these two races that are semi-semitic, etc.—aren't friends. Tigré dominates. Amhara has lost the battle.

§ 31. So we have this complication in this whole system; on top of everything else, Ethiopia becomes communist. Socialist. Encouraged by the Russians, they nationalize everything, all our wealth. We had created an economy. We had houses, what they call an "extra house." Since there were no pensions, every family had its house, created its house in order to have rent wealth. They took all that. They took everything [?]. So, all at once, our economy of a century disappears. We remain one hundred twenty. We maintain our organization. Fortunately, we'd built a big building that gave us 4,000 Ethiopian birrs. Communism took the building, but gave us the rent. It nationalized all our properties, but this building, I managed to convince them [...?]. They said, "that's fine, the building will remain nationalized, but we'll give you the rent." 4,250 every month. So that saved us. The one hundred twenty who remained were able to continue their church and all that. And, little by little, we reestablished ourselves.

§ 32. Unfortunately, they didn't turn over anything of what they'd mobilized. This is a big problem. America says, "turn it over." But they didn't agree. They said, "it's too complicated, etc." So you see that all this effort, all these sacrifices were destroyed by the socialists. We're in a very dangerous situation now. For as long as I remain, I'm there, I'm their president. Since the council members left, I've been left alone. I've continued. I've continued, continued the contact with the socialist government, and I've found five or seven co-workers. They're there, but we've been scattered over three countries: California, Canada, Australia. The bulk of our population is found there. We have a little in France, in Europe, but they aren't many. The bulk are [is made up of] Canada, California, and Australia. There's no possibility that they'll come back. Because the youth is already part of a different life. The old people are dying. And on top of everything else, they aren't succeeding in getting [their properties] back, like Anna. If they managed to, if they succeeded in taking their properties, they could live out their old age right here. So our [?] is beginning. We haven't managed to get even a single house back. So you see that, economically, we're ruined.

§ 33. People like me, like [?], we have historical prestige, all that. So there you see our situation. We were, we no longer are. But! As a miniature, we're complete! We have [the] church. And the government, they're not even aware that we're miniaturized. Since we're active. We don't know how we... How to continue...

§ 34. And since our old friends no longer exist. Because our friendship was in an imperial regime. A feudal life, a capitalist life. All that has disappeared. The grandees who come from Tigré are, yes, they're friends, but they aren't the same. They don't have a past with us. Because our past is tied to the Ethiopian imperial court. Which no longer exists. So there you have our situation.

§ 35. The Americans want to lead these people toward an honest capitalism and all that, but they aren't succeeding... Because there's a big problem. It's very hard to know Ethiopians. Even after a century. Very few of us know Ethiopians; they're a difficult people. They aren't, at bottom, what they seem to be. They're false. They're capable of deceiving you for thirty years. They seem to be your friend but they're not a friend. Even among themselves! They're very shrewd, they're hard to get to know.

§ 36. I'm going to give you an example. When the English left—because I must tell you that [during] the British occupation [they] appointed me Oriental secretary; I was the one who, when the British army occupied Addis Abeba, I was [the] liaison [officer] and they appointed me Oriental secretary. The English weren't of the opinion to put Haile Selassie back on the throne. So throughout this difficult period, I was the one who drew up the treaties. When London decided to put Haile Selassie back in power, thanks to Roosevelt's invitation and thanks to... Goebbels. Do you know Goebbels? I'll tell you why. How Goebbels... [contributed to that]. In any case, when the British government decided to recreate Haile Selassie, there was the question of the legal system. The British officers said in my presence, "*Messieurs les Éthiopiens*, you're two thousand years behind the times. You're still in Biblical ideas. How can we leave our Europeans in your hands?" Because, they said, there was, in the period before the war, before the war with

Italy, there was a law of capitulation. Foreigners had to be judged in the presence of their consul. There was a kind of capitulation that existed [as] in the Ottoman Empire. So the Ethiopians said, "let's remove that." The English said, "What? Should we leave our hands in your judges [sic]? Who are Mosaic [apply Mosaic law]." So they said, "Let us at least create laws that are adaptable to both communities, with Ethiopian judges, assisted by the English and all that." The English agreed. But it was necessary to make a law code. They didn't have a law code. So they invited great French, British, Swiss judges. They came to work, assisted by an Ethiopian judge. After three months of work, the jurists were dissatisfied, they said, "we aren't making progress." They went to see the Emperor, they say, "Give us permission to leave. We don't need your salary, we're here to serve you, we're going to leave." He says, "Why?" "We're not making progress." The Emperor convokes the Ethiopian judge who was working with them. He says, "Majesty, if we accept these jurists' bases, we put the rope around our necks." Because, in Ethiopian law or on the [Ethiopian] understanding, the state isn't subject to the courts. How could they agree that the Emperor should be judged? [...?] Who would apply it? Imagine, they deceive the whole world, they deceive the jurists, they agree. As long as [?], we are the ones who must dispense justice. You see. Europeans don't know that. No European knows, it's the judge who informed me of it. [...?] For their whole lives, it's another mentality. This judge told me, "the laws are for the government's benefit [...?]." So the court system is an element of the administration. And poor jurists, great jurists [?]. They work, they don't know that that one is false. And of all these peoples, we're the ones who had understood, we succeeded in living with them. At the United State embassy, during the capitulation, I was the United States' judge. Since the American judge and consul didn't know the language, they told me, "Why go there? You're the judge." I understood then, it's their mentality. It's an extraordinary thing... America's Negroes come here after Haile Selassie's coronation in the hope that Ethiopia was their fatherland. They're looked down on here, they bring money, they do agriculture, and they had a holiday [sic] where the American Negro was beaten, part of his leg was amputated. There's a trial, the minutes come to the court; before me and the Ethiopian judge. Three pages of minutes that are impossible to translate. Because I'm the official translator, one of the best translators in Ethiopia. Impossible. Because our heads are organized according to Greek, Roman reasoning, an introduction, the subject, and a conclusion. Impossible! Three pages, nothing capable of understanding. It's neither an introduction, nor subject-matter, nor... And they're capable of governing that way. Amid uncertainty. They're masters of uncertainty. How is it possible, [with] our intelligence, our education, [to] accept uncertainty, what isn't clear? Because we look for clarity. Living with them. And we've lived with them.

§ 37. So there you have our situation. We come here, we accept. We produce, we make sacrifices, we create an economy. Naturally, it wasn't the wealth of the big countries, but we were ensured for a lifetime, happy, little work, lots of friendships everywhere. And all of a sudden, our community is destroyed. And as I told you, we maintain everything in miniature form. It's a big effort. Just imagine, if you come to the church on Sunday, you're going to see six people. We hold church with four people. We make choirs that sing, women... All the appearances... And the government thinks that they're strong, that they're well organized. Six people! And since we don't have a priest, we have a gentleman who acts as a priest. Vartkes. It's a big sacrifice, we hold on. And it's an extraordinary thing, our force... We're experts in misfortune, our people. If you tell Anna that: we're experts in misfortune. Not happiness. Amid misfortune, we resist. How we do, I don't know, what is there that makes us resist? Now, with only six people, to hold church. And there isn't a church in Addis Abeba as pretty as that one. And the benefactor is interred in the church. [...?] Why force ourselves? Anna, over there [in France], is concerned about our affairs. She writes things to us. Our graveyard, she took, she had our plan. A miracle, how she was able to have it. In the period when everything was lost, she kept it, she sent it to us. That means an extraordinary force. How, why?... And you, too, Boris, you're the same thing. You have something that drives you... Look here, now, you need other information, there are three or four people here who could give you certain parts of our life.

Context, Stakes, and Resonances of a Collective Autobiography

The preceding text is not just testimony. It testifies to an obvious capacity for narration, in a French that Avedis Terzian spoke fluently, if less naturally than other languages such as Armenian, Amharic, or English.[17] From the first interview on, the "witness" was transformed into a narrator who took charge of a collective history. These remarks were delivered at one go, without interruptions or interferences due to questions. Involved here, obviously, was a narrative that had already been formalized before our meeting, proffered in a version that was, if not fixed, at least carefully thought out, with shortcuts and preestablished transitions from one episode to the next that often create the impression that the narrator is taking pains not to forget anything *of what must be said*. There is, here, material that is the more precious in that it has become unique as a result of the rarefaction of traces of the Armenian presence in Ethiopia and the impoverishment of other testimonies. It is, consequently, not easy to determine whether this material truly comprises a window on the collective memory or whether it contributes, rather, to putting this memory in fixed form, or even to establishing it in an authoritative narration.

My first encounters with these immigrants' descendants soon confronted me with the existence of a Grand Narrative of the past with which various people could identify, beyond the diversity of their trajectories and localities, in Addis Abeba, but also in Marseilles, Nice, or Paris. Thus it seemed possible to speak of a collective memory. But how could one be sure of that? Scholars who look for a collective memory or the identity of a "community" whose existence they presuppose are often tempted to fall back on extensive samplings of oral surveys in order to establish their contours, to the extent they can be defined. There exists a temptation to find "representativeness" in numbers that justify analyses and conclusions, as opposed to the procedure that discerns "the *perfect* type of sociological material" in a life narrative.[18] In the case of the present study, however, the conditions of my investigation, rather than my own methodological choices, determined the selection of testimonies. The ties that the several dozen descendants of Armenian immigrants who were still living in Addis Abeba maintained with each other were comparable to those of a village community: they were based on relations of mutual acquaintance and structured by family ties. The private "power games" and prerogatives of rank, but also the rivalries and oppositions that reigned there, almost mechanically led me to restrict the number of witnesses I consulted orally.

My decision to solicit interviews with Avedis Terzian was neither casual nor arbitrary. Considerations of status came into play here, because Terzian was the last president of Ethiopia's Armenian community council and because he still enjoyed real prestige thanks to this former institutional position. He was aware that he had been granted, with a certain form of deference, the authority to speak in the name of the others. Moreover, from the very beginning of our collaboration, Avedis Terzian spoke of the past of the whole group of Armenian immigrants in the country, not just about his personal life, even if he was also motivated by undeniable autobiographical considerations. The result is that his contribution to the Grand Narrative of the Armenian presence in Ethiopia appears, finally, as a hybrid form between a life narrative that does not identify itself as such and a recapitulation of the history of Armenian immigration, as if he tended to compose a kind of collective autobiography.

Assuming, on the basis of this one narration, that there exists a collective memory of the Armenian presence in Ethiopia involves an obvious methodological risk. The results of the investigation depend on the objectives it has been assigned and the methodology used in carrying it out. As Jocelyne Dakhlia emphasizes, the ethnologist or historian is always a coproducer of the narratives that she would be mistaken to think she merely collects. Even when she dispenses with questionnaires, she involuntarily orients interviews as a function of her own interests, "if not by the quality of her attention." The transcription of the statements, choices about how to divide them up and put them in a particular form, their translation, and even the way one chooses to punctuate them are so many stages of their appropriation by the researcher. They "establish the final text as an interpretation, almost as a hypothesis."[19] I have reproduced the text of my interviews with Avedis Terzian in a form altered by my editorial choices, my own presuppositions, and the subjectivity of my attention, that is, by the way in which, in the context of the enunciation of these narratives, I listened to them. The interaction between the researcher and the person willing to take part in the game of questions and answers is determinant. For the interview, hence the exchange, establishes a kind of parity between the researcher and the person who is the object of his research, and it is not easy for the analysis of the results to diverge from it. The play of mirrors constituted by this interaction relativizes whatever claims to objective knowledge as the researcher might have.

Thus my interviews with Avedis Terzian did not lead me to "collect oral testimony" in the usual sense, as if this type of material differed from written archives only by its form and the fact that the researcher gleaned it as such, in the course of his travels, in a sort of documentary "harvest." This endeavor is not really comparable to collecting a fixed "literature" or an "oral tradition," for the narrators are not writers and are not necessarily guardians of an oral tradition [*traditionnistes*]; they are agents in an unmediated social relationship which implies that the narratives themselves should be considered as acts.[20] This observation also holds for the documentation deriving from private archives that is echoed in the collective autobiography. Photographs, in constant dialogue with oral "knowledge," also help sustain the Armenian Grand Narrative in Ethiopia. Their conservation and divulgation—or non-divulgation—involve the same social issues that oral testimonies do: they are never purely private matters, and they constitute significant acts. The voluminous album painstakingly assembled and annotated in the 1960s by a cousin of Avedis Terzian's, Mushegh Terzian, is a good example.[21] Long jealously secreted away by the lady who owned it, the album was not revealed until 1999, after her death. It should be analyzed as a corpus the many pieces of which form a coherent whole. The collector's motivations, his selection of prints, the way he chose to position them, and the tenor of the handwritten captions that accompany them assign each of them its function in a sort of visual grand narrative *displaying* a memorable past, with its most eminent acts and heroes.

The following analysis of the collective autobiography cannot ignore the personal status enjoyed by Avedis Terzian, who was doubtless one of the people in Ethiopia most often interviewed by historians,[22] Ethiopian students, documentalists, or journalists in the twentieth century (to cite Alessandro Triulzi). Our collaboration was special, because this was the first time, to my knowledge, that Avedis Terzian was interviewed by a scholar whose main interest, not his secondary motivation, was the history of the Armenian presence in Ethiopia. Terzian had manifested a desire to write this history himself, had begun to do bibliographical research to that end—which he did not pursue—and had ended up writing a manuscript a few pages long on the basis of his personal knowledge, even going to the trouble of having it typed up.[23] In his oral account, he by no means intended to produce testimony, but aspired, as he did when he wrote, to recapitulate the collective history from the late nineteenth century on by conferring general meaning on a sum of individual experiences. He expected our collaboration to preserve what he regarded as multigenerational oral knowledge, but also to elevate it to the rank of historical knowledge by casting it in written form. The goal of ennobling and patrimonializing memory that was tacitly assigned to our interviews certainly had a deep influence both on the production of these narratives—one could, to use Jocelyne Dakhlia's words again, talk about a coproduction—and on their tenor. The enunciation of a collective autobiography sought to relate the history of Ethiopia's Armenians to an outsider who would write it down and thereby bestow on this orally narrated past the academic status that it lacked, while also positioning the narrator vis-à-vis his own posterity. It was a question, in sum, of an orality aspiring to written form.

In explaining the slow construction of a memory of the Holy Places in Palestine, Maurice Halbwachs never tires of speculating about the social considerations that govern recompositions of the past. He shows that what he calls "the memory of groups" pursues the enunciation of the past by selecting what is retained and what is consigned to oblivion:

Such memory retains only those events that are of a pedagogic character. The very manner in which memory distorts facts reflects the need to show that each one has a significance beyond the event itself, that it has a logical place in the complete history and that it is part of a chain of events which together culminate in an event comprising all the others. The story hence becomes a logic at work.[24]

I shall attempt to analyze the eminent place that the transversal theme of the Ethiopian kings' friendship for the Armenians holds in the collective autobiography in the light of this reflection. Avedis Terzian assumed the social role of a guardian of memory, the function of a "living archive" of the common past, as he himself put it. By its nature, his narration laid claim to being a kind of teaching. Everything he said in the course of our interviews seems to inscribe itself in one and the same narrative, articulated around a few lines of force that lend it its coherence. His remarks comprise a narration that is sufficiently elaborated to warrant consideration of its elements as parts of a whole. It is a question, then, of a total narrative, all of whose elements converge and work together to demonstrate one and the same thing: the unique nature of the Armenian immigrant experience in Ethiopia, summed up in the idea that, of all the "foreigners," the Armenian immigrants and their descendants were the closest to the Ethiopians.

4

A Past that Engages the Present: The Social Stakes of the Making of Heroes

In Avedis Terzian's narratives, collective identification with a destiny out of the ordinary is embodied in the figure of the sovereigns and the Armenian immigrants who had very close relations to them. Thus these narratives valorize and hierarchize a veritable pantheon of Armenian heroes and heroines in Ethiopia. The checkered posterity of the most famous of them, Avedis Terzian's own father, reminds us that "collective memory speaks of facts that we know are past, that belong to a time that is over and done with, but that still affects us," and that "it is by telling stories about the founding events of our history that we become a historical community."[1]

The Triptych of the Founding Heroes, the Narrative Matrix of Armenian Memory in Ethiopia

The narration of this collective autobiography opens by associating the name of an Armenian, Boghos Markarian, with that of a "king," Emperor Yohannes IV (Narrative 1, § 1). The "second entry," that of the goldsmith Dikran Ebeyan, is also associated with Yohannes, and then with Menelik (§ 2). Shortly thereafter, in the narrative of the capture of Harar, the "third entry" (§ 3), that of Sarkis Terzian, Avedis's own father, is linked to the names of Menelik and *Ras* Mäkonnen (§ 5). The "fourth entry," finally, by way of the railroad from Djibouti to Dire Dawa, the first section of which was completed in 1902, concerns the general run of Armenian immigrants. Occurring after these pioneers' arrival, and less directly tied to the powerful in Ethiopia, it is dispatched in a sentence or two (§ 4). The narrative concentrates on the personalities whose direct relationship with Ethiopia's kings is acknowledged fact, while making short shrift of the others: "I don't know, maybe there were one or two Armenians besides that" (§ 3). The photo album belonging to Mushegh Terzian, Sarkis's nephew, assigns the hero the preeminent place, presenting him, without warrant, as the absolute pioneer, and, in the process, effacing the years he spent in Harar: "1st Armenian who arrived in Ethiopia, on foot: Zeila-Ankober [Ankobär][2] in 2 months, introducing himself as the 1st of them all to Emperor Menelick II. 1882. Died in 1913. Sarkis Terzian the Great."[3] The triptych of founding heroes is posited, and, with it, the idea that the tie established with Ethiopia's powerful from the earliest beginnings of Armenian settlement in the country is in itself a founding act.

In the rest of the narrative, the thread of the narration never departs from this association, which is a veritable leitmotif. All the immigrants seem to appear in its light: "That's how, all of a sudden, with two or three people, a goldsmith, a young man, another who comes from the north [Tigré], Boghos Markarian, who becomes a kind of advisor to Menelik [...] the Armenians start to surround the palace and make it thrive. That way, the contact becomes friendlier and friendlier and the number of Armenians grows." (§ 10) Menelik's response to Sultan Abdülhamid, of sinister memory among the Armenians because of the 1894–7 massacres is, therefore, all the more savory: "Tell him he should send us all those he doesn't like!" (§ 11).

In this narrative, the disappearance of the Ethiopian monarchy and the "feudal life" of the past makes the prolongation of an original Armenian presence in Ethiopia impossible after the 1974 revolution: "Because our past is tied to the Ethiopian imperial court. Which no longer exists (§ 34)." At our first meeting, Avedis Terzian could not know whether I would come back to listen to him again, or whether I would go knocking on other doors, as his last remark, transcribed in § 37, attests. That is why he seems to proceed as rapidly as he can here, singling out the most important names and facts in order to produce a synthesis of the collective adventure that is as edifying as possible. Thus he says only that which, in his estimation, is essential.

Boghos, Menelik's "Comrade"

Boghos Markarian, the first figure in the pantheon of pioneers whom the collective autobiography brings on stage, because he arrived in Ethiopia as early as the 1860s, is one of the rare Armenians to have served both the old and the new master: Yohannes IV, the Tigrayan emperor who dominated Ethiopia from the north, followed by Menelik II, the Amhara "southerner" who had already donned the imperial crown by 1889, when the first real wave of Armenian immigrants arrived. The pioneer's Armenian nickname, *Hayrig* (an affectionate form of "Father") underscores this chronological precedence: "Hayrig! Hayrig means father, because of his beard. They called him Hayrig Boghos. He wasn't called Markarian. Papa Boghos (Narrative 10, § 30)." The nicknames play their part in the collective appropriation and thus the heroization of the tutelary figures, as in the case of Sarkis Terzian, nicknamed *tellik*, an Amharic word meaning "the great," or in that of Hagop Baghdassarian, known as *tellik* Hagop. His long prophet's beard is the most striking feature of *Hayrig* Boghos's photographic portraits (Figure 4.1). It is his beard that *advenes* to us, as Barthes would say;[4] it is on his beard that we spontaneously fasten our gaze. It is easy to recognize *Hayrig* Boghos by the same appendage in a French traveler's description of men of the Armenian colony on their way to the palace on January 1, 1902, "all of them skinny, with a greenish complexion and a sickly appearance [...] in a long, pitiful procession," "guided by their doyen, an old man with a long white beard."[5] At this time, Boghos Markarian was seventy-two years old, if the information that he was born in Sebastia (Sivas, Turkey) in 1830[6] is trustworthy. One would, however, readily take him to be a great deal older, so closely does he resemble, in this description, the Noah of the

Figure 4.1 Boghos Markarian, known as "Hayrig," one of the founding heroes of Ethiopia's Armenian community.

Source: Album of Mushegh Terzian, collection of the Armenian Community in Ethiopia.

Flood or Abraham guiding his people through the desert. This imposing beard is, finally, the only unimpeachable information about a man about whom the eyewitness accounts of his time have little to say. It reinforces his status as a founding hero: Boghos *is* the "Father," because he has a patriarch's beard. Of the other Armenians whom so many nineteenth-century European voyagers noticed in Ethiopia, the collective autobiography tells us nothing, and for good reason: unlike Boghos Markarian and Dikran Ebeyan, who died, respectively, in 1922 and 1926, they were no longer there in the early 1920s, when Avedis Terzian, who had returned home after his studies in Istanbul, began to collect the old-timers' words. Still others, such as Sarkis's uncle Kevork Terzian, who arrived in Harar with the Egyptians around 1875, do not have a place in the triptych of founding heroes, because they did not conspicuously develop direct ties with Ethiopia's notables.

Boghos Markarian appears very rarely in contemporaneous written sources, and then only for his voyages between the port of Massawa and Egypt.[7] He is cited by name in Ethiopia only by an author who avers that he met him near Asmara in 1875:

> Whilst I was sitting outside my tent an Armenian merchant, who, my servants told me, went by the name of Bogos [*sic*], passed by with several mule loads of ivory; he had come from the Shoa [Shäwa] country, and he was one of the best-looking men whom I had ever seen; very fair, at least in comparison with Abyssinians, and dressed in the costume of the country.[8]

Objectively speaking, Boghos Markarian is a great unknown. This does not prevent the narrative of his exploits from playing an eminent part in the memory of the Armenian immigration in Ethiopia.

The Armenian colony's first historiographer, Hayg Patapan, says that he interviewed Boghos Markarian in the autumn of his life, in 1915, and describes him as "the founder of Ethiopia's Armenian colony." In 1871, after spending five years working as a merchant in Adwa, Markarian is supposed to have entered into the service of Emperor Yohannes (who was in fact still only *Ras* Kasa) by going and depositing, in the king's encampment, a large number of gifts chosen from among the wares in his possession: "rifles, ammunition, white linen, and different silk cloths." Yohannes, according to Patapan, forbade him to go to Gojam (where Yohannes's rival Täklä Giyorgis had just proclaimed himself *negusä nägäst* in 1868),[9] but authorized him to go see Menelik, *negus* of Shäwa, entrusting him with a written message and requesting that he accompany a mission charged with transporting valuable gifts, among which there figured "forty parade horses with ornaments of gold." Boghos is said to have arrived without incident in Menelik's royal encampment in Wäräylu, after crossing Wällo. From there, according to Patapan, he accompanied Menelik in his military campaign against Prince Mohamed Ali of Wällo (the future *Ras* Mikaël),[10] before the king of Shäwa tried "to convince him not to return to King Yohannes of Tigré, but to remain by his side." In 1875, Menelik is said to have sent Boghos together with a mission headed by *Ras* Berru to Khedive Ismail in Egypt, in order to convince the khedive to foment an alliance against Yohannes and send a Coptic bishop to Shäwa.[11]

In Patapan's narrative, Boghos Markarian is described as a leading actor in these events. Boghos's treason leads to his persecution at Yohannes's hands and seems almost to have touched off a war:

> In 1877, King Yohannes marched on Menelik and, near Salaydinga,[12] laid siege to the place known as Bakozbeit; he looked for Boghos Markarian in order to take his revenge, but didn't find him. After 1877, Menelik extended his rule over all Ethiopia and Markarian continued to be his favorite. King Menelik II rewarded him with a large tract of land near Mt. Zuquala [Zeqwala], in Leben, where he cultivated fruit trees and planted several hundred thousand eucalyptus trees.[13]

For Avedis Terzian, this episode can only be understood in the context of the struggle between Tigré, in the north, and Shäwa, in the south, for domination of the whole of Ethiopia. In the narrator's estimation, it was a struggle with contemporary stakes, because, in the period in which our interviews took place (between 1997 and 2000), the party in power in Addis Abeba was an emanation of the Popular Front for the Liberation of Tigré, as had been the case since the 1991 fall of Mängestu Haylä Maryam's regime. The victory of the Popular Front appeared as a challenge to the domination exercised by the Amhara aristocracy for more than a century; in this period, "Tigré [Tigré] dominates. Amhara has lost the battle" (Narrative 1, § 30). Boghos's attitude had, therefore, serious implications:

> Boghos Markarian played a false role. [...] He betrayed Yohannes. Markarian, for the Tigré, is a traitor. He went over to Menelik. Because, to understand this passage from Mäqälē to Addis Abeba, everything that is happening now is there: for the Tigrayans, it is an act of treachery, Menelik betrayed Yohannes. And they took revenge. (Narrative 10, § 26)

Conversely, this founding act seems to announce, as a recompense, Menelik's indefectible friendship for Boghos and, by extension, the Armenians.

> Now Markarian was very unceremonious with Menelik. Menelik called him "my comrade." Since they had spent their youth together, he called him "my comrade." And when Menelik took a walk in the city in order to decide, he thought that he could decide [to reserve] the city center [the Arada neighborhood] for the whites. For the merchants. Arada is [today] the Piazza [neighborhood]. And Menelik mounted a mule, Markarian was marching with him, and they made decisions: "we'll do this, we'll do that…" Markarian had become a very close advisor. [...] Things were done in the Ethiopian way. [...] For some things, Ilg was consulted, but, since there wasn't this closeness, Ilg was a foreigner for them. [Whereas] Markarian went to bed with Ethiopian women, like Menelik. [...] He wasn't an educated man. But he had tremendous influence on Menelik. (Narrative 10, § 17, § 30)

Although contemporaneous sources ignore him, concentrating on Menelik's Swiss and French counselors, Alfred Ilg and Léon Chefneux, the close relationship between

Boghos and Menelik here seems to find a reflection in the other immigrants as well, the "ignorant little Armenians" who, unbeknownst to outside observers, also benefited from the king's trust as so many éminences grises:

> The Europeans didn't know. [...] All these books were written through the embassies or the hotels… The Armenians were like Richelieu's Father Joseph. He was in the antechamber. He wasn't seen. (§ 18)

Dikran, the Man Who Crowned Kings

The arrival in Ethiopia of the goldsmith Dikran Ebeyan (Figure 4.2), the second of the figures in the collective autobiography in the order of their appearance, is also a story of kings. Like Boghos Markarian, Ebeyan works for Yohannes before going over to Menelik's service. In the narrative, the choice of an Armenian goldsmith to make the Ethiopian emperor's crown seems inevitable: "Yohannes wrote to the Egyptian khedive, and the Egyptian khedive, since all the goldsmiths in the Ottoman Empire were Armenians, said, 'We'll send an Armenian'" (Narrative 10, § 32). A native of Constantinople, Ebeyan is supposed to have lived in Egypt from 1871 on, and to have become "worthy of Ismail Pasha's attention." During his first journey to Adwa in 1881, he is said to have presented Yohannes with "a royal garment embroidered with gold thread" before withdrawing to the coast, in Massawa, for a year. In 1882, the story has it that he traveled to Ankobär by way of the port of Tadjoura to see king Menelik of Shäwa, "with his comrade, who, coming down with a fever, died en route." Returning to Egypt in 1886, he is supposed to have left for Ethiopia again the following year, with his wife this time, "on 28 March 1887," in order to go back to work in Menelik's service. His only daily recompense was "fifty injira [*enjära*, a local variety of sourdough bread]," a certain amount of other food, and "a jugful of the local drink, taj [*täj*], which they make with honey, water, and the fermentation of a root"—the Abyssinian version of mead.[14]

As in Boghos's case, the narratives about Dikran Ebeyan's arrival in Ethiopia are partly colored by legend and hard to verify. The Armenian sources alone suggest, for example, that Dikran had a hand in making Emperor Yohannes's crown.[15] Dikran started to take an interest in Ethiopia, according to his daughter Arusyag, when an Ethiopian pilgrim en route for the Holy Land made a stop in Cairo, bearing a letter from Menelik to the local Armenian colony in which he asked to be sent a goldsmith. The Armenian made three attempts to get to Ethiopia, each of them aborted after he had disembarked at Massawa. His brother Vartan, who was also a goldsmith, is supposed to have headed back to Constantinople at this point, whereas Dikran finally succeeded in proceeding from Tadjoura as far as Ankobär, where *Negus* Menelik resided. The story has it that he made several crowns for the sovereign and his wife Taytu, including those used during the 1889 imperial coronation, and also a crown which the emperor is said to have donated to the cathedral in Aksum.[16] Dikran's three attempts to make his way to Ethiopia have, here, the same coloration as the magic numbers in fairy tales—the first two to no avail, the third a success. Like a subliminal trinity, they echo the mention of the Ethiopian pilgrim who was traveling to the Holy Land. Here the name of Yohannes

Figure 4.2 Dikran Ebeyan, Menelik's goldsmith.
Source: Album of Mushegh Terzian, collection of the Armenian Community in Ethiopia.

disappears, leaving just Menelik as the explanation for Dikran's arrival in Ethiopia. Furthermore, the request to dispatch a goldsmith is no longer addressed to Khedive Ismail, as it most probably would have been, but directly to Cairo's Armenians, as if there already existed a bond between the Armenians and Menelik.

Like Boghos, Dikran too, in Avedis's narrative, maintains a markedly familiar relationship with Menelik, "who considered him to be a very respectable old man" and "pampered him a lot" (Narrative 16, § 3). Using the familiar form of the second person when speaking with the emperor and the grandees, the goldsmith felt free to ignore court etiquette, with Menelik's indulgence. Dikran's symbolic importance is all the greater in that he is not a simple merchant of arms and cloths, like Boghos Markarian, but the man who will crown two Ethiopian "kings of kings," Yohannes and Menelik, by making their imperial crowns, as a British diplomat sent to Addis Abeba on a mission in 1897 recalled: "The chief Armenian, Tigrane [Dikran] by name, is court jeweler, and works chiefly in gold and silver filagree. Gold ornament is, by the way, the privilege of the royal family, and no one except of royal birth is allowed to wear so much as a gold earring without leave from the Empress, who distributes her permits sparingly."[17] In these founding myths, Dikran's arrival is the result not of a favor but of a request made by Ethiopia's kings. This point echoes the idea, very popular with the descendants of the Armenian immigrants, that their ancestors did not come as refugees or exiles but "on the invitation" of kings.

Sarkis, the Other Victor at Adwa

Avedis Terzian's narrative includes many passages about Ethiopia's situation and its relations with the colonial powers during the period of Armenian immigration: the play of Italian and British ambitions in the Horn of Africa; the revolt of the Mahdi in Sudan, in the struggle with whom Emperor Yohannes, decapitated during a battle near Mätämma, literally lost his head; the annexation of Harar and the surrounding region by the armies of the *negus* of Shäwa, Menelik, in 1887; his expansion southward in the formative years, of the Menelikian empire, 1880-90; and the ticklish question of the Italian-Ethiopian Treaty of Wechalē[18] (Narrative 1, § 5-6). In evoking these events, the narrator presents his father, Sarkis Terzian, the third figure in the pantheon of heroes in the order of their appearance, as Menelik's advisor and savior in the confrontation with Italian imperialism. In order to circumvent the embargo decreed by the Powers in 1890, he himself leaves for Europe to acquire the necessary rifles and ammunition whereas Menelik appears almost timorous and paralyzed by what is at stake: "But Sarkis, how can we procure arms? [...] And how?" (§ 9). The spirit of initiative and force of character are Sarkis's; he appears more like a mentor than a mere servant.

The inclusion of a wealth of details substantiates the narrative. The indication that Menelik entrusts Sarkis with the most prestigious means of payment—gold and ivory—emphasizes that the Armenian is indeed the emperor's personal envoy, his right-hand man. An Italian diplomatic source attests that "the Armenian Sarkis Terzian, with a companion," both well known for smuggling arms "to Africa (Abyssinia and the Soudan), to Asia (Armenia), and the Far East (China)," bought arms in Belgium on the emperor's behalf, "Menelek [sic] paying in ivory and gold dust," and that they were "in correspondence with other European agents at Paris and Marseilles, and in Africa, at Jibuti (E. Perio), Cairo (Ditta Migiudirchian [the Mgrdichian company]), Harrar (Terzian),[19] and the Scioa [Shäwa])."[20] A British report of December 1895—three months before Adwa—notes that "about 7,000 rifles are believed to have found their way from Liège into the hands of the African enemies of Italy," and that they were purchased "by an Armenian gentleman, who is also believed to have procured arms in his country for the insurgents of the Ottoman Empire."[21] The diplomatic archives corroborate, on many points, Avedis Terzian's affirmations about this arms traffic, including those about the complicity of Djibouti's French governor, Léonce Lagarde,[22] and about the places where the arms where bought as well as their transport. The complex toponymy of Sarkis's voyage and the transportation of the cargo—from Obock to Marseilles, then from Liège and Solingen (near Leverkusen, in the Ruhr) to Amsterdam, from Amsterdam to Tadjoura, a port in French Somalia, on a boat leaving for Indonesia—as well as the information about the models of the rifles and the exact quantities of weapons and ammunition imported—are not mere narrative ornaments but participate fully in the "mnemotechnic of the event,"[23] as do the many geopolitical developments that frame it. The most innocent details provided by Avedis Terzian, such as his father's Belgian mistress, mentioned in passing, reveal a narration that has to a great extent been formalized by dint of being often repeated to different people. The story of Sarkis's participation in the arms smuggling is a key moment in the collective autobiography, because this episode seals, for the whole of the coming century, an indefectible friendship between Armenians and Ethiopians.

The highly detailed narrative of the battle of Adwa creates the impression that Sarkis, celebrated in the song improvised by Menelik's soldiers, took personal part in the fighting, although nothing of the sort occurred: "Menelik was aware that he owed the victory to him. And I have told you that, on its way back, the army, the Ethiopian army, sang. They said in Amharic: 'Call, call, call Sarkis / Who crushed them / Delivered them up to the vultures'" (Narrative 15, § 13).[24] Besides the rifles and ammunition, Sarkis had imported swords with a curved blade manufactured by the firm Hoechster of Solingen. The fact that his young nephew stepped in to make hilts for them completes the transformation of the defense of Ethiopia into a family affair: "Because my father had imported eighty thousand swords from Germany. But they didn't have hilts. At the time, hilts were made with cords, and it was Abraham [Sarkis's nephew] who knew how to" (Narrative 33, § 5). These weapons, Avedis makes clear, were of crucial importance to the Ethiopian victory, "because the battle ended up hand to hand."[25] Sarkis's indirect participation in the battle on the Ethiopians' side appears, here, to be the real reason for the miracle of Adwa: "Because it was something really incredible. An African army fighting an army of around twenty thousand well-armed, well-organized Europeans with rifles, modern rifles, whereas ours were scrap" (Narrative 15, § 13). Thus the victory belongs not just to Menelik but also, thanks to the hero Sarkis's mediation, to the Armenians, partisans, and artisans of Ethiopian independence.

The "I" and the "We": Personal Trajectories and Collective Destiny

By weaving individual trajectories into the "Grand History" of kings and wars, dates, battles, coronations, diplomatic negotiations, and other historicizing elements, the collective autobiography creates a stage setting that may seem incommensurate with the handful of late nineteenth-century Armenian immigrants. Avedis Terzian, however, directly aligns their careers with the relationship established between the heroes and the kings. It is therefore difficult to clearly distinguish the use of "I" and "we" in the collective autobiography. The mythical names of Sarkis, Boghos, or Dikran often precede, with no transition, the generic use of terms such as "the Armenians": "Little by little, the Armenians became advisors of a kind" (Narrative 1, § 14). The evocation of the heroic figure of Sarkis lends itself still more readily to this confusion, for it directly implies the narrator and his family: "It was my uncle and my father, they were the founders of the colony in Harar" (§ 3). The son talks about his father as if he were the Father of Ethiopia's Armenians when he relates the arrival of the first Armenian families, natives of Arabkir, in Harar, after the 1894–7 massacres in the Ottoman Empire (§ 11):

> Thirteen years after his arrival, there's a big massacre by Abdülhamid. So he brought his family [...]. So his father was killed, our grandfather was killed. Many members of the family became widows. And it is this group that really constituted the Armenian community. Because it was a group with women, with children, and all that. So Harar becomes... A community's sanctuary. After the relatives arrived. And, that way, the foundation of the community was more or less my family, through Arabkir. (Narrative 15, § 11)

All the personal trajectories form just one trajectory:

> Grandmothers, with the aunts, a whole family at Harar. This is the basis of the community. [...] The Armenian community comes from our family. [...] So we're the result of the 1895 massacre. (Narrative 20, § 7)

When he relates his own life (Narrative 8), Avedis Terzian evokes his familial identity: his childhood, a teenage illness, a first voyage to Cairo with his mother to receive medical treatment; his departure for Turkey, where he was sent by his father after his mother's death; his course of study at the American College of Bardizag (Bahçecik) and Robert College in Istanbul, after the outbreak of the war and the deportation of the Ottoman Empire's Armenians; and lastly, the announcement of his father's death by a family friend on his way through Turkey. The personal elements, however, cannot be dissociated from the rest of the collective autobiography. The narrative of Avedis Terzian's life loses momentum after he recalls his activities during the Italian occupation and his nomination to the post of Oriental secretary by the English when the country was liberated in 1941. What follows is much less vivid. It comes down to an elliptical evocation of his business activities and a highly condensed narrative of the events that occurred after the 1974 Ethiopian revolution. Thus, even when he pretends to narrate his life, Avedis Terzian continues to spin out the collective autobiography, which presents the first generations of the Armenian presence as a golden age in which the tie with the kings of Ethiopia was established. The Italian occupation marks a sharp break in the golden age, before the brief period of British administration creates conditions in which the last flames can burn bright one last time, when Avedis followed in his illustrious father's footsteps.

The Checkered Posterity of an Armenian Hero: *Tellik* Sarkis, Menelik's *Ashkär*

Dated 8 *nähase* of the year of mercy 1893 (August 14, 1901, by the Gregorian calendar), the text accompanying a decoration bestowed by Menelik reads: "We hereby award our friend Särkis Tirziyann the medal of the star of the government of Ethiopia, because he has served us for fifteen years as our *ashkär*."[26]

The Amharic term *ashkär* can be translated both as "servant" and as "soldier." The expression *yä negus ashkär* (literally, "servant of the king") means, according to the historian Berhanou Abebe, that Sarkis is "in our retinue," or else that he is "part of our household." Thus this text echoes the key idea that the Armenians were the best servants of the kings of Ethiopia. The heroization of Sarkis Terzian recalls Halbwachs's observation about the tendency of memory to focus on a place or a person who can serve the group as a point of reference: "A whole period is concentrated, so to speak, in one year, just as a series of actions and events, about which one has forgotten its varying actors and diverse conditions, gathers together in one man and is attributed to him alone."[27] The fame of Sarkis Terzian, the "pioneer" about whom his contemporaries provided by far the most abundant personal testimony, and the eminent place that his son accords him in the collective autobiography, make it possible to explore the social issues at stake in this process in all their complexity.

From Harar to Biyo Kaboba: The Birth of a Hero and the First Shadows

In the collective autobiography (Narrative 1, § 3), Avedis says that his father came to Harar in 1882, when he was still young, to join his uncle Kevork, a baker who had arrived at the same time as the Egyptian garrison that took possession of the city on behalf of Khedive Ismail in 1875. His narrative is faithful to the one that all the Armenians of his generation could read in Hayg Patapan's book: "The families who came from Djibouti, the desert of the Somalis, to settle in Harar were from Arabkir. They were Hajji Kevork and Sarkis Terzian."[28] Sarkis Terzian becomes a hero in the collective memory by taking part in the conquest of Harar. This act seals his entry into Menelik's service. As Patapan wrote in the late 1920s, "the true history of Sarkis Terzian begins with the entry of Emperor Menelik II into Harar."[29] It was supposedly a question, for Sarkis, of freeing himself from the tutelage of Emir Abdullahi, whom the Egyptians had put in control of Harar before leaving the city in 1886:

The petty Muslim chieftain was very fanatical and the Armenians, above all my father and my uncle, found life very unpleasant. He was very fanatical. So my father, who was young, starts to take an interest in Menelik, starts to send messages to Ankobär... and starts to cultivate Ethiopian elements. (Narrative 1, § 5)

It seems to go without saying in this narrative that, of all the foreigners in Harar uneasy about how badly they were faring,[30] the Armenians were the ones who could consider themselves the happiest about a Christian monarch's annexation of the Muslim city: "Since, after the Egyptians" departure, the local emir was a very ignorant, very anti-Christian man, my father tried to find a means of arranging for Menelik to occupy Harar by getting messages to him thanks to his relations with Somalis and Afars outside the city, and by showing himself to be much more daring than his master, as he would again later, during the preparations for the battle of Adwa: "He encouraged him, he said, 'come, we can do it, etc.' Because Menelik was very reticent. He was very much aware of his limited capacities. So he [Sarkis] had to encourage him" (Narrative 15, § 6). A comparable narrative of Sarkis Terzian's exploits may be found in an article, published some ten years after the "facts" in a French newspaper, on which Hayg Patapan and Avedis Terzian explicitly base their accounts:

> Dispatched in a delegation with other Harar notables to the king of Choa [Shäwa] to bring him the act of this city's surrender, he was entrusted by Menelick with the mission of taking possession of the city on his behalf. Followed by twenty carefully selected, resolute men, he entered this city without firing a shot, where, a few hours earlier, he had been treated as a pariah and constantly threatened with death. After seeing to it that the gates were occupied and that their defenders were disarmed, he installed small detachments in various public buildings. The day after this exploit, Menelick II made a solemn entry into Harrar.[31]

No contemporaneous source confirms this story, yet the heroization of Sarkis takes Harar's real situation in 1887 as its setting. For Emir Abdullahi's anti-Christian fanaticism is no Armenian invention.[32] Similarly, the transfer, to the royal residence in Entotto, of the Egyptians' abandoned weapons, which Avedis's narrative attributes to Sarkis (Narrative 1, § 5), echoes contemporary eyewitness accounts.[33] On the other hand, no source provides us with precise information about what was going on behind the city walls while Menelik's army routed Emir Abdullahi's soldiers a few kilometers away.[34] The stage was thus well set, yet bears no trace of the man whom the collective autobiography presents as the young leading actor. A manuscript written in Armenian by Avedis Terzian's cousin Paylag Yazedjian in the 1960s or 1970s nevertheless corroborates this founding myth:

> Sarkis Terzian is from Arabkir. He was living in Harar and sold water in Harar's streets. [...] At this time, however, Harar did not belong to Ethiopia, it was occupied by Muslims. Their chieftain was named Hajji Abdulla Ali. He was a Muslim from the region of Harar who had an army with Muslim soldiers mixed with Turks. In 1895 [sic], Menelik decided to attack Harar and occupy Harar. Harar was almost

surrounded. And when Sarkis learned that Menelik wanted to occupy Harar, he left off work and went to offer Emperor Menelik his services. He joined Menelik. It must be said that Sarkis was not an educated man: he had never gone to school, he did not know how to read and write. Except that he was shrewd and intelligent, like all Armenians! Menelik had canons that he had never used. An Ethiopian was responsible for them, but, seeing that Sarkis was white, he [Menelik] said to himself: "He will surely be more qualified than my Ethiopian." [...] So Sarkis was told to go inspect the canons. Sarkis arrived on the spot. This was the first time he had seen canons. But they were so dirty that they could not function. The first thing he did was to have the canons cleaned. He said to the Ethiopian who was responsible for them, "show me how you operate them, because I of course know canons, but from one canon to the next, it's different." As he had never seen a canon, he learned the trade by watching what the other man did. They went to Harar, but this gentleman knew neither East nor West, so he had the canon fired in the opposite direction [opposite the city] and that created a scandal. Sarkis said, "let me do it." Because he sold water, Sarkis knew every neighborhood well. He fired, he demolished a few houses owned by Muslims, so he was applauded by everyone. He fired at a fort that remained from the time of the Turks and he demolished it. For that moment on, Sarkis's star shone, he became a bosom friend of Menelik's. Menelik entered Harar with Sarkis and the canons. And Sarkis entered Harar on a big mule, dressed like an Ethiopian in gold decorations, just behind Menelik.[35]

Whereas Avedis Terzian's narrative corresponds point by point with the article in *Le Monde illustré*, Paylag Yazedjian's, laced with addenda and comic elements, seems to be the fruit of subsequent elaboration. It evokes the use of artillery, although Menelik occupied the city without firing a shot. Affirming that Sarkis sold water in Harar's streets, something he did later, during the cholera epidemic that raged in Harar in 1892 (Narrative 21, § 2),[36] it explains that the Armenian was able to shell the city with precision. The so-called Turkish fortress that he bombarded was more likely to have been Egyptian. The Armenian narrator, however, takes pleasure in Turkifying it. The most interesting of these addenda concerns Sarkis's entry into Harar "on a big mule," that is, on Abyssinian grandees' traditional mount, "dressed like an Ethiopian in gold decorations, just behind Menelik" and the famous canons. This conclusion in the form of an apotheosis diverges from the preceding narratives. It is strikingly reminiscent, however, of the photograph that accompanies the *Monde illustré* article (Figure 4.3) and offers a striking resume of the memory of an Armenian exception in Ethiopia: "There's a photograph that someone found in an Italian illustrated newspaper, maybe you have seen it? Yes, my father in Ethiopian dress" (Narrative 1, § 5, and Narrative 15, § 4). Sarkis Terzian can be seen in this photograph, shaggy-haired, posing very upright in a beautiful *gabi*, the Ethiopians' white toga, on an ornately harnessed horse, an Abyssinian shield on his arm and a rifle in his stirrup, surrounded by indigenous soldiers armed with rifles, like an authentic Ethiopian military commander.

Let us leave to one side the *studium* that inclines us to regard photos as political testimony or "good historical paintings," for the sake of the *punctum* ("sting, speck, cut, little hole"): "A photograph's *punctum* is that accident which pricks me (but also bruises

104 The Brass Band of the King

Figure 4.3 "Serkis Terzian, Abyssinian grandee, former governor of Geldeissa." Photograph of Sarkis Terzian taken between 1887 and 1891.

Source: Le Monde illustré, supplement to *L'Illustration* of May 22, 1897.

me, is poignant to me)."³⁷ If this photograph captures our attention—and the caption that accompanies it endows it with considerable evocative power: "Serkis Terzian, the Armenian, former Abyssinian grandee, ex-governor of Geldeissa and Bijo-Caboba"— what was it a century long for all the descendants of the Armenian immigration in Ethiopia who looked at it? In an instant, the whole heroicized vision of the Armenian past in Ethiopia advenes to us here. It is most likely this photo, the beautiful harness of this horse and the gold decorations on this shield that Paylag Yazedjian had in mind when he recounted Sarkis's entry into Harar on his mount, accompanying Menelik. The reward bestowed on Sarkis, who was named "governor," seems to take the place of proof:

> "The king gave Serkis territories in Nole and Camboja³⁸ and the tribute that he received from them, then took him with him to his court. A few months later, he was appointed governor of Geldeissa, a post that was very dangerous at the time and feared by the Abyssinians. He was able, thanks to a regime of terror and numerous expeditions, to bring the Somalis to submit to the king's authority, and he extended the conquests of these territories as far as Bijo-Caboba. This photograph was taken on his return from one of these expeditions."³⁹

The fact that Sarkis was made commander of this post as well as his nickname, *tellik* ("the great" in Amharic)—Patapan tells us that "the autochthones called him that"⁴⁰— seem to attest his exploit at Harar. "And Menelik granted the governorship of this city to my father for an express purpose," Avedis emphasizes, for Gildessa and Biyo Kaboba were obligatory stops on the trade route running from Harar to the Somali port of Zeila, which was under British control. Like the *Monde illustré* article, Avedis says that his father fought the Somalis under the orders of Harar's new governor, *Däjazmach* Mäkonnen, in Ogaden, where Menelik was trying to extend his influence: "And he was wounded as well" (Narrative 15, § 4). Once again, Sarkis seems to dictate Menelik's behavior and the way he conducted his foreign policy: "And my father suggested to Menelik that he occupy Zeila. He says, 'What does that represent, England in Zeila? Let's go'. He [Menelik] was afraid." (Narrative 15, § 2)

Contemporary accounts, however, offer a much less flattering image of the "hero" of Harar. In March 1892, two missions, one English, the other Italian, failing to receive authorization to continue their journey to Ethiopia, came to a halt in Biyo Kaboba. The Egyptian or Sudanese chieftain responsible for this frontier post, Mohamed Abdhalla,⁴¹ took his orders from a certain "Cherekis," residing in Biyo Kaboba "in order to protect caravans from attack by the Somalis and the Issas." We can easily recognize Sarkis Terzian in this "Cherekis," "about whom it is hardly necessary to recall that he is a creature as dangerous as a snake," Count Augusto Salimbeni notes in one of his reports. Although, the day after the missions' arrival, the Sudanese officer finally authorized them to continue their journey as far as Gildessa, "an Armenian named Scerchis, the commander-in-chief in Bia-Caboba," just gave them the order to turn back.⁴² Written intervention from the head of customs in Harar and the authority of *Däjazmach* Mäkonnen's replacement there were required to bring Sarkis to let the Europeans pursue their journey unimpeded.⁴³ The Italian envoy Salimbeni's reports, then, contrast with the legend mantling the figure of Sarkis in the Armenian sources. Incidentally, we learn from them that Sarkis was not the "governor" of Gildessa but was in charge of Biyo Kaboba alone. As "governorships" go, command over Biyo Kaboba, a mere camp encircled by huts and defended by an undermanned detachment, was far from being a sinecure. Moreover, Sarkis's many trips to and from Harar, Zeila, and Entotto, to which Rimbaud refers in the period 1888 to 1890,[44] suggest that he exercised the function of a commander in Biyo Kaboba only from 1890 to spring 1892, not beginning with Menelik's January 1887 conquest of Harar as *Le Monde illustré* and the Armenian sources maintain (Narrative 15, § 2). After the incident, the Italians and the English successfully prevailed on Ras Mäkonnen to have "the Armenian Scerchis, the chief of Bia Caboba," condemned to "being stripped of his rank and losing his job."[45]

In the following year, the majority of written sources paint a fairly unflattering portrait of Sarkis. Around 1895, diplomats describe him as a rather unscrupulous arms merchant, whereas the collective autobiography makes him a hero of the Ethiopian cause. It is worth pausing over these contradictions, for they reveal the view that the Armenians of Menelik's day took of themselves by way of the heroization of Sarkis Terzian.

The Epic of *Sarkis Babur*, between Mirage and Fiasco

The adventure of "*Sarkis babur*" emblematizes the gulf between the Armenian memory and the testimony of non-Armenian contemporaries. The importation, in 1904, of this traction engine made in England is a crucial episode in the epic history of *tellik* Sarkis's exploits. His son made sure to recount it in his very first narrative (§ 21) because the *babur*, with its wood boiler and steamroller, symbolizes Ethiopia's entry into modernity: "*Babur* is the word steam in Arabic. Everything that's steam in the Middle East is *babur*. So this steamroller was also called *babur* and the roads they made were *babur mängäd* [routes of the *babur*]" (Narrative 10, § 9).[46] Thus "all the roads bear my father's name" (Narrative 1, § 21). Manifestly, this presentation of the facts is based on the many pages that the French journalist and author Hugues Le Roux devoted to the event.[47]

At the moment recounted by Le Roux, the transfer of the capital to Addis Aläm, planned by the emperor for some time, seemed to be compromised by the difficulties encountered in using an old cylinder filled with lead to level the land for a new road that had become "Ethiopia's fable."[48] After the concession for the railroad had been granted to its initiators, Menelik's Swiss and French counselors, Alfred Ilg and Léon Chefneux, and an Imperial Ethiopian Railroad Company had been created in 1896, pressures exerted in opposite directions by the colonial powers, but also Menelik's fears that this new communication route might become a spearhead of European influence, had held back the construction of the sections of the railroad between Addis Abeba and Djibouti.[49] The line from Djibouti had reached Dire Dawa, but another 350 kilometers of track would have to be laid before it could attain the heights of Addis Abeba, which is located at an altitude of 2,400 meters. Serkis's suggestion to go look for a "locomotive" in England allegedly came at just the right moment for the emperor, because he "took great pleasure in playing this trick, like a childish prank, on the diplomats, who, it seemed, had decided to deprive him of a reward that he himself regarded as the apotheosis of his policies."[50] According to Avedis Terzian, Menelik saw this as an opportunity to modernize his empire while also abrogating the contract with the train company that many members of his court, including Empress Taytu herself, criticized him for signing on the grounds that it opened Ethiopia's doors to foreigners (Narrative 14, § 2). Thus the traction engine's symbolic importance took precedence over its technical function. In fact, there is great confusion in the Armenian sources about this contraption: it is not really clear whether it was a locomobile, a steamroller, or, quite simply, a locomotive. All one can say definitely about it is that it was steam-powered. Hugues Le Roux's narrative does not make matters any clearer. It has Menelik say:

> I'm glad to learn that France wants to see the railway reach Addis-Ababâ as much as I do. That way, the travel times I was afraid of will be shortened. I did not, however, want to wait for everyone's good intentions to allow myself this happiness. I took the initiative. [...] Then someone[51] told me about a land locomotive and what you use it for in Europe. I was shown drawings. I very much wanted to have one while waiting for the other to reach me on the rails that will run from Djibouti.[52]

Le Roux is struck above all by the fact that the engine's arrival functions as a symbol for Ethiopia's modernization. This is the vision of the event that would prevail in the Armenians' memory and resurface in the collective autobiography. Informed at Easter dinner in 1904 that Sarkis had arrived in Dire Dawa, where the Armenian had had the engine transported from Djibouti, Menelik made preparations to go there a month later, on May 18, at four days' distance from Addis Abeba, in order to meet "the locomotive and its accessories," purchased in England, at the head of a magnificent procession comprising all the leading court dignitaries. The multitude, as well as the hubbub created by thousands of men singing as they hauled the vehicle, were all that was needed to complete the scene and invest it with all its grandeur, amid a host of exotic details involving the splendid equipage of the dignitaries of the royal court. Le Roux underscores the striking disparity between the modernity of the engine, decorated with the new Ethiopia's tricolored flag, the staff of which was "planted in the very body of the land locomotive," and the archaic character of the procedure of hauling it. He construes this as a sign of Ethiopia's inevitable march toward progress. The haulers' slow advance evokes the construction of Egypt's pyramids, while the arrival of the monster of steel seems to be ushering Ethiopia into the twentieth century: "Africa will always be the land of pharaohs and miracles."[53] Le Roux says nothing about the forced conscription of laborers in Sarkis's service for the purpose of fulfilling Menelik's wishes.[54] Hence the collective autobiography can unhesitatingly base itself on this narrative.

There is no denying that the *babur*'s arrival in Ethiopia marked a historic date in the collective memory and that it is associated with the name Sarkis Terzian there. The chronicle of the reign of Menelik II reports that "steam-powered vehicles were brought from the land of the *Ferenji* [*färänji* or Franks] and began to circulate between

Addis-Abeba and Guennet [Gännät]." Maurice de Coppet, who published the French translation of this chronicle, points out that the first engine of this kind was imported by "the Armenian Serkis Terzian."[55] Le Roux highlights the "triumphant victor of the day, the daring Serkis," his face "shining with joy and sweat," and the gratitude of the "King of Kings" toward him: "This was undoubtedly the first time in his life that Serkis touched the Master's hand."[56]

The Armenian sources faithfully echo this idyllic description of the event:

> The first man to work in the field of means of transportation was an Armenian, the late lamented Sarkis Terzian, who, in the face of unimaginable difficulties, first brought an engine into the country for the purpose of leveling the roads to Addis Ababa, at a time when the railway was still five hundred kilometers from the capital. On this occasion, Emperor Menelik II, transported by unbounded joy, sent a crowd of thousands to go salute *Tellik* Sarkis.[57]

This interpretation, however, fails to take into account the reservations perceptible in Le Roux's narrative, which affirms that Menelik was disappointed that the engine was so small and astonished that "at its withers, this miraculous machine was hardly taller than the elephants that, in his youth, he had laid low with his bullets," although he was well aware that "nothing serious" would be accomplished in the way of modernizing and industrializing Ethiopia "as long as Ilg's and Chefneux's railroad [had] not scaled the plateau."[58] Avedis Terzian, one of Le Roux's attentive readers, interprets Menelik's slightly disappointed reaction—"it's quite small, it's not big enough" (Narrative 1, § 21)—in the light of the expectations connected with the railroad: "Ninety years afterwards, I say to myself that Menelik, even while he [was] happy, was unhappy [...]. He was happy with the engine, but it didn't replace his railroad" (Narrative 14, § 2). Still more serious, the engine, Le Roux affirms, had refused to start in Dire Dawa, despite the efforts of the train company's engineers: "It was likely that it would never run and that the Emperor would be reduced to building a shed for it." Thus it seemed that "Sarkis's glory" was doomed to being "brief." Aware of this, "the quack broker from the Mediterranean" is supposed to have tried to dupe those around him and then put a good face on things: "Sarkis was not a man of the morrow. The success of the day sufficed, according to his philosophy; and he counted on not postponing the hour of his retribution. [...] Thus what we had before us there was the real-life illustration of a fable as old as the wisdom of men: *The Lion and the Fox*."[59]

Le Roux's reservations are magnified in the narrative of the German engineer Willy Hentze, who came to Ethiopia in 1902 to oversee construction of its mint. Hentz had had to bring steamrollers to the country himself; they were doubtless too small to make as profound an impression as Sarkis's *babur*, yet too heavy to be transported without great difficulty, since they had to be hoisted onto two-wheeled carts drawn by a pair of oxen and a pair of camels. Hentze was still in Addis Abeba in 1904 and present at the ephemeral triumph of Sarkis Terzian, whom he calls, with a touch of scorn, "the Armenian S.":

Since the engine had arrived in pitiful condition, it had, of course, to be repaired, and that is why the aforementioned Armenian S. had brought a man from his country to Ethiopia, a famous "Engineer" who was to take charge of the task. The cherished steamroller, however, did not work.[60]

Hentze writes that he refused the Armenian's offers to pay him to put the engine back in running order, for he knew that Terzian "wished to obtain an important concession for the engine and would have obtained it to the detriment of the country and conscientious businessmen." The emperor, vexed by the Armenian "intriguers" "who had deceived him again" and who were now "roasting in their own fat," supposedly entrusted the job of repairing the engine to the German engineer, who says that he capitalized on the opportunity to hold Sarkis and his Armenian companions up to ridicule, among them an anonymous "Engineer" who seems to have come by his credentials illicitly:[61]

So I told the master that the locomotive was running, as he could now see, and that the Armenians could come back to use it to tamp down the road. I was aware that, because the road was narrow, none of the Armenians would be capable of backing the steamroller out of the shed as far as the first main road [...] and I shared my thoughts with Ras Woldegeorgis [Wälda Giyorgis] and Makonnen, who were royally enjoying this new fiasco. And it is true: Menelik had given orders to tamp down the road and, the following day, the Armenians' joyful whistling announced that there was pressure [in the boiler]. From his palace, the Emperor contemplated the unfolding spectacle. A thousand eyes turned toward the shed from which the engine was supposed to emerge; and, lo and behold, the steamroller appeared to howls of joy from the Armenians, and tumbled into the ditch to the left, for the "Engineer," who had no experience in backing up, was unable to drive straight. So the poor engine was stuck fast there, and the howls of joy gave way to silence. It rolled over onto its side barely eight meters past the door. It seems like a miracle that the boiler did not explode and kill many of those present. With this fiasco, judgment had been passed on the Armenians.[62]

The German affirms that, after he had parked the engine in the shed, "no one went looking for it," and there is no reason to doubt his word.[63] In fact, the breakdown of the *babur* holds at least as large a place in the memoirs as do the routes it helped blaze. Citing a poem that warns an aging prostitute from Addis Abeba that she may end her days as useless and neglected as *Sarkis babur*, the author of a manual of the Amharic language notes that "an Armenian named Sarkis brought some traction engines to Addis Abeba, but they refused to move as soon as they arrived, and so *yäsärkis babur* has passed into a saying."[64] The engine's carcass was left to look after itself for several years, with the result that the neighborhood in which it ended up was commonly referred to by the name of *säbara babur* ("broken-down *babur*"), as attested in the mid-1930s by an American journalist's explanation of the origin of a name given to "a large part of the town": "Broken Wheels."[65]

Figure 4.4 "First locomobile in Ethiopia imported by Sarkis-Ohannes-Apraham-Terzian Bros. 'Fowler' British make [sic]—Leeds (Yorkshire)—England. Driving from Djibouti to Addis-Ababa in 2 1/2 months by Arsen and Apraham Terzian—in great difficulty (1897)."
Source: Album of Mushegh Terzian, collection of the Armenian Community in Ethiopia.

As Hentze's account shows, the importation of the steamroller and its utilization were a matter that concerned not just Sarkis Terzian but a larger group of Armenians as well. In Mushegh Terzian's album, all the many photographs of the *babur* and their captions show several Armenians off to advantage. Among them are one of Sarkis's brothers, Ohannes Terzian, Ohannes's nephew Abraham Terzian, as well as his Armenian journeymen and workers (Figure 4.4). If, in this Armenian reconstruction of the event, the fiasco is passed over in silence and all attention is focused on the mirage created by the *babur's* arrival, the reason is the collective stakes represented by a proclamation of success. Thus it was necessary to defend the hero Sarkis by claiming that his act was well and truly a heroic feat and had truly satisfied the emperor, while also eliciting, incidentally, the admiration of the Ethiopian crowd—this not for Sarkis Terzian's sake but to save the pride of dozens of men and women who, in the period when the steamroller arrived in Ethiopia, or in the years thereafter, could hope to derive a certain prestige from it.

That is why the *babur's* breakdown is only temporary in the collective autobiography: "The steamroller broke down. Abraham set about repairing it with an Englishman. [...] And Menelik marveled at the fact that this young man, Sarkis's nephew, was working. So he appointed him *azaj*" (Narrative 28, § 1).[66] A photograph in Mushegh Terzian's album, "Apraham Terzian receiving 'Azatch' title from Emperor Menelik II" (Narrative 28, § 1), is presented as the immortalization of this event and

A Past that Engages the Present 111

Figure 4.5 Abraham Terzian receiving the title of *azaj* conferred by Emperor Menelik and shaking the British representative Harrington's hand in the presence of Sarkis and Ohannes Terzian and their employees. "In the compound of Sarkis Terzian. Roughly 1900—Addis Ababa."

Source: Album of Mushegh Terzian, collection of the Armenian Community in Ethiopia.

is said to have been taken "in the compound of Sarkis Terzian. Roughly 1900 Addis Ababa" (Figure 4.5). It shows Abraham Terzian, wearing a *kaba* and felt hat like those of the Ethiopian grandees, shaking hands with the British ambassador Harrington in the middle of a group of Ethiopians, Greeks, and Armenians, among them his uncles Ohannes and Sarkis Terzian. This photograph commemorates, however, not the fact that Abraham was awarded a decoration but rather the epic of *Sarkis babur*; and the Armenian memory tries hard to confer a second life on it. Mushegh Terzian displays, on the facing page, several photos of the Fowler in action, including one in which it is driven by two whites before the eyes of a crowd of Ethiopians: "Apraham Terzian rolling [tamping down] the road from Menelik's palace up to Addis-Alem."⁶⁷ Is it really Abraham? Is the Fowler the same vehicle as was imported by Sarkis?⁶⁸ It does not much matter. The *babur*'s breakdown did not prevent it from being recycled in the memory of the ties between the Armenians and the imperial court. Menelik is supposed to have come and admired in person, in the yard around Sarkis's house, a demonstration of the way the same steam engine could be used to saw wood (Narrative 16, § 2).⁶⁹ Later, wishing to test the solidity of the bridge that he had just built over the Käbäna river near Germany's diplomatic mission, the Armenian engineer Krikor Howyan is supposed to have sent his assistant Minas Kherbekian, still an adolescent, down the length of it, perched on the lumbering *babur*.⁷⁰ Passing from Sarkis's hands to his nephew Abraham's, and then those of the young Minas, who would go on to become one of Ethiopia's most famous road builders, the *babur* thus enables the Armenian memory to establish a link between the generations of Armenians who have succeeded one another in the country since the time of the founding heroes. Involved here, beyond the reputation of the very controversial Sarkis Terzian, is the way a group of immigrants and their descendants perceive each other and wish to narrate themselves.

The Bad Reputation in the Pantheon

In the collective autobiography, Sarkis Terzian's acts resemble the Labors of Hercules, (reputedly) accomplished with Ulysses' cunning. Terzian embodies the collective genius of the Armenians in Ethiopia. "A great developer of many activities in Ethiopia" (Narrative 8, § 1), he obtains, in the 1890s, the concession on transportation by oxcart between Harar and Addis Abeba (Narrative 15, § 12).[71] He erects one of the first watermills in the country, in Addis Abeba, using a turbine purchased in France, probably around 1904 (Narrative 21, § 1).[72] That same year, he sets up Ethiopia's first mechanized sawmill, run by his nephew Abraham on the emperor's behalf, forty kilometers west of the capital near the imperial residence in Gännät (Narrative 33, § 5 and 7).[73] Finally, he is said to be the first man to import the sheets of cambered sheet metal used to cook *enjära*, as well as the decanters known as *berillē* that are used to serve *täj* at the big banquets that the emperor organized for his soldiers (Narrative 1, § 23 and Narrative 8, § 30).[74] Yet the majority of the accounts of the day paint the picture of a forger and swindler. On the one hand, we have the pioneer, on the other, the shady concessionary.

The Baths of Fell Woha: Another Mirage?

In Avedis Terzian's narratives, the founding of the thermal baths of Fell Woha appears as a new contribution on the part of the Armenian immigrants to their country of adoption: "It had become a great institution [...] for the Ethiopian Empire." In the collective autobiography, the construction of the thermal baths brings on stage, besides their initiator—the inevitable Sarkis—another Arabkir native, the mason Pilibbos Kherbekian, father of the famous road builder Minas Kherbekian. It is Pilibbos who is supposed to have found a way of capturing the spring water that gushes forth at very high temperatures by making the walls of its basin watertight. "It's our basin down to the present day," Avedis declares, emphasizing that, since then, no other means of capturing the spring water has met with success (Narrative 4, § 45-6). In question, once again, is an initiative by the hero Sarkis that meets the needs of his Ethiopian masters, Emperor Menelik and Empress Taytu:

> "We can't go on this way, we have to make baths." He [Menelik] says, "How?" He [Sarkis] says, "I've been to Austria, to Emperor Franz-Josef's court, they have baths at Badgastein." He [Menelik] says, "And the sovereigns have baths too?" "Yes." "Then make me a bath." (Narrative 10, § 11)

Before Addis Abeba was founded, Menelik and Taytu periodically went down from their residence at Entotto, in the highlands, to the plain of Finfinni in order to take advantage of the hot springs to which the Ethiopians attributed curative powers. That is supposed to be the reason for which Taytu, who greatly appreciated Finfinni, urged her husband to found his capital, the "New Flower," there. In 1906, Sarkis Terzian obtained the concession on baths and was "authorized to construct an establishment at Fill-Ouhoa [Fell Woha] (hot waters)." The contract stipulated that "Serkis Terzian shall construct, at his expense, for the use of the King of Kings of Ethiopia [...], a bath-house and a country house *like those that sovereigns in Europe have*,"[75] and, further, that "the roofing of the aforementioned houses shall be of sheet metal" and "the openings shall have window panes." Thus it can be seen that Avedis Terzian's narrative, while it may somewhat exaggerate the importance of the dialogue between Sarkis and Menelik, does not invent it out of whole cloth, as in the case of the *babur*. The baths are interpreted as a sign of Ethiopia's modernization. Furthermore, says the contract, the concessionary shall "construct at his expense a bath house big enough to be put at the disposal of the Empire's Great Men, soldiers, and peasants," as well as "another bath house for poor sick people. They shall be granted entry to it at no cost."[76] The establishment at Fell Woha seems to have been a place highly esteemed not just by Addis Abeba's Armenian and Greek colonies but also by the Ethiopian aristocracy: witness the handwritten letters addressed to his father and preserved by Avedis Terzian. *Lej* Iyasu is supposed to have regularly patronized these baths. One of the basins was indeed reserved for the indigent and the diseased, notably lepers. The inhabitants of areas nearby came to celebrate weddings there and continued to ascribe curative powers to the baths.[77]

Constructed with rudimentary technology and makeshift means, the Établissement des Bains (Establishment of the Baths) only very distantly resembles an Austrian thermal station. European visitors rarely admire this place with its dubious hygiene, where indigenous men and women come to bathe totally nude.[78] Dr. Mérab further emphasizes the modesty of the installations, given over to the ineffective management of "some Easterner or the other." He notes that the Armenian's concession was finally confiscated in May 1911.[79] Accounts of the day treat the baths as nothing more than evidence of the country's backwardness, whereas they are close to figuring, in Avedis Terzian's discourse, as a place of luxury, a big step forward that his father contributed to Ethiopia's modernization and the imperial court's refinement. The same holds, overall, for the gilded legend of Sarkis "the Great." It does not stand up under examination of the majority of the sources of his day.

From Hero to Swindler

Sarkis Terzian cut a figure as disreputable as he was enterprising. His plans to open a cartridge factory near Addis Abeba in 1906 provide a good example. France's representative in Ethiopia wrote, at the time, that

> a Turkish subject who ranks, more or less, as a French protégé in Abyssinia has obtained a monopoly on the manufacture of cartridges and, at the same time, a preemptive right on all the mines he succeeds in discovering in Abyssinia in territory not yet under concession. This Armenian, whose name is Serkis Terzian,

has created a Franco-Swiss firm in Europe that has sent an Englishman and a Swiss engineer who lives in Paris here to examine the initial installations."[80]

The construction of a cartridge factory was of obvious strategic importance for Ethiopia. The enterprise seemed uncertain, however, because the raw materials could be imported, as in the past, only with the European powers' approval. Thus the plan to found a cartridge factory was, perhaps, just a pretext: "Its promoters are too well informed not to have considered all these problems and I am inclined to believe that the cartridge factory in question will rather quickly cease to be an 'end' in order to become nothing but a 'means' of amusing the Negus and obtaining, elsewhere, mining or other concessions offering, possibly, certain prospects for the future."

At the end of the year, discord did indeed spring up between Sarkis Terzian, "whose business reputation is rather poor in Addis Abeba," and his associates in the Franco-Swiss firm on whose behalf he had succeeded in obtaining the desired concession, when he hit upon the idea of selling the monopoly to a British competitor at a higher price: "It's the usual game in Abyssinia. [...] The Emperor and Sarkis are hesitating, since they're waiting to find out which side the biggest profits will come down on." One month later, it was learned that the Armenian had just "transferred the concession to an English group, thus dispossessing the Franco-Swiss firm behind its back." The affair of the cartridge factory dragged on, with all its ins and outs, for another two years, until Sarkis Terzian, a trickster tricked, discovered that the Ethiopian government was on the verge of stripping him of his privilege in order to cede it to his British interlocutor, a certain Humphreys, himself known for being "a person without scruples."[81]

A far cry from his image as a pioneer, Sarkis Terzian here seems to be motivated solely by the prospect of securing juicy commissions as a middleman by charging European investors high prices in exchange for pulling strings with Menelik, while claiming, as need dictates, to hold imaginary monopolies in order to prevent new competitors from setting up shop.[82] Such was, at any rate, the reputation he had in the diplomatic circles of his time:

> As for Serkis Terzian, he is still the hustler familiar to the Department: he's a man out to get all the concessions in existence, who has contacts with all the Ethiopian personnel, from the humblest to the highest, who is always on the go and, my word, no more dishonest than all these people who gravitate around the Palace and exercise every profession there is—but no more honest, either. His situation never changes: he has money and credit; he is always soliciting French protection, which I am careful not to grant him, for, with people of his kind, one never knows the risks one is taking.[83]

The Armenian sources' silence about affairs of this sort illustrates the fact that the collective memory is built up on forgetting as much, if not more, than on recollection. The only allusion that Avedis Terzian makes to the question of monopolies has to do with his father's putative efforts to cancel those on coffee, salt, and other products essential to Ethiopian trade that Menelik had accorded "to foreigners," ruining, by the same stroke, Harar's merchants:

> The Harari complained. They said to Sarkis, "rescue us." So Sarkis comes to Addis Abeba, he consults the Emperor. He says, "I'm at your disposition to design a plan against these monopolies." Because the embassies, too, considered it illegal to give all the trade to a few individuals.[84]

Sarkis is here crowned with the aura of a savior, far from his reputation as a profiteer. Duplicity seems to characterize Menelik alone, who, on the one hand, has sold off the monopolies, and, on the other, tells Sarkis: "I pocketed a million thalers. Save my thalers; I don't care a whit about the monopoly." After convincing the Harari merchants to take up a collection to come up with an equivalent sum, Sarkis convinces Menelik to abolish the monopolies:

> And from here [Addis Abeba] to Harar, my father was transported on men['s shoulders]. The whole population forbade [him] to go on muleback. He was the hero. Because salt, above all, [was important], since it concerned the population. So he entered Harar as a hero. (Narrative 15, § 16)

A petition addressed to the British government in 1902, however, shows that Sarkis was not necessarily regarded as a hero in Harar. The petitioners demanded that a replacement be found for the British consul in Harar, known for his incompetence, venality, and utter lack of principle.[85] As proof of what they said, they cited the fact that the consul was "a friend and a supporter of one Serkis Terzian, known not only here, but also in Europe as a rogue and a scoundrel." Terzian was accused of being in league with Muslim slave traders and also of being "a thief who buys cartridges and sells them to the Somalis in Somaliland in order that they should become the enemies of the Abyssinians." Thus, in the course of a single night, he was alleged to have sold the Somalis "sixty-two cases of cartridges." The two men "are mixed up in affairs that are anything but commendable; Serkis Terzian having been put in irons several times by the Abyssinian authorities." As the petitioners saw it, the consul's friendship with Serkis Terzian was reason enough to have him recalled. Ultimately, this petition attacked Sarkis as fiercely as it did the consul himself. Signed by twenty-one foreign and Harari merchants, it undermines the myth of the hero borne in triumph by the grateful inhabitants of Harar.[86]

Avedis Terzian did not seem to me to be really aware of the evil reputation that his father had in contemporary accounts. He was not himself an eyewitness of these events or of the life of Sarkis Terzian, since he was only eleven years old when his father died and had been studying in Turkey then and for several years thereafter, cut off from his family and life in Addis Abeba. For the most part, he knew the many anecdotes that he told about his father and the other founding heroes from conversations he held, after returning in 1923, with old men, Armenian and Ethiopian, who had been personally acquainted with him (Narrative 19, § 4–6, and Narrative 26, § 2–5). The selection and deformation of *what had to be said* about *Tellik* Sarkis had probably already begun, carried out by these witnesses themselves.

The Affair of the Seal: From Right-Hand Man to Impostor and Counterfeiter

One of the main features of Sarkis Terzian's heroization consists in the trust that Menelik showed him by dispatching him on missions that often had secret objectives:

> Menelik II and his favorite, the late lamented Ras Makonnen, the father of the current heir to the throne Teferi, discerned special capacities in Serkis Terzian, from which they wished to profit, and they entrusted him with several important commercial missions to Europe. [...] By an edict of Menelik's, he was made a member of delegations dispatched to Paris, London, Berlin, Vienna, Rome, Belgium, and Washington.[87]

It seems, however, that Sarkis Terzian colluded in an imposture when he presented himself in Vienna in summer 1905 in the company of Hajji Abdullahi Ali Sadik, a celebrated Harar merchant who passed himself off, illegitimately, as an emissary of Menelik's on an official diplomatic mission. On Sarkis Terzian's account, his traveling companion was received with great honors by Franz-Josef at the Austrian imperial court. The two men allegedly employed the same stratagem in order to make their way into the court of Kaiser Wilhelm II in Berlin, but were expelled and ordered to leave Germany within twenty-four hours.[88] It was not their first attempt in this line, for, in spring of the same year, the charge of imposture had already been leveled against Terzian in an Italian diplomatic dispatch:

> Mr. Serchis Terzian, a man with a bad reputation and reprehensible morals, likes to give himself the airs of a special envoy of the Emperor of Ethiopia, and, with an objective of the sort in mind, has palmed himself off this time as a member, if not, perhaps, the head, of this mission directed by Abdullhai [*sic*] el Sadik, whom the Negus has sent to Constantinople for an altogether different purpose, and in whose company Serchis has absolutely nothing to do.[89]

The two men later presented themselves as Menelik's emissaries to the United States, with a letter in Amharic to President Theodore Roosevelt as well as two ivory tusks and a lion. Hajji Abdullahi gave himself out to be a high-ranking Muslim dignitary and the "governor of Harar." The career of his companion, "hero of wars," "fearless and merciless warrior against neighboring tribes" of the Empire of Ethiopia, was pompously described in the local press: "Serkis Terzian, although an Armenian by birth, is virtually the Bismarck of Abyssinia [...], whose guns crushed Italy" and "wiped out ten thousand of Italy's finest soldiers a few years ago."[90] It is, nevertheless, probable that Sarkis and Hajji Abdullahi set out on these journeys for the sole purpose of making purchases on the emperor's behalf as simple commercial travelers, not as emissaries or ambassadors. "Things weren't clear. There were no diplomatic contacts, but Abdullahi always presented himself as Menelik's delegate... That was untrue" (Narrative 15, § 8).[91]

The duplicity of the two supposed emissaries came to light during "the affair of the imperial seal," which became public at a time when *Lej* Iyasu had already begun to govern in the place of his much diminished grandfather Menelik:

> In Ethiopia, almost all the Armenians made their livings in petty local trade: they were hardware merchants, saddle-makers, tailors for the indigenous population, goldsmiths, embroiderers, upholsterers, photographers, and—a forger of the Imperial Seal, as was proven at the trial that took place early in 1911, at which it was established that a certain Serkiz had had an imitation of Menelik's great seal made in Paris. He was imprisoned and his whole estate was confiscated.[92]

During this trial, Sarkis tried to put all the blame on Abdullahi, who, however, accused him in his turn of having stolen a large quantity of gold. Imprisoned for several weeks, Sarkis was stripped of the Établissement des Bains in Fell Woha, management of which was entrusted to Täsämma Eshäte, *Lej* Iyasu's favorite.[93] The affair of the seal thus reinforces the doubts about Sarkis's moral principles, belying his heroic image in the Armenian sources.

The Bandit of Trebizond: Questions About the Hesitations of the Memory

The most damning accusations against Sarkis Terzian were leveled in an Italian book published twenty-two years after the death of the accused. The author claims to be writing the true memoirs of a Frenchman named Stévenin. Sarkis, described as a former "leader of a band in his country [Turkey], which he had to flee to escape death," is charged with the murder of a merchant from Marseilles, Antoine Brémond, who was "poisoned during a meal with all his servants for vile reasons by the old Trebizond bandit," "Sarkis [...], former leader of a band of Armenian bandits [...], reduced to performing the humblest and most difficult tasks in Abyssinia in order to escape the guillotine that was waiting for him back there, in a corner of the eastern Mediterranean." Trebizond is no more than a literary artifice here. The passages about Sarkis's stormy past in Turkey are baseless, as is the charge of murder, of which there is no trace in the French archives. The massacre of Brémond's caravan is supposed to have taken place in the period in which cholera was raging, that is, around 1892, when, according to Pariset, "Serkis, an impoverished Armenian [...] was carrying water around on his shoulders in Harar." This element is confirmed by Paylag Yazedjian's manuscript, mentioned earlier, and by remarks of Avedis Terzian's, who, however, said that he did not know Pariset's book: "I don't know exactly, but I know there was cholera, that my father provided the city with supplies. And that he even carried water around on his shoulders. He was a strong man" (Narrative 21, § 2). The difference between the two narratives, which are so similar with respect to this point, turns on the fact that, in Pariset, Sarkis appears to be someone who profits from the epidemic, rather than a good Samaritan. "Serkis, a rank, greedy water-carrier, was to become, in his turn, a rich merchant immediately after the crime of the poisons."[94]

Pariset brings Sarkis on stage in a trial that opposes him to an employee of his store in Harar. It is presided over by *Ras* Mäkonnen, the city's governor. Breaking his word, the Armenian has refused to share his profits with this employee. In a spectacular reversal, the swindler vehemently upbraids the plaintiff: "Have you committed theft? Have you committed murder? No? But that means you've made nothing of your life, and have no right to anything. I, on the contrary, have done all that: and everything is due me!" This quick retort provokes the astonishment and admiration of *Ras* Mäkonnen, who, "in this well-known forger combined with a monstrous murderer [...], sees nothing but a hero," pardons him and lets him go, to the dismay of the "unfortunate store clerk," who leaves "amid the diabolical Armenian's jeers." Asked about this surprising verdict, Mäkonnen justifies rewarding daring as follows: "Sarkis filled me with enthusiasm because of his lack of scruples. He defied my power. He knew well that I could have had him hanged. Thus he richly deserves my unconditional pardon. He has had the good fortune never to have been taken to task by anyone for the murder of Brémond and his servants." In this iniquitous judgment, Pariset sees proof that "we are not in France or in some other Civilized Country!"[95]

The book by Dante Pariset, a former volunteer in the *Fasci all'Estero*, is an accusation brought against the Ethiopia of Menelik and Mäkonnen, Haile Selassie's father. Published in 1937, it has no objective beyond justifying the Italian conquest. The figure of the Armenian bandit provides an opportunity to illustrate the lawless state in which Ethiopia found itself before the conquest and to oppose African barbarity to civilization. Thus when, in the middle of a legal proceeding at the German diplomatic mission,[96] Sarkis is shot and killed with a revolver by a young Armenian whom he has hoaxed and with whom he is embroiled in a court case, "Mamas, Sarkis's brother, plans to bump the young murderer off." The French envoy, little inclined to see the *lex talionis* applied to the protégé of a European diplomatic mission, since this would constitute a deplorable precedent, contests the emperor's right to turn the murderer over "to the family of the deceased, which would torture him heinously." Ultimately, Pariset interprets the tragic death of "the horrible and violent Serkis" as proof that "God's justice is immanent," but also as a demonstration that "the justice of men, in Abyssinia, is an infinitely distressing thing."[97]

Thus Sarkis Terzian, an unalloyed Armenian hero in Ethiopia, simply appears as the quintessential Armenian Levantine in the contemporary European sources, so much so that one is inclined to doubt Patapan's claim that "Sarkis Terzian's murder elicited great emotion in Ethiopian, Armenian, and foreign circles."[98] These contradictions are inherent to the process of reconstructing the past represented by memory, as Halbwachs shows in discussing the various localizations, long in competition with each another, of the Last Supper in Jerusalem: "These contradictory localizations continued for several centuries during which the collective memory remained divided," until one or another of the supposed localizations finally won out, completely eclipsing rival traditions.[99] In the 1920s and 1930s, the years following Sarkis Terzian's death, certain authors continue to portray him as a swindler, while the Armenian sources are already beginning to glorify the "memory" of *Tellik* Sarkis. For as long as it can turn it to advantage, the present appropriates the past and remodels it as it pleases, as is shown by Pariset's narrative, which uses "Serkis" as an edifying digest of Ethiopian barbarity.

Thereafter, this figure is forgotten outside the small Armenian circle in Ethiopia, the only one to continue to take an interest in memorializing Sarkis. Only his gilded legend survives down to our own day, but for a limited audience, whereas the black legend disappears because it no longer finds an echo anywhere. The heroization of Sarkis can, by the same stroke, no longer be tempered by any negative note coming from without. He condenses in his person, like a precipitate, the qualities by means of which the collective autobiography endeavors to underscore the exceptional character of the Armenian presence in Ethiopia: Sarkis is, all at once, cunning, brave, enterprising, a benefactor for Ethiopia, and a friend of kings. Thus he becomes the hero of the same name in whom everyone may be tempted to see himself—beginning with his compatriots from Arabkir and their descendants. The fabrication of heroes, a collective, polyphonic process par excellence, is symptomatic of the way in which the society of the descendants of the Armenian immigration in Ethiopia has perceived itself. The acts of the pioneers necessarily find a reflection in all those who claim to be their heirs.

5

Menelik's Armenians: From the Welcome as Experienced to the Sedentarization of an Imaginary

> *Because we are called "Menelik's Armenians." The Ethiopian people calls us "Menelik's Armenians" [...]*
> *Not this younger generation, they don't know us. The youth, some thirty years, forty years [ago], called us "Menelik's Armenians." [...] Yämenilek armänotch. Yämenilek armänotch. We felt proud.*
>
> (Narrative 14, § 3).

In the late 1920s, the Armenian colony's historiographer was already affirming that Menelik "loved the Armenians and protected them throughout his reign."[1] The theme of the friendship of kings, incarnated by the triptych of the founding heroes, is the product of a memory organized around the idea that, of all the foreigners, the Armenians are closest to the Ethiopians, as if they comprised a sort of "preferred minority." The immigrants' and their descendants' lived experience reflects this "symbolic naturalization."

The Friendship of Kings, a Metaphor for the Hostland

In the collective autobiography, the immigrants' access to the imperial palace functions as a metaphor for implantation. It makes it possible to anchor the memory of a mutual relation of loyalty and exclusive protection in the center of Ethiopian political power, the palace, or *gebbi*.

In the *Gebbi*: On Familiar Terms with Kings and Queens

Forged against the background of a close relationship with kings and the secrecy of imperial court affairs, the heroization of the pioneers grounds their descendants' claim to having a singular bond with Ethiopia. That is why anecdotes involving the court occur so frequently in the collective autobiography. Armenian women occupy a determinant place in it, for it is thanks to them that the Armenians make their way into the sphere of Ethiopian domestic life (Narrative 1, § 23). The feminine presence also

Figure 5.1 Sarkis Terzian and his wife Vartuhi, née Yazedjian.
Source: Album of Mushegh Terzian, collection of the Armenian Community in Ethiopia.

seems to make the relationship between the imperial couple and its Armenian servants more personal, as is suggested by the narrative about the fainting fit of "Madame Serpig," or Srpuhi, the wife of the goldsmith Dikran Ebeyan:

> Madam Serpig has a history… Madam Serpig came to Ankobär, and, from Ankobär, they came to Entotto. Because Menelik transferred his seat from Ankobär

to Entotto—before Addis Abeba [was founded]. They lived in the upper city. And when preparations were being made for the coronation, Menelik said that he wanted European dishes. Madam Serpig takes charge [of cooking them]. Madam Serpig prepares the dishes. There's a big canopy, there are no tents. Thousands of soldiers. Drinking, singing, and... Madam Serpig faints: the heat, the *tädj*[2] ... So the soldiers stand up, they say: "The white woman has died!" They didn't know what fainting [was]. Menelik stands up—he had a little experience of medicine—he goes over to Serpig, who has fallen. And he had a bottle of eau de Cologne... which Ebeyan had brought from Tadjoura. So they poured a little eau de Cologne on her, she comes to. Then Serpig is famous: fainted away during the big banquet! "The white woman has died!" (Narrative 10, § 33)

The factual elements of the narration—the individuals present; the crowd of soldiers; their incredulous, naive exclamations; and, not least, the eau de Cologne that Dikran has brought back for Menelik—reinforce and corroborate the truth of a narrative of striking richness. This anecdote comprises an important episode in the collective autobiography. Narrated in terms that are similar to those of Narrative 1, but more succinct, it makes it possible to drive the lesson home at the moment when the narrative of the arrival of the founding heroes sets out to demonstrate the unique tie established between Ethiopians and Armenians:

And there, you see, the contact becomes closer. [...] So Dikran, on the one hand, becomes very close. Madam Serpig makes Menelik's clothes, Dikran makes the grandees' crowns, and all that. So you see what contact there is, friendlier. (Narrative 1, § 8)

While it seems insignificant, the detail about the bottle of eau de Cologne serves to restate, without calling attention to the fact, the Armenians' role in the modernization and refinement of palace customs. Whereas the establishment of the founding heroes draws the memory of Armenian immigration toward "Grand History," the anecdotes bearing on daily life at the imperial court give "minor history" its chance to even the score. The inordinate importance that the collective autobiography ascribes to them is bound up with the functions that the Armenians exercised at Menelik's court: they are modest but often have to do with the outer appearances of imperial power and spheres involving the sovereign's person—the fabrication of his clothes, the goldsmith's trade, the art of the photographic portrait, the preparation of banquets, and so on.

Although Avedis Terzian knows that he can affirm nothing about the Armenians' political role—for example, in the rejection of the Italian protectorate disguised by the Treaty of Wechalē (Narrative 10, § 20), the prelude to the 1895-6 Italian-Ethiopia war—he is never loath to exaggerate the significance that should be accorded to "minor history" and its petty details:

Just imagine, Haile Selassie's goldsmith was an Armenian, right to the end... You will say, "but, politically speaking, what did that matter?" But it mattered in its day. (Narrative 10, § 34)

The narration becomes expansive at this point, because, better than the events of "Grand History," which leave little room for the modest immigrants, the anecdotes and bedroom secrets underscore the ability of the Armenian servants of the court to perceive behind-the-scenes realities that most foreigners knew nothing about. Armenian women seemed more apt, by dint of their domestic functions, to intermeddle in the imperial couple's private affairs. In one of these anecdotes "that no one knows," Srpuhi Ebeyan sews a nightgown for the wife of an Ethiopian grandee. Scandal in the *gebbi*! The grandee accuses the Armenian woman of cloaking his wife in a shroud. This affair, which makes the rounds, is smoothed over by Empress Taytu in person; she, too, asks Srpuhi to make her a nightgown:

> That is how we created a presentation acceptable to the international world. Because what woman, what queen of Europe, would ever think that the Empress slept naked? (Narrative 33, § 12)

In Avedis Terzian's estimation, this anecdote was important enough to be related at our very first interview. He alluded to it regularly, as if it were evidence of the unique, profound nature of the close relationship between Ethiopians and Armenians: "In spite of all that, we were the only ones to be part of Ethiopian life. As I told you: nightgown!" (Narrative 1, § 13, 28).

This is how Krikorios Boghossian, about whom contemporaneous sources tell us very little, is supposed to have become a servant whom Menelik held in high esteem. The emperor is said to have given him his famous felt hat, which he can be seen wearing in many photographic portraits, as a token of gratitude for a pair of socks that enabled him to mount a horse without bringing on a bout of his chronic rheumatism:[3]

> When Boghossian presented [himself], he [Menelik] was so happy [that] he said, "take that for yourself." [...] Just imagine, he was so happy. You always see him with his felt hat. And since he was bald—Menelik was bald, he always wore a sort of turban.[4] No one knew that he had no hair... So you see, family relations. Socks. Nightgown with the Empress. [...] It was an altogether special relationship. (Narrative 16, § 4)

In anticipation of his diplomatic tour of Europe in 1924, *Ras* Täfäri had supposedly sent the twelve grandees whom he wished to take with him to Boghossian's house, counting on his discretion, so that they could learn good table manners:

> We knew how to serve Ethiopians. They like strong drink, they like salad, they like vegetables and... They like *pastırma*.[5] So they came especially to eat things like that, for a change. [...] [Täfäri] gave the orders. He sent them to Armenian homes. The grandees. [To learn] how to use a fork. A napkin. [...] We had to scold them. Ethiopians make noise when they eat [...] and that's shameful in Europe. And then one does not take things with one's fingers. They didn't know, they took salad, they put [it] on the fork. [...] So the Emperor took them with [him], they learned

to eat. That means, you see, that it is an altogether different relationship. Without affecting their *amour-propre*. Without showing that they're ignorant. (Narrative 6, § 5)

Araxi Yazedjian, "who was present in the palace every day under Menelik and under Zäwditu," whose chambermaid she was, is supposed to have learned one of the most shameful court secrets when she discovered scars on her mistress's legs. Menelik's daughter, according to Avedis, had been subjected to severe treatment by her third and next-to-last husband, *Ras* Webē Atnaf Sägäd, who had whipped her with a leather riding crop:

Only Araxi could see that… No Ethiopian knows […] I assure you that not even the *grandes dames* know that there were scars on the Empress's legs. (Narrative 33, § 10)

A simple piece of gossip becomes evidence of the specificity of the Ethiopian-Armenian relationship. In the same vein, Avedis repeatedly recalls that two ladies of the court asked Sarkis Terzian to provide them with dye to hide their gray hairs, and he attaches the same importance to their request:

It was a secret: the Ethiopians didn't know that European ladies dyed their hair. So the *grande dame*, the wife of a minister, writes to my father. She says, "you know, we're lost: find this dye for me." And my father brought [it] to her from Paris, [where] there was a firm called Richard […]. So just imagine: the *Ras* didn't know that his wife [had her hair dyed] by Sarkis. You see all these little details. We became another world, where semi-whites, semi-blacks… With a lot of influence. (Narrative 10, 19)

The minor services that the Armenians provided the court are understood as a veritable contribution to the modernization of the state and, consequently, to Ethiopia's independence and development: "They didn't have socks. I told you about the Empress's nightgown. We strengthened the palace" (Narrative 8, § 30).

In Avedis Terzian's view, it was essential to relate these anecdotes, for he was convinced that the familiarity that had sprung up between Armenians and Ethiopians came to the fore in them: "Because the husband did not know that his wife had gray hairs! So you see that our friendship went beyond husbands." He was no less aware of the difficulty involved in transcribing such anecdotes and making a place for them in the "Grand History":

So there you see how we were able to worm our way in. It's just to give you an impression. It will be nearly impossible to communicate that in the history. […] No one will know that Madam Araxi has seen the scars of the Empress beaten by her husband. Or if the Empress had a nightgown prepared by Serpig, reluctantly. […] But I don't know whether in your history… You have it now, but you'll never succeed in presenting it. (Narrative 33, § 14 and 16)

Or again, on the subject of the scars on the empress's legs revealed to Araxi Yazedjian:

> History will never be able to know that. Because it's outside history. At most, you'll be able to write one line. That's all. (Narrative 33, § 14 and § 16)

These signs of confidence find expression at so modest, so imperceptible a level that they have no echo in the contemporaneous testimonies of European visitors to the *gebbi*. They nevertheless constitute, in the collective autobiography, vivid proof of an Armenian exception in Ethiopia. Dikran's bottle of eau de Cologne, "Madam Serpig's" nightgown, Krikorios's riding socks, Sarkis's French dye all contribute to demonstrating the same thing: by providing objects or products that touch the bodies of the powerful, by bringing their hidden weaknesses to light—Menelik's baldness, Zäwditu's scars, the fact that Taytu slept naked at night, the gray hairs of the grandee's wife—the Armenian servants seem closer to their masters than if they had held official positions. In his way, the lived experience of a politically privileged status is expressed in a collective vision of the immigrants' past.

The Protection of Kings and Loyalty to the Monarchy

Contrary to what is observable in many diasporan situations, the notables do not stand in the first ranks of the Armenian pantheon in Ethiopia. Matig Kevorkoff, a rich concessionary of the Ethiopian Régie, president of the council of the *kaghoutayin*, and representative of the short-lived Republic of Armenia (1918–20), who built the Kevorkoff National Armenian School in 1935; his uncle and associate Hrant Minassian, the patron of Dire Dawa's Saint Minas chapel; and also Mihran Mouradian, a businessman from Sudan who had the Armenian church of Surp Kevork built at his expense in 1928–30, are all undoubtedly part of this pantheon,[6] which is, however, sharply hierarchized. In the collective autobiography, their names are not honored by inclusion in the inaugural narrative, the purpose of which is to state the essentials. They are benefactors but not heroes, because, in Ethiopia, the Armenian hero is the faithful man, not the rich one. Narrative 1, the anticipatory synthesis of the collective autobiography, highlights only individuals who had a direct relationship with Menelik: Boghos Markarian, his emissary to the khedive; Dikran Ebeyan, the goldsmith who made the three crowns (Yohannes's, Menelik's, and Taytu's); his wife Srpuhi, known as "Madam Serpig"; Sarkis Terzian, the adventurer and arms merchant; Levon Yazedjian, the painter who painted the devil indigo blue in the church of Entotto Maryam (§ 12), and his wife Araxi, who was responsible for the *gebbi*'s rug manufactories and Zäwditu's wardrobe and would later become one of Empress Mänän's familiars; Krikorios Boghossian, the merchant who was a regular visitor to the court and close to the Ethiopian aristocracy; and so on. A photograph of Sarkis Terzian, Dikran Ebeyan, and Krikorios Boghossian taken in Djibouti, probably in 1903, will be regarded with special attention by those "who know" the close relationship that they established with the kings and queens of Ethiopia (Figure 5.2). The obvious bonhomie of Dikran, leaning on his cane; the satisfied demeanor of Krikorios, who lifts his chin a little under his colonial cap, while slightly thrusting out his chest; the manifest self-confidence in Sarkis's gaze; and the

Figure 5.2 From left to right, Krikorios Boghossian, Dikran Ebeyan, Sarkis Terzian, and Gron Khachadurian, photographed in Djibouti in 1903 on the eve of their departure for Europe.

Source: Avedis Terzian papers, collection of the Armenian Community in Ethiopia.

camaraderie that appears to unite all three men—all these impressions created by the snapshot seem to repeat, in the twinkling of an eye, the Armenian epic in Ethiopia and the mighty deeds of its founding heroes. The lifeless group portraits of the community's leaders, these well-established merchants immortalized after each election, pale in comparison.

Even furtive contact with the emperor is a guarantee of posterity. Thus the collective autobiography incorporates Mardiros Aznavorian, whose only claim to fame resides in the fact that he distinguished himself in the fabrication and sale of liqueurs. Menelik, however, spoke to him one day, because seeing the big grandees leaving his bar drunk and emptying their revolvers by firing in the air had made him uneasy:

> So the Emperor summons Mardiros. "Mardiros, what have you made of my people?" To which the Armenian responds, "Your Majesty, I have brought the drinks, and I have also brought little glasses." The Emperor understands. Because they used to drink the whole bottle! (Narrative 5)

Mardiros's bon mot becomes proverbial: "Mardiros's little glasses!"(Narrative 5). The charm of the anecdote aside, however, how are we to explain the fact that it has not been forgotten? Avedis Terzian could have heard it recounted only after returning to Ethiopia early in the 1920s, that is, at least ten to fifteen years after the alleged facts. If Mardiros's contemporaries remembered "Mardiros's little glasses" for so long, and if Avedis Terzian considered them worthy of inclusion in the collective autobiography, it is solely because this episode brings an Armenian immigrant and the emperor into direct relation. The reciprocal familiarization of the Armenians with Ethiopia and of Ethiopia with the Armenians appears to prop itself up on "simple things, but, in those days, they're jewels" (Narration 10, § 13).

Menelik's thoughtfulness lends weight to the theme of the friendship of kings. Thus we have seen that, when "Madam Serpig" faints during the big banquet because of the heat and the mead, the emperor hurries to her bedside and gently brings her to, using the eau de Cologne that Dikran had brought back with him. "Madam Serpig" is not just any servant: she is the spouse of Dikran, the man who made crowns and who uses the familiar second-person form in addressing the emperor. It is, consequently, natural that Melenik should show her such great solicitude. When Srpuhi Ebeyan, newly arrived in Tadjoura from Cairo, is preparing to join her husband in Entotto, she is deemed worthy of favored treatment. The king sends his faithful right-hand man out to meet her:

> Menelik called my father, he says, "Sarkis, take charge! I don't know whether this woman can hold up, and come by way of the Dankali desert, the Afars." Because, from Tadjoura, one came by way of the Afars. So my father went to receive Madam Serpig. (Narrative 10, § 32)

The emperor also arranges for Sarkis's nephew, Abraham Terzian, to receive a decoration, bestowing the Ethiopian title of *azaj* on him, probably in 1905. The same year, he sends, "at his expense," one of Avedis's first cousins, Vahram Terzian, to study "in Europe, in Turkey": "He was so satisfied with Abraham that he said, 'I'm sending your brother'" (Narrative 33, § 7).

The heroes' mighty deeds repeatedly teach the same lesson, in which all the details count. When Menelik asks Sarkis to go get Dikran's wife, who is arriving from the coast in a caravan, he speaks, in this reconstructed or imagined dialogue, in a friendly, almost paternal tone. We see the same lesson in the idea that the emperor was very "unceremonious" with his "comrade" Boghos, or the idea that he considered Dikran to be "a very respectable old man" and was not offended by his use of the familiar form of address. Srpuhi Ebeyan uses the same form of address with the wives of the Ethiopian grandees who come see her in order to solicit her talents as a dressmaker. The simplicity of the oral exchanges between Menelik and his servants suggests the particularly close relationship between Ethiopians and Armenians. When Menelik, wishing to transfer his imperial residence to Addis Aläm, runs up against the reticence of the European diplomatic missions, it is not insignificant that the collective autobiography has him address Sarkis Terzian in the following terms: "Sarkis, you know, the whites don't want to leave" (Narrative 10, § 6; Narrative 1, § 21). We again find the friendly tone, and the familiar second-person form used to address the faithful servant, the one from whom Menelik seeks advice in desperation. The rest of the sentence, which plainly distinguishes Sarkis from "the whites," underscores the specificity of the bond between Ethiopians and Armenians. Thus the familiar form and Menelik's sentence are addressed less to Sarkis than to the Armenians in general, who are not whites like the others, because they are the friends of Ethiopia.

"Menelik's Armenians" are characterized by their unfailing disinterested loyalty to their master. For the old Armenians whom Avedis met on his return from Turkey around 1920—Dikran Ebeyan, Krikorios Boghossian, Hagop Baghdassarian, Abraham Terzian— it was "not a question of making money." The emperor had "a magnetic eye [...]. When he said he needed something, you had to do it" (Narrative 17, § 18). Menelik's great servants receive no retribution other than gifts of land, for "the country wasn't rich" (Narrative 2, § 18). "When Dikran Ebeyan arrives," Avedis Terzian tells us, "Menelik calls him: 'I have no money. Engage in trade; I can give you as much food as you like [but I can't pay you]; I have things to eat.'" Hayg Patapan emphasizes that the goldsmith served Yohannes and then Menelik "almost for nothing," simply in exchange for his daily bread.[7]

> Dikran didn't say, "I don't care, I'm leaving," he kept on... [...] When Menelik told Dikran, "you know, Dikran, I have no money," an intelligent European would have left. Why did he stay? (Narrative 25, § 3)

When the mason Pilibbos Kherbekian, who was unfamiliar with the "Ethiopian system" in which "you have to entreat the boss or give gifts to be paid," impetuously puts himself in the emperor's path during a procession toward the church of Saint George, the emperor's bodyguards nearly run him through with their swords:

> "Your Majesty, have you brought me from Harar in order to make me a beggar? [...] You know, the boss, the clerk, doesn't pay me." [...] Then Menelik says, "Go. Go work, you'll be paid." But the day after, he isn't paid![8] (Narrative 10, § 13)

Menelik's benevolent attitude toward his servants finds its extension in his protection of the Armenians as a group. Thus the arrival of Levon Yazedjian's wife Araxi and their two sons, Paylag and Robert, their daughter Astrig—their second daughter, Anna, would be born in Addis Abeba in 1914—is explained as a favor granted by Menelik. This is the pretext for a famous remark addressed to Sultan Abdülhamid, who is invited to send all the Armenians he no longer wants to Ethiopia (Narrative 1, § 12)[9]: "So you see that the Emperor becomes a protector, even with Abdülhamid." Similarly, Menelik tells the Armenians who are uneasy because they do not have an embassy, "I'm your consul" (Narrative 1, § 15, and Narrative 26, § 29).[10] In the collective autobiography, the Armenian immigration in Ethiopia is never presented as an uprooting. It is the response to an invitation from a king.

Sarkis Terzian's Passport

Avedis Terzian lovingly conserved his father Sarkis's "passport," granted him by Menelik and written in Amharic. The historian Berhanou Abebe has provided me with the following translation of it:

> The lion of the tribe of Juda has conquered,[11] Menelik, chosen by God, Emperor of Ethiopia. Särkis Tirziyan, a native of Armenia,[12] born in the city of Aräbgir [Arabkir], thirty-nine years old, of medium height, with curly hair and a small face, with a whitish scar to the left of his chin. Having long[13] served my kingdom of Ethiopia as a civil servant, he is from now on considered one of the number of the Abyssinians.[14] I have given him this passport so that nothing regrettable happens to him in any country he goes to.[15]
>
> Executed in the city of Addis Abäba on the 28th day of *terr* of the year of grace 1893.[16]

This document will strike the well-informed observer for more than one reason: to begin with, because of the contents of this declaration of citizenship, which concerns a man who, we know, was an Ottoman subject under German protection when this passport was delivered in 1901. Secondly, because the way it is formulated does not respect all the usual rules. Last, and not least, because of the signature affixed to the bottom of the document (Figure 5.3).

At first glance, the most striking thing about these lines is the fact that the emperor expresses himself in the first person singular, contrary to the customs governing documents emanating from the Ethiopian court. Whereas the document accompanying Sarkis Terzian's decoration[17] the same year bore the conventional imperial "we," the author of the letter uses "I" and "my" in *lämängestē* (my kingdom). There is even redundancy in the use of the singular, since the beginning of the third sentence can be translated literally as "having long served *me my* kingdom of Ethiopia." Such a departure from the rules may find its explanation in the desire to confer exceptional status on this document. What is involved is a passport rather than a simple laissez-passer. That is why the description of the peculiar physical features of the individual named in the document is so precise and why the references to his citizenship are so

Menelik's Armenians

Figure 5.3 Sarkis Terzian's "passport," issued by Menelik, with the imperial seal and a signature attributed to Menelik.

Source: Avedis Terzian papers, collection of the Armenian Community in Ethiopia.

repetitive. The text accompanying Sarkis's 1901 decoration spells out, moreover, that he has served Menelik for fifteen years; this brings us to the year 1886 or 1887 and is more or less consistent with the collective autobiography.[18] The date is important, because it coincides with the moment when Menelik annexed Harar and consequently sounds like confirmation of the founding hero's exploit. The scar mentioned in the text, "to the left of his [Terzian's] chin," is also a detail with a certain importance. Avedis Terzian affirmed that his father had taken part in the campaigns against the Somalis in Ogaden under the leadership of *Däjazmach* Mäkonnen and that he had displayed physical courage: "Rifles against spears. And he was wounded as well" (Narrative 15, § 5). Here he followed the articles about Sarkis Terzian in *Le Monde illustré* and *The Washington Times*. This special sign could not but have struck those who considered the epic about Sarkis Terzian to be true.

The second part of the text is a declaration of citizenship. The emperor proclaims that Sarkis "is from now on considered one of the number of the Abyssinians." The most important feature of this document in Avedis Terzian's estimation, however, was the fact that his father had been granted the supreme honor of seeing Menelik's signature affixed to his passport: "Menelik never signed," he emphatically repeated. At the court, prevailing custom was to apply the emperor's seal, which alone made it possible to authenticate the document. It was inconceivable that the emperor should sign the document himself, because the use of writing, regarded as a semi-magical operation, not as a simple means of communication, was reserved for clerics and monks.[19] This did not mean, however, that the emperors did not know how to write, for it was customary for them to be very discreetly ordained as deacons before acceding to the throne.[20] Thus all of them were literate. It is well know that, after 1906, Menelik adopted the habit of having the documents that he issued signed by his secretary, Yosēf Galan. Is what is involved here an instance of this procedure *avant la lettre*? It might be a question, in this case, of the signature of his secretary and interpreter Yosēf Negusē, Yosēf Galan's predecessor in Menelik's service. Berhanou Abebe quite rightly noted that these curlicues and flourishes seem too skillful and sophisticated not to be those of a hand accustomed to signing. One is, moreover, tempted to read *menelik*, although the correct spelling is *menilek*. It would, however, be hard to understand why the letter, clearly drawn up on Menelik's orders, should have been endorsed by someone else. It remains to be proven that it is not a question of a forgery, for, if the passport itself is authenticated by the imperial seal, it seems plausible that the signature was added later by a third party at Sarkis Terzian's request.

Knowing whether this signature really is Menelik's or not is a secondary matter. The question, rather, is to understand how deeply people believed in its authenticity, as well as the significance it may have had for people for whom the collective autobiography was credible. Avedis Terzian's explanation for the bizarre written form of the syllables was that Menelik had created "a modified alphabet" that could serve him as a code. Terzian had compared this signature to one found on a "portrait of Menelik II that he had dedicated to the wife of minister Ilg in his own hand," probably at her request, "in the secret writing invented by Menelik,"[21] which so closely resembles that on Sarkis Terzian's passport that there is no telling them apart (Figure 5.4). If this signature is a fake, a hypothesis that the accusations of forgery leveled at Sarkis Terzian in his day

Bildnis Menileks II. mit eigenhändiger Widmung an Frau Minister Jlg
(Text der Widmung amharisch, Unterschrift in Menileks selbsterfundener Geheimschrift)

Figure 5.4 Signature accompanying the dedication of a portrait of the emperor to the wife of Menelik's former state counselor, the Swiss Alfred Ilg.

Source: Conrad Keller, *Alfred Ilg: Sein Leben und sein Wirken als Schweizerischer Kulturbote in Abessinien*, Frauenfeld and Leipzig, Huber & Co., 1918, n.p.

would tend to bear out, then it has to be admitted that this "fake" was replicated at least once for Mrs. Ilg.

It is, however, possible that Avedis Terzian has provided us, from beyond the grave, with a last element of response to all these questions. Among the papers he bequeathed Ethiopia's Armenian community was a photocopy of a work, composed in the wake of a 1905 German expedition to Ethiopia, on which there appears a facsimile reproduction of the "autograph-signature of Negus Menelik II"[22] (Figure 5.5). The signature seems to be in the same hand as the one in Conrad Keller's book about Alfred Ilg. The signature on Sarkis's passport looks, it is true, as if it has been produced by a slightly more assured hand, but the two signatures are similar.

The fact that Avedis Terzian was in possession of this photocopy at the time of his death indicates that he deemed it proof of the strength of the ties between Sarkis and Menelik. The signature was not considered in isolation but in tandem with the collective autobiography. It meant that the Armenians had been accepted by a Menelik acting as their protector: "Because he never signs! You've seen that it's a very special relation" (Narrative 15, § 19).

Homeland and Fatherland in the Writing of Memory in the Diaspora

A metaphor for implantation, the theme of the friendship of kings reflects the place assigned the hostland in the Armenian memory. It tends to be conflated with the homeland, with the whole of the emotional dimension covered by this term. In contrast, the Armenian Grand Narrative in Ethiopia accords only a reduced place to the fatherland or the ancestors' country. It reflects a memory that was powerfully sedentarized in the country of residence, which was experienced as a genuinely

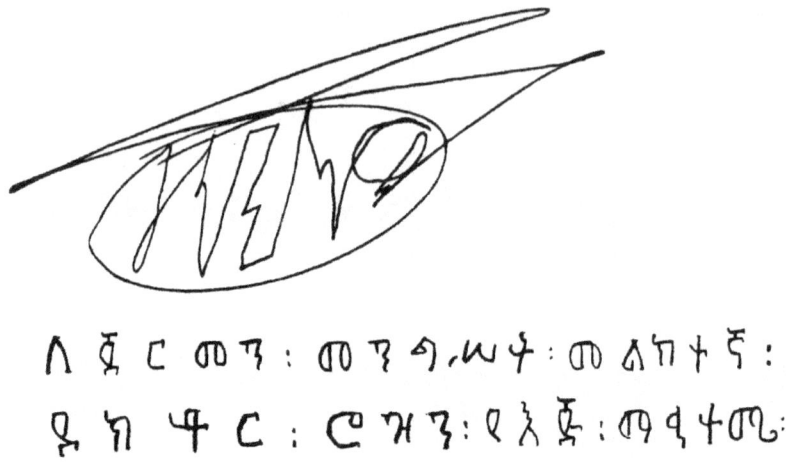

Scherz-Autogramm des Negus Menelik II
Oben: Nachahmung der lateinischen Buchstaben R S N (Rosen) und
darunter: „So schreibt der Gesandte Dr. Rosen."

Figure 5.5 Reproduction of the "handwritten signature of Negus Menelik II."
Source: Felix Rosen, *Eine deutsche Gesandtschaft in Abessinien*, Leipzig, Von Veit & Co., 1907, p. 266.

hospitable hostland. The uniqueness of the tie between the Armenians and Ethiopia is illustrated, in particular, by the Armenians' mastery of Amharic: "Of all the foreign peoples we're the best" (Narrative 1, § 9). Collectively, "the Armenians became advisors of a kind [to the Ethiopians]" (§ 14). This closeness engenders a kind of Ethiopian-Armenian amalgam. It is attested by the fact that many Armenians are granted Ethiopian citizenship and the right to own land, a right that is, in principle, denied foreigners: "You see that we are becoming part of this country" (§ 26). Thus some twenty Armenians took Ethiopian citizenship to support Ethiopia's 1923–4 bid to join the League of Nations:

"You talk about our primitive African justice? We have white subjects.
—Who?
—The Armenians."
Thus we were the subjects of the slaveholders! (Narrative 6, § 16, and Narrative 26, § 11)

Despite the apparent intractability of the "question of color" and the "inevitable racism" spawned by the Armenian families' endogamy (Narrative 1, § 27), the collective autobiography tends to demonstrate that, of all foreigners, Armenians were "the only ones to be part of Ethiopian life" (§ 28). The narrative as a whole has no purpose other than to highlight "how all that ties together" (§ 29). In a good many respects, then, the sedentarization involved here is distinct from what specialists of diasporas mean when they speak of territorialization.

Many studies of diasporas point to the recreation of a territory on which the diasporans are at home or "among themselves" in exile,[23] to the will "to open new places in non-places,"[24] to carve out new places of residence with reference to an elsewhere that preceded exile. This reconstruction, they argue, is rendered necessary by the loss of landmarks due to the migratory experience, especially when the uprooting is associated with a violent, traumatic break "with a structuring territory." Exile then appears as an experience of the "*hors-lieu*" [outside place] in which the transmission of a "national imaginary" or collective imaginary is based on the crucial episodes of the "exodus from the territory" of origin, and it generates myths such as that of the "return" or the "eternally stateless person."[25]

The Grand Narrative of the Armenian presence in Ethiopia, however, leaves little room for the fatherland. The Armenian immigrants came, between the 1880s and the 1920-1930s, from areas that were very dissimilar at the cultural or dialectical level, a circumstance Avedis Terzian takes care to underscore. The collective memory, however, tends to efface these difference by focusing more on the hostland than on the places associated with the pre-migratory experience. This hostland has become homeland.

A photograph in Mushegh Terzian's album that can doubtless be dated to 1908 immortalizes a moment of arrival of Armenian immigrants in Addis Abeba. It shows a crowd of men, women, and children under the boughs of an imposing wild fig tree (Figure 5.6):

Before the creation of the railroad, the Armenians traveled from Harar to Addis Abeba on muleback. It took sixteen days. It was a caravan, and before entering Addis Abeba, there was a big fig tree, it's a *shola*, with very broad branches, and the last encampment was pitched under this tree so that friends from the city could go out to meet them. Then there was a big banquet, a picnic, and we still have photographs of this [meeting] in which a family came together there. Under the *shola*. And not just Armenians. There were also Ethiopians who were friends with the gentlemen here and who went out to meet the families. (Narrative 3, § 3)

The *shola* was, in this period, the place where every new arrival was met, but also "the good-bye tree for anyone leaving for the coast, because it was customary to part here from friends who had come to bid one a last farewell."[26] Basing themselves on the smiles in these photographs and the pleasant atmosphere of an outdoor holiday emanating from them, the narratives of the arrival of the immigrants reconstruct this moment as a happy time. Are we not tempted to associate all these smiling faces with Menelik's proverbial riposte to Sultan Abdülhamid, which, in the collective autobiography, punctuates the arrival of Araxi Yazedjian and her children in Ethiopia (Narrative 1, § 11)? We are far removed, here, from the painful memories elicited by the photos of child survivors in rags after the Great War, or the mental image of the refugees disembarking in Marseilles, in the cosmopolitan big city, and looking,

Figure 5.6 Sarkis Terzian, his wife Vartuhi, and their two children, Yervant and Avedis, welcomed by the Armenian community on their arrival from Harar around 1906 in a locality near Addis Abeba known as Shola.

Source: Marcerou collection.

on the insalubrious quays, for temporary furnished lodgings for the whole family, in hopes of avoiding the uncomfortable conditions of the camp on Oddo Boulevard. The immigration to Ethiopia is engraved on the collective memory as a moment of tranquility rather than a difficult transition, and it is symbolized by the reunions under the *shola*.

What we see at work here is the photographs' visual contribution to the collective process of implantation or taking-root. The part they play in this silent endeavor grows over time, in the same measure as the era of the pioneers recedes. A photo retains its incomparable evocative power, even without a caption. It can dispense with precise identifications of the faces figuring in it, of the place and time it immortalizes. It seems to stimulate the receptivity of the addressees of the collective autobiography all the more when its caption is laconic or when it lacks one.

The composition of the group photos and family portraits is revelatory of this choice of the host country in a land of collective renewal, as in a photograph taken in Aqaqi, on the porch of Krikorios Boghossian's country house (Figure 5.7). We recognize the master of the house surrounded by his children, accompanied by other mature men standing the length of the balustrade, among them the engineer Krikor Howyan and, easy to recognize among all others thanks to his debonair figure, Dikran Ebeyan, Menelik's goldsmith. Below the balustrade, a row of poverty-stricken Ethiopian servants waits, squatting, wrapped in their grayish wool robes. The Ethiopians figuring in the family albums, however, are not just servants; they are also often ministers and renowned grandees, as in the photograph of picnickers gathered around the illustrious *nägädras* Haylä Giyorgis, a moment of relaxation liberally washed down with drink, in which those present are divided equally between Ethiopians and Armenians (Figure 5.8). His relatives or a practiced eye will recognize Mihran Hazarian, an artisan in the palace; the Behesnilian brothers, famous merchants in Ethiopia; or, again, the manufacturer of liqueurs Mardiros Aznavorian, holding the memorable "little glass" that Avedis Terzian told us about. These group portraits against a background of eucalyptus forests (Figure 5.9) valorize not just the Ethiopian setting, but, above all, a condition it would have been impossible to experience in the immigrants' country of origin or any place of exile other than this one.

The Memories of the Banished and the Memory of the Guest

How should we understand the Grand Narrative of the Armenian presence in Ethiopia, which is not based on the narrative of the original Catastrophe of the genocide but on that, as embellished and idealized as possible, of the "invitation" that the Ethiopian kings extended to the founding heroes and their families? The collective autobiography that Avedis Terzian's narrative comprises makes no appeal whatsoever to "the themes of the lost fatherland, a genealogical unthought, or to territories abandoned, confiscated, and engulfed, to say nothing of the theme of perpetual migratory wandering" that are supposedly constitutive of the Armenian diaspora's "collective imaginary."[27] We are not confronted here with a memory of the banished or exiled but with a memory of guests who privilege an emotional relation to their adopted Ethiopian homeland. For, in the context of the enunciation of the collective autobiography, the segment of the

Figure 5.7 On the porch of the Boghossian family's house in Aqaqi, around 1908.
Source: Boghossian collection.

Figure 5.8 Picnic with *Nägädras* Haylä Giyorgis (number 11, center, seated).
Source: Album of Mushegh Terzian, collection of the Armenian Community in Ethiopia.

Figure 5.9 Picnic with Dikran Ebeyan (number 10).
Source: Album of Mushegh Terzian, collection of the Armenian Community in Ethiopia.

past that it was important to valorize had to do not with the rupture of exile but with the immigrants' joyful arrival and their reception in Ethiopia. This was not the case in major countries of immigration such as France or the United States, where, after the Great War, Armenian immigration served as a source of mass labor for industry and ran up against xenophobia and increasingly strict state control over the conditions of residence and entry into the country.

It is not easy to interpret the place assigned to the exodus and the Turkish massacres as founding acts of the emigration, or, again, to the theme of the lost country—in short, to everything comprising, according to the expression I have used, a "memory of the banished" as opposed to the "memory of guests" observable in Ethiopia. It may, however, be noted that the scholars who foreground these themes have produced their works in social contexts in which cultural assimilation was perceived as a real threat, and where resistance to this phenomenon seemed to constitute a legitimate object of study. The memory of the exodus or past suffering accordingly appears as a rampart against the "dilution of identity," to borrow Martine Hovanessian's phrase. This need for differentiation seems the more urgent in social contexts in which there is marked dispersion, as in Western Europe or North America, due to the size of cities, the dimensions of migratory flows, or even the absence of clearly identified Armenian neighborhoods or localities. For descendants of immigrants confronted with their own invisibility, reference to the massacres perpetrated by the Turks becomes "a sort of ritual expression of collective adversity"[28] in the affirmation of an abiding

Armenian identity. In the United States, where the first generations of immigrants also experienced a difficult socioeconomic situation, xenophobia, discrimination, the insalubrity of housing and forms of ghettoization,[29] their descendants' affirmation of a distinct collective identity seems to go hand-in-hand with acknowledgment of their own assimilation, via focalization on the fatherland and the genocide.[30]

In Greece or France, the Armenian refugees' proletarianization fueled hopes of a "return" to Soviet Armenia in the early 1930s and again in 1946–7.[31] In major countries of immigration such as France or the United States, the Armenian immigrants were subject to stigmatization spawned by governmental policies that categorized them as "exotic," "unassimilable," and "undesirable."[32]

In the collective autobiography in Ethiopia, there are no camps or slums, and even fewer customs officers or long, humiliating administrative procedures such as the physical examination inflicted on hopeful immigrants in France or the United States. It is true that Levon Yazedjian's daughter tells the story of the privations that her father endured in a struggle to survive after being forced to leave Turkey, where a price had been put on his head for revolutionary activities; these difficulties are, however, smoothed over as if by magic as soon as Yazedjian hears about Ethiopia:

> My father managed to get out, and then he went through every possible kind of adversity, and, finally, he arrives in Alexandria. [...] He sees a newspaper where they tell him about a Christian country, Ethiopia, where the emperor is Christian. "Ooo!" he says, "that's terrific; I'm going to go there." And so he takes the boat from Alexandria, washing dishes the whole time and all that. He arrives in Djibouti. From Djibouti, it took him twenty days to arrive in Addis Abeba, because there was no railroad. [...] There was an Armenian who had a good reputation in the palace, he could approach Emperor Menelik. My father had found the photo [of Menelik] in the newspaper, they had enlarged all that. Then as that other fellow, the Armenian Krikorios[33] said, "wait there, in front of the gate, the Emperor's going to go to church, I'll introduce him to you." So he introduced him and the Emperor accepted him. Really, he made a friend of the Emperor with that photo. [...] That's my father's story.[34]

The narrative of the passage from the "outside" to the "inside" thus goes straight to the heart of the matter without lingering over possible difficulties or the vicissitudes of the voyage. The "junction" between the emperor and the immigrant seems virtually immediate, again showing how the theme of the friendship of kings dilutes the narrative of individual experiences. The only hardship of the voyage seems to have to do with the fact that, because construction of the railroad between Dire Dawa and Addis Abeba had not yet been completed, the immigrant had to finish his trip on muleback. Thus what emerges from this narrative is a smoothed over vision of settlement in Ethiopia, as if the favorable socioeconomic conditions that the immigrants found in the country softened the hardships of exile. To be sure, the handful of Armenian immigrant families mentioned as present in Harar in the 1880s and 1890s associated neither with the kings of Ethiopia nor with ambassadors, and one's impression is, rather, that they lived in very modest conditions. What is more, the Armenians who arrived in Ethiopia after the First World War were refugees, as in Europe. The collective memory of this immigration, however, organized around the idea of welcome, echoes the "symbolic nationalization" of the Armenians that I have hypothesized.

The social impact of public discourses on memories must nevertheless be taken into account. The "sedentary" nature of the Armenian memory, attested by the collective autobiography and incarnated by Menelik's pro-Armenian attitude and the theme of the friendship of kings, is perhaps less the result of a transmission from generation to generation than the reflection of an era and an enunciatory context that must be taken into account. If my investigation had been carried out in the interwar period, it would certainly have revealed a much more fragmented memory, constructed with reference to places of origin located for the most part in the towns and rural areas of Turkey, and more heavily oriented toward these fatherlands and toward periods of departure and immigration in the proper sense of the word—in short, a memory of exiles, and perhaps not this memory of guests that I observed in the 1990s and the 2000s. The importance that the theme of the "friendship of kings" came to acquire in the Armenian Grand Narrative may in part result from the increasingly rigid distinction between the "national" and the "foreign" that became apparent in Ethiopia from the 1950s or 1960s on, and from the policy known as "Ethiopianization."[35] From that time on, the construction and expression of a "memory of guests" rather than, and in opposition to, a memory of exiles or the uprooted could very aptly serve to reaffirm that the Armenians were well and truly in *their* country in Ethiopia. Malleable, and subject to reversals, memory is indissociable from the social issues of its time.

Establishing the Golden Age

In the collective autobiography, Menelik's illness and subsequent death mark the decline of the singular tie that the Armenians established with Ethiopia by way of the symbolic intervention of the families of Armenian "grandees" present at the imperial court. This break in the ideal order of things occurs just before the deaths of the pioneers, as if intentionally. The death of Sarkis Terzian, who had, according to his son, "outlived his period of importance" in the palace (Narrative 17, § 4) and seemed bound not to survive his illustrious protector, almost seems to be a sign heralding the other founding heroes' disappearance. Thus there is a before and an after Menelik. In 1923, Avedis Terzian, on his definitive return to Ethiopia after ten years of study in Turkey and at the moment when he attained the age of majority, was able to observe the fading away of the generation of pioneers of the communitarian adventure. Sarkis Terzian died in 1915, two years after the date generally taken to be the date of Menelik's death. Of Sarkis's three brothers, who might have continued to embody the past revered by his son, only Mamas Terzian was still alive in 1923, when he turned forty-six. Garabed Terzian had died before Avedis left for Turkey in 1913, and Ohannes Terzian probably died before 1923, for he does not appear in the Armenian church's death register, which was kept from 1923 on. Pilibbos Kherbekian, who had been Mäkonnen's and Menelik's mason, died in 1923. Boghos Makarian, the celebrated *Hayrig*, gave up the ghost in 1922 at the venerable age of ninety-two. The engineer Krikor Howyan, the goldsmith Dikran

Ebeyan, and the photographers Levon Yazedjian and Bedros Boyadjian, illustrious servants of Menelik's, breathed their last in that order in 1925, 1926, 1927, and 1928. Even the manufacturer of liqueurs Mardiros Aznavorian, whose "little glasses" the reader will recall, died in his fifties in 1926. The interviews that Avedis Terzian was able to conduct with Hagop Baghdassarian and Krikorios Boghossian, who lived until 1932 and 1940, respectively, doubtless had a strong influence on the construction of the collective autobiography, as did the testimony of Levon Yazedjian's and Dikran Ebeyan's wives, who had also long worked at the palace: Srpuhi Ebeyan, who died in 1937, and Araxi Yazedjian, who passed away in 1955. We must also underscore the importance, for Avedis Terzian, of his interviews with Krikorios Boghossian's first three sons, Khachig, Khosrov, and Aghassi, all of whom were born in Addis Abeba, in 1900, 1904, and 1905, respectively; with Pilibbos Kherbekian's son Minas, born in Arabkir in 1887, who probably arrived in Ethiopia with his father in 1899; and with Dikran and Srpuhi Ebeyan's daughter Arusiag, who came into the world in Entotto in 1890. All these people had had enough contact with the "old-timers" to be able to contribute to establishing Menelik's reign as the golden age of the Armenian presence in Ethiopia.

> As you can see, from Ebeyan, Sarkis, Markarian, Yazedjian on, we're intertwined. It's not a normal relationship. [...] Baghdassarian, Boghossian... [...] Under Haile Selassie, times changed. [...] Haile Selassie, to begin with, as a character, was quite different from Menelik. Secondly, the times were changing. In 1916, relations with the world were changing. The embassies, the arrival of the railroad in Addis Abeba. Then the Armenians weren't as important as before. There were more important elements. There were the embassies. The country's character was changing. And then the leading grandees were disappearing. There were young people, etc. So Armenian influence was diminishing. Losing its character. (Narrative 16, § 8–10)

Collective memory subdivides time, organizes it, and determines the historical breaks in the common past. The measure for the fabrication of heroes, like that for establishing a golden age, depends on the preoccupations of the present. It is by no means a neutral act. Born in Harar in 1904, Avedis Terzian, his community's doyen when our interviews took place, says almost nothing about the period after Haile Selassie's restoration to the throne in 1941 in narrating his own life, as if what happened thereafter were not edifying subject matter. A similar subdivision punctuates the collective autobiography in its entirety. The golden age of the Armenians of Ethiopia is clearly put in the time of Menelik's reign, which serves as the stage for the founding myths. The childhood of the community's adventure further corresponds to the narrator's childhood in Harar, which is presented as the true cradle of the Armenian presence in Ethiopia. Avedis Terzian has the most to say about this period, in which he still had his father, his mother, all his uncles and aunts, and his maternal grandmother, who arrived from Arabkir in 1895. Thus the collective autobiography arranges for the collective golden age and the narrator's personal golden age to coincide. It speaks to us about a time that people under the age of one hundred cannot have known.

> For some twenty years, we lived a completely Ethiopian life, with the Ethiopian sovereigns. But we did not even have houses, we had huts. And we constructed only gradually. No houses, no floors. Earth! We started to have floors in 1920. (Narrative 2, § 11)

The twenty years of "completely Ethiopian" life correspond, roughly, to Menelik's reign. Nostalgia for the golden age leads to the celebration of the most archaic Ethiopian ancien régime, the one in which the Armenian immigrants who frequented the *gebbi* were given slaves as gifts: for example, "Fayça Sarkis," who, after being given to Avedis Terzian's father by Menelik, "became a son of the family" (Narrative 30, § 2), or, again, his own nanny, "a girl whom Menelik gave to my father" (Narrative 26, § 5).

> Because in our families, in our family, we had domestics who were tied to us. They even bore their boss's family name... Ebeyan had some. Boghossian had some. We had maids and men who were very close to our family. They bore our family name. Because they were not [just] servants. The system was such that they were [part] of our family. [...] We had contacts with people of the lower classes all the way up to the grandees. (Narrative 19, § 4)

Like "Mamo," "the son of my grandmother's slave," they learned to speak Armenian: "Because they were, as one says, *ashkär*. *Ashkär* is soldier and [servant] at the same time. Our servant was an *ashkär* [...]. Even Sarkis was an *ashkär* of Menelik's" (Narrative 30, § 5–6).

The period that follows this happy community childhood appears as a kind of silver age in the collective autobiography. It corresponds to the one that saw Avedis Terzian's return to the land of his birth as a young adult, after he had completed his studies in Turkey and after the death of his parents, but also to that of most of the "great" Armenians of Menelik's day. This second period in the Armenians' common history still serves as the stage for a few brilliant episodes, such as the epic of the Forty Children, in 1924. Basically, however, the break with the golden age was consummated with the change of generations. It was also a result of the veritable demographic revolution that the small group of the Armenians of Ethiopia underwent after the Great War, with the massive arrival of new immigrants who had backgrounds different from those of the immigrants of the first period. After 1941 and the end of the Italian occupation, the last of the epic periods of the collective adventure, it seems that economic, political, and social transformations in Ethiopia tipped the Armenian presence over into a kind of normality with no particular profile.

Menelik's Catafalque

The place of the theme of the friendship of kings was of such importance in the construction of an Armenian Grand Narrative in Ethiopia in the twentieth century that the death of the pro-Armenian emperor Menelik could *not* leave a mark on it. Like the founding myths, veritable eschatological myths are thus grounded on the inexhaustible theme of the alliance between the Armenian immigrants and the Ethiopian kings.

Pursuing the same logic at work (*logique en action*), they continue to make "Menelik's Armenians" people who were initiated into the imperial court secrets:

> There was something mysterious for us Armenians [when Menelik died]. One night, at midnight, officers from the palace went to see Boghossian. They said, "We need a joiner" to make a coffin. Boghossian understood that it's a secret. Why don't they announce who the coffin is for? [...] He knew Menelik was dying. He understood. (Narrative 17, § 11–12)

"An extraordinary thing": the night the emperor dies, they go knocking on "an Armenian's" door in order to ask for "a coffin at all costs." "For two years," however, Menelik's death was kept secret:

> That means, all that, that means trust. You see: they have to keep the Emperor's death [secret], and they have to turn to Armenian friends to make a coffin. You see how things are advancing. (Narrative 1, § 19)

Like the anecdotes about life in the imperial palace, the legend of Menelik's coffin has the value of a lesson. Symbolically, it puts the king's body in the hands of one of his Armenian servants:

> So you see again the Armenians' closeness [to the court]. The only person they trust is an Armenian family. [...] You know, [en]trusting state secrets to an Armenian... That means, to show you the great trust they had. [En]trusting a state secret. (Narrative 17, § 12 and 14)

Albeit completely unverifiable, this story was familiar to, and repeated by, various people in the period when I was conducting my research. Three of Krikorios Boghossian's surviving daughters confirmed it for me when I encountered them in their old family home in Addis Abeba. Over tea and petits-fours, between old-fashioned adobe walls studded with somewhat intimidating trophies of stuffed deer, they told me, in their tranquil little way, how the emperor's coffin had been placed on the big living room table (which was in front of me as they spoke) before it was carried off to the palace amid the greatest possible secrecy.[36]

The coffin is supposed to have been made, at Boghossian's request, by an Armenian joiner, Matheos Karamanian. We know next to nothing about him, except that he owned a mill and farmed land in Addis Abeba (Narrative 17, § 16). In a photograph in Mushegh Terzian's album (Figure 5.10), he appears, old and shaggy-haired, in a tattered suit. After hearing the story of Menelik's coffin told many times over, are we not tempted, as others before us may have been, to discern a trace of it in the deep, meandering wrinkles that crease Matheos's face? The photo's caption comprises nothing but a name ("Matheos Karamanian"), a date ("1912"), and a profession ("joiner"). For anyone familiar with the story of Menelik's coffin, however—and there is no reason to suppose that Mushegh Terzian was not—Karamanian's name was no doubt enough and required no commentary. As for the date, it can in no case be that of the photo.

Figure 5.10 "Matheos Karamanian 1912 [sic], Joiner"
Source: Album of Mushegh Terzian, collection of the Armenian Community in Ethiopia.

It shows Matheos Karamanian as an old man; we know, however, from the register of deaths in the Armenian church in Addis Abeba, where he died in 1961, that he was born in Caesarea (present-day Kayseri, Turkey) in 1875.[37] Thus he was at most thirty-seven or thirty-eight at the end of Menelik's reign. The year 1912, mentioned under this portrait that apparently has no history, more likely refers to the year that the emperor died and was secretly placed in his coffin, an episode that ensured Matheos's fame in the group of descendants of the Armenian immigration in Ethiopia.

Krikorios Boghossian's closeness to the imperial court doubtless helped make the legend of the coffin credible in the Armenian milieu. Married to an Ethiopian, Charlotte Boghossian, Krikorios maintained close ties with several members of the country's aristocracy, whom he regularly saw in the context of a religious brotherhood, the *mahbär* of Täklä Haymanot: "So the leading grandees felt at home in the Boghossian house, because they went there every week to eat with their fingers" (Narrative 17, § 20). After Menelik's death, Krikorios Boghossian donated, for the decoration of his mausoleum, one of the stone lions he had ordered in Belgium: "So one of these lions is the gift of Boghossian. He said, 'It's my duty to give at least something to our patron'. All this to show you the relations that existed, extraordinary" (§ 17).

It is undeniable that Menelik's death was long matter for speculation. The historians now agree to date it to the night of December 12–13, 1913.[38] However, as Avedis Terzian points out when he affirms that "he died in [19]13, but it was announced in [19]15," it was several years before the emperor's death was officially admitted. It was an open secret: everyone knew that Menelik's body had been "hidden in a nook of the palace" in 1913 and that, because his grandson *Lej* Iyasu had ruled out a funeral celebration, his death was revealed only in 1916, when his daughter Zäwditu acceded to the throne.[39] The pretenders to Menelik's succession had no interest in announcing his death before making sure that they would be able to establish their dynastic legitimacy. The official chronicle notes that *Lej* Iyasu, who was enjoying the hot springs at Fell Woha at the time, deemed it preferable to conceal his grandfather's death for fear of seeing his enemies immediately join forces against him. "And all who heard of the King's death pretended not to have heard"[40] on *Lej* Iyasu's orders, at the risk of displeasing the country's people, who wished to pay their last respects to the deceased emperor. "He himself, the same day, went galloping at the racecourse. Pretending nothing [was] bothering him" (Narrative 17, § 11). Iyasu was criticized for his attitude three years later, at the time of his dethronement, when Täfäri attacked him for failing to organize a mass in Menelik's honor. On December 12, 1920, Täfäri and Zäwditu made a great show of distancing themselves from Iyasu's attitude by seeing to it that the seventh anniversary of Menelik's death was commemorated with great pomp.[41]

Well before 1913, announcements of Menelik's imminent death had become everyday occurrences. Since 1906, it had been widely known that the emperor, who had suffered a serious stroke in May, would doubtless live only a few more years at best. From 1908 on—he was sixty-four years old at the time—he was frequently seen walking with a cane, and he left the business of government to his entourage and the Empress Taytu. He was hardly ever seen in public after 1910, and the government soon had to issue regular denials of rumors of his death. In the early 1920s, Dr. Mérab, the former "personal physician of Negus Menelik II," dedicated a book of his "to the memory of my august client, Negus Menelik II [...] who died in the fullness of his glory and amid the love of his subjects on 25 November 1909," a Friday, the feast day of Saint Gabriel, at five o'clock in the evening, he felt duty-bound to add—that is, four years before the officially admitted date. This was proof, according to Mérab, of "the Abyssinian people's incredible stock of innate diplomacy."[42] In the same period, it was still possible to write, as if what was involved were acknowledged fact, that Menelik's death went back to 1908.[43] Traveling through Ethiopia in 1930, Evelyn Waugh doubted whether the mausoleum in which Zäwditu's and Menelik's coffins had been placed "contain[ed] the body attributed to it, or indeed any body at all": "The date and place of Menelik's death are a palace secret, but it is generally supposed to have taken place about two years before its formal announcement to people."[44] Until 1914, the term *lej* ("child") continued to be attached to the name of Iyasu, heir apparent to the throne, the better to conceal his grandfather's death.[45] The Ethiopian aristocracy, however, was accustomed to this practice in the early twentieth century.[46] The body of *Lej* Iyasu, who died in the early 1930s after a long imprisonment on *Ras* Täfäri's orders, was itself concealed after his death.

In the oppressive atmosphere that marked the end of Menelik's reign, all the foreigners in Ethiopia feared the disorders that would not fail to erupt as soon as his death was announced, leaving shops and estates prey to looters.[47] Meetings were organized to meet the crisis at the legations of various European states in order to finalize plans to defend their citizens and buildings with armed force. These fears undoubtedly created a context that bred rumors. What, however, explains the fact that the Armenians alone bruited the strange story about Menelik's coffin? Extending Durkheim's reflections about the necessarily objective bases for myths considered as social constructs,[48] we may assume that the Armenians alone felt the need to do so. For their situation differed from that of the other foreigners. As Ottoman subjects who did not benefit in any way from the protection of the Turkish consul in Harar, their legal situation was precarious. Little inclined, until this time, to accept the German legation's offer to register them on its lists, the Armenians suddenly changed their attitude in late January 1909, when "Menelik's advanced age" seemed "to be of a nature to justify certain fears."[49] At year's end, the French legation deplored the fact that the Armenians, who, together with the Greeks, "displayed rather intense fears from the day that the Emperor's alarming condition" had become public knowledge, had "topped up their supplies of ammunition" and taken refuge "with people whose houses seemed, thanks to their solidity, to offer some guarantee of safety. [...] Despite the assurances given them, a number of Armenian families, abandoning their homes, have taken up quarters near the Legation of Germany in order to protect themselves from unforeseen attack."[50]

The fact that this legend emerged, circulated, and was perpetuated only in Ethiopia's Armenian milieu reflects the adhesion of a group of individuals to one and the same vision of the collective past and present. It is significant that Avedis Terzian, when addressing an external public, did not necessarily mention the stories that nevertheless give the collective autobiography all its meaning and charm, such as the anecdotes about palace life or the legend of Menelik's coffin. Thus he confines himself, in the short account of his community's history that he wrote at the end of his life—in English, and thus presumably for an audience of non-Armenian, non-Ethiopian readers—to verifiable, incontestable matters, such as the Armenians' role in the crafts, trade, and so on. We do not, however, ever find in this account the charm of the anecdotes and legends recounted in Addis Abeba's Armenian families. The disparity between the aridity of this short text and the collective autobiography's great narrative richness reveals the influence of the interrelational context on the narration: the narrator recounts his story or, rather, tells it to the end, when and only when he thinks he will be believed. Thus he speaks freely, in the true sense, only in the circle of trust formed between the narrator and his audience. When the narrative is addressed to a broader public, its contents are poorer; they are reduced to what might be called a lowest common denominator of credibility. The legend of Menelik's coffin gives expression to the memory of an Armenian exception in Ethiopia. It is addressed only to an audience already convinced of the reality of this exception. Like the fabrication of the founding hero, the legendary story of Menelik's coffin is part of the "record of resemblances" that Halbwachs evokes when he explains that collective memory "retains from the past only what still lives or is capable of living in the consciousness of the groups keeping the memory alive," and that it "provides the group a self-portrait."[51] A rumor that originated in the years following Menelik's death and that likewise involves an Armenian will allow me to illustrate what this means.

Lej Iyasu's True False Portrait

Menelik's problematic succession inaugurated a kind of "time of troubles" in Ethiopia. It culminated in the short but very controversial reign of his grandson *Lej* Iyasu (1913-16).[52] A persistent rumor has it that an Armenian who was often present in the imperial palace, Levon Yazedjian, participated directly in dethroning *Lej* Iyasu by producing a photomontage that showed him wearing Muslim dress. The photomontage is said to have helped bring about the replacement of Menelik's designated heir by his eldest daughter, Zäwditu, and to have consecrated the victory of the partisans of *Lej* Iyasu's rival, *Ras* Täfäri Mäkonnen. In its way, this rumor, too, plays its part in marking the end of an Armenian golden age in Ethiopia.

In an article that has become famous, Marc Bloch argues that fake news and its propagation comprise an object of study par excellence for historians, because "the error propagates itself, grows, and ultimately survives on just one condition—that it finds a favorable breeding ground in the society in which it is spreading." Elsewhere, Bloch calls this "a collective mood."[53] The question as to whether Yazedjian did in fact produce this photomontage is secondary. It is far more important to discern the "collective mood" revealed by the rumor.

The rumor that a fake portrait of *Lej* Iyasu was fabricated at the instigation of the English, with an Armenian photographer's direct involvement, began to make the rounds in 1916 and was propagated throughout the interwar period, because there existed conditions that made it credible. *Lej* Iyasu's ancestry helped fuel the suspicion that he had converted to Islam. His father, the mighty *Ras* Mikaēl of Wällo, who was honored with the title of *negus* in 1914, had abjured the Muslim faith during the reign of Yohannes IV (1872–1889), but his conversion to Christianity was regarded as a baptism of convenience. *Lej* Iyasu had inherited solid relations with the empire's Muslims from his father. Between 1913 and 1916, his policy of "national reconciliation," which aimed to re-equilibrate the distribution of power between his Muslim and Christian subjects in the empire, aroused the Ethiopian Church's mistrust and led to the spread of a great many rumors about his supposed apostasy.[54] Furthermore, the fact that he had conspicuously adopted a position in favor of the Central Powers in 1914, when the Ottoman Empire had just officially declared a *jihad* against the countries of the Entente, frightened the Ethiopian government, which, brought up short, thought it wiser to wait and see how the conflict in Europe developed before taking sides.[55] The British could only be alarmed by the sympathy Iyasu showed his Muslim subjects at a time when they had their hands full with Mad Mullah's rebellion in Somalia. They might begin to fear that their access to their route to the Indies would be blocked, something that would, in the long run, have resulted from any rapprochement between *Lej* Iyasu and the Young Turk government. The rumor of British intervention in Ethiopia was, therefore, plausible. People were mentally prepared for it.

In the interwar period, a report had it that, in the wake of a short visit that Colonel Lawrence paid Ethiopia in 1916, the emperor had been "photographed in Gibbi [*gebbi*] when he was surrounded by his Arabian favorites wearing Mohammedan costume," and that "prints were made of this photograph in Khartum and distributed in hundreds of thousands among the people" on the initiative of the British, an act that "probably accelerated the fall of Lidj Yassu."[56] In the same vein, the British ambassador reported, three months before the fall 1916 coup d'état, that *Lej* Iyasu was "slowly drifting back into his old ways, eating and sleeping in Moslem houses, wearing the turban and so forth," and that he had

> recently been photographed in a fez and ha[d] had the photograph mounted with the pictures of six of his Mohammedan ancestors surrounding it, and it is reported that 100 copies are to be made for circulation among the Somali tribes. It will be interesting to see if these photographs with their Arabic inscriptions are sent also to our tribes and to the Mullah.[57]

By no means intended to defame Iyasu, the photomontage is supposed to have served his pro-Muslim policy. Rumors of Iyasu's pan-Islamic designs and his presumed apostasy were still thriving in the 1930s:

> His father's Mohammedan origin added color to this report, and proof was supplied in the form of his portrait wearing a turban which purported to have been taken at Harar. Many, however, declare that this conclusive piece of evidence was fabricated in Addis Ababa by an Armenian photographer.[58]

The fact that Armenian photographers had maintained close relations with the *gebbi* since early in the twentieth century substantiated the hypothesis that they had produced a fake. From a technical standpoint, nothing contradicted the idea. Bedros Boyadjian, and, later, sons Haygaz and Tony and daughter Dikranuhi ("Dicky") excelled in the art of retouching official portraits at the request of those who had commissioned them.[59] If the existence of photographs of *Lej* Iyasu dressed "like" a Muslim is not subject to doubt, no one has ever succeeded in proving that, thanks to a trick, a photomontage made it possible to show him wearing such dress.[60] The absence of proof, however, stimulates imaginations rather than restraining them. Individuals are said to have submitted crude collages—"fake fakes," as it were—to the expertise of collectors trying to find Yazedjian's mythic photomontage.[61] Nevertheless, in Ethiopia's Armenian families, the idea that Levon Yazedjian fabricated a true false portrait of *Lej* Iyasu is never called into question.

Here is how Levon Yazedjian's daughter recounted, in 1996, her father's role in these events:

> We were very close to the royal family. The reason for this is quite remote. [...] *Ras* Täfäri was a minor governor: he was *qäñazmatch*—a minor title. [...] My father was a photographer, as I've told you. There was *Lej* Iyasu, the one who succeeded to Menelik and who put Menelik's daughter [Zäwditu] in prison. [...] He had come to see my father to have his picture taken as a Muslim. [...] So he had his picture taken with a turban, with a cutlass, bare-breasted, with a spear. As a Muslim, a Somali. He had his picture taken, he asked for a lot of copies for distribution in the country. [...] So my father took the picture, made copies, but, in those days, we didn't have what was required for photos. We left photos to dry, like this, you know, with a clothespin, on the couch. *Ras* Täfäri—he wasn't a *ras* yet—*Qäñazmatch* Täfäri arrived. While he waited for my father, he walked around, saw photos, and so he saw *Lej* Iyasu dressed like a Muslim. He took one of the photos, he put it in his pocket without saying anything. And he showed it to the grandees: *Lej* Iyasu become a Muslim. [...] They came and asked for eight hundred copies of this photograph. My father said, "No, I can't, absolutely not, he's a friend. What?! We eat together, can I do something like that? No, I won't give them [to you]." They had to requisition them: "You must give them to us or else it's prison." They took what there was, they left, and they distributed these photos. And *Lej* Iyasu had to go to the interior [to the provinces], he was arrested. The son of *Ras* Mäkonnen, the one who won the war of Adwa against the Italians, was in a good position to become king, regent. He [*Ras* Täfäri] became regent, Iyasu was arrested, and the first thing the regent did was to have Menelik's daughter released from the convent, the prison where she was. And he became regent; she [Zäwditu] reigned but, in fact, he was the one who ruled. That's how it was.[62]

The Yazedjian family could consider itself close to the royal family. After Levon Yazedjian entered the palace as a painter in Menelik's and Taytu's service, his wife, Araxi Yazedjian, headed the *gebbi*'s carpet workshops for many years. Levon began a career as a photographer and was fairly successful:

> Levon Yazedjian was appointed Mikaël's official photographer. Since Bedros [Boyadjian] had Menelik, he [too] wanted to have a sovereign. So Yazedjian had letterhead saying: "photographer for the king of Wällo"... But he used that against Mikaël! (Narrative 27, § 4)

In his daughter's narrative, Levon Yazedjian is compelled, under duress, to help Täfäri perpetrate the infamous act against Iyasu. These narrative precautions are understandable, because this is the narration of a betrayal. Levon Yazedjian violates his loyalty to one reigning family—Iyasu's and his father Mikaēl's—for the benefit of another—the family of Täfäri, the son of Ras Mäkonnen, who seizes power thanks to this stratagem. "Many Ethiopians accuse Yazedjian of behaving badly," Avedis explains. They say, "He didn't have the right to overthrow an emperor" (Narrative 16, § 5). In the Yazedjian family, the preceding narrative was doubtless elaborated at a time in which it was deemed dangerous to demonstrate too overtly that one favored one or the other of the pretenders to the throne, that is, before 1930, when Haile Selassie was crowned emperor, shortly before *Lej* Iyasu's death. In the interval, the narrative canvas took set form with certain crucial details, such as the number of copies (eight hundred) that were made of Iyasu's portrait, or, again, the reconstructed dialogue between Täfäri and Yazedjian, "in a set of facts which are retained, shared, and retransmitted, although it is impossible to designate the exact source or author," and which, because they were constituted at a time still close to the event, "serve as the matrix for later evocations" of it.[63]

Similar motives explain, perhaps, the fact that the legend of Menelik's coffin remained confidential and was rarely divulged outside Armenian circles. For, by providing a coffin for Menelik secretly, by night, Krikorios Boghossian in fact objectively served *Lej* Iyasu's interests, since Iyasu did all he could to suppress the news of his grandfather's death. Thus the Armenian and his family had no reason to boast about playing such a role, neither at the time nor in the years thereafter, when, on the contrary, it was necessary to demonstrate one's loyalty to Zäwditu and Täfäri, who, in the 1920s, criticized Iyasu for having imposed this silence.

The stake was no longer the same when I carried out my investigation. Himself Levon Yazedjian's nephew by way of his mother, Avedis Terzian affirmed that the Armenian participated actively and willingly in preparing the coup d'état:

> One way or another, one had to show the leading Ethiopian military grandees that *Lej* Iyasu was a Muslim. *Lej* Iyasu traveled to the region of the Afars a lot. He wore a loincloth [...] like a Muslim. [...] So the English approach Yazedjian, my uncle. They say, "Can you make a photomontage for us?" He says, "yes." So they take *Lej* Iyasu wearing a loincloth, and they put a turban on his head. (Narrative 16, § 5)

For Avedis Terzian, there could be little doubt that Levon Yazedjian had been paid by the English, as the English had paid the head of the Ethiopian Church, *Abunä* Matëwos, to agree to release the Ethiopian grandees from their oath of loyalty to the emperor (§ 5).[64] In his view, the further course of the Armenian photographer's career was telling evidence of this and proved that he had been directly mixed up in this affair: "When *Lej* Iyasu was sent packing, there were riots here. So, immediately, he was considered anti-Iyasu. And Haile Selassie appointed him police chief. [...] Naturally, this family became a friend of the [imperial] family's." This is why Levon Yazedjian's daughter, "the Empress's godchild," according to Avedis Terzian,[65] was "very closely tied to Haile Selassie's dynasty [...]. They are very close." One of his sons, Paylag, had become "deputy police chief": "Father and son, they were the police" in Addis Abeba. "Later he became a friend [of the] government, he had a very good reputation with Haile Selassie," becoming director of the tobacco régie, and then a customs official, a tax official, and even vice-governor of the municipality of Addis Abeba. "So he had Haile Selassie's support. Since his father had contributed to the victory" (Narrative 16, § 6–8).[66]

This appointment to the post of police chief in the capital has left no material traces.[67] The explanation may lie in the fact that Levon and his twenty-year-old son Paylag are said to have held this eminent office for only a few months. Certain "indications," however, have convinced the Yazedjian family and Addis Abeba's Armenians of the veracity of the appointment. Avedis Terzian explained this choice as a consequence of the "tremendous disorder" reigning in Addis Abeba at the time of the October 27, 1916 battle of Sägälē, which saw the eighty-thousand man army of *Negus* Mikaēl, determined to put his son back on the throne, confronting the forces of the rebellious grandees: "So they appoint [...] our uncle police chief! Léon Yazedjian! You see how things… Paylag, second!" (Narrative 1, § 20). Levon Yazedjian's daughter kept a letter with the following letterhead: "L. M. [Levon Mardiros] Yazedjian, Ethiopian Chief of Police" in French and Amharic (*lēwon yazedjyan yäzäbäña aläqa*), stamped with the seal of the Addis Abeba police. She also had a portrait of Levon Yazedjian wearing—on her account—a police chief's uniform (Figure 5.11).[68]

In the same perspective, we may ask about the significance acquired by a photograph taken at Levon Yazedjian's funeral. It, too, was transmitted by his daughter (Figure 5.12). It is January 25, 1927. Levon Yazedjian has just died at the age of fifty-six, overcome by typhus.[69] A procession is conducting his mortal remains to the cemetery. A crowd of onlookers wearing white robes, thronging both sides of a broad avenue, is being held back by armed policemen, while a chauffeur seems to be waiting for the coffin to be placed on the open platform of his vehicle. In the center of the picture, Addis Abeba's Armenians are marching down the road, shaded by luxurious vegetation, in order to bid the deceased a final farewell. In the distance, we can make out, between the choirboys and the church banners, the Armenian priest's somber conical cowl and his processional cross. We are struck, above all, by the presence of *Ras* Täfäri's royal brass band at the head of the cortege, led by its musical director wearing a colonial hat, with its gleaming instruments and its most beautiful uniforms. It puts the finishing touch on the tableau, lending it all its solemnity and pomp. Did the man who would soon be committed to the earth deserve such exceptional consideration? In the "collective mood" that reigned in the interwar period among the Armenian immigrants and their children, it is not impossible that this photograph brought back memories, by the association of ideas, of the affair of *Lej* Iyasu's fake portrait, in which, it was suspected, Yazedjian had been involved. The royal brass band's participation in the funeral procession could have seemed like a final gesture of appreciation, on Täfäri's part, for the man who had helped him seize the throne using methods too shameful to be openly acknowledged.

Thus it appears that the legends and rumors propagated in the 1920s can be interpreted as the remote echo of preoccupations that arose among the Armenians as a result of their diminishing influence at the palace and the fragilization of their political situation after Menelik's death. The memory of the friendship of kings, however, may also be the consequence of later reconstructions, shaped by more recent issues that we cannot accurately assess, as is suggested by the place the royal brass band came to hold in the collective memory.

Figure 5.11 Portrait of Levon Yazedjian in the uniform of Addis Abeba's "police chief," around 1916.

Source: Marcerou collection.

Figure 5.12 The royal brass band at the head of Levon Yazedjian's funeral procession in Addis Abeba, January 25, 1927.

Source: Marcerou collection.

6

Arba Lejoch: The Logical Apotheosis of a Collective Destiny

The place that *Ras* Täfäri's brass band occupies in the collective memory provides a striking illustration of the term *logique en action* ("logic at work") that Halbwachs uses to define memory when he observes that it "retains only those events that are of a pedagogic character" and attributes, to each one, "a significance beyond the event itself" by suggesting "that it is part of a chain of events which together culminate in an event comprising all the others."[1] The inscription of this very poorly documented event in people's memories plays a teleological part in the invention of a collective destiny.

Children of the Negus: The Social Resonance of the Myth of Adoption

At the price of contortions and acts of forgetting, the arrival of the *arba lejoch* or "forty children"—to borrow the Amharic name by which the young musicians of the royal brass band have been known in Ethiopia since the 1920s[2]—was imposed on the collective memory as the adoption of "forty orphans" by the crown prince. Thus it stealthily inserted itself in the preexisting memorial framework of an Armenian exception in Ethiopia.

The Adoption of the Forty Orphans, or, the Euphemization of a Work Contract

Unlike most of the heroes, anecdotes, legends, and rumors mentioned so far, the fame of the *arba lejoch* goes far beyond the narrow circle of descendants of the Armenian immigration in Ethiopia. The current popularity of Ethiopian music is not without bearing on the fact that the "forty children" have not been forgotten. The adventure of the *arba lejoch* is often treated as the first chapter in the history of modern Ethiopian music (*zemenä muziqa*), a prefiguration of the "Swinging Addis" of the 1960s.[3] The available information about the event is, however, quite nebulous. According to a letter from the Armenian General Benevolent Union (AGBU), which shared responsibility for these orphans with the Armenian patriarchate in the Holy Land, "after the brass band made up of forty schoolchildren from our orphanage in Jerusalem performed in honor of the crown prince of Ethiopia, His Highness Ras Taffari, during his visit to Jerusalem, the prince proposed to the Armenian Patriarch of Jerusalem, Monseigneur Tourian, that he take the brass band and its two teachers into his service."[4] The rare contemporary accounts, however, demolish the image of the young musicians as infant prodigies. Contemporary observers note that "the Armenian orchestra's cacophonous pom-poms" were very diversely appreciated.[5] Nicod deplores the lack of taste attested by its repertory and the negative influence that its musicians and their conductor, "who played the violin reasonably well," had on those of their Ethiopian peers for whom Nicod himself was responsible.[6] Kevork Nalbandian, the royal brass band's conductor, reports in handwritten autobiographical notes that he had observed that only six of the forty children had an adequate command of instrumental music on their arrival in Ethiopia. Once there, the forty children and their conductor had to wait five or six months for a complete set of musical instruments, which came, perhaps, from France.[7] Intense rehearsals were required to bring this first official Ethiopian orchestra up to snuff. The brass band's conductor wrote, however, in a letter to the AGBU's Central Council posted shortly after his September 26, 1924, arrival in Addis Abeba together with the children, that

> the day after our arrival, His Highness Crown Prince Ras Tafari, surrounded by his ministers, received the orphans in his palace, where they stood in front of him and played a military march. His Majesty the Prince addressed the following words to them, among others: "You are my children; do not ever worry about anything; I shall watch over you as if you were my own children."[8]

Kevork Nalbandian also affirmed that, on October 2, the children were invited to a banquet in the palace, where "Her Highness the Princess" [Mänän] had received them and been so good as to sit down beside them "for a period of five minutes." "Although the instruments had not yet arrived," he added, "we performed twice with the few instruments we had to hand, eliciting the Ethiopian people's enthusiasm and joy."[9] This much suffices to give purchase to both the myth of the infant musical prodigies and that of their adoption by the king and queen of Ethiopia. The event, about which there is little information, is, consequently, all the more malleable, and can be invested with very different meanings, depending on the interests at stake. From this point on, descendants of the Armenian immigration in Ethiopia will hold the *arba lejoch* up as a sort of emblem, presenting their arrival as "a kind of adoption" and "the proof" that Täfäri was "the Armenians' friend."[10]

In the chronicle of Zäwditu, the reference to the "forty Armenian orphans who had lost mother and father and whom His Highness the Crown Prince had brought to Jerusalem" highlights the Christian charity of the crown prince, protector of the Church and the weak.[11] This reading of the event has triumphed on the many internet sites dedicated to glorifying Haile Selassie, be they the work of people nostalgic for the Ethiopian imperial regime, of fans of reggae, or of Rastafarians convinced of the divinity of the last emperor of Ethiopia, the incarnation of a liberated Africa.

Jerusalem is, obviously, a place that is particularly conducive to reconstructions. The ideological background to Täfäri's 1924 visit, a veritable return to the sources of an Ethiopian monarchy that claimed the heritage of King Solomon and the Queen of Sheba, is not without bearing on the idealization of the "adoption." There is a round number of orphans, the easier to remember in that it echoes a multitude of Biblical and hagiographical references: the forty days Jesus spent in the wilderness, Lent, the Forty Martyrs, and so on. This Christian reading of the event offers an edifying illustration of the Black sovereign's generosity. The good King Gaspar of the Nativity is not far to seek.

In the collective autobiography, the idea of adoption comes into view in a reconstructed dialogue between *Ras* Täfäri and the patriarch of the Armenians of Jerusalem, Yeghishe Tourian:

"Father, who are these children?" He [the Patriarch] says, "They are children saved from the Turkish genocide. We are educating them. They are happy to meet you." He [Täfäri] says, "Would you let me take these children to Ethiopia?" He [the Patriarch] says, "yes." So the Emperor [sic] says right away, "organize everything; [while] I travel to France, take these children to Ethiopia." (Narrative 24, § 1)

The narration is quite elliptical here. It limits itself to suggesting Täfäri's tender feelings and does not trouble itself with details or precise historical information, although Avedis Terzian is usually at pains to include both when he recounts the founding heroes' exploits. It is as if the young musicians' tender age led him to simplify the narrative: "The forty children reach Addis Abeba. They're lodged in a palace where there's a tied-up lion. Poor children!" (Narrative 1, § 29). Forty beds had been laid out in an outbuilding of the palace with a dirt floor, according to a number of matching accounts, twenty on each side of the big room that was to serve them as a dormitory.[12] One is immediately reminded of the beds of Snow White's Seven Dwarfs, or those of Tom Thumb and his brothers, lined up opposite the seven little beds of the Ogre's daughters. Emperor Haile Selassie is supposed to have rewarded each musician with a villa on a tract of land in his capital city located not far from the present-day site of the Ghion Hotel, on the very spot where, formerly, a residence of *Lej* Iyasu's stood (Narrative 24, § 9). Another version has it that the emperor only gave the orphans the land, on which they built their villas themselves, using their own savings.[13] The Armenians' memory, propping itself up on narrative procedures related to those used in folktales and fairy tales, strives to euphemize events. Yet the Negus's brass band was not created without regard for material considerations.

The patriarchate and AGBU had a clearly perceived interest in accepting *Ras* Täfäri's suggestion. For the Araradian orphanage (Figure 6.1), which had been established within the perimeter of Saint James' Armenian monastery in Jerusalem, was too small to accommodate the 816 boys and girls whom the English had brought from the camp of Baquba in Mesopotamia in February 1922. The orphanage appeared to be a potential source of epidemics. Six lethal cases were recorded in the first four months after it opened. It was this overcrowding that had led to the July 1922 creation of an orphanage reserved for girls, the Vasburagan, located outside the walls of the monastery and the old city. In the meantime, the AGBU arranged to send many of the orphans to other reception centers in Soviet Armenia, Aleppo, and Beirut.[14] The AGBU's correspondence clearly shows that the forty young orphans' departure

Figure 6.1 The brass band of the Araradian Orphanage in Jerusalem, around 1923.
Source: Bibliothèque Nubar de l'UGAB, Paris.

for Ethiopia was motivated by the same concern, and that it had been the object of veritable "negotiations" and "an acknowledged agreement with representatives of His Highness Ras Tafari."[15] This agreement made provisions for the orphans' upkeep in Ethiopia. Shortly after the contract was signed, Täfäri let the patriarch know that he refused to provide for the orphans' material needs from June 1924 on and considered himself under an obligation to do so only as of October 1, that is, from the moment the orphans actually arrived in Ethiopia. He also made it clear that he refused to pay the travel costs of the family of the Armenian priest who had been chosen to accompany the children to Ethiopia.[16] According to Nicod, "the Negus allocated each of them an allowance of fifteen thalers monthly" and "provided the instruments" as well as "the costume of navy blue wool cloth" that would serve them as a uniform. The salary granted them was not insubstantial for work that, according to him, was limited to providing the music during the festival of the Discovery of the Cross (*Mäsqäl*) once a year in September, "and to very rare official performances," when "the average Abyssinian lives perfectly well on six thalers."[17] This salary came to thirty-five thalers monthly, according to the Armenian sources.[18] It seems, however, that the musicians were not entirely satisfied by their salary: "They thought that they could profit from the situation created by the approaching coronation festivities, judging that it was the right moment to ask for a raise, but the Negus refused outright, something that led to the dissolution of this group in 1929."[19] A former member of the brass band affirms that the orphans performed, to their disappointment, much more often than they had initially been given to understand: "They had told us that we would march out ahead of the Queen on her way to the church with the orchestra only on religious holidays, but, for the Ethiopians, every day is a religious holiday, and, every day, in the mud, we brought the Queen or the heir to the throne to church and then to the palace."[20] It is also possible that the Armenians' salaries, which seemed relatively attractive on paper, were not paid regularly, a recurrent problem for the Ethiopian monarchy's servants in this period. The signed contract officially engaged the musicians for only four full years, that is, until July 31, 1928. The brass band was bound by no contractual obligation after this date, although it continued to perform for some time thereafter, until 1929.[21]

Although Kevork Nalbandian writes about the "superb reception" that the Ethiopian government and the Armenian community in Djibouti and Dire Dawa gave the group,[22] Mardiros Vagharshagian evokes, rather, the children's disappointment after their arrival in Djibouti, where they had to wait several days under a blazing sun, without immediately finding "the new work and new instruments" that had been promised them. In Dire Dawa, to which they traveled by train, they did not receive, according to Vagharshagian, the reception that they had a right to expect from their compatriots: "There were many Armenians who simply waved to us and then went their way." They had to walk in the rain for a long time after their arrival, in the cold and the mud, before reaching the crown prince's residence, where the meal they were served was too spicy: "But what could we do? We ate it, our mouths on fire." The orphans even complained about the new conductor who had accompanied them from Port Said, maestro Kevork Nalbandian.[23]

A clause in the contract stipulated that the adolescents would be given an opportunity to learn a trade in the Ethiopian government's workshops during their stay.[24] It seems, however, that this promise was not kept. On the strength of a report from "Ethiopia's Armenian priest," the AGBU committee and Patriarch Tourian expressed their alarm over the fact that "the forty orphans in our Jerusalem orphanage's brass band, who were transferred to Abyssinia at the request of H. H. Prince Tafari," found themselves, a year after their arrival, "in a deplorable situation as a result of the Queen of Ethiopia's [Empress Zäwditu's] refusal to ratify the contract concluded between the Prince and the patriarch of Jerusalem." The situation was so bad that the patriarch suggested sending the children to Soviet Armenia "in order to put an end to this situation and save the orphans from inevitable degeneration." Such an operation was, however, hypothetical, for the government of the Soviet Socialist Republic of Armenia demanded payment of one hundred dollars for each orphan thus "repatriated." The AGBU Council deemed that it did not have the means to cover this expense in addition to travel costs and suggested "turning to Prince [Täfäri] and asking him to pay the costs of these orphans' travel to Armenia as compensation for his abrogation of the contract that required him to provide these orphans' upkeep."[25] The Ethiopian government, however, was clearly unresponsive to the Armenian request: five months later, the AGBU Council took anxious note of reports from "compatriots returning from Ethiopia" who described "the situation of these unfortunate orphans in very somber terms." The reports indicated that "the majority of these adolescents" had "contracted venereal diseases" or would in the very near future, "given local conditions." Under these circumstances, the AGBU Council gave up the idea "of entreating the government of Armenia to open its doors to these adolescents."[26] After the brass band's dissolution, most of the *arba lejoch* found themselves without employment or any qualifications other than their ability to sing and play an instrument.[27]

The Success of a Myth: Chronicles of an Announced Adoption

The myth of the adoption of the forty orphans "took hold," notwithstanding its many improbable features, because it accorded with the way the Armenians' relationship to the Ethiopians was experienced or perceived, in both Jerusalem and Addis Abeba, as if it were simply the logical consequence of a set of events that heralded it.

In Jerusalem, the adoption of the forty orphans by the king of Ethiopia took its place in the long-standing relation of reciprocity between the Ethiopian and Armenian Christian communities. The Ethiopians benefited from a special authorization from the Armenian patriarch to celebrate mass on Pentecost in the Armenian church of the Holy Savior on the hill of Zion. It remained in effect until the 1948 war and the transformation of this part of the city into an Israeli military zone. On several occasions, Ethiopian doormen stood guard at the entry to the Armenian monastery. Without going back to the ancient donations of food still customary in the nineteenth century,[28] let us note that the Armenian patriarchate occasionally distributed financial aid to an Ethiopian monastic community that was particularly enfeebled after the 1974 revolution.[29] The traces left by these events are added, like pieces of a puzzle, to a collective memory of the subordination of the Ethiopian monks to the Armenian patriarchate. They make it plausible that the orphans were adopted as recompense for the assistance and protection that the Armenians are said to have extended the Ethiopians in the Holy Places from time immemorial—as if the adoption were the Armenians' just reward.[30] This is perhaps how we should interpret the gift of five sacks of coffee and fifty Egyptian pounds that Täfäri made during his visit to the Armenian monastery of Jerusalem,[31] as well as the honors he conferred on Patriarch Tourian

> on behalf of her Majesty, Empress Ouazerou Ouditou [Wäyzäro Zäwditu], by presenting Us with a beautiful Cross and decorating Us with the insignia of the Great Sash of the Order of the Star of Ethiopia [...]. This mark of high esteem conferred on Us reflects on the whole Armenian Nation, which feels honored, in the Person of its Spiritual Head, and shall always stand ready to attest, as in the past, its profound sympathy with, and boundless attachment to, the Glorious Empire of Ethiopia, where several of its children are living under the tutelary aegis of Your Imperial Dynasty, and display the greatest possible devotion to Your Imperial Highness.[32]

In Addis Abeba, the myth of the adoption of the forty orphans was grafted onto a Grand Narrative based on the idea of the Ethiopian sovereigns' friendship for the Armenians. Beginning with his first narrative, Avedis Terzian seized on it as evidence that, "of all the foreign peoples, we're the closest to the Ethiopian people" (Narrative 1, § 29). The immigrants' descendants found it advantageous to link the creation of the royal brass band to the collective epic's most glorious episodes, marked by the figures of the founding heroes.

Figure 6.2 The forty children before their departure for Ethiopia, in front of the entrance to Saint James Armenian Cathedral in Jerusalem, 1924.

Source: Bibliothèque Nubar de l'UGAB, Paris.

Figure 6.3 Crown Princess Mänän visiting Patriarch Yeghishe Tourian in Saint James Armenian Monastery in Jerusalem, accompanied by Araxi Yazedjian, 1923.

Source: Marcerou collection.

Figure 6.4 Crown Princess Mänän and Archbishop Papken Guleserian (center) in Jerusalem, accompanied by Araxi Yazedjian (on the right).

Source: Album of Mushegh Terzian, collection of the Armenian Community in Ethiopia.

Once it had become the stuff of epic, the *arba lejoch*'s adventure, of which the Ethiopian national anthem composed by Kevork Nalbandian served as a permanent reminder down to the 1974 revolution, seems to have resisted ending with the brass band's dissolution. The collective memory took pains to provide it with a sequel perpetuating the central idea of the Grand Narrative: the brass band of Addis Abeba's police force, the *arada zäbäña*, made up of children performing under the baton of Garabed Hakalmazian,[33] who had earlier been one of the forty orphans himself (Figure 6.5). After the royal brass band's conductor, Kevork Nalbandian, called an end to his career as a musician around 1949,[34] his nephew Nerses Nalbandian, today regarded as one of the greatest Ethiopian musicians of his time, appears as the upholder of the tradition of this original musical epic.[35]

The myth of the adoption of the forty orphans thrived on Ethiopia's fertile soil, where the conviction of the immigrants', and their descendants', alliance with the Ethiopian sovereigns had already struck deep roots. Thus the transmission, through narratives or photographs, of the memory of the forty orphans seems simply to be intended as the prolongation of the Grand Narrative inaugurated with the triptych of the founding heroes, Sarkis Terzian's conquest of Harar, the goldsmith Dikran Ebeyan's crowns, and the anecdotes and legends connected with the past of the Armenian presence in the imperial palace. In this perspective, the adoption of the forty orphans is merely another chapter in a very old history. Like the memory of the Cévennes

Figure 6.5 The brass band of the *arada zäbäñña*, Addis Abeba's police force, and its conductor Garabed Hakalmazian.

Source: Hayg Patapan, Արդի Եթովպիա եւ Հայ գաղութը [Modern Ethiopia and the Armenian colony], Venice, Saint Lazarus Printing Press, 1930, p. 267.

region, which "continues to recount the War of the Camisards, even when it is not the subject of discussion,"[36] the Armenian memory continues to elaborate on the theme of the friendship of kings, the time of "Menelik's Armenians," by way of the brass band. Driven out of Turkey, where their relatives were massacred, but welcomed with open arms by the king of Ethiopia, the forty orphans are adopted in the way that Menelik seems to have prophesied when he urged Abdülhamid to send him all the Armenians he no longer wanted (Narrative 1, § 11).

The Federating Virtues of a Belated Pantheonization

The Grand Narrative of the Armenian emigration to Ethiopia makes Arabkir, in Turkey, the original homeland, and Harar, in Ethiopia, the cradle of a newly founded collective life. The cult of the founding heroes coincides with this geography of the past, with names as famous as Kevork and Sarkis Terzian, Pilibbos Kherbekian, or Levon Yazedjian. Thus "it is possible to say that Ethiopia's Armenian colony was founded with the *Arabkertsi*.[37] But, beginning with the 1908 constitution and after the World War, the Armenian colony was made bigger by Armenians from many different localities."[38] As the collective autobiography notes: "After the genocide, they came from Beirut, from Syria. [...] Armenians from the South who had escaped to Syria and southern Armenia, not to the North. [...] There are many from Ayntab. The people from Ayntab overtook those from Arabkir later on" (Narrative 2, § 6).

Radical Transformations in the Armenian Presence in Ethiopia after the Great War

The way in which the forty orphans were inscribed in the collective memory seems to account, negatively, for the radical transformations that the small Armenian population of Ethiopia underwent after the Great War, when it abruptly rose from one 150 or 200 to, roughly, over 1,000. According to the registers of Addis Abeba's Armenian church, only four of the years between 1923 and 1963 saw fewer than ten births. The most fertile years (1927, 1931, 1935, 1938, and 1946) each saw over twenty births. The average number of births reached 15,5 annually between 1923 and 1935. Indications are that the Armenian presence attained its apogee in the mid-1930s. Increasing in size, it also changed its aspect with the fanning out of the places of origin of the immigrants, who were, from now on, divided by profound cultural differences. Arabkir (in the Harput/Kharpert *vilayet*) and Ayntab (in the Adana *vilayet*) are the two poles around which the memory of the very diverse migratory trajectories is organized.

About half the sixty-four Armenians known to have been living in Harar around 1910 came from Arabkir.[39] The same holds for 40 percent of the eighty-four Armenians present in Addis Abeba, according to a count made by the French legation in 1908.[40]

After the genocide, however, the second wave of Armenian emigration to Ethiopia displays a shift toward the south, with the increasing importance of the *vilayets* of Adana (Cilicia) and Aleppo. Natives of Ayntab were the most heavily represented in this group. After the Second World War, Armenian immigration from the traditional Turkish localities disappears in favor of new centers, mainly Syria, Lebanon, and Palestine.[41]

Thus the Armenian population in Ethiopia, although it seemed nondescript to outside observers, comprised, from the 1920s on, a mosaic of extremely diverse regions. Avedis Terzian acknowledges that "groups were created"; they brought these people from very different localities and regions together on the basis of their cultural affinities, social level, dialects, culinary habits, family networks, and parochial spirit:

> There were those who were more capable, better educated, more advanced. You couldn't compare those who came from a big city like Istanbul or Smyrna with the villagers. So there was all that. But gradually, since there were marriages, they married among themselves. (Narrative 2, § 8)

The register of marriages has virtually nothing to say on this subject, since it mentions the birthplace of only a small percentage of the women who married before 1941. The register of births, in contrast, shows that, for Armenian couples married in Ethiopia, unions between people from different localities and regions became the rule only slowly. In more than 40 percent of the ninety-seven couples examined who had children between 1900 and 1941, the parents were natives of the same or neighboring localities.

A good one-third involved people born in the same city in Turkey. This propensity was especially pronounced among *Ayntabtsi*. Thus the effacement of regional demarcations by marriage was still relatively slight in this period. A mere 27 percent of these couples comprised individuals from different regions in Turkey. This reticence to contract "mixed marriages" reflects divisions stemming from the radical transformation of the internal social composition of the Armenian population in Ethiopia in the interwar period. The pantheonization of the forty orphans, whose arrival coincided with this period of transformations, shows how memory attenuated these antagonisms.

Restoring Order Amid Disorder, Reconciling Ayntab and Arabkir

According to Maurice Halbwachs, the birth of Jesus was put in Bethlehem, like King David's, because, at the time the Gospels were written, when the Jews of Palestine were divided as to whether he was truly the Messiah, "it seems that Christian memory could only have taken root in Jewish memory."[42] The memory of the second phase of the Armenian immigration to Ethiopia was similarly grafted onto the memory of its first phase, that of "Menelik's Armenians." Inscribing the *arba lejoch* in the Grand Narrative made it possible to integrate families who did not necessarily consider this narrative theirs, because they had only just settled in Ethiopia.

The heroes making up the pantheon of the Armenians of Ethiopia all belong to the first generation of the immigration, that is, to Menelik's reign. With the end of the golden age, the collective autobiography presents the 1920s as a time of "fierce struggles" among the Armenians (Narrative 4, § 1). Regional antagonisms seem to have intersected with, and reinforced, partisan divisions between supporters of the Armenian Revolutionary Federation (A.R.F. or *Tashnagtsutiun*), hostile to Armenia's Sovietization, and supporters of the conservative *Ramgavar* party, who chose to accommodate themselves to it. Reflecting this division, there were two Armenian elementary schools. One was the Ararat school, built by the engineer Krikor Howyan and opened in 1918 on the premises of the small Surp Asdvadzadzin (Holy Mother of God) chapel, where a nursery school had existed since 1915.[43] The other, named after the inventors of the Armenian alphabet, was the Sahak Mesrop School, responsible for some forty schoolchildren. Nothing justified the parallel existence of these two schools, apart from the fierce opposition between *Tashnags* and *Ramgavars*.[44] The schools did not merge until 1928.

These internal divisions are evoked in the collective autobiography to explain the existence of Armenian collaborators under the 1936–41 Italian occupation, which contradicts the theme of the friendship of kings:

> These were elements who weren't attuned to Ethiopian life. They were the latest arrivals, who had nothing but making a fortune in mind. So they had no sympathy for the Ethiopians. So they were encouraged, a few of them became spies. Others claimed to be Fascists. But not many. (Narrative 2, § 13)

In this discourse of a son of the first wave of *Arabkertsi* immigrants, it is easy to recognize, among these "latest arrivals," natives of the Ayntab area, or, again, of

Syria and Lebanon, who provided the largest contingents in the late phases. The belated pantheonization of the *arba lejoch* made it possible to unite, discursively, this immigration's pre-Menelikian cohort and its post-Menelikian cohort, and thus to overcome the heterogeneity characteristic of the immigrants' trajectories. This process may have begun at the very beginning of the 1930s, just after the dissolution of the royal brass band, as is attested by a photomontage that probably dates from this period and already has a commemorative character (6.6). For the Armenian population now increasingly witnessed marriages between people from different cities or provinces of the former Ottoman Empire. Marriages involving one and sometimes two people born in Ethiopia had represented one-third of the couples who had children between 1900 and 1941. Thereafter, they became largely predominant, because, from the mid-1920s on, the number of births outside Ethiopia was negligible. The peak of Armenian immigration had passed. Year by year, conditions increasingly encouraged the immigrants' descendants to recast their past in a single mold.

Figure 6.6 Photomontage commemorating the royal brass band, with medallions of Kevork Nalbandian and *Negus* Täfäri, 1929.

Source: Bibliothèque Nubar de l'UGAB, Paris.

We should not underestimate the fact that the pantheonization of the royal brass band made it possible to incorporate the genocide—the reason that the "forty children" were also the "forty orphans"—in the Grand Narrative of the Armenian immigration in Ethiopia. This happened, for example, when Avedis Terzian affirmed that the children had refused to play Turkey's national anthem at the imperial coronation, despite the emperor's insistence and the intervention of his Armenian secretary Abraham Koeurhadjian:

> The children say no. So the Emperor calls the leading grandees [...]. All the grandees say, "no! The children shouldn't play [it]!" So the *Turkish March* wasn't played [...] The Ethiopian grandees, all together, say, "the children are right." [...] Because they say, "How can you ask a child to play the march of his father's murderer?" (Narrative 24, § 5)

It is not certain that the children's refusal to play the *Turkish March* would have been so prominently foregrounded before 1930, when the memory of the massacres of the Great War had not undergone the politicization that characterizes it today. By opening the Armenian Grand Narrative in Ethiopia up to the set of themes associated with the genocide, the Armenians' memory made it possible to unite those whose relatives had not experienced the deportation and reconstructed their past with reference to the friendship of kings alone, and those whose families came to Ethiopia only after the Great War. Including the orphans in the collective pantheon wrote a new chapter in the story of the friendship between the Armenians and the kings of Ethiopia and performed a double function for the use of descendants of the two successive phases of the Armenian immigration. To the heirs of the first phase, the "Old-timers," it offered an unhoped-for extension of their Grand Narrative, all of whose founding events and heroes harked back to a period closed off with the end of Menelik's reign. It reaffirmed the original Covenant concluded with the kings of Ethiopia. To the descendants of the second phase, the "Newcomers," pantheonization of the *arba lejoch* made it possible to forge an artificial link to the glorious past of "Menelik's Armenians" and thus to lay claim to part of the heritage. Descendants of the immigrants of the final period could, in their turn, take pride in a connection established with the sovereign in the persons of Crown Prince Täfäri and Empress Zäwditu, who together replaced the figure of Menelik. It is not insignificant that the participation of several of the orphans in the war with the Italians, in 1935–36, notably as drivers of the trucks that transported the Ethiopian army's arms and provisions to the front, remained engraved in the collective memory: "Some of them took part in the war. There was even a death, on the southern front, he lies buried in Jijiga. [...] His name is Papken Babayan"[45] (Narrative 24, § 9). By dying for Ethiopia, this former member of the brass band appears as someone who sustains the tradition of the Armenians devotion to their hostland as celebrated in the collective memory by way of the association of Sarkis Terzian's name with that of the battle of Adwa. Let us note, as well, that the family of Täfäri's master musician, the brass band's conductor, Kevork Nalbandian, who composed Ethiopia's national anthem and the *March Täfäri*, was a native of Ayntab. Thus, with this new chapter of the Armenian Grand Narrative, Ayntab succeeds Arabkir not just in the immigrants' demography but also in their pantheon. The *Ayntabtsi*, in their turn, enter into the service of Täfäri, now Emperor Haile Selassie, as Levon Yazedjian, a famous *Arabkertsi*, did during the affair of *Lej* Iyasu's true false portrait. They themselves become servants of *Ras* Mäkonnen's son, as if the friendship that his son maintained with the founding hero Sarkis Terzian and other famous *Arabkertsi* prefigured what happened in 1924. It can thus be seen how the *Ayntabtsi*, despite their belated arrival in the country, succeeded in appropriating for themselves, as Armenians, Menelik's putative love for the Armenians, as if the *Arabkertsis*' arrival, three or four decades earlier, had simply paved the way for their own. The immigrants of the second wave succeeded in making a place for themselves in the ideal Grand Narrative forged by their predecessors, as if they had felt the need to come to resemble them by identifying with the founding myths and providing them with a sequel. Like the other founding myths, which invest individual trajectories with a collective meaning, the epic of the *arba lejoch* helps create a sense of "us" amid disparity.

This study of a collective memory was carried out on the basis of material to which I would not necessarily have had access if I had undertaken my research a few years later. I had to be present at the right moment, but also to be accepted, to enter a circle of trust, to acquire the capacity to measure the social resonance and historic interest of the spoken narratives. There was not, once again, a "tradition" ready to be collected by an "ethnographer on his way through."[46] The material comprising the collective autobiography, which is so original and so rich, emerged thanks only to a profound effort of "coproduction" with Avedis Terzian. My fieldwork thus had a decisive influence on the orientation of my investigation. Analysis of memory as a reconstruction of the past shows that the Ethiopian monarchy's social discourse about the Armenians did not make a difference only on the surface of things. The theme of the friendship of kings was not merely a system of signs and beliefs. As the "eminent form" of the sedentarization of a collective memory, it represents, to borrow Durkheim's phrase about religious life, "the epitome of collective life,"[47] which is necessarily founded, beyond discourse, on an objectivizable social reality. This reality is that of a space of interstitial sociabilities that puts the Armenians of Ethiopia halfway between the indigenous and the foreign. It finds verification not just in the immigrants' lived experience but, equally, in the materiality of their daily lives, and even in the influence that collective representations can have on it.

Part 3

The Sedimentation of the Ungraspable

7

From Threshold to Interstice: A Space of Decompartmentalized Sociabilities

"Among the 60,000 inhabitants" of Addis Abeba, an American wrote in the 1920s, "are large numbers of Levantines, Armenians, Greeks and Syrians, as well as Indian and yellow-skinned Yemenese, but they are superimposed on the native life and remain detached from it, an excrescence, though they control the business and industry of the capital. Were they swept away tomorrow, the essential Addis would be unchanged."[1] Henry de Monfreid, never loath to fall back on cliche, proffers no brighter image of these "Levantines who have wormed their way into the country":

> Abyssinia includes a number of them. [...] They are perfectly adapted parasites: they are invisible, they are no bother, they can be crushed from time to time, when they become overly invasive, but they are always there; they are part of the life of the country.[2]

By no means confined to one segment of society, contrary to what the concept of "middlemen minorities"[3] tends to suggest, the Armenian immigrants and their descendants had access to a broad spectrum of sociabilities from the first half of the twentieth century on. Together with the Greeks, Indians, and Arabs, they appeared to benefit from "an enviable situation in Ethiopia,"[4] precisely because they were confined to neither a restricted segment of society nor a rigid liminality. The Armenian immigrants' places of residence, the evolution of the occupational profiles observable among their descendants, and also their burial practices contradict the notion that Ethiopian society was structurally closed to foreigners.[5]

The Diversity of Places of Residence and the Blossoming of Family Life

The Armenians in Harar, beginning in the 1880s, lived side-by-side with indigenous Ethiopians, not segregated from them. Although foreigners were not allowed to settle outside the city walls,[6] Greek and Armenian immigrants owned and cultivated land there. An example is provided by a certain Artin, nicknamed Shopi Artin,[7] who owned and operated a coffee plantation located forty-five minutes from Harar. He was "a very simple man, an Armenian by birth" who "spoke no European language," had "lived for a long time in Egypt, and has been residing here for fifteen years," that is, since 1892, with his wife. "He and his wife are weavers by trade. They work for Menelik and Ras Makonnen. He obtained his concession from Ras Makonnen." Yesayi Garikian is another example: he was a man "with considerable influence and experience" who was "fluent in Armenian, Turkish, Arabic, and French" and owned a banana plantation half an hour from Harar's city walls, where he set up a tannery in 1904.[8]

The Armenian immigrants settled in Harar to stay, with their families, despite the fact that "this wretched town that the Amhara have turned into a cesspool" seemed to have little to offer: it was a "strangely twisting and turning" city that was "cluttered up and full of bumps and potholes," with rather unattractive, "gloomy" houses that made it look like "a pile of troglodytic habitations."[9] Yet Greeks and Armenians "seem to have the power of flourishing in strange places."[10] Harar had a population of 30,000 to 40,000 at the time, but the number of foreigners living there year-round was very low because of the growth of Addis Abeba and Dire Dawa. The Terzian, Yazedjian, Kherbekian, Semerjibashian, Yerzingatsian, and Kasabian families, who had come from Arabkir in the late 1890s, were still living there early in the twentieth century.[11] Yesayi Garikian's old mother went with her to Harar, where the climate was better than in Djibouti or Aden. She died there in 1906.[12] Marriages were contracted between Armenian immigrants and Harari women. Armenag Zamanian, a native of Tamzara (near Shabin Karahisar, in the *vilayet* of Sivas in Turkey) married a woman who was born in Harar, say the Armenian registers, without mentioning her family name; her Armenian forename, Srpuhi, was probably given her when she married. Their children had Armenian forenames. Their oldest son, Menagar Zamanian, came into the world in Harar in 1894. His birth was followed by those, also in Harar, of their daughters Satenig and Hranush, in 1905 and 1912, and of their second son, Hrand, in 1908. The Armenians did not hesitate to undertake a search for a bride in their home towns in Turkey in response to the request of a brother or cousin who had come to Ethiopia as a pioneer. Thus Stepan Yazedjian arranged a marriage between his sister Vartuhi, who was still living in Arabkir, and his employer, Sarkis Terzian. Collating the registers, which, to be sure, are incomplete, reveals that there was at least one Armenian birth in Harar in 1903, another in 1904,[13] two in 1905,[14] at least two in 1909, one in 1910, two in 1912, and five between 1913 and 1916.[15] The education of some of the children was taken in hand by French Catholic missionaries established in Harar since the late nineteenth century, who ran a school for boys in which Ethiopian children were in the majority and the rare white children were, around 1900, mainly sons of Armenian immigrants, such as Minas and Karekin Kherbekian, Vahan Kalustian, and Vahram Terzian. In the same period, the nuns associated with the mission "opened a little school for Abyssinian, Harari, and Armenian girls" that was already in operation around 1901.[16] Thus the children of Armenian immigrants mixed with indigenous youth; they, too, went barefoot, and all the children sat at the same school desks. The Armenian women, who remained in Harar longer than their husbands did, learned to speak Harari before moving to Addis Abeba.

This early family life in Ethiopia is a strikingly original feature of the Armenian immigration. The sources suggest that, in 1910, only some fifteen of Ethiopia's three hundred Greeks, who represented the country's biggest European population, were women. The result was a large number of Greek-Ethiopian mixed-races, but also the unruliness of a population of young, unmarried men. The immigration of their families to Ethiopia, which took place relatively late, began in the period 1910–20.[17] Dr. Mérab says of the Armenians that "their marriages with indigenous Ethiopians are much more rare" than in the case of the Greeks: "There are scarcely a dozen mixed-races; the reason is that most are here with their wives and children, a result of their emigrations during the Armenocidal Sultan's reign."[18] At the end of Menelik's reign, Addis Abeba's Armenian population was becoming increasingly younger and female. Leaving aside children born in Harar whose parents had only recently moved to the capital and collating registers and epitaphs indicates that there were at least fifty-two Armenian births in Addis Abeba, in thirty-one different households, between 1890 and 1915. The birthrate increased from 1907 on, when the families in Harar began to migrate to the capital for good. From 1907 to 1915, there were forty-five births; there was not a single year without a birth. The most fertile years were 1909 (twelve births) and 1911, 1912, and 1915 (six births each year). Taking all this data into account (some thirty mothers and some forty births, at a minimum) and collating it with that provided by the French legation in 1908 (eighty-four adult males), we can advance the solid estimate that the capital's Armenian population was between 150 and 200 at the end of Menelik's reign. The small Armenian colony, with the high percentage of children characterizing it (between one-quarter and one-third of the whole), distinguished itself even more sharply than the colony in Harar from the Greek population and the bulk of the foreign population.

No kind of spatial or residential confinement of foreigners is observable in this period, in contrast to the situation of racial segregation that would be created in the big Ethiopian cities under the 1936–41 Italian occupation. It was, nonetheless, possible to identify an Armenian neighborhood in the nascent capital from Menelik's reign on: "The Armenians, a colony that is still growing and that is, perhaps, the most populous, have formed an entire neighborhood in Addis Abeba, known as the Armenian quarter." It was originally sprinkled with Abyssinian huts, which were replaced by wood cabins, and with the first stores selling liqueurs, weapons, and hardware; there followed stone-built houses "with eucalyptus groves and big vegetable gardens and paddocks." This "quarter," however, was by no means an enclave. Its houses "formed a veritable village, with a kind of Siberian cabin with a pointed roof, built, perhaps, in the intention of turning it into a church, but subsequently adapted to serve as a habitation."[19] This was the residence of the family of Krikorios Boghossian, one of Menelik's first servants, whose estate—two very beautiful houses set in a garden, with a thatched roof in one case and a wooden roof in the other—was handed down to his heirs. In the interwar period, the Kevorkoff school and the Ararat club were erected here, followed by Addis Abeba's Armenian church. This was, originally, land located on a hill that Menelik handed down to *Ras* Mäkonnen, the governor of Harar. The hill stood to the north of the bridge known as "Mäkonnen" that is located in the present-day Piazza neighborhood and extended as far as *Abunä* Matēwos's residence, today the seat of the Ethiopian patriarchate, near Amist Kilo. The collective autobiography associates the choice of this place of residence with a reaffirmation of allegiance to *Ras* Mäkonnen,

Menelik's favorite and Haile Selassie's father, about whom Patapan already claimed in his day that he had won "the Armenians' love and sympathy":[20] "We think that the Armenians who came from Harar came to settle in the neighborhood belonging to Harar's governor" (Narrative 3, § 2), beginning, doubtless, in 1905. A description of the capital made a few years later singles out only three big complexes: the business district, lying between the bank and the church of Saint George (Giyorgis); the quarter of the European legations; and "the Armenians' quarter, surrounded by greenery, with the house of Abuna Matheàs [Abunä Matēwos]."[21] The Armenian quarter appears on an Italian map of this period, and also on a plan of the city drawn up by the Ethiopian government's engineer, Khachig Papazian, in 1931.[22] No comparable neighborhood has been identified or indicated for either the Greeks or the Indians in this period, although they seem to have been more numerous than the Armenians. Despite its name, this neighborhood was never populated by Armenian immigrants alone. A majority of its inhabitants were doubtless Ethiopians.

In the 1920s and 1930s, Greeks and Armenians seem to have been everywhere, even in the country's most out-of-the-way localities. They were often among the first people that European travelers encountered, on the Red Sea or in Ethiopian border towns.[23] The Greeks, above all, attracted notice, because they were more numerous and were present, in small groups, in every small town or crossroads of any importance: in Addis Aläm, for example, in the vicinity of the capital; in the localities of southern Ethiopia, such as Jimma; near the Sudanese borders in the southwest, in Burē, Gorē, Dembidollo (Sayo), or Gambēla, despite the isolation, the insalubrity of the climate, and the risks of contracting malaria there; in northern Ethiopia, near the Eritrean border, in Adwa or Addi Ugri; and even in the villages and train stations that dotted the length of the railroad, such as Aqaqi, Mojo, Awash, Dawenlē, or Afdäm.[24] The sources indicate that there were, in the province of Jimma in the mid-1930s, six Armenian firms (Seferian, Kevorkian, Ohan Israelian, Kegham Israelian, Atsyan, Papazian), nine Greek firms, and many Indian and Arab firms, but no European company among the fifty foreign businesses in existence. A total of ninety-seven foreigners had established themselves in this region, including twenty-six Greeks, twenty-three Indians, twenty-one Arabs, eight Italians, and seven Armenians. Of the ten foreign merchants in Jijiga, in the province of Harärgē, the most numerous were the Greeks, Indians, and Armenians (three). In Harar itself, "where there [were] few foreigners" after the railroad arrived in Dire Dawa, all the hotels were owned by Greeks, together with eleven of the sixteen commercial firms (three others were Armenian and one was Indian). In the city of Dire Dawa, twenty-three of the forty biggest merchants were Greek and five were Armenians. There was a significant Greek and Armenian presence even in the regions where the fewest foreigners lived. Thus, in Gorē, the capital of the province of Illubabor, there were only 40 foreigners out of a population of 25,000, among them a fairly large number of Greeks and a few Armenian and Syrian merchants, sometimes accompanied by their wives and children. The city's Ethiopian grade school, with some fifty schoolchildren, employed one Armenian and three Ethiopian teachers. Six of Gorē's twelve commercial firms were Greek, four were Armenian, and one was Syrian. Most were in the business of exporting coffee, and sometimes also imported various articles for the local population. The Selim Tabet (1912) and Bedushian (1915) companies were the first to establish themselves in the area. The small town of Burē (three thousand inhabitants, only fourteen of them foreigners) boasted four Greek commercial firms (established between 1926 and 1932) likewise specializing in the coffee trade. Also located in Burē were the agencies of firms in Gorē, such as Seferian & Co., whose agent was an Armenian, Rupen Vorperian. There were also a private Greek physician and four resident Greek families. The village of Mättu, the last station before Gorē on the road from Addis Abeba, counted fifteen foreigners among its one thousand inhabitants and nine commercial firms, all of them Greek. In several villages in the environs, the extremely rare foreigners were virtually all Greeks; the same holds for Gambēla, a river port in western Ethiopia near the Sudanese border, where the Seferian company and a few of its Greek competitors were the best represented. The same observations can be made about Yirga Aläm, in the Sidamo region; in Tigré, where "the rare foreigners, all Greeks, did the trading"; in Läqämtē and Dembidollo, in the Wällägga region; in the Wällamo region; and, finally, in Däsē, in the Wällo region, where Astrig Karabian, the widow of an Armenian immigrant, ran a movie theater and a cafe-restaurant.[25]

Transformations in the Armenians' Professional Profile

In the 1880s, according to Hayg Patapan, the Armenians were basically traders who imported arms and ammunition, silk, and linen, and exported local products such as ivory and wax. In a second phase, which seems to correspond, roughly, with the reign of Menelik II, the Armenians had acquired, according to Patapan, "an enviable position" in Ethiopia, since they had begun to open stores and engage in less primitive forms of trade, while also taking part in the creation of means of transportation for merchandise before the railroad was built. Finally, in a third phase, the proportion of commercial activities is supposed to have diminished, while that of "public and state employment"—that is, civil service and administrative posts——and "crafts"—that is, artisanal and technical activities—increased. "And, today [in 1930], it is an obvious fact that the Armenians, compared to foreign communities, hold the best place in the civil service."[26]

At over 52 percent, merchants heavily dominated the list of the eighty-four Armenians counted by the French legation in 1908. They represented only 22 percent of economically active Armenians in 1930, if Patapan's figures are accurate, and 30 percent in 1935, according to the directory of foreigners in the capital established by Zervos. Conversely, the proportion of craftsmen doubled, rising from 19 percent in 1908 to 36 or 37 percent in 1930–5. The register of births shows that the proportion of merchants, who predominated in 1920, sank steadily over the next twenty years. The proportion of artisans, markedly inferior to that of merchants in 1920 (30 percent as opposed to 47 percent), exceeded it from 1927 on. It remained higher until the early 1940s. Artisans accounted for a solid one-third of the ninety-seven fathers of families still economically active in 1934, as opposed to only one-quarter who were merchants. These transformations reflect the high social mobility of the Armenian immigrants and their descendants.

Transformations in One sector of Activity, Trade

Albeit on the decline, trade remained the immigrants' predominant sphere of activity; the petty retailers who represented the majority of merchants in 1908, however, comprised only around one out of three merchants twenty to twenty-five years later. In the same period, the proportion of those employed by commercial firms made up nearly 60 percent of the category of merchants. Armenian petty trade continued to meet the needs of foreign residents, but also those of the Ethiopian population, by way of sales of paper, perfume, shoes, clothing, locally produced umbrellas, blankets, woolens, foodstuffs, wines, alcoholic drinks and liqueurs, and so on. In the 1930s, however, the old stalls were replaced by real stores with evocative names, such as M. Matikian's "International Bazaar," Y. Eliazarian's and Hayg Tulumbajian's "Popular Grocery Store," Vache Tarpinian's "Economical Grocery Store," or Sarkis Kenajian's "Franco-Oriental Grocery Store."[27] Big, respected import-export firms were now thriving. The oldest were those owned by Matif Kevorkoff and Krikorios Boghossian (founded in 1895), Hayg Aynajian (1898), Yervant Hagopian (1901), Avedis Sevadjian (1909), Kevork Muradian (1912), Maksud Kassabian (1920), and Hrant Minassian (1924). These commercial firms had branches in all the country's big cities, such as the Kevorkoff and Minassian companies, present in Harar and Dire Dawa; the Israelian brothers' company and the Muradian company, established in both these cities and in Jimma as well; the Maksud Kassabian company, which had been founded in Aden before it established itself in Ethiopia, and which also had agencies in Zeila, Berbera, and Djibouti; the Boghossian company, which represented European automobile firms in Ethiopia; and the Hagopian company, an Ethiopian partner of German, Belgium, and French firms. Mention should also be made of the Behesnilian brothers, Samuel, Yeghia, and Rupen, each of whom had his private commercial firm.[28] These family enterprises helped structure the Ethiopian market by stimulating trade between the country's capital and its various regions.[29] Their proprietors and associates frequented European high society in Ethiopia, were often guests of the embassies, had seats on the Armenian colony's council, and were invited to official Ethiopian ceremonies and the celebrations of national holidays in the various legations. Some, such as Matig Kevorkoff, Mihran Muradian (based in Khartum, in Sudan),[30] and Hrant Minassian, were philanthropists who sponsored the construction of schools and churches. Matif Kevorkoff, a French citizen who had been established in Djibouti since 1896 and in Addis Abeba since the early 1900s, seems to have been the biggest Armenian merchant thanks to his very lucrative monopoly, granted to him in 1909 or 1910 by Menelik for a fifty-year period, on the import, manufacture, and distribution of cigarettes and tobacco throughout the Ethiopian Empire; he ran it together with a number of Armenian partners.[31] He was appointed representative of the ephemeral Republic of Armenia (1918–20) in Ethiopia after the Conference of Sèvres. His business career and his connections prefigured those of several big Armenian merchants in the interwar period, who cut a figure as notables, altogether unlike the petty merchants of Addis Abeba's and Harar's turn-of-the-century markets.

The Crumbling and the Renovation of the Armenian's Professional Profile

In all professional categories, the diversification of the Armenians' occupations is noteworthy. Occupations in trade aside, the Armenians engaged in eighteen different forms of economic activity in 1908, thirty-five in 1930, and twenty-nine in 1935, according to the sources at our disposal. Among the new professions, the best represented involved artisans (especially gunsmiths, cobblers, cabinetmakers, and chefs), but also petty manufacturers such as tanners, and the distinct category made up of chauffeurs and mechanics. The liberal professions (lawyers, architects, pharmacists, physicians, dentists, and veterinarians),[32] non-existent at the turn of the century, had made their appearance by the 1930s, but represented only 3 percent of the occupations indicated by Patapan, outside civil service jobs. A new professional group also emerged with the appearance of some fifteen teachers, at least three of whom had posts in the Täfäri Mäkonnen Lycée in 1930, while the rest worked in the Armenian school.

While occupations that had earlier been privileged tended to decline, the blossoming of new professions showed the immigrants' capacity to adapt to transformations of the local economy. Famously, Armenians in Ethiopia had since the late nineteenth century plied the goldsmith's trade, the most prestigious of the crafts. The proportion of goldsmiths declined, leveling out at between 12 and 14 percent of all Armenian artisans in the 1930s, although they had still comprised a quarter of the total in 1908.[33] In the same period, the metallurgical trades (tinplating, tinplate-making, ironworking, the blacksmith's trade) saw their relative share of the total increase, although it had been negligible at the turn of the century, with only one blacksmith per sixteen artisans in 1908, a proportion that rose to nearly one-sixth of all Armenian artisans after 1930. The Greeks (32 percent) and Armenians (24 percent) alone represented more than half of the 622 people on the list of Addis Abeba's merchants and independent businessmen drawn up by Zervos. They monopolized cafe-restaurants (eleven of sixteen were run by Greeks, the remaining five by Armenians),[34] grocery stores, smithies and hardware shops (four out of six), and tailor's shops (thirteen out of eighteen). Certain professions seem to have been uncontested Armenian specialties, such as tinplate-making (seven out of eight), clock-making and jewel-making (nine out of eleven), photography (four out of seven), tanning (two out of three),[35] and, above all, shoemaking, which seems to be the most emblematic (twenty to twenty-five Armenian cobblers for thirty cobbler's shops),[36] in a country in which the use of shoes was a luxury still in its infancy.

There were also many Armenians among chauffeurs and mechanics: this was a sign of the times. Some were former members of the royal brass band. The children of Armenian immigrants born in the country, or those who had arrived there with their parents at a young age, were well placed to work as chauffeurs, a position that called both for imported technical savoir-faire and mastery of several languages in order to communicate with customers and serve as a guide in the country. For the first time, cars and trucks loaded with merchandise and driven by Armenians reached a good many of Ethiopia's remote localities or regions, among them the coffee-growing region of Jimma in 1929, Däbrä Marqos (in the Gojam region), Goba (in the province of Balē), Yirga Aläm (in the province of Sidamo) in 1934, the areas on the borders of Kenya and Italian Somalia in 1935, and so on.[37] Several garages were also run by young

Armenians, often born in the country, who surrounded themselves with Ethiopian apprentice mechanics.

Like the Europeans, the Armenian had a hand in introducing new technologies that were sometimes of great economic and social importance. With the help of their Armenian-Ethiopian employees, the Seferian, Behesnilian, and Yerzingatsian firms established, even in the most remote countryside, large numbers of small, light mills, fitted out with diesel motors.[38] New Armenian photographers opened studios in Addis Abeba.[39] They targeted not just the European clientele but also the newly urbanized fringes of the Ethiopian population, benefiting, according to Avedis Terzian, from "their facility for the language and their contact with the Ethiopians" as well as their ability to satisfy the local conventions governing the art of the portrait:

> The Ethiopians patronized that with their wives, with certain standards: the woman and the man [were] seated, on condition that their hands were visible and their ears were visible. They thought that hiding them showed a defect. [...] And now the Ethiopians became great lovers of photos.[40]

Moreover, the Djerrahian brothers, Elias and George, profiting from their "profound knowledge of several languages," founded the Imprimerie Artistique [Artistic printing house] in 1930 and introduced "the first Offset, the first Clichographe, the first and the only Linotype with Ethiopian characters."[41]

The Steady Growth in the Number of Office Workers and Civil Servants

Often better educated and, because they had been born in Ethiopia or had grown up there, better versed in Amharic than their elders, the Armenian immigrants' children no longer confined themselves to professions in business and the crafts in the 1920s: "Thanks to their capacities and manifold qualities, the Armenians secured the biggest share of foreigners' overall contribution to state institutions."[42] Armenians occupied a remarkably large number of posts in public administration or the administration of private companies (as accountants, customs officers, bank employees, etc.) requiring a command of spoken and written Amharic—which few foreigners had in this period—as well as international languages such as French or English. Certain minor government or palace officials even had a reputation for their detailed knowledge of Amharic, such as Vahram Terzian, a cousin of Avedis Terzian's and an accountant in Addis Abeba's customs office, who "had beautiful handwriting" and was, of all the Armenians, the one who wrote this language best: "The Emperor knew, as soon as he saw a petition, 'Ah', he would say, 'it's Vahram.'"[43] Avedis Terzian himself was considered to have expert knowledge of Amharic and was designated translator of the Anglo-Ethiopian Treaty of 1942.

In the 1920s, at least ten Armenians were employed by the municipality of Addis Abeba, among them the surveyors Minas Kherbekian and Amasia Sukiasian and the engineer Khachig Papazian, or by various ministries as legal advisors, accountants, secretaries, policemen, instructors, civil engineers, and so on. Mihran Kaymakian was the only veterinarian holding a civil servant's post in the Ministry of Agriculture. Suren Chakerian was an employee of the Ethiopian Post Office, Hayg Patapan was employed by the Bank of Abyssinia in Addis Abeba, Stepan Yazedjian held a post in its Dire Dawa branch, and Stepan Papazian was a counselor at the Ministry of Public Education and the Fine Arts.[44] Papazian was an architect who also designed some of the characteristic iconography of the Ethiopian state, certain elements of which figured on the stela commemorating Haile Selassie's imperial coronation, as well as on stamps and bank notes printed during his reign. Three other Armenians had posts in Dire Dawa's customs office. The most famous of them, Abraham Koeurhajian, a Francophone who had graduated university in Marseilles and settled in Ethiopia in 1908, was, in the 1920s and 1930s, the Ethiopian government's accountant, a post that dovetailed with that of general steward of the royal properties. This "very learned Armenian who spoke and wrote seven different languages perfectly" simultaneously served as the emperor's "confidant and secretary" and received the requests of the sovereign's foreign visitors before presenting them, when appropriate, to the palace.[45] On the eve of the Italian invasion of Ethiopia, he was also the administrator of customs on Addis Abeba's forests and hot springs (the famous thermal baths of Fell Woha), succeeding another Armenian, Vahan Kalustian, in this post. Furthermore, the only Armenian to direct a department in the Ministry of Commerce (the former Customs Office) was Levon Yazedjian's son Paylag Yazedjian, who was at the head of the General Inspections Office, which was responsible for supervising customs procedures both in Addis Abeba and the provinces.[46] In the 1950s, he held the post of vice-governor of the municipality of Addis Abeba. In the same period, Khachig Boghossian exercised important functions in the Ministry of Agriculture.

The Armenian immigrants' preeminence as interpreters is a well-known phenomenon in Ethiopia, as it was in Palestine under the British mandate in the same period; their distinction in this field was also exemplified by the Armenian dragomans in the Egypt of the khedives or in certain Arabic-speaking regions of the Ottoman Empire in the nineteenth century. "The Armenians' knowledge of Amharic was appreciated by the various foreign legations that employed them as interpreters and intermediaries," writes Adrien Zervos.[47] In the 1920s and 1930s, almost all the legations' interpreters were Armenians, with the exception of the Greek, Belgian, British,[48] and Turkish missions. Samuel Behesnilian, followed, from 1927 on, by Avedis Terzian, held the post of interpreter in the legation of the United States. Ardashes Peshdilmaji held the same post in the French legation, where he was also the secretary of the Armenian bureau. Hovhannes (or Johannes) Semerjibashian was the interpreter in Germany's legation, while Antranig Papazian held this office at the Egyptian consulate. As for Suren Chakerian, a resident of Ethiopia since 1902, he was the interpreter in the Italian legation until 1936, after serving in the same post in the French legation in the 1910s.[49] The presence of these interpreters was indispensable in the mixed courts that associated consuls and Ethiopian judges to judge litigation opposing Ethiopian subjects to foreign citizens or protégés.[50] Avedis Terzian was appointed Oriental Secretary when the British liberated Ethiopia from Italian occupation in 1941. He was an auxiliary agent whose role was to facilitate contacts between the Occupied Enemy Territory Administration (OETA), in place until 1943, and the Ethiopian authorities.[51]

By employing Greeks or Armenians in such posts at this time, the British avoided creating the impression that they intended to make liberated Ethiopia a protectorate.[52]

Thus one observes, by way of the evolution of the professional profile of first-generation and second-generation Armenian immigrants, an obvious permeability of the "frontiers" that should, in principle, have separated the Ethiopian population from foreigners. The immigrants' ability to melt into the host society, however, manifested itself not just in their professional lives but in the whole set of their social practices, from the cradle to the grave. Funeral customs are a revealing example.

Liminality and Interstitiality in the Beyond: The Armenian Cemeteries in Gulēlē

From 1913 on, Addis Abeba's foreigners—and Catholic Ethiopians as well—were buried in a cemetery of their own in Gulēlē, a few kilometers from the city center, as was, moreover, also the case in Harar and Dire Dawa.[53] The Armenians, who had, two years earlier, fitted themselves out with a national committee comprising seven elected members, marked off their separate section of Addis Abeba's international cemetery, a concession that the Ethiopian government granted them for ninety-nine years.[54] Subsequently, in 1961, the concession was extended by the grant of a second piece of land that was not contiguous with the first but was located in the same funereal complex in Gulēlē. It was given the name Surp Hagop's (St. Jacob's) cemetery, in memory of Hagop Baghdassarian, the donor who had made it possible to acquire it.[55]

At the turn of the century, there were no rules governing inhumation of non-Ethiopians, nor did there exist cemeteries properly so called, that is, areas reserved strictly for the repose of the dead and segregated from the hurly-burly of the world of the living by an enclosure: "Before 1913, the dead were buried just anywhere."[56] The first Armenian immigrants interred their dead in line with local custom, in the churchyards of the churches in their neighborhoods, mainly in those of the church of Giyorgis (Saint George) and the church of Sellasē (the Trinity).[57] Garabed Terzian, one of Avedis's uncles, as well as his brother Yervant, who died at an early age in 1903 or 1904, repose in the churchyard of the church of St. George. Since it was too small to accommodate the mortal remains of all the neighborhood's dead, a big Ethiopian cemetery later sprang up spontaneously just outside its walls. Sarkis Terzian and his wife Vartuhi, who died in 1915 and 1913, respectively, were initially buried there. This area, however, offered no guarantee that the graves would be preserved. The "city's big cemetery," which surrounded the basilica of St. George before the basilica's reconstruction in 1905, was thus "gradually closed down, passing into the hands of the Indians, who desecrated it by putting up stores and rental apartment buildings" on it.[58] Still located outside the city limits at the turn of the century, Gulēlē offered, in contrast, a site suitable for a new cemetery reserved for foreigners.

After the Armenian cemetery was opened in Gulēlē, the mortal remains of some of the dead interred in the churchyards of Ethiopian churches were transferred to it. A concern for peace and quiet and the preservation of the graves is, however, not sufficient explanation for the creation of a separate cemetery for Armenians, whom

Mérab advised to "simply" attend "the Abyssians' religious services' rather than worrying about securing their own place of worship, "since they are—what is more, unawares—purely and simply Monophysites, like the Copts, Syrian Jacobites, and Ethiopians."⁵⁹ In the absence of a priest of their own Church, the Armenians turned to Swedish or French missionaries and Greek Orthodox priests to celebrate weddings, christenings, and funerals,⁶⁰ but also to Ethiopian priests, and even, occasionally, to the *abun* in person.⁶¹ It was, however, "a very funny thing," according to Avedis Terzian, that the Ethiopian priests were willing to bury only Armenians with Biblical names in the churchyards of their churches: "In the case of Arsen," a worker in his father's employ, "we perhaps gave him [the name] Jacques or Jacob. [...] So many of these old-timers are buried under combined names" (Narrative 11, § 2).

Thus it seemed necessary to open a separate Armenian cemetery. The opening of the Surp Asdvadzadzin (Holy Mother of God) chapel and the fact that Hovhannes Gevherian, an Armenian priest, settled in Addis Abeba in 1923 also seems to have contributed to the creation of a cemetery of the Armenians' own. Yet the baptismal register shows that a non-negligible number of the 751 infants mentioned in it were baptized by non-Armenian priests, usually Ethiopians, not only before but also after 1923. Ethiopian priests in fact performed more than two-thirds (twenty-nine) of the forty-one christenings performed by non-Armenian priests. Between 1902 and 1937, nineteen Ethiopian baptisms were celebrated by at least seven different priests in the churches of Sellasē, Giyorgis, Balä Wäld, Maryam, Estifanos, and Mikaēl in Addis Abeba, as well as in remote provincial cities such as Däsē and Läqämtē, where there was no Armenian priest in residence. The register of deaths shows that, despite the existence of an Armenian cemetery, the Armenians sometimes still buried their dead in Ethiopian cemeteries, as happened on August 10, 1929, in the case of the child of an Armenian father and an Ethiopian mother who died in infancy. Recourse to non-Armenian priests did not completely cease after 1923; non-Armenians officiated at about 10 percent of the burials that took place in Gulēlē. Thus, between 1957 and 1973, eight funeral ceremonies (out of 166) were performed by Greek priests in periods when no Armenian clergyman was present, because an Armenian priest had left or died and his successor had not yet assumed his office.⁶² People also frequently turned to Ethiopian priests, as on December 5, 1961, for Simon Kazanjian's burial; on July 22, 1962, for Hovhannes Misakian's; or on November 16, 1970, for Garabed Hakalmazian's. Between April 16, 1975, the date of the last funeral service performed by the priest Zareh Basmajian, and December 29, of the same year, the date of the first funeral celebrated in the presence of Father Vahan Topalian, Armenian funerals in Gulēlē were carried out four times by an Ethiopian priest and twice by a Greek priest. Certain ceremonies were entrusted to Ethiopian priests even when an Armenian priest was to be found in Addis Abeba at the same time. Turning to an Ethiopian priest was thus sometimes, perhaps, a meaningful choice for people who had been born in Ethiopia or had spent a large part of their lives there in the service of the imperial court and government. Garabed Hakalmazian was a former member of the forty orphans whom *Ras* Täfäri had "adopted" for his royal brass band; he had himself served as the conductor of orchestras of young Ethiopians, including the municipal orchestra. Similarly, Mushegh Terzian, born in Harar in 1905, and, later, Garabed Atamian, were buried in Gulēlē in an Ethiopian priest's presence in 1965 and 1969, respectively, although Father Goriun Manuelian officiated regularly, and with no apparent interruption, between August 1962 and October 1970. Thus the existence of an exclusively Armenian cemetery, if it seems to attest a search for a place of the Armenians' own, does not exclude individuals' implantation in the society in which they lived. The complex reality that finds expression here is that of an in-between, which is the product not of cultural dispositions but of an evolving social configuration.

8

Between Stateless Person and Citizen: The Belle Époque of a Legal Gray Zone

At the turn of the twentieth century, the mobilization of long-standing collective representations for contemporary political purposes opened up an interstitial space of sociabilities for the Armenians of Ethiopia. Changes made thereafter, in the first half of the twentieth century, to the laws applying to foreigners favored the emergence of a legal gray zone. The short period of Italian occupation that, from 1936 to 1941, followed the 1935–6 conquest of Ethiopia by Mussolini's troops is a privileged moment for observing the freedom of action that this space offered individuals. This period shows that, far from penalizing them, the effect of the absence of any clear definition of the status of Ethiopia's Armenians was, paradoxically, to protect them.

The Legal Regime of Foreigners and the Sedimentation of a Gray Zone

The archives of the former *Ministero dell'Africa Italiana* help us define more precisely the legal status of the Armenians and other groups, such as the Greeks or Arabs. For fascist ideology made the Italian colonial administration's agents more attentive to the classification of individuals in racial and national categories. The way these agents applied the legal categories and norms that were in force in Europe reveals the confusion that had, until then, reigned over the situation of Armenians who had long since immigrated to, or been born in, Ethiopia, where the borderline between citizens and foreigners was blurred.

The Diversity and the Imprecise Character of the Legal Statutes

The confusion surrounding the status of the majority of Armenian immigrants and their children first became problematic with the Italian occupation. This is revealed by a request for the ratification of a marriage contracted one year earlier by an Armenian immigrant, Agop Sivrissarian, and a Hungarian citizen, Etel Schreiner. Since the marriage contract signed on August 18, 1935, in the presence of the former Ethiopian head of the municipality of Addis Abeba stated that the husband was an "Ethiopian subject," the Italian administration contended that he should be considered a colonial subject by virtue of the organic law of June 1, 1936, for Italian East Africa (IEA) and that the same held for his wife. It followed that they came under Ethiopian law. It remained to establish how Agop Sivrissarian, "a merchant residing in Addis Abeba," born in Smyrna in 1901 as "the eldest son of the late Mr. Artin Sivrissarian and Mrs. Dicranichi [Dikranuhi] Sivrissarian," both of whom had died in Turkey,[1] had become an "Ethiopian subject."

The registers of Addis Abeba's Armenian church often mention the Ethiopian "citizenship" of the Armenians listed in them, but their nomenclature, which is rather imprecise, does not necessarily reflect these Armenians' official legal status. That this information was not regularly compiled before the 1950s may reflect the small importance attached to this question in Ethiopia until a late date. The register of Dire Dawa's Armenians, which was essentially kept up-to-date between 1930 and 1950, specifies the "nationality" of 106 of the 109 individuals registered but does not leave us any less uncertain for that. Those mentioned in it are assigned some fifteen different statuses. Only one individual is said to be of Ethiopian "nationality"; two others are declared "Ethiopian subjects." The biggest groups are made up of individuals said to be of Lebanese (eighteen) or Syrian (thirteen) nationality, a little less than one-third of the total, or identified as French subjects or protégés (sixteen individuals, about one-sixth of the total). Mention is also made of four Egyptians or Egyptian subjects, four Iranian subjects, three Turkish subjects, and one Greek subject. Almost half the individuals listed (forty-four), however, are simply declared to be of "Armenian" nationality, a category that, at the time, did not correspond to any legal reality. It is probable that a good many of these individuals were in fact stateless.

In the register of births of Addis Abeba's Armenian church, nearly two-thirds of the children born between 1920 and 1929 are declared to be Lebanese, Syrians, French or French protégés, or stateless. Beginning in the 1930s, new nationalities (notably Egyptian and Italian) make their appearance, while more than half the newborn children are identified as Ethiopian. The proportion of children said to be Ethiopian subjects comprises nearly two-thirds of the total in the 1940s, levels off at around 60 percent in the 1950s and 1960s, and, at nearly 85 percent, preponderates in the final period, 1970–80. According to the same source, the number of French protégés rises to about 20 percent of the total in the 1920s and completely disappears in the following decade, subsisting at a residual level between the 1940s and the 1960s.[2] Yet, on the eve of the Italian invasion, the French envoy in Ethiopia estimated the number of French protégés in the capital at four hundred, and there is every reason to believe that the Armenians held a preponderant position among them.[3] Still more surprising is the fact that fourteen of the twenty-three newborn children (out of sixty) whose nationality is indicated in the registers between 1936 and 1941 are said to be "Ethiopians," whereas the autochthones in the Italian territories in Africa were, from this period on, simply deemed colonial subjects of IEA. It is, consequently, hard to establish the meaning to be given to these declarations of nationality. One finds, in the sources, individuals "of Armenian nationality" who are simultaneously "Ethiopian subjects" and, sometimes, "French protégés." Ultimately, the question of how the status of Ethiopian subject was acquired remains unanswered.

Becoming an "Ethiopian Subject" in the Interwar Period

In the wake of a request that he addressed to the General Government of IEA, Garabed Gugiughian [Kiuchiukian], born in Zeytun, Turkey in 1908, a resident, from the age of fourteen, of Addis Abeba, where "he came in 1924 and was one of the forty orphans brought from Jerusalem by Tafari in order to create the orchestra of the imperial guard," is successively and, it seems, with some indifference identified as being "of Armenian nationality," an "Italian subject," an Armenian subject, a "former Armenian," and a "subject of Italian East Africa." If he became an Italian subject after the conquest of Ethiopia, he must previously have had the status of Ethiopian subject. The trajectory of Vartan Garabedian and Artin Derderian, who returned to Ethiopia, where they still had family, as holders of Ethiopian passports, and, after the invasion of Ethiopia, asked to be made Italian subjects, reveals something "about the way that, since they were of Armenian origin, they managed to acquire Ethiopian citizenship." Garabedian was born in Constantinople in 1876, while Derderian was born in Bardizag in 1900. Both stated that they "had acquired Ethiopian citizenship thanks to a 'Gracious Dispensation' accorded by the former Emperor, who had given all the 'stateless persons' of Armenian origin the opportunity to acquire Ethiopian citizenship after making application for it." In order to legitimize their declarations in the Italian authorities' eyes, they said that they had "preferred to acquire Ethiopian citizenship rather than remain 'stateless.'"[4]

These declarations clearly show that being granted Ethiopian citizenship in the interwar period was tantamount to being granted a privilege: the bestowal of citizenship depended solely on the emperor's will. Prevailing customs did not differ, it seems, from those observed under Menelik's rule, when the emperor could single-handedly decide that his servant Sarkis Terzian would be "considered one of the number of the Abyssinians." This decision had real legal validity, as is confirmed by a document signed by an Ethiopian consul in Djibouti, Josef de Galan (Yosēf Galan), on August 14, 1903; Galan "requested that the civil and military authorities of friendly states and states allied with Ethiopia grant free passage to Mr. Serkis Terisian and his wife, Ethiopian subjects, and provide them assistance and protection in case of need." The acquisition of the status of Ethiopian subject by Vartan Garabedian and Artin Derderian was also the result of a "gracious dispensation" accorded by Haile Selassie, probably in 1930 or 1929, perhaps earlier. This testimony echoes the collective autobiography, according to which *Ras* Täfäri, through his Armenian secretary Abraham Koeurhadjian, encouraged the Armenians to become Ethiopian subjects in 1923 or 1924 in order to prove to the European governments that Ethiopia deserved to be admitted to the League of Nations. "Täfäri urged us on and the Armenians immediately presented themselves [in order to] register [as] Ethiopian subjects."[5]

The first Ethiopian law on nationality, which seemingly served to put an end to this discretionary naturalization procedure, was adopted on July 22, 1930, a few months before Haile Selassie's reign began. It remained in force to the end of the imperial regime. By the terms of this legislation, a foreigner who wished to be naturalized had to have resided for at least five years in Ethiopia and to "know perfectly, speak and write Amharic."[6] An October 3, 1933, amendment to the law stipulated that these clauses could be set aside by the Naturalization Commission "on condition that there exists a need or special reason" to grant Ethiopian nationality. The result was that, by the time the Italian occupation began, a significant proportion of Armenians had acquired the status of Ethiopian subjects and hoped to pass it on to their children.[7] Armenians nonetheless continued to seek the protection of one or another European legation present in the country.

The Regime of Extraterritoriality and Its "Play"

A result of agreements concluded between the Ethiopian government and the great powers, the establishment of an "appropriate legal regime" for foreigners was intended to reassure European governments about the lot of their citizens in a day and age in which eminent jurists deemed it "obvious that an individual who is a member of a developed society could not, without negative consequences, purely and simply live under the rule of the laws governing Ethiopian society."[8] It was a matter "of making it possible for foreigners to settle and co-exist peacefully with the natives" while "protecting them against the imperfections and incompatibilities of a law code corresponding to a primitive civilization [...], without, however, ignoring the sovereign rights of an independent nation on its own territory, and without prejudice to the legitimate interests of its native population."[9] Article 7 of the treaty signed on January 10, 1908, by Emperor Menelik and the French plenipotentiary on special mission to Ethiopia, Antony Klobukoswski, stipulated that all litigation between French citizens or protégés would henceforth come under "French jurisdiction, until the legislation of the Empire of Ethiopia is in conformity with the legislations of Europe." Litigation opposing French citizens or protégés and Ethiopian subjects would be "brought before an Abyssinian magistrate sitting in a special location, assisted by the French consul or his delegate."[10] The creation of this special, or mixed, tribunal took effect only with the beginning of the regency, in 1922, at a time when the government headed by *Ras* Täfäri felt the need to respond to the critiques of the iniquity of the Ethiopian courts being brandished as weapons by opponents of Ethiopia's admission to the League of Nations.[11] As French protégés, the Armenian immigrants and their children could thus be subjects of the emperor of Ethiopia and, at the same time, appeal to consular jurisdictions.

The Franco-Ethiopian Treaty of January 1908 simply took its place in a tradition of extraterritoriality that several older treaties between the country's kings and the great powers had established in Ethiopia: the Anglo-Ethiopian Treaties of 1849 and 1897; the treaty concluded between Menelik, king of Shäwa, and the king of Italy in Ankobär on May 21, 1883; and the Treaty of Ucciali (Wechalē) of May 2, 1889. This regime of extraterritoriality is comparable to the capitulations put in place for French merchants in the Ottoman Empire in the seventeenth century. Additional treaties concluded with Ethiopia extended these arrangements to cover citizens of other foreign states, so that these states, too, secured the advantages of the status of most favored nation. By virtue of prevailing custom and consular protection, the benefits of the Franco-Ethiopian Treaty were likewise extended to citizens of countries that had not signed treaties with the Empire of Ethiopia, such as Turkey, Egypt, and Sweden, so that they were "treated on a perfectly equal footing with other foreigners who were citizens or protégés of a state that was a beneficiary of the Klobukoswski Treaty," for their governments had come to an understanding with the states bound by the Franco-Ethiopian Treaty stipulating that the latter would grant consular protection to citizens of the former as well. Thus, in the early 1930s,

> France accorded consular protection to Dutchmen, Swiss, Czecho-Slovaks, Poles [...], Romanians, Russian émigrés, Persians, citizens of states under French mandate, Syrians and Lebanese, émigrés of Armenian origin, and all citizens of countries without consular representation who apply for it. [...] The result was that there was, in the end, not a single foreigner in Ethiopia who was not entitled to the protection of one of the Powers represented with the Imperial Government.[12]

From 1900 to 1930, protection of the Armenians was a diplomatic issue disputed by the different legations, for it seemed to be a source of influence. In 1908, the head of the French legation was alarmed by the prospect that Germany's legation might assume protection of the "Ottoman colony," consisting mainly of Armenians, many of whom worked in the imperial palace. "From the special standpoint of French influence," he emphasized, "Germany's conduct in this matter is most regrettable." For these immigrants, "ordinarily mild-mannered, timid, and of humble appearance," seemed to constitute "an appreciable force, a disciplined factor, and a docile tool for whoever unties them in a group."[13]

Unwarranted extension of this extraterritoriality "to political ends" had, however, perverse effects, according to one of the special tribunal's foreign advisors, who spoke of "deplorable consequences": "It is well-known that the majority of the French legation's protégés in Ethiopia is made up of a large number of people who are neither French citizens, nor French subjects, nor even citizens of countries that have been placed under French mandate, but, rather, émigrés of Russian or Armenian origin." "It is not rare," he regretfully noted, "to see certain natives, bearers, simultaneously, of several certificates of nationality or protection issued by different consulates, use these certificates at their discretion and according to the interest they have at a given moment in claiming such-and-such a consulate's protection rather than another's."[14]

Toward the Restriction of an Interstitial Space

The increasing rigidity of the rules for acceding to Ethiopian nationality after the Second World War, however, reduced the space of the liberties created by the regime of extraterritoriality. Abruptly suspended by Italy's conquest of Ethiopia, this regime was not reestablished by the Ethiopian government, which wished to reaffirm its complete recovery of its sovereignty in 1941. In the 1950s and 1960s, the imperial regime pursued a policy of "Ethiopianizing" managerial staff and civil service jobs (e.g., in banks, transportation, and administrations). Children of Armenian immigrants who had reached majority now preferred to expatriate to further their careers, a trend that was even more pronounced under the *Därg* regime (1974–91). The requirement that foreigners obtain a residence permit and authorization to exercise a professional activity encouraged individuals to exit the legal gray zone of an earlier day. Acquiring

Ethiopian citizenship became an imperative necessity for a number of families who wished to remain in Ethiopia because they had been settled there for one or two generations.[15]

In the early 1950s, because the French authorities had not renewed the protection that they had committed themselves to providing before the war, many Armenians acquired Syrian or Lebanese passports before deciding to go through the procedures required to obtain Ethiopian nationality. The attitude of the responsible Ethiopian authorities, however, had become more restrictive. Under the imperial regime, they seem to have applied the law on nationality flexibly. Witness the decision to facilitate the naturalization of Armenians in 1965, after Catholicos Vazken I personally submitted the problem posed by their situation to Haile Selassie.[16] Children of naturalized Armenians did not automatically acquire Ethiopian citizenship until the *Därg* regime. Even if most Armenians officially enjoyed Ethiopian nationality thereafter, however, the distinction between these naturalized citizens and the others persisted de facto and in administrative practice.[17] In the same period, the question of property belonging to Armenians that had been nationalized under the *Därg*'s socialist regime was treated the same way as that of property belonging to any other Ethiopian: whereas foreigners were able to obtain compensation from the new Ethiopian regime after the 1991 fall of the *Därg*, this was not the case for naturalized Armenians or their children. Thus it appears that, as the legal norms constitutive of the modern nation-state solidified, the interstitial space from which the Armenians in Ethiopia had been able to benefit until the mid-twentieth century shrank.

The Consular Waltz

In the early twentieth century, Armenians were not treated differently than other Ottoman subjects. They comprised, according to the head of the French legation, "the main element of the Turkish colony," and, "a few individuals aside, all the Sultan's subjects in Abyssinia."[18] The application of the provisions of the Franco-Ethiopian Treaty to other powers' citizens and protégés, however, encouraged them to engage in a veritable consular nomadism which saw them pass, officially, "from Turkey to Germany, from Germany to Russia, from Russia to France,"[19] even while many of them acquired the status of Ethiopian subjects (or, in a later day, Lebanese or Syrian passports), as if the aim were to entrust the right to protect them to the highest bidder. When, in June 1908, the German legation informed the emperor of Ethiopia that it had just made an agreement with the Sublime Porte to extend its protection to Ottoman subjects who applied for it, the Armenians regarded this as "forced protection" imposed by the sultan and seemed "more inclined to turn to France than Germany to this end."[20] Three months later, only fourteen of them had completed the required procedure; the others seemed to consider themselves "as falling naturally under the French legation's jurisdiction."[21] Only in winter 1909, after the most alarmist rumors about the deterioration of the state of Menelik's health had begun circulating, rumors "of a kind that justified certain apprehensions," did Armenians start going in greater numbers to the German legation in order to register with it, since registration alone guaranteed that they would be "allowed to appeal to" the Kaiser's representative and "take refuge in the legation in the event of danger."[22] Thus it was that, at the outbreak of the First World War, the great majority of the Armenians found themselves, willy-nilly, under German protection.[23] At the moment when Sarkis Terzian was shot and killed by another Armenian on the premises of Germany's consular court in 1915,[24] he enjoyed, concurrently, the status of an Ethiopian subject, which Menelik had bestowed on him in 1901, and that of a German protégé (as an Ottoman subject), a status he had probably had since 1908. This had not prevented him from regularly soliciting the French legation's protection in the period 1906-15, which the ambassador had been careful not to grant him because of Terzian's shady reputation as a businessman.[25] After his death, the Turkish consul in Harar, who still considered him an Ottoman subject, had his land, securities, and personal papers seized.[26]

The Armenians, albeit officially citizens and protégés of the Ottoman Empire and Germany, nevertheless, made a public display of their sympathy for the Allies during the Great War: "Deeming this an unfriendly act, the German ambassador deprived these Armenian visitors of his defense. Addis Abeba's Armenian colony thereupon collectively renounced the German representative's protection."[27] It was then granted Russian protection until, in 1919, following the creation of the Bolshevik regime in Russia, the Czar's last representative in Ethiopia, Winogradoff, turned the defense of Russian matters over to the legation of France. At the same time, in February 1920, the president of the Republic of Armenia's delegation to the Peace Conference, Avedis Aharonian, designated, with the French government's consent, a French citizen of Armenian origin, the merchant Matig Kevorkoff, as the newly created Republic of Armenia's representative in Ethiopia. The French government had a "Notice to the Armenians of Ethiopia" published in the May 28, 1920, *Courrier d'Éthiopie* in which it declared that "all Armenians from all parts of Armenia who live in Ethiopia or are temporarily residing there, shall register, until new orders are issued, at the legation of France, which shall protect their interests."[28]

The previous year, the French chargé d'affaires had declared that "while the defense of Russian interests in Ethiopia did not present serious problems for the legation of France, given the small number of Russian subjects residing in this country, the same would not appear to hold for the protection of Armenian subjects who are Russian protégés." It nonetheless seemed advisable to him for the French legation to undertake to protect the Armenians, whose "National Committee, elected by popular ballot," represented "a force and a means of influence that it would no doubt be possible to turn to advantage." It was important that the decision to extend diplomatic protection to the Armenians be made in Paris before it occurred to the British to claim responsibility for it, in the event that the United States government, whose interests in Ethiopia were defended by the British, accepted a mandate over Armenia.[29] The decision to extend protection to a large, industrious population could not be made lightly, however, for the burden it might come to represent was all too obvious, as is shown by British complaints about the turbulent Greek population that Great Britain had agreed to protect.[30]

In theory, delegating protection of Ethiopia's Armenians to France was a temporary measure. The ephemeral Republic of Armenia's untimely demise, however, led to the prolongation of this situation until Italy invaded Ethiopia. The burden represented by consular protection of the Armenians, among whom there were one hundred family heads, rapidly proved too onerous for the French representation. It had to employ "a serious auxiliary agent who spoke and wrote Armenian" and to build an annex to the chancellery in order to maintain a consular court reserved for litigation between Armenians.[31] In the 1920s, the legation seemed to be chronically overwhelmed by the countless trials pitting its protégés against each other: "At a time when the political crisis taking shape in Ethiopia should occupy all my time and attention," the ambassador complained, "I have become a judge charged with settling private suits, most of which involve Armenians and Russians."[32] The ambassador accordingly proposed to prohibit new registrations by Armenians or Russians, reserving "the right to deprive them of French protection by a simple administrative measure if they show themselves to be unworthy of it." In his estimation, "the Armenians who have not availed themselves of the opportunity to acquire a nationality" offered by the 1923 Treaty of Lausanne, which confirmed the Republic of Armenia's disappearance and gave Armenians two years to exercise this option, "must, it seems, be regarded as Ottomans [sic] or as local subjects,"[33] that is, as subjects of the emperor of Ethiopia. The majority of Armenians living in Ethiopia during the interwar period, however, were still in a position to acquire full French protection by right or to benefit from it de facto. Their particular situation as stateless persons or former Ottoman subjects who could no longer be referred to a Turkish diplomatic representation indefinitely extended the legal gray zone in which they found themselves. In theory, foreigners who were not citizens of a state benefiting from the provisions of the 1908 Franco-Ethiopian Treaty, "or who, albeit entitled to place themselves under a beneficiary state's consular protection, have not registered with its consulate, should ordinarily be considered subject to ordinary native tribunals as far as their litigation with Ethiopian subjects is concerned." For "non-protected foreigners were, in that case, described as 'local subjects' or, in the current but inexact phrase, as 'Ethiopian protégés' and assimilated to the status of Ethiopian subjects."[34] The French legation was the less likely to remove Armenians from its registers of protégés, in that, given the then prevailing colonial context, the representatives of European governments had little desire to create too many precedents by abandoning whites to the sole status of Ethiopian subjects falling under the jurisdiction of indigenous courts.[35]

"Ethiopians with a Separate Constitution"?

In obedience to the logic created by this regime of extraterritoriality, Armenians fitted themselves out with an organization that was supposed to represent them all with the Ethiopian authorities and the different legations, whatever their personal legal status. The "National Committee (Ephor) of the Armenian Community in Abyssinia" was created in 1911; its president at the time was Ethiopia's imperial court photographer, Bedros Boyadjian. The committee was initially placed under the control of the Armenian patriarchate of Constantinople, which ratified the election of its seven members, to be held every four years, until this responsibility was delegated to the Armenian Prelacy of Cairo during the Great War. In 1923, the archbishop of the Armenians of Egypt reaffirmed that the committee had, "like its predecessors, authority to represent [...] the Armenian colony of Abyssinia and to act on its behalf with respect to everything bearing on its members' collective interests."[36] In the course of the 1920s, however, the committee broke off its relations with the archdiocese and renamed itself "Council of the Armenian Community in Ethiopia," more commonly referred to as the *kaghutayin khorhurt*, or "colony council."[37] The council served as an interlocutor for foreign legations and the Ethiopian government and delivered birth certificates and identity papers when Armenian immigrants or their children were asked to produce them.[38] It honored commemorations and ceremonies organized in Addis Abeba's diplomatic circles with its presence, such as the July 14 festivities at the French legation.[39] Even before official creation of this representative organ, Armenian delegations were invited to attend official receptions whenever representatives of the legations were.[40] In 1908, an Armenian "committee" invited the legations to celebrate the proclamation of the constitution in Turkey.[41] Whatever their actual legal situation, the Armenians were collectively considered one of the "foreign colonies" established in the country. The council of the *kaghutayin* was also recognized as a legitimate interlocutor by the Italian authorities between 1936 and 1941,[42] and by the British OETA between 1941 and 1943. It obtained the Ethiopian government's authorization to draw up a "constitution" governing the status of the "Armenian community in Ethiopia" in 1930, at exactly the same time that the first imperial constitution and first imperial law on citizenship were proclaimed. The Armenian constitution was amended for the first time when the country was liberated in 1941, and again in 1963. It made the council of the *kaghutayin* the "Armenian community's" recognized legal representative with the Ethiopian authorities. It granted this council alone the competence to deliver "birth, baptismal, marriage, and death certificates, but also certificates of good conduct, residence, and identity," all of which had legally validity in the eyes of foreign legations and the Ethiopian government. The constitution also granted the *kaghutayin* authority to stand in for the Ethiopian authorities in settling matters deemed internal to the community, such as disagreements over inheritances, "in accordance with the Armenians' ancient traditions," but also the domestic disputes that might crop up in Armenian families as well as divorce cases, which were to be submitted to the religious head of the diocese to which Addis Abeba's Armenian church was attached, the archbishop of the Armenians of Egypt. In this sense, it contributed to making the Armenians "Ethiopians with a separate constitution":[43] "The Armenians living in Ethiopia are organized as a separate community called 'The Armenian Community of Ethiopia,' in conformity with their ancient traditions and acknowledged rights."[44] The evolution of the Ethiopian legislation on the status of foreigners and the creation of a regime of extraterritoriality early in the twentieth century thus practically culminated, a few decades later, in what might be called a state within a state for the Armenians and the descendants of the Armenian immigration in Ethiopia.[45] This legal exception plainly did not trouble the Ethiopian administration, nor did it prevent descendants of Armenian immigrants from acquiring Ethiopian nationality. In the same period, these individuals continued, without apparent contradiction, to be represented, from cradle to grave, by a distinct "national committee." The period of the Italian occupation nicely brings out the legal and political paradoxes spawned by this situation.

The Armenians Under the Italian Occupation of Ethiopia

From 1936 to 1941, foreigners suspected of spreading anti-Italian propaganda or of standing in close relation with indigenous Ethiopians were especially closely watched. The fascist administration directed its efforts against everything that "detracted from the race's prestige," as is shown by an investigation of the Armenian Yervant Atamian, a French protégé accused of "blindly" obeying "the will of the native grandees" and of showing "great attachment to, and respect for, the Galla and Amara population," a circumstance that allegedly earned him "a very bad reputation."[46] Surveillance of foreigners was intensified after the abortive February 19, 1937, assassination attempt on Italian Africa's viceroy, Marshal Graziani, which served to justify brutal, murderous repression of the Ethiopian populace. In this difficult period, however, far from being a handicap, the fuzzy definitions of the Armenian immigrants' legal status seemed to work in their favor by providing them with wider margins of maneuver than those enjoyed by citizens of clearly identified states.

Toward According Preferential Treatment?

Many expulsion orders were issued for "security reasons" or "disturbing the peace," sometimes accompanied by more precise accusations of declared or alleged support for the Ethiopian resistance. They applied to all the Italian territories in Africa.[47] The collective autobiography presents the Italian occupation as a period of suffering that led to numerous expulsions and a drop in the Armenian population from 1,200 to about 600.[48] In reality, the great majority of expulsions were of Greek subjects, far more than of Armenians.[49] It is true that the large number of Greek mixed-races conflicted with the fascist policy of racial segregation. Many expulsion decrees were also issued against Italians, who were repatriated to Italy by force for behavior or language deemed harmful because it diminished the "prestige of the race": for example, the fact of having indigenous mistresses or maintaining excessive contacts with Ethiopians, of contracting debts with them or vaunting their merits, of abandoning a job or engaging in illicit activities, and so on.[50] In contrast, expulsion orders targeting Armenians are extremely rare in the files found in the Italian archives, although these files are otherwise well filled. A number of Armenians were sent to Italian colonies rather than being expelled, such as Kevork Nalbandian, who was temporarily exiled to Eritrea.[51] The reason for this may have been that the personal legal status of many Armenians in IEA made it difficult to expel them to a third country, and that the Italian Minister of the Interior demanded that the administration take care to "limit the influx of undesirable foreigners into the Kingdom to what is strictly necessary."[52] The same asymmetry is evinced by the files on the 1940–1 internments of foreigners in the Italian "concentration camps" in the Harar region, such as the Hurso camp near the village of Sarkama, or the Quoram camp for inhabitants of Addis Abeba.[53] Eighty percent of internment orders found in this archive concerned Greeks, while only a dozen concerned Armenians.[54]

This difference in treatment finds its explanation in the deterioration of relations between the Kingdoms of Italy and Greece in the wake of Mussolini's expansion into the Adriatic and Albania. The 1,000 to 1,500 Greek subjects were now considered to be "enemy subjects" and came under suspicion of promoting anti-Italian, pro-English propaganda. It was pointed out that the Greeks, who "made their way into the territories that today constitute" the Italian empire in Africa "well before we did, and who have thorough knowledge of not just the inhabitants of these territories, but also of their languages, customs, and practices, to which they adapt with great facility, without attaching any importance to the prestige of the race [...] elicit far more sympathy from the indigenous peoples than we Italians, who are more feared than loved." This was why surveying almost all the Greeks living in IEA, women and children included, and confining them in a camp reserved for them in May Habar, Eritrea, "for the duration of the war," seemed to be measures of elementary prudence, while confiscating their assets seemed to be a measure of retaliation against the Kingdom of Greece.[55] In contrast, the fact that the Armenians, like the Arabs residing in Ethiopia, were not legally bound or assimilable to an enemy state seemed to guarantee them relative leniency on the part of the Italian authorities.[56] This was the reason, as an internal note pointed out, "that *the clauses concerning people who are nationals of an enemy state and their assets are not to be applied to those who* hold Syrian or Lebanese citizenship, *are of Arab or Armenian origin*, and reside in the Kingdom, Colonies, or Possessions, except in cases resulting from circumstances that justify denying them *the above-mentioned preferential treatment*."[57] The Armenians who were not nationals of a recognized state benefited from this legal imprecision, since it was not possible to consider them "enemy subjects" at any time during the war. Even those who were clearly judged to be hostile to Italian interests were in many cases not expelled when their individual status as stateless persons made it impossible to find another country prepared to admit them. It is noteworthy that individuals were evaluated here as a function not of their nationality but of their "origin": the same note spells out that "Greek subjects of Armenian origin should receive comparable treatment," although they were, as Greeks, citizens of an enemy state. This is a clear indication of the preferential treatment that the colonial administration wished to apply, collectively, to the Armenians in Ethiopia, with an eye to instrumentalizing them later.

From Protection to Instrumentalization

A memorandum drawn up on this subject by the Inspector for Propaganda and the Press of the Fascist Federation of Scioa [Shäwa], Giuseppe Martucci, emphasizes the services that the Armenian population could render Italy in its effort to establish and increase Italian influence not just in Ethiopia but in the whole Middle East.[58] According to the inspector, before the Italian occupation of Ethiopia, "Armenians, like Europeans in general, had always been "tolerated" individuals held in suspicion by the fundamentally xenophobic native population" and had been "subjected to all sorts of harassment and humiliation." "With the proclamation of the Italian Empire of Ethiopia, the Armenians came to know a new life. The community promptly demonstrated that it wished to orient itself toward the new Regime, collaborating with it on the task of improving society and valorizing the vast territories wrested from negusite [*sic*] barbarity and opened up to civilization at last." This way of presenting matters minimizes the expulsions and the banishment orders pronounced against certain Armenians: "As if in a natural physiological process, the community is carrying out its own selection, losing elements inclined to resist the new history that is getting underway with the advent of Fascist Italy."⁵⁹ The author adopts Zervos's exaggerated estimate that there were 2,800 Armenians in Ethiopia in 1935, doubtless in order to make his remarks seem more convincing.⁶⁰ The objective was to profit from the successful integration of a population "made up of prolific families living in stable fashion in Ethiopia" and from "the moral and economic position that the Armenians" had secured under the old Ethiopian imperial regime. According to Martucci, this position "was markedly superior in comparison with that of the other foreign communities," thanks to the many prosperous businesses run by the Armenians; the fact that they often served as advisors in various state administrations, especially in the fields of finance, public education, and the arts and sciences; and their privileged positions as interpreters working for foreign legations: "The Armenians' knowledge of the local environment and language will be exploited more and more effectively by the government organs in conducting political action vis-à-vis the indigenous subjects. It will be possible to make use of the Armenians' experience of the markets of the East to develop our imperial economic policy."⁶¹ The projected policy of Italianizing this population and winning it over to Fascism, which is simultaneously suggested in small touches, was largely based on the idea that "the Armenians, who know the natives' language well and also enjoy their trust, are the most apt to meet their demands" and serve as auxiliaries in Italy's penetration of Ethiopia.⁶²

In this period, conferring the status of "subject" of the Italian possessions in Africa was an integral component of imperial policy.⁶³ It sought to offset the influence of foreign or hostile powers. "The possibility offered foreign subjects—Arabs, Indians, and Yemenis—of accepting the status of Italian subject" should be understood in this sense.⁶⁴ The prospect of granting this status to Armenians does not, however, seem to have been seriously envisaged, for it clashed with the Fascist ideological principles that made it imperative "to avoid declaring Aryan individuals who are of the white race to be colonial subjects." The consequence of such an arrangement would have been to reduce such individuals to the indigenous status common to all Africans in the Italian colonies in Libya, Eritrea, Somalia, or Ethiopia. It would have placed the Armenians in a situation of "legal equality with the natives," thus inflicting a "moral, racial, and also a political wrong" on them, and, above all, contravening the new "provisions of the law on the preservation and prestige of the race with regard to subjects of color." It was dismissed for these reasons.⁶⁵

The question as to whether it might be opportune to accord Armenians full Italian citizenship, rather than the status of subjects of IEA, was briefly considered in 1939, when it appeared "indubitable that a projected law was being prepared at the Quai d'Orsay to grant French naturalization to citizens of other states and to the stateless persons listed as protégés in the registers of the French consulates in Ethiopia." The Italian authorities feared that "if such a law were adopted, several thousand Armenians, White Russians, and Levantines of all sorts residing in Italian East Africa [would] acquire French citizenship and thus come to form a large French colony in an artificial way here." This threw up the question as to "whether or not it is opportune to anticipate the French initiative by facilitating rapid acquisition of Italian citizenship by those who apply for it."⁶⁶ A draft of the text of this projected law declared that the Viceroy of Ethiopia has the power to confer Italian citizenship by decree on foreign subjects and citizens, and also on former stateless persons, foreign subjects, and foreign citizens who became Ethiopian subjects before 9 May 1936, on condition that they are not of the Jewish race and do not belong to the populations of Italian East Africa or populations with traditions, customs, and religious, legal, and social concepts similar to those of the natives of Italian Africa. (article 1)

The aim, plainly put, was to grant the many Armenians who had since the 1920s or 1930s been French protégés, stateless persons, or Ethiopian subjects rapid access to Italian citizenship while dismissing applications that "native" Ethiopians might make. In the end, preference was given to granting Aegean citizenship not just to individuals of Greek origin but also to those who came "from this ethnic and geographical environment," such as Armenians, White Russians and "Levantines."[67]

The attitude adopted toward the Armenians was the administrative pendant to political projects that saw control of this well-implanted group as a vehicle for Italian influence in Ethiopia. Greeks and Armenians were encouraged to send their children to Italian schools. In the very first months of the invasion of Ethiopia, Harar's Italian Residence transformed Dire Dawa's Greek school into an Italian school.[68] The following year, Addis Abeba's big Greek school was closed down on hollow pretexts.[69] The Kevorkoff national Armenian school,[70] rebaptized "Scuola Elementare Vittorio Emanuele," was requisitioned in the same way.

Adult "courses in Italian and fascist culture reserved for Armenians" were also organized. January 1938 saw the foundation of a sporting association for young Armenians, which was "given the glorious name of Vartan and put under the control of the Office for Sport of the Fascist Federation of Scioa [Shäwa]."[71] On December 19, 1939, the secretary of the new community council, Berj Babayan (an employee of the Armenian-Italian Seferian company), who was appointed by the Italians after Matig Kevorkoff was expelled,[72] gave a pro-fascist speech in the presence of Inspector Martucci. In January 1940, a commemoration of the 1,500th birthday of the Armenian Catholicos Saint Sahak was organized under the auspices of Addis Abeba's Fascist Federation. It was punctuated by recitations of poems in Italian and by various allocutions, among them an address about the Armenian people's immortal genius delivered by Father Vahan Hovhanessian, who had made the trip from Venice.[73]

The Venice Mekhitarist congregation of Catholic monks of the Armenian rite was mobilized in Ethiopia, with the support of the Holy See, for the influence it was apt to have or to acquire on Armenians living there. It was deemed all the more opportune to send Father Vahan Hovhanessian to Ethiopia at the expense of the Italian Ministry for Africa because "several thousand Armenians live in Ethiopia" and were being wooed by France. As the Italian administration saw it, collaboration with the Mekhitarists would make it possible "to make contact with the Armenian community" and "draw it within our orbit," "something that would not fail to produce, as well, a beneficial effect on the more general terrain of our policy of penetrating the Middle East."[74] Father Hovhanessian himself highlighted the "valuable services" that the Armenians of IEA could contribute to "the stabilization and valorization of the Empire, whether by affording the local authorities the benefit of their knowledge of the natives" language, customs, and mentality, or by serving as a liaison between the Italians and the natives in exploiting the country's resources: "Since a majority of them are stateless persons, they have every interest in cooperating with the Italian Empire's colossal plans."[75] Even if it seems doubtful that such plans to instrumentalize Ethiopia's Armenians were often translated into action, it is plain that the Armenians' interstitial legal situation made them seem like the ideal auxiliaries for the implementation of this policy. Thus, in less than half a century, these immigrants passed collectively from the symbolic status of "privileged minority" that was symbolically accorded them by the Ethiopian monarchy to the practical state of a community privileged by the Italian colonial administration. The representations of this abiding gray zone were not without effect on the social agents' conduct and trajectories.

9

Between *Färänj* and *Habäsha*: Representations and Social Practices of Hybridity

The trajectories of the Armenian immigrants and their descendants in Ethiopia reveal the existence of collective representations of a kind of hybridity, located in an undecidable place between the "we" and the other, the inside and the outside. Far from constituting mere images of a social reality, which are sometimes deceptive, these representations must be studied, just as juridical and legal frameworks must be, with an eye to their social effects. Beyond figures of style and beyond stereotypes, the mark of collective representations on the behavior of individuals makes it possible to reveal the possible incarnations of this hybridity, bring out its social character, and lend it human form.

From the *Färänj* to the "Semi-White": The Uncertain Discursivization of the Interstitial

By definition, this gray zone cannot be unambiguously superposed on the boundaries traced by administrative categories. It also defies the terminologies in common use. It is not easy to define a vocabulary of alterity in Ethiopia with precision, for national affiliations are not always decisive criteria, no more than skin color is. Thus the Armenians do not really find their place in the binary lexical opposition between *Färänj* and *Habäsha*, which partially coincides with that between a national "we" and the others in Ethiopia.

The term *Habäsha* (from which the word "Abyssinian" is derived) is not the name of an ethnic group but is generally used to identify the Christian populations of the Ethiopian high plateaus who speak languages that have come down from *Ge'ez*, *Tegreñña*, and *Amhareñña* (or Amharic). Thus, in principle, the appellation "*Habäsha*" does not apply to the populations in the regions conquered and colonized in the late nineteenth century in the southern and western parts of the empire of Ethiopia, although the term was sometimes used in the twentieth century to designate, comprehensively, all the subjects of the emperor of Ethiopia.[1] Similarly, the term *Färänj* or *Färänji*, a calque on the word "Frank" also attested in Arabic from the time of the crusades on, can be interpreted in different ways, depending on the period and those who use it.[2] In the mid-seventeenth century, the German scholar Job Ludolf observed that it was used mainly for Roman Catholics, but that was also extended to cover all Europeans, Protestants included.³ He notes that Greeks and Armenians were not considered to be *Färänj*. In the nineteenth century and early in the twentieth, the term seems to be applied to all Europeans without distinction of confession, although it is "always" used, as Antoine d'Abbadie notes in his *Dictionnaire de la langue amhariñña* (1881), "in an insulting sense."⁴ In the mid-nineteenth century, the inhabitants of Harar "apply this term to all but themselves." Its usage, which is rarely well-meaning, is elastic, as is attested by an Indian merchant who complains that he was "always called a Frank by the Beduins, because he wore a *shalwar* [baggy trousers] or short pants."⁵ A *Färänj* was still very vaguely defined under Menelik's reign. Thus a priest named Gäbrä Yohannes, who was the principal of a school in Harar in 1903, "was able to recite whole books of the New Testament, but his knowledge of geography did not extend beyond Jerusalem and Suez. In his view, everything located farther off than that was lumped together under the title *frangi* or foreigner."⁶ This imprecision notwithstanding, it was noted at the time that "the Abyssinians call the French, English, Italians, Russians, Swiss, and Germans 'Frengi,'" whereas they count Greeks and Armenians as "Griks."⁷ In 1922, at his first train stop in Ethiopia, Avedis Terzibashian was harassed by children who had only two words on their lips: "Fereng! Armen!" He affirms that "when travelers are not Abyssinians, they are *Fereng* [*Färänj*] or *Armen* [*Armän*]" in the view of the children who beg travelers for coins.⁸ It would seem that this terminology was refined in proportion as the number of foreigners increased with the construction of the railroad. The word *Grik*, the linguist Marcel Cohen affirms in 1924, was "only recently naturalized in Amharic," but "it is very often used today to designate all manual workers, owners of cheap restaurants, and European petty traders, be they, moreover, really Greek (a majority of the last-named are), Armenian, or Italian." In his view, the word expresses a social rather than a physical distinction: Abyssinians distinguish *Griks* "from other Europeans, whom they call *Frang̈(i)* [*Färänj*]—diplomats, civil servants, travelers, and merchants—by their way of life and their dress." The linguist had "heard it said of such-and-such a person, whose business had taken a turn for the better and who had adopted the manners corresponding to his prosperous situation, that he had once been a *grīk* but had become a *frang̈i*," which would indicate that the term was used to designate "social classes rather than different nationalities."⁹ Representations of otherness vary with contexts and actors. Witness the commentary offered, around 1910 in Madji, by the leader of an indigenous rebellion against raids by slave traders organized, since the Ethiopian conquest, with the authorities' approval: "He had no idea of the differences between French, German, or English, but regarded them all indiscriminately as 'white men.' [...] He thought Greeks were a sort of race half-way between the white and the black."¹⁰ Thus it is not certain that skin color sufficed to distinguish what was "white"—if one maintains "white" as the definition of the word *Färänj*—from what was not.¹¹

It might be asked whether the collective representations, European and Ethiopian, of this gray zone did not feed off each other. Early in the century, the Europeans themselves seem not to have considered Greeks and Armenians as being of their number, as their equals; they were more likely to speak of "semi-whites" or "half-breed Europeans."¹² Many authors point out the Indians', Greeks', and Armenians' ability to live like the autochthons, speak their language, anticipate what they might need or ask for, and, consequently, achieve greater success than the Europeans: "Also it must be said that the natives are less suspicious of these men than they are of European traders, in whom they never put absolute trust. In a way they look upon Greeks and Turks as belonging almost to their own race," whereas "anything European brings bad luck upon the country, they believe."[13] Moreover, wrote Charles Michel in 1900, "the Abyssinians and the Gallas always prefer a Hindu, or even an Armenian or Greek stall, to a store run by a European, for they can bargain over the price more comfortably with a merchant *who is like them in his mind set and habits.*"[14] For the American anthropologist Carleton Coon, writing in the 1930s, "in the first place, Greeks and Armenians are not considered true Europeans, and are as a rule excluded from all significant social functions" in Ethiopia.[15] Greeks and Armenians, like Indians and Arabs, are distinguished from Europeans, that is, from *Färänji*, by their apparent flexibility with respect to the country's constraints and customs, their modest living standards, and, of course, their "keen business instinct" as much as their absolute "unscrupulousness."[16] Here we find, thirty years later, the same stereotypes and recriminations as are expressed in the parable about the "thaler-men" and the "mean-spirited,"[17] which coincides, although the parable does not say so, with the dichotomy between the *Habäsha* and the *Färänj*; the "mean-spirited" are located at a point somewhere between the two extremes, and are, as it were, close to the *Griks*.[18] These differences, which are usually described as if they were natural phenomena, seem to find their reflection even in individual temperaments. Thus the Greeks are supposed to be more patient with the natives, "to a degree where a European would lose his temper and use his fist or his feet freely."[19] They seem to be impervious to Djibouti's suffocating heat, to the humiliations inflicted on them by the Ethiopian grandees, to the mediocrity of their own social condition, and even to the malaria in Ethiopia's western regions.[20] Greeks and Armenians can be easily told apart from Europeans, because they are "ever distinguishable by their unshaven faces and ill-fitting clothes and hats."[21] The "Levantine," who "carries on every part of himself an indefinable patina [...] made up of imponderable elements, neutral tints, moral traits in which his abandonment of all dignity finds very distinct expression, or, more exactly, the absence of the least pretension of superiority to the native whose parasite he is," blurs the division between whites and black that its defenders would like to draw as clearly as possible: "In the same measure as the European strives to preserve his moral ascendancy, the Levantine pretends to lower himself and to degrade himself. [...] They are the ones who have forever destroyed the prestige of our race."[22] The same idea emerges from the words of a son of Ras Haylu of Gojam, Zäwdu, who returned from the United States in 1933: "Greeks and Armenians, he murmured, were the lowest forms of humanity. Their presence in Ethiopia was a lechery and a curse. Someday the Ethiopians would rise up and get rid of them."[23] A British diplomat describes Ethiopian intellectuals' new contestation of white superiority as a baneful consequence of the fact that these young people of Addis Abeba "consort on terms of equality with the riff-raff of Armenia and Greece, and in some cases France and Russia."[24] Amharic sayings evoke, in the same sense, "the plague of the Greeks and the pestilence of the Armenians,"[25] or affirm that "cabbage from food stuff and Armenian from the human race are the lowest."[26] "The

Armenians," Landor notes with surprise, "are not so popular as the Greeks, and they are somewhat looked down upon by the natives, this being, I think, merely a racial dislike, which is difficult to explain."[27] It must of course be taken into account that these reports, all of them indirect, about such collective representations are to some extent oriented by cliches and stereotypes. The existence of such representations is, however, attested by the fact that the Armenian of Ethiopia became a handy literary figure of hybridity in this period.

How the Armenian of Ethiopia Became a Literary Character

This end result was the culmination of a long tradition that established "the Orient" and "Orientals" as the ideal stuff of dreams, mystery, and literary digressions.[28] In nineteenth-century travel narratives about Ethiopia, the description of Armenian, Greek, Indian, or Arab stalls and bric-a-brac in Harar's or Addis Abeba's markets sought to satisfy a readership fond of the picturesque and Orientalizing detail. However, the development thanks to which Armenians are transformed, beginning in the 1930s, into literary embodiments of hybridity, goes beyond mere conformism on the part of the publishing industry. The writer who most often uses the figure of the Armenian as an element in those of his stories and novels that (more or less overtly) take Ethiopia as their setting, Evelyn Waugh, is, precisely, an author whose African travel narratives depart from the conventions of the genre. In *Black Mischief*, he makes an imaginary "Krikor Youkoumian" one of the main characters in a fierce parody of Haile Selassie's Ethiopia, in which Youkoumian appears as, all at once, extraordinarily resourceful, a forger, the manager of a seamy hotel, and an unscrupulous merchant of adulterated liquor who has become the very influential, dishonest Financial Secretary of the ineffective "Ministry of Modernization."[29] This literary use of the figure of the Armenian of Ethiopia differs from the simple evocation of an Armenian presence, mentioned in passing and intended only to embellish the narrative with titillating details or local color, of the sort one finds in classic travel narratives. It seems to be fueled, more directly, by collective representations of the symbolic gray zone with which Armenians in Ethiopia were identified. The expressive qualities of literary writing are thus useful when it comes to grasping an interstitial reality that it is difficult to objectivize.

The two novels set in Ethiopia or its environs that Jean-Christophe Rufin published in the 1990s both bring Armenian characters on stage. The famous traveler Khodja Murad and his nephew, also named Murad, are incorporated into the plot of a historical novel, *L'Abyssin* [The Abyssinian], loosely inspired both by the memoirs of the French physician Charles Jacques Poncet, who was sent to Ethiopia in 1699 to treat Emperor Iyasu I, and also, no doubt, by the memoirs of the French general consul in Cairo, Benoist de Maillet. In a later, more contemporary novel (*Les causes perdues* [Lost causes], 1999), whose story unfolds in Eritrea during the 1984 famine, Rufin again includes an Armenian character. Imaginary this time, he serves as both the narrator and a foil for the hero, who is young, naive, and ignorant of the part or the world where he has come to work as a doctor for an NGO. The narrator, in contrast, is an old man for whom Abyssinia no longer holds any secrets. He is ending his life in solitude: "I, Hilarion Grigorian, an Armenian from Africa and a retired arms merchant—if it is ever possible to give up this profession when it is a calling and almost a sacred mission—have been faithfully keeping this century company since it was two years old." Grigorian's ostensible origins aside—he declares that his family settled in the Hamasēn region in the mid-eighteenth century and that one of his ancestors received the Abbadie brothers in his home in the nineteenth century—he seems, as portrayed in the novel, to be an altogether plausible figure. The Armenian from Abyssinia here incarnates the interpreter at the junction of two worlds who helps the young French hero understand a strange universe that it is hard to penetrate. This approach to the subject derives, perhaps, from the author's own experiences and encounters in Ethiopia. It is somewhat reminiscent of the relationship which, in the 1840s, binds Arnauld d'Abbadie to his Armenian interpreter, a native of Baghdad who saved the Frenchman's life when he offended an Ethiopian grandee, only to severely reprimand him thereafter:

> Astonishing! Astonishing! It still has me reeling! To have eyes, ears, all five senses, but to make no use of them! Our ancestors put it well: Never make a companion of a hothead. You Franks, you're always boiling over. [...] Does one have to know people's language to realize what's going on? Let me explain to you what you failed to understand."[30]

"I calmed him down," Abbadie concludes, "by admitting that I had been thoughtless, and we returned to Adwa as the best friends in the world."[31]

We are presented with a new incarnation of this figure straddling two worlds in the guise of "the Armenian-Ethiopian Garbiz Budurian," "a Copt and the Negus's former secretary—or so he claimed." Living in the Belleville of the 1930s as portrayed by the writer Clément Lépidis, Budurian is a distinguished, cultivated character who clashes with his immigrant and working-class Paris neighborhood. He is the very opposite of the book's hero, the cobbler Aram Tokatlerian, a humble Armenian refugee who, after losing his family and everything he owned in the massacres in Turkey, arrives penniless in Paris, where he manages to survive only by working illegally for a compatriot in his *chambre de bonne*. Budurian, too, has been living in dire poverty since arriving in France, but only as a consequence of a terrible reversal of fortune that he suffered in the days when, in Ethiopia, "he lived at the court of the King of kings," "enjoying his esteem and trust," and, according to the novelist, was fabulously rich: "What adventure was responsible for the fact that he ended up in Paris? That was a riddle for everyone." The attic apartment that he rents in the Passage Julien-Lacroix is still plastered with portraits of Haile Selassie that Budurian has clipped from magazines. He has preserved his passion for coffee, drinking it as ceremoniously as is the custom in Ethiopia, and, when he hears the announcement of the Italian invasion, which makes him "the first victim of Italian fascism in Belleville," he recites in a low voice in "Armeno-Abyssinian"—a new tongue invented by Lépidis—"his hapless country's Constitution."[32] Of all the characters in this novel, he is the one who seems, by far, the least at home in his surroundings. He is also the one who allows the author to shake off the constraints of plausibility and the otherwise realistic presentation of all the other actors in his story (French and foreign workers, Armenian refugees, Greeks and Polish or German Jews). An imaginary character, a former Armenian from a fantasized Ethiopia painted with broad strokes of the brush, Garbiz Budurian nevertheless recalls, thanks to certain decisive traits, Abraham Koeurhadjian—who, after studying in France, in Marseilles, had indeed been *Ras* Täfäri's and then Emperor Haile Selassie's private secretary for many years, before being deported to Calabria by the Italians and held captive there during the war, together with some of the leading Ethiopian grandees in the emperor's entourage.[33] Thus the novelist seems to have taken his inspiration, if not from reality, then at least from prevailing representations of an Armenian-Ethiopian amalgam.

Literature seizes on the figure of the Armenian of Ethiopia as an apt means of expressing this original amalgam. Henry de Monfreid's books, which take their place halfway between travel narrative and fictional narrative by presenting their author's personal experiences as so many "adventures," employ similar devices. In his *Terres hostiles* [Enemy territories], de Monfreid devotes many a page to the "fat Armenian Kherbeguian," whom the Ethiopians familiarly call "Mina" because he represents, in their view, the unique case of a foreigner "who came to Abyssinia at the age of seven" and "succeeded in adapting to the Abyssinians' character," intimate knowledge of which Monfreid proudly claims for himself at every turn. Kherbeguian affords him the chance to illustrate his very general argument about the "perfectly adapted parasites" who, he says, "are part of the life of the country," with the fortunate difference, in his opinion, that Minas, in contrast to the general run of "Levantines," "has brought off the admirable exploit of remaining subaltern without making himself contemptible," so that "he has managed to maintain his dignity as a European." Monfreid explains, with a certain admiration, how this autodidact went about things, finding "the means of acquiring, on his own, the elementary education required to learn the basics of the engineer's profession," so that he could set about constructing buildings—among others, the new residence in which the dethroned emperor *Lej* Iyasu was to be interned—and roads running through the mountains and countryside, in record time and with "a remarkably practical turn of mind." It is, it seems, because he does not act like a European and is not considered to be one that the Armenian engineer has proved capable of a "tour de force that would have been impossible in our part of the world, but is very simple here," which consists of marking off the course of a future road by setting out "on his mule," traveling from village to village, and requisitioning thousands of Oromo peasants living to either side of it for a true corvée, in line with "custom": "the route was laid out in three days."[34] Minas Kherbekian, born in 1887 in Arabkir as the son of the mason, Pilibbos, who built the baths in Fell Woha, holds a prominent place in the pantheon of the Armenians of Ethiopia. He still is a well-known figure in Addis Abeba, where he long served the municipality and Emperor Haile Selassie as a surveyor. His activity in this field earned him the Amharic nickname *Minas bēt afrash*, "Minas the demolisher of houses," which has since acquired a proverbial dimension. The zigzags in the route indicate, the story goes, the location of the houses in which Minas kept a mistress and which he had consequently chosen to spare.[35] Avedis

Terzian, who knew him well, described him as "a quasi-Ethiopian Armenian" who had "created an Ethiopian family" and was capable of filling the many orders of the Ethiopian government "without an office, without European complications": "he had no road plans, but he spoke Amharic perfectly, he knew their mentality, he became the most important man in the empire when it came to roads."[36] Thus Monfreid's assessments of Minas Kherbekian reflect not only his personal judgment but also his contemporaries' shared feeling that this "fat, unshaven man with an expressionless face, doubtless because of his strange toad's eyes," embodied the symbolic gray zone that other writers have sought to portray.

"Men of the World": Evelyn Waugh's Armenian Encounters in Ethiopia

The Armenian characters peopling the Ethiopian segment of Evelyn Waugh's literary work shed light on some of the ways this symbolic gray zone has been put to use. In 1930, Waugh was sent to Ethiopia by the London magazine *The Graphic* to observe the festivities surrounding Haile Selassie's coronation as emperor. From this experience, he drew the material for part of *Remote People* (1931), memoirs of his travels in Ethiopia and Kenya. He went to Ethiopia as a journalist again when the Italian-Ethiopian war broke out in 1935, an experience he reports on in *Waugh in Abyssinia* (1936). The extreme irony with which he describes Haile Selassie's Ethiopia, which later served as a source of inspiration for very acerbic parodic novels, has not helped create an image of him as a serious writer. Observing matters as an outsider, Waugh leaves the impression that details interest him more than major events.[37] In 1935, he seems unable to really follow the evolution of the war then underway, preferring to describe, in a disabused, sarcastic tone, the atmosphere of the end of a reign and the small world of European diplomats or journalists in Addis Abeba. This is perhaps why, more than any other author of his day in Ethiopia, he paid so much attention to certain Armenians he met.

Neglecting the celebrations of the imperial coronation, Waugh assigns an important place to an excursion he made to the monastery of Däbrä Libanos in the company of an American scholar,[38] but also, and above all, in that of "a bullet-headed Armenian chauffeur, and a small native boy, who attached himself to us without invitation." This banal trip to the countryside provides the pretext for a reflection, between the lines, on Europeans' and Abyssinians'—that is, on *Färänjs*' and *Habäshas*'—basic inability to understand each other. Waugh's Armenian chauffeur manifestly intrigues him because of his conspicuous detachment and the strangely reassuring nature of his presence, as when rifles are pointed at them after they run, in the middle of the night, "straight into a caravan bivouacked round a camp-fire" and cause a general panic: "The Armenian strode into their midst, however, and, after distributing minute sums of money as a sign of goodwill, elicited directions." Addressing the two tourists in French, the chauffeur punctuates all the difficulties they meet along their way with an "*ah, Monsieur, ça n'a pas d'importance*" [ah, sir, that's of no importance]—for example, when he narrowly avoids running over beggars who flock round the automobile. At the monastery, his knowledge of Amharic enables him to make the visitors' stay among the monks go more smoothly by taking charge of the small talk and "speedily establish[ing] relations of the utmost geniality" while refraining from translating the tactless remarks of the American professor who prides himself on his knowledge of Eastern theologies. The chauffeur/interpreter conducts himself exactly the same way as the young Ethiopian boy accompanying them who scatters, with a hail of rocks, a troop of baboons that the two tourists were gazing at in admiration and threatens to apply the same treatment to the deacons who crowd around them. One of the most illuminating moments of this narrative is the story of the meal that the monks offer the two tourists, who have no choice but to eat it, however unappetizing it looks:

> At last supper arrived; first a basket containing half-a-dozen great rounds of native bread, a tough, clammy substance closely resembling crêpe rubber in appearance; then two earthenware jugs, one of water, the other of *talla*—a kind of thin, bitter beer; then two horns of honey, but not of honey as it is understood at Thame; this was the product of wild bees, scraped straight from the trees; it was a greyish colour, full of bits of stick and mud, bird dung, dead bees, and grubs. Everything was first carried to the abuna for his approval, then to us. We expressed our delight with nods and more extravagant smiles. The food was laid before us and the bearers retired. At this moment the Armenian shamelessly deserted us, saying that he must go and see after his boy.[39]

Waugh and his companion, famished, but repulsed by the food offered them, wait until they are alone to open a can of grouse and a bottle of European beer that they have brought with them, when the Armenian comes back:

> With a comprehensive wink, he picked up the jug of native beer, threw back his head, and without pausing to breathe, drank a quart or two. He then spread out two rounds of bread, emptied a large quantity of honey into each of them, wrapped them together, and put them in his pocket. "Moi, je puis manger comme abyssin" [as for me, I can eat like an Abyssinian], he remarked cheerfully, winked at the grouse, wished us good night, and left us.[40]

It is worth noting that, to the present day, the Armenian families of Addis Abeba eat Ethiopian bread, *enjära*, every day. They did so in the 1930s as well, at a time when all these families lived with the Ethiopian servants who prepared their meals.[41] Thus we have here the example of someone perfectly at ease in both a European and an Ethiopian environment, whose activity is limited neither by linguistic barriers nor by culinary preferences. The place that Waugh makes for him in his narrative shows how striking he found this.

In the same narrative, Waugh dilates on the profound impression that another encounter with an Armenian in Harar, a certain "Bergebedgian," left on him.[42] Bergebedgian was "a stout little man in a black skull-cap," the owner of one of the two inns in the city, "both universally condemned as unsuitable for European habitation," who "spoke a queer kind of French with remarkable volubility."[43] Waugh avers that he was sincerely attached to this man: "I found great delight in all his opinions; I do not think that I have ever met a more tolerant man; he had no prejudice or scruples of race, creed, or morals of any kind whatever." In fact, despite his hotel's rather unattractive appearance, the coarseness of his excessively fatty and spicy cuisine, and the insalubrity of the adulterated drinks he serves, his character matches Waugh's personal conception of the true gentleman. He turns out to be the ideal guide to the old Muslim city and the person best qualified to initiate the British writer into an understanding of its inhabitants' customs, but also to gain him access to the Greek, Indian, and Armenian merchants' businesses, and even to the most wretched native hovels or bars:

> He was a remarkable guide. We went into the shops of all his friends and drank delicious coffee and smoked cigarettes; he seemed to have small financial transactions with all of them, paying out a thaler here, receiving another there. [...] We went through the bazaar, Mr. Bergebedgian disparaging all the goods in the friendliest way possible, and I bought some silver bangles which he obtained for me at a negligible fraction of their original price. We went into several private houses, where Mr. Bergebedgian examined and exhibited everything, pulling clothes out of the chests, bringing down bags of spice from the shelves, opening the oven and tasting the food, pinching the girls, and giving half-piastre pieces to the children. We went into a workshop where three or four girls of dazzling beauty were at work making tables and trays of fine, brilliantly-patterned basketwork. Everywhere he went he seemed to be welcome; *everywhere he not only adapted but completely transformed his manners to the environment.*[44]

Waugh comments: "I was surprised to realize that the two most accomplished men I met during this six months I was abroad [...] should both have been Armenians." He imagines that he has found, in this "race of rare competence and the most delicate sensibility [...] the only genuine 'men of the world.'" He regrets that he will never be able to be one of them, because he knows that he will always be vulnerable to life's small inconveniences, and that, as he admits, "I shall always be ill at ease with nine out of every ten people I meet [...]—then I comfort myself a little by thinking that, perhaps, if I were an Armenian, I should find things easier."[45] Further on in the same text, Waugh confirms, when he befriends a Turk living in Zanzibar, the affinity with Armenians that he has acquired in the course of his journey: "The warmth of my admiration for Armenians clearly shocks him, but he is too polite to say so. Instead, he tells me of splendid tortures inflicted on them by his relatives."[46] Waugh does not seem to realize that it is only in a particular context that the Armenians he admires are able to conduct themselves as they do. It is in a very precise social configuration and historical context, not at all because of certain racial or national traits, that the most Ethiopianized Armenians—as a rule, people who came to Ethiopia at a very young age, like, no doubt, Waugh's chauffeur in Däbrä Libanos—found themselves in a position to evolve socially in the company of Ethiopians as easily as in that of Europeans. This propensity is an indication of how far the interstitial space of sociabilities opened up to them had come by the interwar period. The collective representations of this symbolic gray zone, however, could sometimes work to the disadvantage of the individuals involved.

The Fate of Three "Abyssinized" Families under the Italian Occupation

The decisions that the Italian administration in Ethiopia took with regard to certain Armenian families seem to have been prompted, in part, by these representations. After the February 19, 1937, attempt on the life of the viceroy of Italian East Africa, Marshal Rodolfo Graziani, more than four hundred notables, aristocrats, and dignitaries of the former Empire of Ethiopia were banished to southern Italy. Most of the Ethiopians detained after being charged with complicity in the plot against Graziani were found innocent and, beginning in summer 1938, were authorized to return to Ethiopia, at a time when the Italians wished to institute a form of indirect administration entrusted to appointed autochthonous leaders. Only a handful, the "incorrigible," as well as the emperor's family or close associates, around ninety people in all, were kept in exile in Italy.[47] Included in this group were those whom the Minister of the Interior had thought it wise to transfer from the camp in Asinara, in Sardinia, to another in Longobucco (near Cosenza), Calabria as early as 1937, because they had been classified as "dangerous internees." The administration recommended that they not be treated "with half-measures." Of twenty-four of these "particularly dangerous Ethiopians who had been transferred for assignation to Longobucco," all had Ethiopian names and, in most cases, an honorific title, with the exception of four: Abraham Koeurhadjian, Khosrov Boghossian, and the Baghdassarian brothers, Armenag and Aramast. Koeurhadjian and the Baghdassarian brothers were later joined in exile by their families. In 1939, there were still thirty-four names on the list of Longobucco's male internees; ten of them were those of members of these families of Armenian origin. Khosrov Boghossian's and Armenag and Aramast Baghdassarian's names were preceded by the Ethiopian title *Lej*, which underscored the importance of the ties that these heirs of Menelik's old Armenian servants had to the imperial court. The Koeurhadjian family had eight members at the time: the father, his wife Aishè, and their sons Yervant, Nerses, Torkom, Haygaz, Toros, and Hrant, to which we must add Khosrov Boghossian, who was still in detention. Thus, in April 1943, of the nineteen people still interned in Longobucco, nearly half were of Armenian extraction.[48] To the best of my knowledge, these Armenians were the only people of foreign origin interned in Italy, except for the Russian-Ethiopian Babitcheff family, which had been deported to Libya in late 1936 and had spent time in various places of banishment in Italy thereafter.[49] The case of this family, however, resembled that of the families of Armenian origin. All had been residents of Ethiopia for at least two generations. These families comprised Ethiopian subjects or people who had remained stateless. Moreover, all were the products of intermarriage with Ethiopian families.

If these people were interned in Longobucco together with the Ethiopian leaders who were deemed the most "incorrigible," it was because they were regarded as being very close to Ethiopia's imperial family and considered, for all practical purposes, to be Ethiopian, their Armenian origins notwithstanding. In their correspondence with the Italian administration, these exiles generally present themselves as "detained Ethiopians" or as "Armenians, interned Ethiopians," while the Italian officials variously describe them as Ethiopians, natives of Italian East Africa, or Armenians and mixed-race Armenians. In a police report, Abraham Koeurhadjian is identified as "an Italian colonial subject," meaning that he did not have a valid nationality and was not a protégé of any foreign state; the report states that he was "born in Turkey of Armenian parents, in his fifties, a Coptic Christian, married to Aishè Koerdajian [sic], the daughter of Mogos Koerdajian [sic][50] and Amettè Tzion, approximately forty-three years old, born in Addis Abeba, by whom he has had six sons." The man figures as an "Ethiopianized element [elemento abissinizzato], for although he arranged to have his sons study in Europe, he brought them up in the Coptic faith"; thus he embraced the religion of the Ethiopian Christians, like Lépidis's Garbiz Budurian. His entire entourage was Ethiopianized, since "his wife, an Armenian mixed-race, dressed in the manner of Ethiopian ladies" [delle uozerò abissine],[51] a detail that did not plead in the Koeurhadjian family's favor. Similarly, Khosrov Boghossian, "a half-breed Armenian," is mentioned in a list of "Abyssinian personalities who arrived on May 3 and 4, 1936, in Djibouti," to which they had followed the emperor when he went into exile, together with one of Babitcheff's mixed-race sons, who had become a pilot in the Ethiopian air force.[52] It was the fact that Italian civil servants considered them to be very close to the Ethiopians, or even Ethiopianized, that seems to have legitimized the special treatment reserved for them, rather than any real political threat that they might have represented.

Beginning in 1937, the Minister of the Interior had pointed to the need to "evacuate the seaside resort of Asinara, where groups of Ethiopians have been confined," and "to send no more Ethiopian internees to Italy, in view of the difficulty of providing premises for their internment." Thus the minister had to make an exception to the rules, in response to requests that Graziani had expressly formulated and duly justified, in order to authorize the dispatch of the Koeurhadjian and Baghdassarian families to join Abraham, Armenag, and Aramast in Italy. Graziani described the members of the Koeurhadjian family as people "imbued with extremist ideas, who maintain relations with the Abyssinian refugees in Djibouti, who propagate false news in the intention of diminishing our prestige among the native elements, and whom it does not seem possible to intern in a locality in Eastern Africa because they are politically dangerous." His justification for sending a third son of Hagop Baghdassarian, Ardashes, to Italy together with Ardashes's mother and his niece was similar; this measure seemed all the more urgent in that "the above-named person can neither be expelled, because he has held an Italian passport since 1929, nor interned in Italian East Africa, because he is politically dangerous." Thus it was "in view of the special nature of their case and for serious reasons" that the Interior Ministry authorized these exceptions to the rules; the Koeurhadjian and Baghdassarian families had, under close surveillance, to be "incorporated into the group of internees in Longobucco," that is, the notorious "incorrigible" internees.[53] Abraham Koeurhajian's activity in the Ethiopian government's service, at the beginning of the war, left no doubt about his political sympathies: "When large numbers of Italians had to abandon Addis Abeba, he initiated and then headed a government commission to carry out appropriations at our citizens' expense, seizing—according to reports—a great deal of landed property."[54] Apart from this unsubstantiated accusation, however, which appears only once, there is nothing concrete in the files on the "incorrigible" internees with which they might be reproached. Before Ethiopia was occupied, Khosrov Boghossian had had no official functions other than his position as the "jockey of the former negus and former director of the racecourse." Abraham Koeurhadjian "was the administrator of the former negus's private assets" and "held, under the old negusite government, various posts, as director of the quarter of Filohà [Fell Woha], administrator in a factory, and Haile Selassie's chief accountant, secretary and confidant." His various functions do not ever seem, however, to have given him a sensitive political role. In May 1940, that is, three years after the beginning of an internment that had seen them transferred from a prison in Addis Abeba to the internment camps in Asinara and Longobucco, the General Government of Italian East Africa admitted that no particular charge could be lodged against them. They should therefore be treated with "clemency," the General Government declared, and authorized to return to Ethiopia.[55] That return was, however, delayed until such time as normal communications could be reestablished between Italy and Italian East Africa. As a result of the escalation of the international conflict and the fact that the Italian administration was, for material reasons, unable to send them back to Ethiopia, these people were interned at least until 1943.

The Life and Death of an Armenian Patriot in Ethiopia

Hovhannes Semerjibashian's career bears witness to forms of social mobility that were very highly developed by the Armenian immigrants who found themselves in this configuration. It is typical of careers in the first phase of the Armenian immigration in Ethiopia. Semerjibashian was born in Arabkir in 1893, before his father Avedis, a merchant who had lived in Egypt, settled in Harar around 1899.[56] After entering the American high school in Bardizag in 1906, he returned from his eight years of education in Turkey as a polyglot: in addition to Armenian and Amharic, he spoke French, English, German, and Turkish. In 1914, he was employed as assistant interpreter in the British legation in Addis Abeba. Held in high esteem by the British ambassador to Ethiopia, Wilfred Thesiger, he was left in charge of the British consulate in Harar during the consul's occasional absences. After a voyage to Europe, he worked, from 1919 to 1923, as the Ethiopian representative of the Anglo-American Oil Company, which was planning a campaign to prospect for oil in the country. In 1925, he entered the service of the German legation as chief interpreter. His new duties saw him attending the special tribunal when litigation involving German citizens came to trial. He was part of a German delegation charged with concluding a trade agreement with Yemen in 1930. That same year, he attended Haile Selassie's coronation as emperor as an official member of the German delegation. After the German diplomatic representation in Ethiopia was closed in 1941, he worked in the service of Sweden and, thereafter, for the United States embassy. Like many Armenians of his generation, he established close ties and many friendships with Ethiopians close to the imperial court. He was part of the same relatively Ethiopianized fringe of the small Armenian colony to which, as we have briefly seen, the Koeurhadjians, Boghossians, and Baghdassarians also belonged. In 1917, he married a high-ranking aristocrat, Wäyzäro Atsädä Maryam Wäsän Yälläh.

Their children were given hyphenated Armenian-Ethiopian names, such as that of their oldest son, Vahakn-Aklilu Semerjibashian. According to a manuscript belonging to Semerjibashian *fils*, based in part on an autobiographical text that his father left behind at his death,[57] Hovhannes Semerjibashian was so closely tied to Ethiopian aristocratic circles that he played a role, in 1916, in organizing secret meetings of the aristocrats who were in favor of dethroning Emperor *Lej* Iyasu. He was thus ideally placed to serve as an intermediary between the legation of Great Britain, his employer at this time, and *Ras* Täfäri's partisans. In the interwar period, moreover, Hovhannes Semerjibashian was close to Haile Selassie, was decorated with the Star of Ethiopia by the emperor in 1930, and ranked, as the conventional formula had it, among the "patriots and the new Emperor's servants and friends."[58] Several photographs show Hovhannes Semerjibashian and the emperor side by side in public. Personally smitten early in the 1935–6 Italian-Ethiopian war by the deaths of several of his Ethiopian friends, notably that of his brother-in-law, *Däjazmach* Afä Wärq Wäldä Sämayat, he wholeheartedly espoused the Ethiopian cause and, shortly before Emperor Haile Selassie's went into exile on May 2, 1936, went to see him together with other supporters in order to assure him once again of his loyalty on the steps of the church of the Holy Trinity.[59]

After Italian troops marched into Addis Abeba on May 5, 1936, Semerjibashian seems to have lost no time making contact with members of the Ethiopian resistance. He is said to have remained in the capital because he thought he could be of greater use to the cause there, thanks to his post in the German legation,[60] which had been reduced to the level of a consulate general. From there, he is supposed to have helped expedite ammunition and medicines to those fighting in the resistance, with whom he corresponded under the Ethiopian pseudonym *Abba* Gäbrä Sellasē.[61] He was arrested by the Italians in July 1936 together with the former Ethiopian interpreter in the British legation, Täfärra Wärq Kidanä Wäld, "because he was strongly suspected of conniving with the rebels; His Excellency Graziani released him, however, after the German consulate interceded,"[62] although Graziani had earlier proposed, in a telegraph to Rome, to have the two prisoners executed.[63] The close surveillance of Semerjibashian and his oldest son was maintained after his release. A telegram from the governor of Italian East Africa presented Semerjibashian as "an element representing a danger to our national interests," noting that "he has been living in Ethiopia for about twenty years," knows several foreign languages, and has an Abyssinian wife. "According to a credible source," the governor added, "one of his sons, a mixed-race, is studying in Paris with financial aid from the former negus," a circumstance that speaks volumes about the ties that bound the Semerjibashian family to the emperor's, as well as the suspicions that he could excite among the Italians. From the outbreak of the war, he is supposed to have collaborated with the Ethiopian information service, which was headed by a Greek officer, Moscopoulos, and to have been involved "in an intense pro-Abyssinian propaganda campaign," behind which the Italians discerned, as was their wont, the hand of the English and the Intelligence Service.[64] Beginning in June 1940 and the United Kingdom's entry into war with Italy, Semerjibashian helped found, with Armenian and Ethiopian friends, an underground newspaper published in Amharic, *Amdä Berhan zä'Ityopeya*, which was designed to provide information to the resistance movement led by Abäbä Arägay in the Addis Abeba region.[65]

After the British consented to authorize Haile Selassie's return to Addis Abeba on May 5, 1941, Semerjibashian was one of the many Ethiopians troubled by the fact that people who had spent the war years in exile and who even, in the case of certain dignitaries, had actively collaborated with the Italians, were quite simply put back in positions of power. Although he was decorated, together with other former members of the resistance, with the Imperial Order of Merit on the Grand Esplanade of Janhoy-Mēda in November 1944, and was effusively celebrated in the *Ethiopian Herald* of December 9, 1946, which passed the adventurous history of the newspaper *Amdä Berhan* in review,[66] his relations with Haile Selassie's government deteriorated sharply after the country's liberation. Openly critical of the government, he was declared persona non grata in a November 13, 1946, circular addressed to the entire diplomatic corps. Residing openly in Addis Abeba, as he had in the past, and going about his activities without any apparent change, he was still working at his post in the US embassy, which he had held since 1941, when he was assassinated, on the evening of October 9, 1947, in all probability on orders from the government. Indications are that his murderer was a member of the imperial guard.[67] In this sense, his case was no different from that of many other Ethiopian veterans of the resistance who were sidelined or eliminated in the postwar years. Hovhannes Semerjibashian, who arrived in Ethiopia at a young age, developed deep familial ties and personal relationships there. His career is representative of the interstitial situation in which the Armenian immigrants and their descendants found themselves. He pursued it to the point of making, unreservedly, the cause of Ethiopia's independence his own.

Attending to the ways individuals use the configuration of which they have become an integral part helps free us from the stereotypes conveyed by the majority of written sources, but as well from the inevitably idealized vision perpetuated by the memory of the Armenian immigration in Ethiopia. Asking the question in terms of social space forces us to consider the external, collective factors that, everywhere and at all times, orient individuals' choices and trajectories. The contours of this space evolve. As the legal question shows, they can give rise to reversals, running from the expansion of the field of available possibilities in a space that authorizes all sorts of variations in forms of belonging to the contraction of this field. Observation of the effects that this configuration induces in its agents, effects that are sometimes emancipatory or protective and at other times restrictive, diverges from identity-based readings of the social. By way of the attempt to establish empirical proof of the existence of an interstitial space, it allows us to objectivize a social reality that is palpable but hard to grasp.

Conclusion

At the end of this investigation, the Negus's brass band seems to play a kind of music very different from anything we could have suspected when set out. However strange it may seem, this migratory experience, transformed into an epic, is rich in lessons on the social formation of communities and the fabrication of collective identities. Choosing to consider the creation of this brass band not as an isolated act or an inexplicable curiosity of contemporary Ethiopian history, but as a political event in the full sense of the word, allows us to pose questions about the uses of the past and the invention of Ethiopian traditions that actively mobilize foreigners' collective representations. Hypothesizing a symbolic nationalization of the Armenians in Ethiopia entails deconstructing the way that the history of the foreign presence in Ethiopia is written and, equally, taking one's distance from the typological categories employed by specialists of diasporas.

One of the major difficulties of this investigation has to do with the fact that such subtle phenomena do not engender an abundant documentation that historians can readily consult. There are no official archives of the invisible. That is why our study of the Armenians' memory has had to make detours. The collective autobiography, or the result of my collaboration with Avedis Terzian, constituted inestimably rich raw material. It was neither a resume nor a photograph of *the* collective memory, but a source that revealed the vivacity and social character of the Armenian Grand Narrative in Ethiopia. The multiple meanings of the theme of the friendship of kings, a metaphor for the taking-root of the immigrants and their descendants as they themselves experienced it, made it possible to reveal the construction of a "sedentary memory" or a "memory of guests" in Ethiopia, as opposed to the "memories of exile" or "memories of the banished" of which the literature on refugees, and on the Armenian diaspora in particular, offers countless examples. This active recomposition of the past is not exempt from the forms of politicization of memories of immigration observable in other contexts. Mobilizing *Negus* Täfäri's brass band of forty children, for example, makes it possible to reestablish, today a connection that had not appeared earlier between the memory of the Armenian immigration in Ethiopia and that of the genocide. In the same perspective, we can continue to interrogate the influence that the growing formalization of the legal borderline between the foreign and the national in

Ethiopia had on the recompositions of the Armenian Grand Narrative over the second half of the twentieth century.

The immigrants' and their descendants' ways of being and acting—it would doubtless be more exact to speak of their *possibilities* for being and acting—underscore the need to refine ways of looking at the question of the "foreigner" in Ethiopia and to admit that what distinguishes it from the "national" is neither obvious nor indifferent. Here we broach questions that have been raised about integration in studies on immigration, that is, on the different forms of social mobility and individuals' participation in collective life.[1] There are many indications of the Armenians' Ethiopianization in very different domains, running from domestic to political life. Here there is matter for complexifying the schema of an Ethiopian society said to be systematically closed to "foreigners." These rich, complex forms of the socialization of individuals also cast doubt on the theoretical validity of the model of "middlemen minorities" that are supposedly oriented, by their very nature, toward their country of origin; are not capable of taking root in their society of residence; and never fully accepted by the autochthonous population. Classifications of this kind, because they lead us to view the social in terms of collective entities alone, do not allow us to grasp the complex reality of an interstitial space that blurs the borderline between the national and the foreign. The uses of this "interstitiality" show that the legal and political definition of nationality in Ethiopia was only feebly developed prior to the Second World War and that it was more precisely defined much later than in the countries in which large numbers of immigrants settled. That is why the "non-definitions" of their legal status long seemed to redound to the Armenian immigrants's benefit, although they seem to have penalized immigrants in other political contexts.

Beyond drawing up a balance sheet of the most empirical aspects of this book, it seems to me important to insist on the questions of method that it poses, for this investigation takes its place neither in the sphere of community studies nor in a defined cultural domain, be it Armenian or Ethiopian. The questions it poses are transversal. How are we to define the situation of individuals in a diaspora who are not, in the proper sense, foreigners in the society in which they reside—this alchemy of the process of taking root that was revealed by the initial, ethnographic stage of the investigation, yet, pending a more precise description, remains a sort of mystery difficult to objectivize? How are we to conceive of the construction and social uses of this gray zone without falling back on an identity-based paradigm? What is the study of diasporas likely to contribute to the understanding of their societies of residence?

Since the 1980s, works on nationalism have exerted renewed influence on the discussion of the social construction of "communities." Their conclusions have been rather too facilely put to use in studies of both nation-states and infra-national, supranational, or even transnational constructs such as diasporas. This holds for Benedict Anderson's celebrated text on "imagined communities," which purports to ask, "in an anthropological spirit," why nations, "these particular cultural artefacts[,] have aroused such deep attachments."[2] Simply invoking a collective "imaginary," however, does not suffice to explain the sedimentation, in Ethiopia, of an Armenian "community," these "white Ethiopians" who became "an Ethiopian minority of Armenian tradition," to cite Avedis Terzian's words. For there is no eluding objective determinations in analyzing allegiances of this kind. Ernest Gellner's reflection on nationalism, which is often too hastily summed up in the notion that it leads us to take nations to be pure inventions, shows that what we commonly tend to consider as the creation of ideologues or the awakening of passions is the product of exogenous factors. The "we," which a good many social scientists content themselves with explaining, tautologically, in terms of a "sentiment of belonging," cannot be understood as the mere emanation of a common culture (in the linguistic sense, e.g.), or, more vaguely, a "cultural heritage," a simple will (the desire to live together dear to Ernest Renan), or, again, the fantasy of "the imaginary." If it is to be truly understood, it must also be envisaged as the surface manifestation of "structural requirements" of the society in which this phenomenon is produced.[3] This remark is fundamental because it invites us to keep our eyes trained on the relations established between the collective and the individual, by means of the play of ties of interdependence, and, sometimes, of constraints. Conceiving of the Armenian presence in Ethiopia in terms of social space, rather than identities, allows us to go further toward an understanding of its original features. Thus we avoid grounding our analysis on collective entities such as ethno-national communities, middlemen minorities, and other preconceived diasporan categories whose existence seemingly needs no demonstration. Therein resides, beyond a doubt, the principal contribution of the socio-historical approach, which makes it possible to bring the individual into an analysis of social transformations. Broached with this methodological concern in mind, in a sedentary approach attentive to the contexts in which outsiders take root in their country of adoption, the study of the forms of socialization of individuals in diasporas can prove particularly fecund when the aim is to produce historical knowledge of the societies in which they reside. It is in this sense that, I hope, the present book will find its place in discussions to come.

Notes

Preface to the Second Edition

1. Vartkes Nalbandian's recent book (2019) is the one that best explains the evolution of Ethiopia's Armenian community from the 1960s to the 2000s.
2. See, for example, Harre (2015); Bezabeh (2015); Bonacci (2008); De Lorenzi (2008 and 2016). See also Berhe and De Napoli (2022).

Introduction: From the Sedentary Logic of Diasporas to the History of the Nation-State

1. Amharic vowels are here transliterated as follows: *ä* (pronounced like the a in "ago"; *u* (pronounced like the u in "boost"), *i* (pronounced like the "e" in "be"), *a* (pronounced like the a in "father"), *ē* (pronounced like the "a" in "sane" or like the "ier" in "Perrier," depending on the case), *e* (close to the Turkish "ı," as in *rakı*), and *o* (pronounced like a short English "o"). For ease of reading, Amharic consonants are spelled phonetically (sh, ch, j, ñ, and so on); plosives are not noted. Exceptionally, certain personal and place names are spelled the way they usually are in English: Addis Abeba (Addis Abäba), Harar (Harär), Dire Dawa (Derē Dawa), Massawa (Mätsäwa), Menelik (Menilek), Haile Selassie (Haylä Sellasē), and so on. The spelling of Armenian family names and other Armenian words is based on the way they are pronounced in Western Armenian. See also the glossary at the end of the book.
2. In its modern sense, this term designates a mountainous area a majority of whose inhabitants are Christians speaking one of two Semitic languages derived from Ge'ez, Tegreñña, and Amhareñña. It is located partly in the state of Ethiopia and partly in the state of Eritrea.
3. See the map of Ethiopia and the bordering countries, p. xviii.
4. Green (2002). For a fuller bibliography, see Adjemian (2011a).
5. Dufoix (2003, pp. 43–61). Cohen (1997).
6. Bordes-Benayoun (2002); Tölölyan (2005).
7. Hovanessian (1992; 2005, p. 67; 2007c, p. 449).
8. Elias (1991, pp. 10–11, 154–61).
9. Geertz (1973, p. 22). Emphasis in the original.
10. Gaston Bachelard, cited in Garcia (1989, pp. 17–8).
11. Ginzburg (1979, p. 280).
12. Revel (1996).
13. Bloch ([1924] 1973, p. 3).
14. Ibid.
15. Wachtel ([1971] 1992, pp. 306–7).
16. Bensa (2006, p. 9).

17. Amselle (1999, p. 61).
18. Halbwachs (1941, pp. 189 and 9).

1 Wax and Gold: The Royal Brass Band's Unsuspected Political Role

1. Hobsbawm and Ranger ([1983] 2012).
2. Cannadine ([1983] 2012, p. 133).
3. Gebre-Igziabiher Elyas (1994, p. 461).
4. The Ethiopian calendar runs seven to eight years behind the Gregorian calendar.
5. Ullendorff (1976, pp. 70–1); Haylä Sellasē (1972, illustration no. 26, pp. 160–1); Gebre-Igziabiher Elyas (1994, pp. 436, 438, 442).
6. Gustave Bertrand, *Les nationalités musicales étudiées dans le drame lyrique*, Paris: Didier (1872), cited in Francfort (2004).
7. Vovelle (1997).
8. Thiesse (1999, p. 15); Anderson (1983, p. 22).
9. Ihl (1996); Dompnier (1996); Francfort (2004).
10. Patapan (1930, pp. 211, 213, 266, and 269).
11. Liano (1929, pp. 183–4).
12. Nicod (1937, p. 119); Monfreid (1933, p. 218); Falceto (2001, p. 39).
13. Nicod (1937, p. 199).
14. Gebre-Igziabiher Elyas (1994, chap. 2).
15. Gebre-Igziabiher Elyas (1994, chap. 72, pp. 471–2) (emphasis added). The phrases in brackets in the quotations from this Ethiopian chronicle have been added by the editor (and translator) of the Amharic text.
16. Ibid.
17. Nicod (1937, p. 50).
18. Gebre-Igziabiher Elyas (1994, chap. 97, pp. 538–41).
19. Nicod (1937, pp. 93–4).
20. According to the personal testimony of a former member of the royal brass band, Mardiros Vagharshagian, who was interviewed by Francis Falceto on June 26, 1994, in Addis Abeba.
21. *Wäyzäro* is a term designating a lady of the Ethiopian aristocracy.
22. Gebre-Igziabiher Elyas (1994, chap. 88, p. 505); Nicod (1937, pp. 74–5).
23. The *abun* or *abunä* has for centuries been the head of the Ethiopian clergy. Until 1951, it was customary for the Coptic patriarch of Alexandria to name an Egyptian bishop to exercise this function. See Chap. 2.
24. Gebre-Igziabiher Elyas (1994, chap. 95, pp. 533, 544, and chap. 98).
25. See Gebre-Igziabiher Elyas (1994, chap. 89, pp. 511–14).
26. Marcus ([1987] 1995b); Bahru Zewde (2002 and 1991). See also Gebre-Igziabiher Elyas (1994, chap. 51, pp. 425–6, and chap. 53, p. 432). Täfäri's personal tutor in his youth in Harar was the vicar apostolic of the Gallas, in the person of the French bishop André Jarosseau.
27. Esme (1928, pp. 109–13).
28. Nicod (1937, pp. 196–8); Gleichen (1898, p. 251); Farago (1935, p. 27).
29. Armandy (1930, p. 172).
30. Falceto (2001, pp. 33, 37).

31. Témoignage d'Avedis Terzian, interviewed in Addis Abeba, May 27, 2000.
32. Marcus ([1975] 1995a, pp. 82–3).
33. Esme (1928, p. 111); Waugh (1931, pp. 28, 45–7); Nicod (1937, p. 50).
34. Jean Doresse, personal communication of March 12, 2007.
35. Gebre-Igziabiher Elyas (1994, chap. 86, pp. 501–2).
36. See the portrait of it painted by the monk Bahrey in his overview of the Christian society of the sixteenth century in Conti Rossini and Guidi (1907).
37. Nicod (1937, pp. 54–8).
38. Falceto (2002, pp. 717–19).
39. See (De Castro 1915), which contains a reproduction of a photograph of the orchestra (vol. 1, table 50, illustration 75); Nicod (1937, pp. 198–9).
40. Falceto (2002, p. 720).
41. Nicod (1937, p. 198) (emphasis added).
42. See Gebre-Igziabiher Elyas (1994, chap. 67).
43. The denunciation of the Treaty of Ucciali (Wechalē), which Menelik signed in 1899, was one of the factors leading to the first Italian-Ethiopian war. The dispute between the two signatories, which has spawned an abundant bibliography, arose from possible differences of interpretation between the Amharic and Italian versions of the treaty, some of which could have made Ethiopia a form of Italian protectorate. See especially Conti Rossini (1935).
44. Sohier (2007b, pp. 301–2, 331).
45. Gebre-Igziabiher Elyas (1994, chap. 53, p. 431).
46. In 1868, the crisis that opposed Great Britain to Emperor Tewodros (1855–68) ended in a victorious British army expedition and the emperor's suicide in his besieged fortress. See Chap. 2.
47. Ministère des Affaires étrangères [MAE], Series K, Ethiopia, vol. no. 14 (June 1, 1924, to August 31, 1924), letter from Gaussen to the Foreign Minister, Addis Abeba, August 9, 1924, cited in Sohier (2007a, pp. 209–10).
48. Gebre-Igziabiher Elyas (1994, chap. 69 and chap. 71, pp. 469–70).

2 The Long Time of an Event: From Jerusalem to Jerusalem

1. Shack (1979, pp. 43–7) and his introduction to Shack and Skinner (1979, pp. 12–13).
2. Marcus (1995b, pp. 73, 94); Bahru Zewde (1991, p. 129 and 2002, pp. 95–8); Sohier (2007b, p. 267).
3. Cerulli (1968, pp. 7–8) (preface to the third edition).
4. Isaac (1976); Conti Rossini (1942); Gruntfest (1984); Ricci (1955–8, p. 82); Olderrodge (1974).
5. Ullendorf ([1967] 2006, pp. 74–6); Colin (2002).
6. Cerulli (1968, pp. 212–20); Basset (1915); Esteves Pereira (1901).
7. Lusini (1993, pp. 45–7, 52, 61–7); Fiaccadori (1985 and 1984–5); Taddesse Tamrat (1972, pp. 197–8 and 206–10).
8. Sapritchian (1871, vol. 1, p. 3); Cerulli (1943–7, vol. 2, pp. 329–40).
9. Sapritchian (1871, vol. 1, preface).

10. Between 1527 and 1543, after declaring a jihad, Imam Ahmad ibn Ibrahim al-Ghazi of Harar, known as Grañ (the left-handed man), carried out a series of devastating raids on the Christian Kingdom of Ethiopia.
11. Cerulli (1943–7, vol. 1, pp. 379–81).
12. Hintlian (1989, p. 40).
13. Cust ([1929] 1980, pp. 23–4, 26) The term *yamak* (plural *yamaklar*) can be translated as "assistant" or "dependent" and can designate the subordinate rank of a person or an adjutant vis-à-vis his superior. Here it seems to refer to the notion of clientelism.
14. Cerulli (1943–7, vol. 2, p. 281).
15. Cerulli (1943–7, vol. 2, p. 277).
16. Cerulli (1943–7, vol. 2, pp. 107–17, 120–42, 197, 239–73, 275–81, 346); Appleyard, Irvine and Pankhurst (1985, pp. 101–3 and 105–8).
17. Sapritchian (1871, vol. 2, p. 165).
18. Cerulli (1943–7, vol. 2, pp. 341–2).
19. Bairu Tafla (1977, p. 179).
20. In addition to Dimotheos's narrative, the course of the voyage is described in letters that the two churchmen sent Patriarch Garabedian from Jedda and Suakin. They appear in volume 3 of the review *Sion*, published by the Armenian patriarchate of Jerusalem, notably no. 4 (April 30, 1867), pp. 48–54, no. 6 (June 30, 1867), pp. 89–90, no. 8 (August 31, 1867), pp. 121–2, and no. 12 (December 31, 1867), which also contains a letter from Patriarch Garabedian to Emperor Tewodros.
21. Sapritchian (1871, vol. 1, pp. 78–9).
22. Ibid., pp. 72–3.
23. This was no isolated case. Kevork Hintlian has brought the case of "Kapriel vartabed Yetovbiatsi" (in Armenian, "Father Gabriel of Ethiopia") to our attention, evoked by Mgrdich Aghavnuni in *Miapank yev aytseluk* [Monks and visitors to Armenian Jerusalem, in Armenian], Jerusalem, 1929, p. 57. This Ethiopian secular monk learned Armenian from Patriarch Giragos Mnatseganian, who ordained him a priest according to the Armenian rite in 1843 before dispatching him to Ethiopia as the emissary of the Armenian patriarchate of Jerusalem in 1850. This information is carved on his tomb opposite the Coptic church of Saint Minas in Cairo, where he died in 1855.
24. According to Dimotheos, Kasa expressly seconded the two visitors' request. It is noteworthy that the only people to boast that they had seen through this mystery were, at a century's interval, two Armenian authors of travel narratives. The first was the jeweler Hovhannes Thovmajian, who did so following his journey to Ethiopia in the 1760s. See Nersessian and Pankhurst (1986, p. 615).
25. Sapritchian (1871, vol. 1, pp. 121, 128–30, 135–44, 149, 177).
26. For a discussion, see also De Lorenzi (2008).
27. Ibid., pp. 152–3.
28. Rubenson (1976, pp. 34, 62–3); Erlich (2000, pp. 24–8); Bahru Zewde (2002, pp. 108–9).
29. Sapritchian (1871, vol. 1, pp. 153–5 and 160–4).
30. Bairu Tafla (1977, p. 87).
31. Lefebvre (1845a, p. 15).
32. Sapritchian (1871, p. 92).

33. Pankhurst (1978–9, pp. 277–8), who cites the narratives of Reverend Joseph Wolf and Charles Beke. According to Richard Pankhurst, Hovhannes may well be the "Persian" priest by the name of Abba Mahlem mentioned in Combes and Tamisier (1838, vol. 3, p. 27).
34. Sapritchian (1871, vol. 1, pp. 80, 82, 91–2, 127–8); Zewde Gabre-Sellasie (1975, pp. 30–1); Matteucci (1880, pp. 178–9); Rubenson (1976, pp. 66, 131–6). See also Conti Rossini (1916, pp. 452, 472).
35. Geertz (1983, pp. 9–10).
36. Geertz (1967, p. 14) (reprinted in Geertz 1973, pp. 327–41).
37. Geertz (1973, p. 408).
38. Levine (1965).
39. Braudel (1984, pp. 50–1).
40. Combes and Tamisier (1838, vol. 2, pp. 345–52). See also Getatchew Haile, Lande, and Rubenson (1998); Rubenson (1976); Pankhurst (1966); Crummey (1972).
41. See Taddesse Tamrat (1998).
42. Rochet d'Héricourt (1846, p. 143).
43. The king of Portugal sent a contingent of 400 arquebusiers under the orders of Christovão da Gama, the son of the famous navigator, who arrived to lend a hand to the young king Gälawdēwos's armies in their conflict with the Muslims. See also Chap. 2, n. 10.
44. The Jesuit mission, led by Pedro Paez from 1603 on, set out, with the successive conversions to Catholicism of the Emperors Zä Dengel, Ya'eqob, and Susenyos (together with the latter's brother, Se'elä Krestos), to bring about a complete Latinization of the Ethiopian Church's liturgy and doctrines, insisting, notably, that all the emperor's subjects be baptized anew by Jesuits and decreeing that ordinations of priests and sacraments carried out by Egyptian bishops were null and void. In 1626, Afonso Mendez was enthroned as patriarch of Ethiopia and Emperor Susenyos took an oath of submission to the papacy.
45. See Conzelman (1895, pp. 158–9, 169, and 184); Ludolf (1684, pp. 317–65); Pennec (2003); Merid Wolde Aregay (1998).
46. See Thévenot (1665, p. 746); Ludof (1684, pp. 230–1, 368–9); Basset (1882, pp. 184–5 and 311–12); Tedeschi (1966, p. 109); Prutky (1991, pp. 92–102, 306–23).
47. See Caix de Saint-Aymour (1886, p. 179, n. 1 and p. 106).
48. Ibid., pp. 209–54; Bruce (1790, vol. 3, p. 112); Tedeschi (1966, p. 102); Basset (1882, pp. 308–9).
49. See, inter alia, in Alboyadjian (1946); Van Donzel (1979, pp. 177–84); Canard (1983); Tedeschi (1990). See also Avedik Paghtasarian's 1690 travel narrative in Alishan (1896–7). See also Topouzian (1974).
50. Guidi (1903, pp. 39–40); Tedeschi (1990, p. 7, n. 26).
51. See Donzel (1979); Alboyadjian (1946).
52. Ludolf (1684, pp. 397–8); Bruce (1790, vol. 2, p. 315).
53. Bruce (1790, vol. 2, pp. 310–11). In his *Mediterranean* ([1949] 1990, vol. 1, pp. 55–6), Fernand Braudel says much the same thing, citing Jean-Baptiste Tavernier's *Six Voyages*.
54. See Cini (2007); Curtin ([1984] 2002, pp. 198–204).
55. Agonts (1802–8, vol. 10, pp. 527, 533, 540–1); Nersessian and Pankhurst (1986); Adjemian (1998).

56. Bruce (1790, vol. 3, pp. 273–4).
57. Cited in (Van Donzel 1979, p. 158); see also (Van Donzel 1974 and 2007).
58. Bruce (1790, vol. 2, p. 310).
59. Ludolf (1684, p. 227).
60. See Chap. 2, n. 10.
61. Bruce (1790, vol. 2, pp. 310, 312–4); Ludolf 1684 (pp. 227–8); Beckingham and Huntingford (1961); Sergew Hable Selassie (1974). The chronicle of Emperor Gälawdēwos (1541–59) also notes that he built a palace with the help of "Syrian and Armenian" artists and engineers (Conzelman 1895, p. 143).
62. See Bruce (1790, vol. 3, pp. 87–90, 103, 129–30); Tedeschi (1966, pp. 102, 108); Caix de Saint-Aymour (1886, pp. 107–57).
63. Thévenot (1665, p. 476).
64. Caix de Saint Aymour (1886, pp. 294–6), who cites a "Mémoire sur les veuës que l'on a de pénétrer d'Égypte en Éthiopie par les routes du Nil ou de la mer Rouge par rapport à l'introduction du commerce des Indes orientales" that the French consul in Cairo drew up in 1697 and sent to Pontchartrain.
65. See Gulbenkian (1994–5).
66. There are counter examples, of course, as is shown by the detailed narrative of an Armenian working for the British consulate in Massawa, Margos, whom Hormuzd Rassam met in July 1864. This Armenian said that he had gone to Ethiopia to make his fortune and had introduced himself to Emperor Tewodros II "as an Armenian professing the same doctrine as he did." He had also told the emperor, he said, that he "had visited the Holy Sepulcher in Jerusalem"; "and, to prove it, I showed him the tatoo on my arm—the mark identifying a Christian pilgrim." Margos declared that, despite this display of doctrinal orthodoxy, Tewodros had accused him of being a Turkish spy, with the result that he was imprisoned and, later, thrown out of the country. See Rassam (1869, vol. 1, pp. 17–19).
67. Matteucci (1880, p. 251); Soleillet (1886, pp. 99, 105, 131).
68. See Lefebvre (1845b, vol. 1, pp. 47 and 51–2); Abbadie (1868, vol. 2, pp. 16, 43, 21–2, 62–3); Combes and Tamisier (1838, vol. 1, pp. 195–8, 206, 245, 251, and vol. 4, p. 231); Gobat (1834, p. 331); Ferret and Galinier (1847, vol. 2, pp. 69–75); Rubenson (1976, p. 68).
69. Combes and Tamisier (1838, vol. 1, pp. 195–6, 206); Lefebvre (1845b, vol. 1, pp. 53–4, 322 and vol. 2, p. 48); Ferret and Galinier (1847, vol. 1, pp. 439–44); Parkyns (1853, vol. 1, pp. 43, 45); Abbadie (1868, vol. 1, p. 37).
70. Sapritchian (1871, vol. 1, pp. 11, 14, 18, 34–5, 95, 124, 128–9, 144, 149, 165–6); Rassam (1869, vol. 1, pp. 77–8, 102); Abbadie (1868, vol. 1, pp. 36–7, 48, 601–2); Rochet d'Héricourt (1846, p. 142).
71. Justin de Jacobis was the head of the Lazarist mission in Tigré from 1839 on. His influence on *Ras* Webē, whom he converted to Catholicism, earned him the hostility of the head of the Ethiopian Church, *Abunä* Sälama.
72. See Brayer (1836, vol. 2, pp. 429–36); Torkomian (1928); Sapritchian (1871, vol. 1, pp. 149–52); Conti Rossini (1916, p. 482); Rubenson (1976, pp. 61–2); Halls (1831, vol. 2, p. 348); Markham (1869, p. 165); Powell-Cotton (1902, p. 391); Wylde (1888, vol. 1, p. 276). For greater detail, see Pankhurst (1977, p. 344, and 1978–9, pp. 260–9).
73. Douin (1941, vol. 3, pp. 720, 752, 793, 1046); Mayo (1876, p. 234); Rubenson (1976, pp. 315–17); Pankhurst (1978–9, pp. 291–3).

3 Of Immigrants and Kings: Toward a Symbolic Nationalization

1. See Bonacich (1973); Schnapper (2001).
2. See Van der Laan (1975); Horowitz (1985, pp. 113–21).
3. See McCabe (1999 and 2007).
4. See Pankhurst (1967, 1968, 1977, 1978–9, 1981, and 2003).
5. Pankhurst (1981).
6. Pankhurst (1968, p. 63).
7. As Bahru Zewde has recently acknowledged in his preface to Ydlibi (2006).
8. Mérab (1920–9, vol. 2, p. 178).
9. MAE, NS, Éthiopie 62: "Application de la juridiction consulaire en Éthiopie," Brice to Pichon, Addis Abeba, March 31, 1909; "Protection des Grecs dans la province du Harrar," Perrot to Cruppi, Dire Dawa, March 19, 1911. See also Garretson (1974, pp. 164–75); Ghanotakis (1979, p. 34); Wolynsky (1903a, p. 282); Michel (1900, p. 522).
10. Addis Abeba's population could exceed 100,000 when provincial governors came to spend part of the year there with their armies and retainers. It was estimated to lie between at least 45,000 and 60,000 toward the end of Menelik's reign. See Gleichen (1898, p. 156); Duchesne-Fournet (1909, vol. 1, p. 50); Collat (1905a, p. 427); Henin (1907, p. 87); Cohen (1912, p. 8); Annaratone (1914, p. 149).
11. Wolynsky (1904, p. 49); Collat (1905a, p. 427); Cohen (1912), p. 5; Annaratone (1914, p. 168). Of a total of 40,000 inhabitants, there were, according to Skinner (1906, p. 22), "1,000 Armenians, Greeks, Turks and Europeans." See also Landor (1907, vol. 1, pp. 25–7). The foreigners' numbers are doubtless exaggerated. By another estimate, there were, in the same period, 100 Greeks and Armenians over against some 50 Europeans. A few years later, there was supposedly only somewhat "more than two hundred foreigners, including 60 Greeks, 50 Armenians, the same number of Indians and a dozen French people, Italians and others." See Collat (1905b, p. 500); Mérab (1920–9, vol. 1, p. 167).
12. See Norberg (1977).
13. Mérab (1920–9, vol. 2, p. 104) counts 1,083 foreigners in Addis Abeba, including 334 Greeks and 146 Armenians, basing what he says on information gathered in 1909 "in the chancelleries or from competent individuals"; Henin (1907), however, counts only 205 in October 1906, while Orléans (1898, p. 142) says that there were no more than 20 or so in 1897. According to Pease (1902, vol. 3, p. 68), there were only "four French people, four Arabs, three Greeks, two Indians and seven Armenians" in Addis Abeba on December 31, 1900. Yet Collat (1905b, p. 500) declares that there were 450 foreigners. Escherich (1921, p. 36) estimates the number of Europeans in the capital at 200 in 1909, to which, he says, one must add "around five hundred Indians and Armenians," that is, significantly more than Mérab's figures suggest. Cohen (1912, pp. 8–9) plumps for 700 to 800 Greeks and Armenians out of a total of nearly 1,000 Europeans in 1910–11. Although it is highly improbable, the figure of 2,800 Armenians in 1935 is cited in several studies, following Zervos (who, moreover, contradicts himself, citing another, more plausible figure of 1,200). See Zervos (1936, pp. 14, 415, 497); Pankhurst (1968); and, in his wake, Norberg (1977).
14. Orléans (1898, pp. 18, 142); Mérab (1920–9, vol. 2, p. 106); Armandy (1930, p. 89, 152, 160–1); Nesbitt (1934, p. 30).
15. Said (1978).

16. Wolynsky (1903b, p. 373).
17. Wolynsky (1903b, pp. 372–3).
18. Du Bourg de Bozas (1906a, p. 4).
19. Gleichen (1898, p. 56).
20. Wellby (1901, p. 34); De Castro (1898, p. 157 and 1915, vol. 1, p. 41); Michel (1900, pp. 68–9); Bardey (1981, p. 141); Orléans (1898, p. 56); Rosen (1907, p. 68); Vanderheym (1896, p. 43); Wolynsky (1904, p. 49 and 1903b, p. 375); Mérab (1920–9, vol. 1, p. 167); Rodd (1923, p. 137); Du Bourg de Bozas (1906a, p. 4); Borelli (1890, p. 242).
21. Mérab (1920–9, vol. 2, p. 108). See also Forbes (1925, p. 130) and Mazade-Roussan (1936, p. 62).
22. MAE, Nouvelle Série [NS], Éthiopie 62: "Protection des sujets ottomans," Brice to Pichon, Addis Abeba, September 17, 1908.
23. Duchesne-Fournet (1909, vol. 1, p. 211).
24. Hentze (1908, p. 85).
25. Du Bourg de Bozas (1906b, pp. 197–8).
26. Decaux (no date [1907], pp. 185–6).
27. Henin (1907, pp. 135–6); Kouri (1906, pp. 37, 39); De Castro (1915, vol. 1, pp. 217, 219); Mérab (1920–9, vol. 2, pp. 104, 110, 146, 176); Michel (1900, pp. 68, 522); Wellby (1901, pp. 34, 104); Powell-Cotton (1902, pp. 117–8); Farago (1935, p. 55); Duchesne-Fournet (1909, vol. 1, p. 262); Wolynsky (1903b, pp. 374–5); Landor (1907, vol. 1, pp. 17–8); Rosen (1907, p. 68); *Djibouti, Journal Franco-Éthiopien*, May 31, 1902, pp. 2–3; Archivio del Ministero dell'Africa Italiana [ASMAI], Éthiopie, 38/1/11: "Commercio russo in Etiopia," Ciccodicola au Ministre, Addis Abeba, October 10, 1900; MAE, NS, Éthiopie 71, "Étude sur le commerce en Abyssinie (mission du Lieutenant Collat)," Appendix to political dispatch no. 22, March 28, 1905.
28. Nesbitt (1934, p. 38).
29. Arthur Rimbaud, letter to Alfred Ilg, Harar, December 20, 1889, in Rimbaud (1995); Loti ([1921] 2006, pp. 186, 229–30).
30. Wolynsky (1903b, p. 376).
31. MAE, NS, Éthiopie 62, telegram from Brice to Pichon, Djibouti, December 12, 1910; "La légation britannique et la colonie grecque à Addis Abbeba," Brice to Pichon, Addis Abeba, January 4, 1911; Ghanotakis (1979, p. 46).
32. See Armandy (1930, pp. 46, 89, 190–1); Montandon (1913, p. 375).
33. Rey (1923, p. 199).
34. Mauco (1932, p. 172); Noiriel (2007, pp. 319–25).
35. Nesbitt (1934, p. 43).
36. See the translation by Ottavio Cerroti (1894, p. 847).
37. See Salimbeni (1956, p. 143). See also ASMAI 39/1/9 and 31/9/10; 39/2/12; 39/3/23, 39/3/26 and 39/330; 39/4/43.
38. See Norberg (1977).
39. De Castro (1915, vol. 1, p. 219 and 1909, p. 410).
40. ASMAI 36/10/80, "Missione Salimbeni ad Harrar (Gennai-Marzo 1892)," Salimbeni to the Minister, Zeila, February 26, 1892 and Bio Caboba, March 7, 1892; Felter to Salimbeni, Harar, February [March] 10, 1892. ASMAI, 36/10/81, Salimbeni to the minister, Harar, April 21 and June 13, 1892. The reasons for the "Bia-Caboba incident" were never made explicit, but Terzian seems to have suspected that he was dealing with spies. Ethiopia's sovereignty over Ogaden had yet to be fully secured, since Italy

and the United Kingdom regarded its occupation of Biyo Kaboba as illegitimate. See Swayne (1900, pp. 286-7).
41. See Vanderheym (1896, p. 38); Bardey (1898, p. 9); Swayne (1900, pp. 144-5); Gleichen (1898, pp. 24-7); De Castro (1898, pp. 138, 146 and 1915, vol. 1, p. 31).
42. Arthur Rimbaud, Letter to Alfred Ilg, Harar, September 13, 1889 (in Rimbaud 1995). See also Alfred Ilg's letters to Rimbaud of August (Entotto) 21, and September 10, 1889 (Ait-Amba), as well as those of Rimbaud to Ilg of September 12, December 11 and 20, 1889, in which Sarkis Terzian is repeatedly referred to as someone who carries mail and newspapers between Harar, Shäwa, and the coast.
43. *The New York Herald* of October 23, 1905 and *The Washington Times* of November 23 and 26, 1905. Prouty (1986, pp. 272-3); Patapan (1930, p. 230); Eadie (1924, pp. 148-50); Bairu Tafla (1994, pp. 112-4). ASMAI 38/2/28, "Mission éthiopienne à Vienne," Cateani to the minister, Addis Abeba, May 20, 1905. MAE, NS, Éthiopie 72, February 27, 1911: "Falsification d'un sceau impérial. Très confidentiel," Brice to Pichon, Addis Abeba, February 27, 1911, as well as the second appendix to the dispatch of the French legation in Ethiopia of February 27, 1911: "Contrefaçon du Sceau de l'Empereur Ménélick."
44. Montandon (1916, p. 12).
45. Foreign Office [FO] 371/190, Clerk to Grey, Addis Abeba, May 15, 1907. Mérab (1920-9, vol. 2, p. 99 and pp. 63, 100, 106-7).
46. Conti Rossini (1935, pp. 37-8, 45); Salimbeni (1956, p. 188). On the Treaty of Wechalē, see *supra*, Chap. 1, n. 43.
47. This is notably true of Sarkis Terzian in Le Roux 1914, and also holds for Pariset 1937.
48. MAE, NS, Éthiopie 65, "Monopole des tabacs concédé à un turc protégé allemand. Indications diverses," Lagarde to Bourgeois, Entotto, April 17, 1906. See also FO 371/20/83, Thesiger to Grey, Addis Abeba, May 14, 1910, which denounces "a band of unscrupulous concession-hunters who work together and are omnipotent now," among them the Syrians Ydlibi and Baldassare.
49. MAE, NS, Éthiopie 21, "Cartoucherie. Difficultés," Lagarde to Bourgeois, Entotto, October 24, 1906; "Monopole de cartoucherie et concessions annexes," Lagarde to Bourgeois, Entotto, April 8, 1906; "Cartoucherie-Annexe," Lagarde to Bourgeois, Entotto, May 21, 1906; "Annexe à la dépêche politique du 21 mai 1906," Lagarde to Bourgeois; "Au sujet d'un monopole des cartouches, poudre, plomb et explosifs en Abyssinie," note from Captain Martin-Decaen, June 28,1906, n. p.; Anonymous, "Au sujet de Serkis Terzian, arménien en instance de naturalisation," November 30, 1906; "Réponse à la lettre du Département du 9 juillet n° 59 (cartoucherie)," Klobukowski to Pichon, Addis Abeba, August 2, 1907; "Établissement d'une cartoucherie à Addis-Abbeba," Brice to Pichon, Addis Abeba, November 8, 1909; "Au sujet d'une cartoucherie à Addis Abbeba," Brice to Pichon, Addis Abeba, March 25, 1910.
50. MAE, NS, Éthiopie 65: "Privilèges concédés sur les alcools et les vins," Lagarde to Bourgeois, Entotto, September 28, 1906; "Privilège des liquides spiritueux," Roux to Pichon, Addis Abeba, March 18, 1907; "Monopole des alcools et des liquides spiritueux," Roux to Pichon, Addis Abeba, April 2, 1907.
51. Borelli (1890, p. 152). See also Le Roux (1914, p. 102).
52. See Salimbeni (1956), Rome, September 19, 1889: "Promemoria personale per lo Scioa e lo Haràr presentato dal conte Pietro Antonelli ad Alberto Pisani Dossi, capo gabinetto del ministro ad interim degli Affari Esteri, Francesco Crispi."
53. See, among other sources, Gleichen (1898); Orléans (1898); Rodd (1923); Le Roux (1914); Skinner (1906); Landor (1907, vol. 1, pp. 79-80).

54. Norberg (1977); Monfreid (1933, pp. 217–18).
55. Salimbeni (1956, pp. 106–7, 145, 174); Gleichen (1898, p. 248), which mentions the Armenian jeweler "Tigrane."
56. Guèbrè Sellassié (1930–1, vol. 1, p. 269, n. 3, and pp. 275–6, 322).
57. Pankhurst (1967, pp. 36, 44); Patapan (1930, p. 170); Annaratone (1914, p. 158).
58. See De Castro (1898, p. 147 and 1915, vol. 1, p. 31); Orléans (1898, p. 34).
59. Salimbeni (1956, p. 188).
60. Duchesne-Fournet (1909, vol. 1, p. 211).
61. See Hentze (1908, pp. 90–2) and Le Roux (1914, pp. 102–5). I analyze the many traces that this machine's arrival in Ethiopia left in the Armenian memory in Chap. 4.
62. Du Bourg de Bozas (1906b, p. 201); Nicolopoulos (1923, p. 77); Herzbruch ([1907] 1925, p. 178); Rodd (1923, p. 134); Gleichen (1898, pp. 46–7).
63. Powell-Cotton (1902, p. 97); Duchesne-Fournet (1909, vol. 1, p. 53); Gleichen (1898, p. 147); Rodd (1923, p. 154); Orléans (1898, p. 200). MAE, NS, Éthiopie 64, "Les Allemands en Abyssinie," the Administrator of the Legation of France to Pichon, Addis Abeba, March 8, 1907. See also Armandy (1930, p. 234).
64. Pariset (1937, pp. 166–7).
65. Collat (1905a, p. 429). See also (Patapan 1930, p. 164, 212) and Zervos (1936, p. 495).
66. Victor-Hummel (1995).
67. Pinguet (2011).
68. Institut du monde arabe (2007).
69. See, for example, Mérab (1920–9, vol. 2, p. ix); Monfreid (1954, pp. 65, 192–3); Zervos (1936).
70. Sohier (2007b, pp. 45–50). See also Sohier (2012).
71. Patapan (1930, p. 255). On the Italian Secondo Bertolani, who seems to have played the same role early in the century, see Sohier (2007b, pp. 50–1).
72. Sohier (2007b, pp. 51–2). See also Sohier (2012).
73. See Berhanou Abebe (2003, pp. 30–2).
74. Sohier (2007b, pp. 211, 233, 249) and Sohier (2012).
75. Sohier (2007b, p. 265).
76. See Berhanou Abebe (2003, p. 31); Sohier (2007a, p. 32).
77. Boudjikanian (2007, pp. 828–33). An influx of new immigrants from Turkey breathed new life into the Armenian presence in Egypt early in the nineteenth century, in a context that Mehmet Ali's relatively liberal policies rendered auspicious. There were some 4,000 to 5,000 such immigrants in Egypt in the 1810–20 period. See Kazazian (2007, p. 133).
78. From 1805 to 1853, three Armenians succeeded each other without interruption in this post. In the same period, a majority of high-ranking officials in this ministry were Armenians; there were so many of them that foreign observers referred to it as the "Armenian palace" (Boudjikanian 2007, p. 831).
79. Le Gall-Kazazian (2011).
80. See, among other sources (Marcus 1995a).
81. See Patapan (1930, p. 170).
82. Neither Guèbrè Sellassié (1930–1, vol. 2, p. 508) nor Hentze (1908, p. 86) mentions Baghdassarian's role, but it is explicitly cited in De Castro (1915, vol. 1, p. 219), Zervos (1936, p. 494), and Patapan (1930, p. 212).
83. Patapan (1930, pp. 211–12). See also Norden (1935, p. 33), who avers that, in the dining room of Täfäri's palace, furnished in the European manner, "the crockery

of gold and silver was the work of the court jeweler, who is not an Abyssinian. He is Armenian, and he also made the crown that Ras Tafari recently attributed to himself."
84. Boudjikanian (2007, p. 829).
85. See Berhanou Abebe (2007, pp. 3–12).
86. Patapan (1930, p. 212).
87. Zervos (1936, p. 496); Patapan (1930, p. 212). Avedis Terzian also mentions this.
88. Zervos (1936, p. 498); Patapan (1930, p. 212). See also Nicod (1937, pp. 37–41), who gives a long account of an interview with Täfäri and also with "Monsieur Abraham," "a man who had the government's full trust."
89. Patapan (1930, p. 7).
90. Levine ([1974] 2000, p. 26). See also (pp. xxi–xxiv, 20–5, 40).
91. Triulzi (2002); Gascon (1995, pp. 88–93); Bureau (1987, pp. 119–48).
92. Gellner (1983, p. 46).
93. Decorations are supposed to have been awarded to fourteen Armenians before 1930, including six servants of the palace distinguished by Menelik (Sarkis Terzian, Dikran Ebeyan, Avedis Yamalian, Dikran Hazarian, Krikorios Boghossian, and Abraham Terzian), one by *Lej* Iyasu (Levon Yazedjian), and eight by *Negus* Täfäri (Krikorios Boghossian, for the second time; his son Khachig Boghossian; the merchants Matig Kevorkoff and Hrant Minasian; the goldsmith Hagop Baghdassarian; the conductor of the royal brass band Kevork Nalbandian; the Armenian archbishop of Istanbul, Kevork Arslanian; and a personal friend of Emperor Haile Selassie's, Hovhannes Semerjibashian, whom I discuss in Chap. 9). See Patapan (1930, p. 215).
94. Mérab (1920–9, vol. 2, p. 129).
95. Ibid., p. 131.
96. See *supra*, Chap. 1.
97. Geertz (1973).
98. Geertz (1972, p. 29).
99. This film, part of the Berhanou Abebe collection, was shown at the exhibition about the Boyadjians organised in June 2007 by the Paris Museum Jeu de Paume.
100. I have not consulted the brochure by Bishop Terenig Poladian, the former director of the Ethiopian seminary in Addis Abeba, which describes this day: *Iteke Menen, Empress of Ethiopia: Her Funeral Ceremony, her Achievments, and the Participation of the Armenian Community of Ethiopia in the Ceremony* (in Armenian, with a resume in Amharic), Addis Abeba, Artistik, 1962, 43 pages, with illustrations.
101. The two churches are about one kilometer apart.
102. See the account of this visit in Arslanian (1930).
103. This can be neither *Abunä* Matēwos, who died in 1926, nor his successor *Abunä* Qērelos VI, consecrated by the patriarch of Alexandria in May 1929. See (Erlich 2000, p. 28).
104. Del Boca (1995, p. 167). See also ASMAI 91, folder 287.

Prelude to the History of a Collective Memory

1. This premise informs Oscar Lewis's pioneering work (1961).
2. The whole set of these narratives is currently being prepared for separate publication.

3. It is in fact not the Italians but the Egyptians who left Harar in 1885, not 1875, while Menelik conquered the region of Harar in 1887, not 1877.
4. The Treaty of Ucciali was signed in 1889.
5. A diminutive form of the forename Srpuhi. According to Avedis Terzian, this was the name given to her by the Ethiopians at court.
6. There is an obvious mistake here. Avedis Terzian meant 1895.
7. The Coptic Christians: this is an allusion to the nineteenth-century dispute about the keys to the monastery of Dayr el-Sultan. See Chap. 2.
8. This was one of the missions to Istanbul undertaken by *Däjazmach* Mäshäsha Wärqē in 1903, 1905, and 1907. In question here must be the last one. See Bahru Zewde (2002, p. 186).
9. Abdülhamid II ruled the Ottoman Empire from 1876 until he was dethroned in 1909. Under his rule, between 1894 and 1897, the Ottoman Empire's Armenians were subjected to large-scale massacres.
10. Anna Marcerou, born Anna Yazedjian in Addis Abeba in 1914, was Avedis Terzian's first cousin. I met and interviewed her in Nice in April 1996.
11. Let him travel without restriction.
12. The decline in the state of Menelik's health makes such a conversation unlikely at so late a date.
13. *Ras* Mikaël of Wällo, proclaimed *negus* in 1914.
14. The reference is to the battle of Sägälē, which took place on October 27, 1916.
15. Levon Yazedjian's oldest son.
16. Inaudible. Terzian must mean the Empress Zäwditu, accompanied by the Crown Prince Täfäri. This ceremony took place in 1928. See Figure 3.5.
17. He also spoke Turkish very well, and, probably, Italian.
18. Thomas and Znaniecki (1919, vol. 3, p. 6). Emphasis in the original.
19. Dakhlia (1990, p. 30).
20. Bensa and Goromido (2005, p. 13).
21. This album assembles some 500 prints of irregular format on 110 pages.
22. For example, in Pankhurst (1967, 1968, and 1981); Garretson (1974); Prouty (1986), and Bahru Zewde (2002), which cites "Ato (Mr.) Avedis Terzian, a highly knowledgeable informant of Armenian origin" (p. 222).
23. This is a sixteen-page booklet in English entitled *The Armenian Community of Ethiopia*, completed around 1997.
24. Halbwachs ([1941] 1992, p. 223), trans. modified.

4 A Past that Engages the Present: The Social Stakes of the Making of Heroes

1. Valensi (1992, pp. 276–7).
2. The residence of *Negus* Menelik of Shäwa in the 1880s.
3. Sarkis in fact died in 1915. The year 1913 corresponds to Menelik's official date of death.
4. Barthes ([1980] 2010, pp. 16–17, 38).
5. Du Bourg de Bozas (1906b, pp. 197–8).
6. Patapan (1930, p. 165).
7. Douin (1941, vol. 3, pp. 752, 793, and 1046); Rubenson (1976, pp. 315–7).

8. Mayo (1876, p. 234).
9. After the suicide of Emperor Tewodros II (1855–68), several different pretenders disputed the title of emperor, among them *Ras* Kasa of Tigré (the future Emperor Yohannes IV) and *Wagshum* Gobäzē of Gojam (emperor, under the name Täklä Giyorgis, from 1868 to 1871).
10. Mohamed Ali converted to Christianity and married one of Menelik's daughters, Shäwa Rägga.
11. Patapan (1930, pp. 165–7). This request was intended to make it possible to legitimize Menelik's rule and, should the occasion offer, facilitate his accession to the dignity of the imperial throne.
12. Säla Denga is one of the principle localities in the Mänz region of Shäwa. Yohannes's and Menelik's troops briefly confronted each other there in February 1878 (Marcus 1995a, p. 54).
13. Patapan (1930, p. 168). See also Pankhurst (1967, p. 35 and n. 34), which cites Avedis Terzian: "Tradition says that he [Boghos] acted as an agent for the King of Shoa and had sent messages on his behalf secreted in a cane"; "some people have gone so far as to assert that Bogos [*sic*] Marcarian was implicated in the death of the Emperor Yohannes at Metemma."
14. Patapan (1930, pp. 169–70).
15. Yohannes's chronicle does not mention Dikran Ebeyan. See Bairu Tafla (1977).
16. See Pankhurst (1967, pp. 35–6), who cites Arusyag Ebeyan's narrative, which he heard in 1965.
17. Gleichen (1898, p. 248).
18. See *supra*, Chap. 1, n. 43.
19. In question here is the firm Terzian Brothers, founded in Harar by Sarkis and Ohannes Terzian.
20. FO 403/239, Memorandum from the ambassador of Italy, August 17, 1896.
21. FO 403/221, Sir F. Plunkett to the Marquis of Salisbury, Brussels, December 15, 1895. The last accusation, which is improbable, is reiterated in Pariset (1937, pp. 107, 141).
22. FO 403/329, Adamoli to General Ferrero, Rome, February 10, 1896. Gleichen (1898, p. 197). FO 403/298, Harrington to the Marquis of Salisbury, Addis Abeba, April 7, 1900.
23. See Valensi (1992).
24. See the similar versions of this song (but in which Sarkis is not mentioned) in Vanderheym (1896, p. ii) and Thesiger (1987, pp. 41–2).
25. Interview with Avedis Terzian, Addis Abeba, May 23, 2000. See also (Narrative 1, § 9) and De Castro (1898, p. 158).
26. Translated by Mihreteab Tsighe.
27. Halbwachs ([1941] 1992, p. 223).
28. Patapan (1930, p. 163).
29. Ibid., p. 225. At the time, he was only *negus*.
30. Bardey (1898, pp. 47–55).
31. "Au Harar," *Le Monde illustré* (supplement to *L'Illustration*), May 22, 1897, p. 334. A very similar story was published in the *Washington Times* on November 23, 1905.
32. FO 403/89, The King of Shoa to Consul Hunter, Harrar, January 8, 1967. On Grañ, see Chap. 2, n. 10 *supra*. Monfreid (1933, pp. 163–4).
33. Gleichen (1898, p. 196).
34. The battle of Chalänqo of January 6, 1887, saw the victory of 20,000 of Menelik's men over the Emir's 3,000 soldiers, who were armed with 600 rifles and 2 canons

left behind by the Egyptians. According to Borelli, Menelik entered Harar without encountering resistance. No source mentions Sarkis, but two Greeks and an Italian, who had until then been detained by Abdullahi, are supposed to have been dispatched to Menelik by Harar's inhabitants in order to beg him for mercy. See FO 403/89, Baring to Salisbury, Cairo, February 9, 1887. Borelli (1890, pp. 200, 214); Arthur Rimbaud, "Lettre au directeur du Bosphore égyptien," August 20, 1887 (*Le Bosphore égyptien*, August 25-7, 1887); Marcus (1995a, p. 92).

35. Manuscript by Paylag Yazedjian, translated by Anna Marcerou, Nice, April 20, 1996.
36. See also Pariset (1937, pp. 107, 142). ASMAI, 36/10/81, Salimbeni to the minister, Harar, April 28, 1892.
37. Barthes (2010, pp. 48-9).
38. The domain of Kombolcha was one of *Däjazmach* Mäkonnen's residences. See ASMAI, 36/10/81, Salimbeni to the minister, Harar, June 3, 1892. It may be that Sarkis had the usufruct of it.
39. *Le Monde illustré*, May 22, 1897. The *Washington Times* of November 23, 1905, offers a similar narrative.
40. Patapan (1930, p. 225). See also Terzibashian, (no date [1944]), pp. 293-9).
41. ASMAI, Éthiopie, 36/10/80, Salimbeni to the minister, Zeila, February 26, 1892, and Harar, March 19, 1892.
42. ASMAI, 36/10/80, Felter to Salimbeni, Harar, March 6, 1893, and Salimbeni to the minister, Harar, March 19, 1892.
43. ASMAI, 36/10/80, Felter to Salimbeni, Harar, February 10 [*sic*, probably March 10] 1892.
44. Rimbaud, who lived in Harar in 1888-90, repeatedly had recourse to Sarkis's services in his regular correspondence with Alfred Ilg. He does not mention him at all in his correspondence of 1890 and 1891.
45. ASMAI, 36/10/81, Salimbeni to the minister, Harar, June 3, 1892. After 1892, no European traveler ever notes the presence of an Armenian officer at Biyo Kaboba.
46. Trains are known as *babur* in Ethiopia even today, although they are no longer steam driven.
47. Le Roux (1914).
48. Ibid., p. 112; Annaratone (1914, p. 158); De Castro (1915, vol. 1, p. 219); Mérab (1920-9, vol. 2, pp. 206-7).
49. Marcus (1995a, p. 159, pp. 200-4).
50. Le Roux (1914, pp. 102-5).
51. In Le Roux's account (Le Roux 1914), this "someone" is "Serkis."
52. Le Roux (1914, pp. 112-14).
53. Le Roux (1914, p. 114). See also (Mérab 1920-9, vol. 2, p. 133).
54. See Collat (1905a, p. 431):

> In May 1904, in order to improvise a trail and haul the components of a steamroller all the way to Addis-Abbeba, peasants were commandeered *en masse* over an area extending to six days' travel by foot to either side of the route. This was an immense task, admirably accomplished in the desert and over the mountains. Thousands of men blazed the trail. Two hundred dragged a wheel behind them. Eight hundred were harnessed to the motor, and the multitude hauled it as they sang, urged on by their leaders' exhortations. Every

man had brought his own flour, but there was no water, and many died: the corvee was murderous.
55. Guèbrè Sellassié (1930–1, vol. 2, p. 509).
56. Le Roux (1914, pp. 285–7 and pp. 289–94). See also De Castro (1915, vol. 1, p. 221).
57. Patapan (1930, p. 270).
58. Le Roux (1914, p. 299, n. D).
59. Ibid., pp. 293–4.
60. Hentze (1905, pp. 90–1).
61. This is probably the engineer and architect Krikor Howyan, born in Constantinople in 1849, a graduate of the Paris École des ponts et chaussées and a friend of the astronomer Camille Flammarion. According to Avedis Terzian, he was the architect who designed the Empress Hotel (the Itēgē Hotel, the present-day Taytu Hotel).
62. Hentze (1908, pp. 90–2).
63. See Mérab (1920–9, vol. 2, p. 133), according to whom Hentze's narrative is comical but honest.
64. Eadie (1924, pp. 246–9); Pankhurst (1981, p. 378).
65. Farago (1935, p. 27).
66. See Patapan (1930, p. 215); Zervos (1936, p. 496).
67. According to Landor (1907, vol. 1, p. 72),

> since the arrival of two traction engines in the capital, Menelik, followed by many Abyssinian grandees, spends most of his time walking behind these engines while they are at work crushing stones upon the road. Sometimes Menelik himself gets on the platform of the engine and takes the keenest interest in its working, including the stoking. Thousands of soldiers and a great portion of the population form a procession behind the Imperial chauffeur.

68. A few years later, other Fowlers were imported by way of the United Kingdom's diplomatic mission. MAE, NS, Éthiopie 64, "Industrie de l'automobile en Abyssinie," Klobukowski to Pichon, Addis Abeba, August 20, 1907.
69. Landor (1968, vol. 1, p. 72) confirms this part of Avedis's narrative:

> Menelik certainly gets a deal of amusement out of the traction engines. He uses them for all sorts of purposes besides road-making. I have seen the Emperor sawing wood with a circular saw driven by one of these engines upon the racecourse where a stand was being erected. When he did not actually work, hours were spent by the Emperor watching the saw at work, and he did not restrain his admiration at the evenness of the divided planks.

70. Interview with George Israelian in Addis Abeba on August 29, 2002.
71. See also Pariset (1937, p. 144); Montandon (1913, p. 376).
72. See Pariset (1937, p. 141); Henin (1907, p. 119).
73. Its only competitor was the sawmill opened by the Swiss Evalet and Faller further off, in Jamjam, at a distance of sixty kilometers from Addis Abeba.
74. This is a dubious claim. Dufton (1867, p. 173) indicates that they were already in use around 1862. In a November 13, 1889, letter to Rimbaud, Ilg complains about a "flood of birillis [berillē] in Shoa today" that "are debilitating commerce, merchants as well as consumers."
75. Emphasis added.

76. MAE, NS, Éthiopie 21, "Source thermale d'Addis-Abbeba," Roux to Pichon, Addis Abeba, March 12, 1907: "Convention concernant les eaux chaudes d'Addis Abeba."
77. Duchesne-Fournet (1909, vol. 1, p. 58); Liano (1929, pp. 112, 116–17, 122–3); De Castro (1915, vol. 1, p. 239); Mérab (1920–9, vol. 2, pp. 150–7); Escherich (1921, pp. 41–2).
78. Liano (1929, pp. 112–15); Esme (1928, pp. 58–9); Herzbruch ([1907] 1925, pp. 125–6); Rey (1923, p. 154).
79. Mérab (1920–9, vol. 2, pp. 151–2). I shall come back to this confiscation later.
80. MAE, NS, Éthiopie 21, "Monopole de cartoucherie et concessions annexes," Lagarde to Bourgeois, Entotto, April 8, 1906.
81. MAE, NS, Éthiopie 21, "Monopole de cartoucherie et concessions annexes," Lagarde à Bourgeois, Entotto, April 8, May 21, and October 24, 1906; "Au sujet d'un monopole des cartouches, poudre, plomb et explosifs en Abyssinie," note from Captain Martin-Decaen, June 28, 1906; "Au sujet de Serkis Terzian, arménien en instance de naturalisation," November 30, 1906; Brice to Pichon, Addis Abeba, November 8, 1909. See also ASMAI, 38/3/28, Caetani to the minister, Addis Abeba, May 27, 1905; FO 371/20/823, Thesiger to Grey, Addis Abeba, May 14, 1910; Montandon (1913, p. 376); Mérab (1920–9, vol. 2, p. 204); Rodd (1923, p. 160); Le Roux (1901, p. 177).
82. MAE, NS, Éthiopie 64, Brice to Pichon, Addis Abeba, May 13 and July 3, 1908.
83. MAE, NS, Éthiopie 21, Brice to Pichon, Addis Abeba, March 25, 1910. Still considered an Ottoman subject, Sarkis Terzian had applied for naturalization as a French citizen, but his application was rejected in 1907: Klobukowski to Pichon, Addis Abeba, August 2, 1907.
84. Peter Garretson (2000, p. 131) reports Avedis Terzian's remarks, recorded in the early 1970s, in similar terms.
85. At this time, the consul of the United Kingdom in Harar was the Greek merchant Gerolimato.
86. FO 1/40, "Residents at Harrar: Petition to Secretary of State," December 22, 1902.
87. Patapan (1930, pp. 226–7).
88. Bairu Tafla (1994, pp. 112–4); Eadie (1924, pp. 148–9).
89. ASMAI 38/3/28, Caetani to the minister, Addis Abeba, May 20, 1905.
90. *Washington Times*, November 23, 1905; *New York Herald*, Octobre 23, 1905. Patapan (1930, p. 230); Prouty (1986, pp. 272–3); Eadie (1924, p. 150).
91. The two accomplices rejected such accusations in the *Washington Times* of November 26, 1905.
92. Mérab (1920–9, vol. 2, pp. 108, 151).
93. Eadie (1924, pp. 135–62); MAE, NS, Éthiopie 72, "Contrefaçon du Sceau de l'Empereur Ménélick," February 27, 1911; Brice to Pichon, Addis Abeba, February 27, 1911; the Chief of Police to the minister, Paris, May 18, 1911.
94. Pariset (1937, pp. 107, 142).
95. Ibid., p. 142.
96. See also Patapan (1930, p. 231).
97. Pariset (1937, pp. 144–7).
98. Patapan (1930, p. 231).
99. Halbwachs ([1941] 1992, p. 222).

5 Menelik's Armenians: From the Welcome as Experienced to the Sedentarization of an Imaginary

1. Patapan (1930, p. 20).
2. A sweet, fermented, low-alcohol drink that is usually compared to mead.
3. Stirrups in Ethiopia consisted of a simple metal ring in which the horseman, who had to be barefoot, stuck his big toe.
4. This was in reality a white diadem that covered the top of his skull. Menelik wore it over his black felt hat.
5. An Armenian specialty whose basic ingredients are dried beef and fenugreek.
6. Patapan (1930, pp. 184–8).
7. Patapan (1930, p. 170).
8. Pilibbos arrived in Ethiopia in 1899. Patapan (1930, p. 163).
9. Arusiag Ebeyan related this episode in much the same terms in 1965. See Pankhurst (1967, pp. 74–5).
10. Hapet Ghurlian, born in Constantinople in 1900, told a similar story in the 1980s. See Fikremariam Estifanos (1986, p. 37).
11. Literally, "the conquering lion of the tribe of Juda."
12. 'agäru armän. Literally, "from the country of the Armenians."
13. bäzuqän: literally, "for many days," but it is obviously a question of several years (Berhanou Abebe).
14. This sentence might also be translated "he is now counted among the Abyssinians," "he now belongs to the number of the Abyssinians," or "he is included in the number of the Abyssinians."
15. Berhanou Abebe also suggests another translation: "I have given him this passport so that no evil confronts him" or "so that nothing regrettable [or untoward] happens to him in all the countries he travels through."
16. February 5, 1901, by the Gregorian calendar.
17. See *supra*, Chap. 4, p. 101. Emphasis is added.
18. With the exception of one detail: Sarkis is supposed to have been born in 1862, not in 1868, as Hayg Patapan affirms.
19. See Gleichen (1898, p. 233).
20. This ordination played its part in the medieval legend of Prester John in Europe.
21. Keller (1918).
22. Rosen (1907, p. 266).
23. Hovanessian (1992 and 1995); Ma Mung (1996).
24. Hovanessian (2007a, pp. 449–50, and 2007c, pp. 17–18).
25. Hovanessian (2007c, pp. 17–19).
26. De Castro (1915, vol. 1, p. 52 and pp. 237–8). See also Gleichen (1898, pp. 117–18); Duchesne-Fournet (1909, vol. 1, pp. 50–1); Skinner (1906, p. 72); Mérab (1920–9, vol. 1, p. 120). The name of the present-day neighborhood of Shola-Käbäna in Addis Abeba preserves a trace of the fig tree.
27. Hovanessian (2007b, p. 6).
28. Talai (1989, pp. 5, 96, 125–31).
29. Mirak (1983, pp. 89, 123–47, 272–83).
30. Bakalian (1993, pp. 319–92).
31. Ter Minassian (1997, p. 30); Hassiotis (2007); Antoniou (2007).
32. Noiriel (2007, pp. 311–64); Adjemian (2020).

33. Krikorios Boghossian.
34. Anna Marcerou, Nice, April 19, 1996.
35. See Nalbandian (2019) and De Lorenzi (2016).
36. My informants were Elise, Louise, and Suzanne Boghossian, born, respectively, in 1907, 1910, and 1914 in Addis Abeba, where they all died in 1999. The other children of Krikorios and Charlotte Boghossian still living in Addis Abeba were Hampartsum Boghossian (1912–2003) and Sahag Boghossian (1911–2009).
37. According to a letter of Mihran Hazarian's dated Addis Abeba, December 21, 1907, and published in the Armenian daily *Arshaluys* (Smyrna) on January 17, 1908, Matheos Karamanian was born in Talas (near Cesarea) and spent almost twelve years in Tigré before moving to Addis Abeba in 1907. A farmer, dressed like an Abyssinian, he was more or less unable to express himself in Armenian or Turkish and found it easier to speak "in Ethiopian" (i.e., either in Amharic or Tegreñña).
38. See Marcus (1995a, pp. 250, 261); Prouty (1986, p. 340). This is also the date that figures in the chronicle of Iyasu and Zäwditu. See Gebre-Igziabiher Elyas (1994, p. 343).
39. Esme (1928, p. 83).
40. Gebre-Igziabiher Elyas (1994, p. 344).
41. Ibid., chap. 25, p. 357 and chap. 44, pp. 402–10.
42. Mérab (1920–9, vol. 2, pp. 240–1).
43. Darley (1926, p. vii).
44. Waugh (1931, p. 60).
45. See Mérab (1920–9, vol. 2, p. 66), which cites a work, published in January 1914, by a Montmartre cabaret singer:

> What's this I hear? Poor Menelik / Just breathed his last!… / They're burying, I see / The Negus of Abyssinia; / It's the thirty-sixth time; / It's becoming an odd habit!… / There's no fooling me any more / The gimmick's too well known; / […] / Every time they kill this sprightly chap off / He comes back, like onion soup.

46. In 1906, *Ras* Mäkonnen's death was kept secret for a short time in Harar. See (Mérab 1920–9, vol. 2, p. 40). Similarly, when *Ras* Täsämma, designated regent of the empire by the Ethiopian government, passed away on the night of April 10–11, 1911, arrangements were made for his body to be carried off amid great secrecy and discreetly buried in the Monastery of Däbrä Libanos. See Cohen (1912, p. 63).
47. Montandon (1913, p. 22); Annaratone (1914, p. 155).
48. Durkheim (1912, p. 117).
49. MAE, NS, Éthiopie 62, Brice to Pichon, Addis Abeba, February 10, 1909.
50. MAE, NS, Éthiopie 62, "Au sujet de la population européenne," Addis Abeba, November 14, 1909.
51. Halbwachs ([1949] 1980, pp. 80, 86).
52. Menelik had two daughters by an earlier marriage, contracted when he was still king of Shäwa, but no son. His second wife, Empress Taytu, did not give him any children. *Lej* Iyasu must have been thirteen years old when, in 1909, he was named heir to the throne. He was born of the marriage of Menelik's second daughter Shäwa Rägga with *Ras* Mikaël of Wällo.
53. Bloch (1921, pp. 17, 26).
54. Gebre-Igziabiher Elyas (1994, pp. 357–8); Haile Sellasie (1976, p. 49).
55. See Marcus (1995a, pp. 270–4 and 1995a, pp. 15–19); Greenfield (1965, p. 132).
56. Farago (1935, p. 61); Berhanou Abebe (2001, pp. 323–5).

57. FO 371/2593: "Lidj Iasu's Moslem intrigues," Thesiger to the minister, Addis Abeba, July 20, 1916.
58. Waugh (1931, pp. 30–1).
59. See Berhanou Abebe (2003).
60. Reidulf K. Molvaer (Gebre-Igziabiher Elyas 1994, pp. 560–1) attributes a photo of Iyasu dressed like a Muslim to an Armenian photographer whom he mistakenly confuses with the Indian J. G. Mody.
61. According to my conversation of May 2000 with Denis Gérard in Addis Abeba.
62. Anna Marcerou, Nice, April 19, 1996.
63. Valensi (1992, p. 267).
64. In 1986, Avedis Terzian declared that Yazedjian had received three thousand thalers from the English. See Fikremariam Estifanos (1986, p. 32). In 1984, Hapet Ghurlian spoke of fifteen thousand thalers. See Berhanou Abebe (2003, pp. 24–5).
65. In fact, Anna Marcerou, née Yazedjian in 1914 in Addis Abeba, was the godchild of the Justice Minister, Sahlä Tsedalu. Later, Täfäri's wife, after becoming Empress Mänän, stood godmother to Marcerou's daughter.
66. See also Patapan (1930, p. 212); Zervos (1936, p. 496). According to Avedis Terzian, Paylag Yazedjian was appointed vice-governor of the municipality of Addis Abeba in 1956.
67. Except for Patapan (1930, p. 270), who mentions that Yazedjian was a "policeman."
68. According to Avedis Terzian, it was the uniform of Levon's father, Mardiros Yazedjian, a lawyer in Turkey (Narrative 16, § 6).
69. Armenian church register of deaths.

6 *Arba Lejoch*: The Logical Apotheosis of a Collective Destiny

1. Halbwachs ([1941] 1992, p. 223).
2. Patapan (1930, p. 243, n. 1).
3. See Falceto (2001).
4. Bibliothèque Nubar [BNu], Minutes of the AGBU's Council meetings, session of June 3, 1924, vol. 2, p. 240.
5. See Esme (1928, pp. 112–13) and *supra*, Chap. 1.
6. Nicod (1937, pp. 60–1).
7. According to Mardiros Vagharshagian (interviewed by Francis Falceto on June 26, 1994 in Addis Abeba), the instruments were provided not by the Ethiopian government but by the AGBU.
8. "The arrival of the AGBU's brass band in Ethiopia," *Miutiun* [newspaper published by the AGBU, in Armenian], no. 101, September–October 1924, pp. 78–9.
9. Ibid.
10. Sarkissian (2005).
11. Gebre-Igziabiher Elyas (1994, p. 461).
12. Patapan (1930, p. 244). Mardiros Vagharshagian, interviewed by Francis Falceto on June 26, 1994, in Addis Abeba. See also Sarkissian (2005, p. 10), in which Vagharshagian repeats this anecdote.
13. See Patapan (1930, pp. 244–5); Nicod (1937, p. 50).
14. Kévorkian and Tachjian (2006, pp. 158–9).

15. BNu, General Correspondence of AGBU, vol. 63, pp. 526–7, letter of the See to the President of the local committee of the AGBU in Addis Abeba, Paris, November 8, 1924.
16. BNu, General Correspondence of AGBU, vol. 62, p. 714, Central Council to Patriarch Tourian in Jerusalem, Paris, July 3, 1924.
17. Nicod (1937, p. 50).
18. Patapan (1930, p. 244). See also "The Brass Band of the AGBU's Araradian Orphanage," *Miutiun* [in Armenian], no. 99, May–June 1924, p. 42.
19. Nicod (1937, p. 50).
20. Sarkissian (2005, p. 10).
21. The forty "children" were from eighteen to twenty-five years old in 1930. See Patapan (1930, p. 244).
22. "The arrival of the AGBU's brass band in Ethiopia," *Miutiun* [in Armenian], no. 101, September–October 1924, p. 78.
23. Sarkissian (2005, pp. 9–10).
24. Patapan (1930, pp. 243–4).
25. BNu, Minutes of the AGBU's Council meetings, session of October 20, 1925, vol. 2, pp. 308–9.
26. BNu, General Correspondence of AGBU, the AGBU's managing director, Krikor Sinabian, to Yeghishe Tourian, patriarch of the Armenians of Jerusalem, Paris, March 24, 1926.
27. Interview with Mardiros Vagharshagian, Addis Abeba, August 17, 1997. Only twenty-eight of the orphans remained in Ethiopia after the brass band was dissolved.
28. See *supra*, Chap. 2.
29. Interview with Kevork Hintlian, Jerusalem, March 2010.
30. See Figures 6.2, 6.3, and 6.4.
31. Armenian Patriarchate of Jerusalem [APJ], Correspondence, letter from the Reverend treasurer of the patriarchate to the secretary of the Empire of Ethiopia in Jerusalem, April 30, 1924.
32. APJ, undated letter [May 1924] from Patriarch Tourian to *Ras* Täfäri.
33. See Patapan (1930, pp. 213, 267).
34. Exiled to Eritrea by the Italians, Kevork assumed the direction of the imperial guard's brass band again in 1941, followed by that of the army and of the police, in which he held the rank of captain. His brother Hagop Nalbandian replaced him in 1949. Hagop Manugian, a former teacher in the Armenian primary school, served as instructor of the police's brass band in the 1950s and 1960s. See Avedis Terzian (Narrative 7, § 7); Interview with Piuzant Nalbandian, Addis Abeba, September 4, 1997; Nerses Nalbandian, "The biography of Captain Kevork Nalbandian" (manuscript, in Armenian), 1964.
35. Born in Ayntab in 1915, Nerses Nalbandian, who played several different instruments, arrived in Ethiopia in 1937. He carried on his uncle's work in the Ethiopian theater and pursued the renewal of modern Ethiopian music. Kevork Nalbandian composed or arranged some fifty Amharic songs and wrote musicals, among them *Gebre-Maryam the Gondare* (1933–4). In 1946, Nerses became the head of the municipal orchestra, which provided the foundations for the Theater of Haile Selassie I under the direction of the Austrian Franz Zelwecker from 1955 on. He helped form most of the institutional orchestras of the period and had a decisive influence on younger generations of musicians. See Falceto (2002, pp. 726–7); Interview with Piuzant

Nalbandian, Addis Abeba, September 4, 1997. See also his obituary in *The Ethiopian Herald*, November 18, 1977.
36. Joutard (1977, p. 316).
37. Natives or inhabitants of Arabkir. In Armenian, the suffix *-tsi* designates origin.
38. Patapan (1930, pp. 163-4). The restoration of the Ottoman constitution in 1908, was imposed on Sultan Abdülhamid II by the "Young Turk" revolution and the Committee of Union and Progress. The following year, the Adana massacres led to heavy emigration of Armenians from Cilicia.
39. Patapan (1930, pp. 163-4).
40. MAE, NS, Éthiopie 72, First appendix to the September 17, 1908 dispatch of the French legation in Abyssinia, "Sujets ottomans à Addis-Abeba."
41. Epitaphs in the Armenian cemetery and registers of the Armenian church in Addis Abeba. See B. Adjemian 2011b.
42. Halbwachs (1941, pp. 61, 74, 80).
43. Djerrahian (1991, pp. 5-6); Fikremariam Estifanos (1986, p. 16).
44. Terzibashian (no date [1944], p. 64). See also Avedis Terzian (Narrative 4, § 1 and 7).
45. Avedis Terzian is mistaken about the name. The slain soldier was Papken Seferian.
46. Dakhlia (1990, p. 26).
47. Durkheim (1912, p. 421).

7 From Threshold to Interstice: A Space of Decompartmentalized Sociabilities

1. Forbes (1925, p. 130).
2. Monfreid (1933, p. 136).
3. Bonacich (1973).
4. Patapan (1930, p. 223).
5. See Shack (1979).
6. Wellby (1901, p. 34).
7. According to Avedis Terzian.
8. Kulmer (1910, pp. 40-1, 75-7, 81-2, 91-2, 96).
9. Borelli (1890, p. 242); Michel (1900, pp. 68-9); Mérab (1920-9, vol. 1, p. 167); Burton (1856, pp. 321-2); Vanderheym (1896, pp. 41-2).
10. Gleichen (1898, p. 56).
11. Patapan (1930, p. 164).
12. Kulmer (1910, p. 76).
13. 1904 was the year of Avedis Terzian's birth in Harar. His parents already had a son, Yervant, who, however, died in his infancy. The following year saw the birth of Antranig, the son of a dentist from Constantinople, Dr. Emmanuel Terzian (no relation to Sarkis Terzian) and his wife Ovsanna, according to the registry of Armenians living in Dire Dawa.
14. Those born in 1905 were Satenig Zamanian, already mentioned, and Mushegh Terzian, the son of Ohannes and Nartuhi Terzian. Mushegh was Avedis Terzian's first cousin.
15. According to Avedis Terzian, the first Armenian birth in Ethiopia was that of Arusiag, the daughter of Dikran and Srpuhi Ebeyan, who were then living in Entotto with their master and mistress Menelik and Taytu. Arusiag was born around 1890.
16. Du Bourg de Bozas (1906a, p. 21).

17. See Ghanotakis (1979, pp. 25, 27, 35–6, 50, 61, 70, 106); Natsoulas (1977, pp. 149–51).
18. Mérab (1920–9, vol. 2, p. 112). The allusion is to Sultan Abdülhamid II and the 1894–7 massacres. See also De Castro (1915, vol. 1, p. 219).
19. De Castro (1915, pp. 218–19, 237–8). This pseudo-isba may be the first Armenian chapel in Addis Abeba, built on the site of the present-day Armenian club and restaurant.
20. Patapan (1930, p. 22).
21. Annaratone (1914, pp. 151).
22. De Castro (1909, unpaginated map; Zervos 1936, p. 26).
23. See Leiris ([1934] 1988, pp. 291, 313, 627); Nizan ([1931] 1990, p. 115); Hallé (1913, p. 14); Landor (1907, vol. 1, p. 1).
24. Landor (1907, vol. 1, pp. 15, 191, 200, 218–20; Nesbitt (1934, p. 27); Darley (1926, p. 97); Maydon (1925, pp. 28–9, 34); Esme (1928, pp. 45–6); Monfreid (1933, p. 248); Armandy (1930, p. 210); Ghanotakis (1979, pp. 38–9, 102–3).
25. Zervos (1936, p. 340–1, 355–61, 367–70, 391, 395, 399, 401–2, 405, 408).
26. Patapan (1930, pp. 223–4).
27. See, for example, Esme (1928, p. 61); Coon (1936, p. 107); Armandy (1930, p. 152); Nesbitt (1934, p. 36); Zervos (1936).
28. In 1911, the Delsizian brothers, Garbis and Vahan, established their company, founded in Milan around 1896, in Eritrea; it extended its activity over the whole of East Africa before being put into liquidation in 1923.
29. Zervos names thirty-one companies among the exporters and importers of coffee who plied their trade between different provinces and Addis Abeba. Seven were Armenian, ten were Greek, and at least six were Indian. See (Zervos 1936, p. 156).
30. He made his brothers in Europe partners in the Kevork Muradian company before opening a branch of the business in Egypt in 1908 in association with Krikor Seferian. He later moved to Khartum and, finally, Ethiopia. See Patapan (1930, p. 185).
31. The Ethiopian empire's Tobacco Régie was directed by three Armenians, in the interwar period: Matig Kevorkoff, Hrant Minassian, and Markar Mirza, and, thereafter, by Mirza's heirs. It had two factories, located in Addis Abeba and Dire Dawa, and employed a large number of Ethiopian workers. See Zervos (1936, pp. 212–3); Patapan (1930, p. 188, 218–19). Kevorkoff was expropriated by the Italians. See ASMAI, Box 95, File 344, "Ditta Matig Kevorkoff, Monopolio Tabacchi, 1939–1940."
32. Patapan (1930, p. 222); Nicod (1937, pp. 88 and 98); Zervos (1936, pp. 126, 140–2, 275–9).
33. Zervos mentions only seven goldsmiths in 1935, whereas Patapan puts their number at sixteen five years earlier.
34. The same holds for nightclubs and illegal gambling establishments. See Coon (1935, p. 127).
35. Zervos (1936, pp. 144–5, 211, 495). Patapan puts the number of Armenian tanners at six, among them Stepan Darakjian, Avedis Sevadjian, and Kevork Kehiayan.
36. Zervos (1936, pp. 208–11); Patapan (1930, p. 221).
37. Zervos (1936, p. 496).
38. Avedis Terzian (Narrative 7, § 13). See also Zervos (1936, p. 144); Maydon (1925, pp. 174–7).
39. Patapan lists seven, including Piusant Abuseifian; Aram Shahbazian, the owner of the "Chahbaz" studio; Vazken Kevorkian; and Jirayr Mekhjian, as well as Bedros Boyadjian's sons, Haygaz and Tony. We may add the photographer "Shant" and Hrant Wararanian, whose studio was, according to Zervos, "the Ethiopians' and the autochthons' favorite." See Zervos (1936, p. 493).

40. Interview with Avedis Terzian, Addis Abeba, May 23, 2000.
41. The Djerrahian brothers also founded the Papeterie Artistique [Artistic stationer's shop], which found itself in competition with the Surmeyan Stationer's shop. The Imprimerie Artistique employed more than 250 employees after the war, when the Djerrahian brothers built, at their expense, the Artistic Building in downtown Addis Abeba. Djerrahian (1991, pp. 14, 19); Zervos (1936, p. 107).
42. Patapan (1930, p. 267).
43. Avedis Terzian (Narrative 33, § 7).
44. Zervos (1936, pp. 26, 289–91, 495, 498–9); Patapan (1930, pp. 130, 213, 267); Armandy (1930, p. 160). Avedis Terzian (Narrative 32, § 6).
45. A. Nicod (1937, pp. 37–41).
46. Zervos (1936, p. 149).
47. Ibid., p. 496.
48. The British employed several Greeks in this post.
49. Mérab (1920–9, vol. 2, pp. 100, 105); Patapan (1930, p. 267); Zervos (1936, pp. 419, 424, 429, 433, 473, 496). In Asmara, Hagop Segulian was an interpreter for the Office of Political Affairs of the Government of Eritrea from 1911 to 1913, before being employed for several years by the firm Delsizian Brothers. See Puglisi (1952, pp. 270–1).
50. Nicod (1937, p. 179). Nicod himself was represented, in a suit heard by this special court, by "the dragoman" of the legation of France, a certain "Monsieur P.," probably Ardashes Peshdilmaji.
51. From 1904 to 1933, the post of Oriental or Abyssinian Secretary of the legation of the United Kingdom had been held by the Greek Photios Zaphiropoulos (or Zaphiro), a former pharmacist in Harar who had acquired British citizenship. See Natsoulas (1977, pp. 151–60). Greek merchants such as Ioannis Gerolimato served as British consular agents in Harar and Dire Dawa. Similarly, Hovhannes Semerjibashian was Oriental Secretary at the German legation from 1932 to 1936.
52. FO 371/27524. The Greek Minister to Sir O. Sargent, Addis Abeba, December 4, 1941.
53. Zervos (1936, pp. 359–60); *Guida dell'Africa Orientale Italiana* (1938, p. 447).
54. Patapan (1930, p. 261); Mérab (1920–9, vol. 2, p. 202).
55. The older of these two cemeteries boasted 264 graves in 2002, to which the 231 graves in St. Jacob's cemetery must be added, for a total of 495 graves.
56. Avedis Terzian (Narrative 11, § 1).
57. Patapan (1930, p. 261).
58. Mérab (1920–9, vol. 2, pp. 135–6).
59. Ibid., p. 108.
60. See Ghanotakis (1979, pp. 35–6, 44, 59).
61. Patapan (1930, p. 202).
62. For details, see Adjemian (2011b).

8 Between Stateless Person and Citizen: The Belle Époque of a Legal Gray Zone

1. ASMAI 181/58, folder 287. "Promemoria" about the question of the husband and wife Schreiner-Sivrissarian, Rome, June 4, 1937; marriage contract of Etel Schreiner and Agop Sivrissarian, Addis Abeba, July 14, 1936.

2. The protection extended by the French government in fact ceased after the Second World War.
3. MAE, Série K, Éthiopie 122, Box 82, Bodard to Coppet, Addis Abeba, June 5, 1935.
4. ASMAI, 181/66, folders 335, 335 and 336. For greater detail, see Adjemian (2011a, 2013, and 2022).
5. Avedis Terzian, Narrative 4, § 27 and Narrative 26, § 11, and *supra*, Chap. 5.
6. Zervos (1936, pp. 122–3).
7. Despite the law's silence on this subject (Vanderlinden 1971), the children of Armenian immigrants probably benefited from the naturalization of their parents.
8. Auberson (1936, p. 23).
9. Ibid., pp. 32–3.
10. Ibid.
11. Scholler (1985, pp. 11–41).
12. See Auberson (1936, pp. 24–36).
13. MAE, NS, Éthiopie 62, Brice to Pichon, Addis Abeba, September 17, 1908.
14. Auberson (1936, pp. 84, 96–7).
15. See Nalbandian (2019); De Lorenzi (2016).
16. In 1965, the head of the Armenian church paid an official visit to Addis Abeba to attend the meeting of the heads of the five Eastern non-Chalcedonian Churches. Let us note that none of the Rastafarians who had come from Jamaica, although they considered themselves "true Ethiopians," were ever granted Ethiopian citizenship. Bonacci (2007, pp. 588–94).
17. See Nalbandian (2019). Nationality by birth and nationality by acquisition do not give access to the same rights, because jobs in the state administration and civil service are not open to naturalized citizens (Vanderlinden 1971). Nor do they involve the same obligations: no Armenian has served in the Ethiopian army since the end of the imperial regime.
18. MAE, NS, Éthiopie 62, Brice to Pichon, Addis Abeba, September 17, 1908, and February 10, 1909.
19. Avedis Terzian, Narrative 4, § 3.
20. MAE, NS, Éthiopie 62, Brice to Pichon, Addis Abeba, June 8, September 17, and December 22, 1908.
21. MAE, NS, Éthiopie 72, "Sujets ottomans inscrits à la légation d'Allemagne," Addis Abeba, September 15, 1908 (second appendix to the dispatch of September 17).
22. MAE, NS, Éthiopie 62, Brice to Pichon, Addis Abeba, February 10, 1909; "Au sujet de la population européenne," Addis Abeba, November 14, 1909.
23. Patapan (1930, p. 232).
24. See *supra*, Chap. 4.
25. MAE, NS, Éthiopie 21, "Au sujet de Serkis Terzian, Arménien en instance de naturalisation," Addis Abeba, November 30, 1906; Brice to Pichon, Addis Abeba, March 25, 1910.
26. FO 371/50AB/3494, "Estate of Mr. Terzian in Abyssinia," Gates to Ryan, Constantinople, December 17, 1918.
27. Patapan (1930, p. 232).
28. Proclaimed on May 28, 1918, the first Republic of Armenia was recognized de facto by the Allies in January 1920. Kevokoff's declaration is dated May 24, 1920.
29. President Wilson's plans, discussed during the preliminary negotiations over the August 10, 1920, Treaty of Sèvres, had initially provided for a US mandate over Armenia.

30. MAE, NS, Éthiopie 62, Brice to Pichon, Addis Abeba, January 4, 1911; Mérab (1920-9, vol. 2, p. 98); Ghanotakis (1979, pp. 46, 49).
31. MAE, Series K, Éthiopie 21, Coppet to the minister, Addis Abeba, February 4 and 20, 1920; MAE, Series K, Éthiopie 1, Boucoiran to the minister, Addis Abeba, August 25, 1923.
32. MAE, Series K, Éthiopie 1, 79, Reffye to the minister, Addis Abeba, n.d. [1928]. See also Armandy (1930, pp. 127-8).
33. MAE, Series K, Éthiopie 83/1, Reffye to the president of the council, Addis Abeba, 17 November 1928; "Inscription d'Arméniens en Éthiopie," note of the MAE, Paris, January 14, 1929; Reffye to Briand, Addis Abeba, March 8, 1929.
34. Auberson (1936, pp. 98-9). These individuals came under the jurisdiction of Ethiopian law and legal procedure but—the fact bears emphasizing—"without application of physical constraint."
35. Thus Sarkis Terzian's murderer, Missak Parunagian, was extradited to Eritrea in 1915 so that a white would not be turned over to Ethiopian courts and hanged. The Italians expelled him to the USSR in 1936.
36. MAE, Series K, Éthiopie 1, Boucoiran to the minister, Addis Abeba, May 13, 1923. On this date, the fourth committee to be elected comprised Yervant Hussissian, Hayg Tulumbajian, Krikorios Boghossian (Treasurer), Shemavon Kevorkian (Secretary), Hrant Papazian (President), Krikor Howyan (Honorary President), and Mihran Hazarian.
37. Patapan (1930, p. 255); Unpublished manuscript of Avedis Terzian (1997).
38. MAE, Series K, Éthiopie 21, box 82/7, Coppet to the minister, Addis Abeba, February 4, 1920.
39. MAE, Series K, Éthiopie 1, box 79, Boucoiran to the president of the council, Addis Abeba, July 15, 1923; Reffye to the minister, Addis Abeba, July 23, 1928. See also *Le Courrier d'Éthiopie*, July 21, 1923, p. 2.
40. Du Bourg de Bozas (1906b, pp. 197-8).
41. MAE, NS, Éthiopie 72, Appendix 5 to the dispatch of the French legation in Ethiopia on September 17, 1908: "Réponse du chargé d'affaires d'Allemagne au comité organisateur d'une fête en l'honneur de la constitution," Zintgraff to the Armenian Committee, Addis Abeba, September 6, 1908.
42. See ASMAI, 95, folder 344, telegram of January 11, 1939, to Benito Mussolini extending New Year's greetings from the president of the Armenian community, Matig Kevorkoff, together with the Duce's expressions of gratitude to the Armenian community.
43. Avedis Terzian, Narrative 4, § 21.
44. "Statutes of the Armenian community in Ethiopia" (revised on February 6, 1963), articles 1, 4, and 6.
45. See Auberson (1936, p. 85), who notes that "the different foreign colonies placed under the authority of one and the same consulate thus comprise, within the Ethiopian state, so many little states subject to the administrative authority and jurisdiction of the consul at their head." See also Avedis Terzian, Narrative 9, § 1-5.
46. ASMAI, 180/42, folder 136, "Sudditi stranieri," July 21, 1939. Yervant Atamian was a member of *Ras* Täfäri's brass band in 1924 (Patapan 1930, p. 245).
47. Many different cases of expulsion of Greek subjects are noted in ASMAI 181/55, folder 260, folder 262; 181/58, folder 287; 180/42, folder 136, expulsion orders, or plans to expel, Yervant Hagopian, Yervant Norarevian, Melidos Ohanessian, and Yervant Atamian.

48. Avedis Terzian, Narrative 2, § 12–13; Narrative 12, § 15.
49. The "Records of residence permits" of the Ethiopian Immigration Office show that 454 people of Armenian origin entered Ethiopia between 1944 and 1949, as opposed to 1,041 Greeks, a disparity that may be due to the difference in the number of expulsions during the war. See Norberg (1977, pp. 89–90).
50. ASMAI 181/55, folder 261. These expulsion decrees also concerned Italians residing in Eritrea.
51. See also in ASMAI 181/58, folder 287: Agop Sivrissarian and Vahram Terzian were relegated to Somalia in 1936.
52. ASMAI 181/55, folder 262, the case of Artin Partikian; the case of Avedis Kenajian, his wife Azniv Derballian, and their children in 1936–7.
53. ASMAI 180/44, folder 154. Borruso (2003, pp. 27–31).
54. See ASMAI 180/44, folder 155 and ASMAI 84, folders 249–50. Among the Armenians interned were Avedis Terzian, Minas Kherbekian, Aramast Baghdassarian, and so on. For more detail, see Adjemian (2022).
55. ASMAI 180/44, folder 155. For greater detail, see Adjemian 2022.
56. The Armenian merchant Matig Kevorkoff was, however, because of his status as an "enemy subject," deprived of his monopoly on tobacco and saw his assets confiscated because he was a French national. He was expelled from IEA on November 29, 1935. ASMAI 95, folder 344.
57. Emphasis added. ASMAI 180/44, folder 156, "Applicazione delle leggi di guerra. Sudditi siriani et libanesi di origine armena e araba, e sudditi greci di origine armena," Governo della Libia, Tripoli, April 23, 1941.
58. Martucci (1940).
59. Ibid., pp. 6–7.
60. He admits, later in his memorandum, that "the Armenian community of Addis Abeba currently comprises around eighty families totaling five hundred fifty individuals," a figure that confirms that the Italian conquest destabilized the community, even if we add to the total "the other five hundred Armenians living in other territories of Italian East Africa" (a figure that is exaggerated in its turn). Martucci (1940), pp. 5 and 8. Another Italian source puts the number of Armenians living in Addis Abeba at 830 in 1938. See *Guida dell'Africa Orientale Italiana* (1938, p. 479).
61. Martucci (1940, pp. 5, 8, 15).
62. ASMAI 73, folder 190, letter from Father Hovhanessian to Benito Mussolini and the minister for IEA, Rome, July 29, 1938.
63. See Berhe and De Napoli (2022).
64. ASMAI 91, folder 288, "Promemoria relativo ad alcune situazione createsi in seno alla colonia araba di Addis Abeba," Addis Abeba, July 22, 1940.
65. ASMAI 92, folder 293: Alice Papazian's rejected application.
66. ASMAI 91, folder 288 and Adjemian (2022).
67. Aegean citizenship was attributed to natives of the Italian islands of the Aegean on the basis of a October 19, 1933 decree. It did not give access to the same political rights as those Italian citizens enjoyed but offered the advantage of exonerating those who held it from military obligations. ASMAI 91, folder 288, "Greci, armeni e levantini in A.O.I.—Cittadinanza," Rome, May 8, 1939. See also Espinoza 2022 and Castiglioni (2022).
68. ASMAI 181/55, folder 261, Nasi to the minister for the colonies and the governor of IEA, Harar, 2 December 1936.
69. Archivio centrale dello Stato [ACS], MAI, 28, p. 10, Scuola greca di Addis Abeba.

70. Martucci (1940, p. 7).
71. Ibid., pp. 14, 19, 27. Avedis Terzian, Narrative 8, § 44 and 47.
72. After the war, Berj Babayan long held the post of president of the Armenian community.
73. Martucci (1940, pp. 12–13, 16–20, 22–6, 28–32).
74. ASMAI 73, folder 190, "Armeni," governor of IEA to MAI, Addis Abeba, April 22, 1938; Serapion Uluhogian to MAI, Venice, June 10, 1938. Some thirty Armenian children were sent from Addis Abeba to the Mekhitarists in Venice to continue their education. See Martucci (1940, pp. 8, 15–5). Avedis Terzian, Narrative 7, § 15 and 20; Narrative 8, § 47 and Narrative 31, § 4. Testimony of George Israelian (Addis Abeba, August 29, 2002), born in Addis Abeba in 1927.
75. ASMAI 73, folder 190, Vahan Hovhanessian to Benito Mussolini, Addis Abeba, July 29, 1938.

9 Between *Färänj* and *Habäsha*: Representations and Social Practices of Hybridity

1. Levine ([1974] 2000, p. 118). Levine tends, it is true, to argue for the historical unity of Ethiopia as a whole, above and beyond the country's cultural heterogeneity.
2. Leslau (1976) translates *Färänj* as "Westerner," "foreigner," "European," or "white man" and translates its plural form, *färänjoch*, as "white people."
3. Ludolf (1684, p. 392).
4. Pankhurst (1983 and 2005).
5. Burton (1856, p. 145). Doughty (2002, pp. 958, 1087, 1237) mentions different uses and definitions of the word *frenji* (the plural form of *el-afrenj*) in Arabia in 1876–8. According to him, the term designates both people who have come from Europe ("Frankistan") and, for the Beduins whose words he cites, "the exotic customs or items that Turks and foreign pilgrims bring with them to the Holy Places" (Mecca), such as tobacco.
6. Skinner (1906, p. 21).
7. Collat (1905b, p. 500); Guèbrè Sellassié (1930–1, vol. 2, p. 515, n. 2); Hess (1970, pp. 26–7).
8. Terzibashian (no date [1944], pp. 47–8).
9. Cohen (1924, pp. 27 and 30–2). Faïtlovitch (1910, p. 125) notes that the indigenous population seems to distinguish Greeks and Armenians from Europeans by their customs and social level. See also (Pankhurst 1967, pp. 82–5).
10. Darley (1926, pp. 79, 80, 97, 105).
11. People from the Caribbean and American Blacks who had "returned" to Ethiopia were also considered to be *Färänj* by the Ethiopian peasants of Shashämänē, who saw in them, above all, new landowners. Bonacci (2007, pp. 187–8 and 448–9).
12. Portal (1892, p. 21). Orléans (1898, p. 18) mentions, in the same tone, the "Greeks, Maltese, and semi-Arabs" that he encountered at Djibouti.
13. Landor (1907, vol. 1, pp. 8, 17–18, 31, 65, 118).
14. Michel (1900, p. 522) (emphasis added).
15. Coon (1936, p. 69).
16. Farago (1935, pp. 54–5).
17. See Wolynsky 1903b and *supra*, Chap. 3.

18. Wolynsky (1903b, pp. 372–3).
19. Landor (1907, vol. 1, p. 18).
20. Coon (1935, p. 37); Landor (1907, vol. 1, pp. 6, 218).
21. Landor (1907, vol. 1, p. 25).
22. Monfreid (1933, pp. 135–6).
23. Coon (1935, p. 31).
24. Bahru Zewde (2002, p. 195), who cites FO 371/13111, Annual Report for 1927, Bentinck to Chamberlain, December 6, 1928.
25. Cited in Eadie (1924, pp. 237–8).
26. Fikremariam Estifanos (1986, p. 36).
27. Landor (1907, vol. 1, p. 18).
28. Thus Nicod (1937, pp. 127–9) transforms the descriptions of his encounters with Armenians in Dire Dawa into an evocation of a mysterious Orient.
29. Waugh ([1932] 1962). Youkoumian seems to be a character inspired by someone Waugh met in Harar and also, perhaps, by Haile Selassie's personal secretary, Abraham Koeurhadjian.
30. Abbadie (1868, vol. 1, pp. 601–2).
31. Ibid.
32. Lépidis (1973, pp. 50–2, 57).
33. See *infra* the section "The Fate of Three Abyssinized Families under the Italian Occupation."
34. Monfreid (1933, pp. 111–12, 129, 135, 141, 156).
35. Berhanou Gebressellasié, personal communication, February 2008, Lyons.
36. Patapan (1930, p. 213). Register of deaths of the Armenian church of Addis Abeba. Avedis Terzian, Narrative 4, § 47; Narrative 10, § 12 and 15; Narrative 19, § 6–9.
37. Thesiger (1987, pp. 91–2).
38. Waugh calls this scholar "Professor W." Indications are that it was the archeologist and specialist in Byzantine history, Thomas Whitemore. See Lang (1988, p. 77).
39. Waugh (1931, p. 82).
40. Waugh (1931, pp. 77–83, 91).
41. Avedis Terzian, Narrative 6, § 8. See also Parkyns (1853, vol. 1, pp. 43, 45) and Combes and Tamisier (1838, vol. 1, p. 197) on the subject of Greeks and Armenians used to Abyssinian customs and fond of raw meat.
42. This may have been Berj Bedushian. Waugh's encounter with him was, his book suggests, the most memorable of all his encounters during his African voyages. The account of this episode is, moreover, reproduced in *When the Going was Good*, a later compilation of extracts drawn from the writer's various works.
43. This description is in every respect similar to that of Youkoumian in Waugh's *Black Mischief*.
44. Waugh (1931, pp. 106–8) (emphasis added).
45. Ibid., pp. 110–11.
46. Ibid., p. 162.
47. Borruso (2003, p. 59).
48. ASMAI 84, folder 249.
49. See Angelo Del Boca, preface, in Borruso (2003, pp. 13–14). The family could return to Ethiopia only after 1945.
50. Aishè was in fact the daughter of Boghos Markarian.
51. ASMAI 84, folder 250, the prefecture of police to the minister, Rome, May 23, 1939.

52. ASMAI 91, folder 287. This was Miska Babitcheff. A certain "Jacob," a "mechanic-aviator," also appears on this list; "Jacob" is no doubt Hagop Sarafian (Avedis Terzian, Narrative 33, § 28).
53. ASMAI 84, folder 250, Graziani to the Ministry, Addis Abeba, June 23 and July 3, 1937.
54. ASMAI 84, folder 250, the prefecture of police to the minister, Rome, May 23, 1939.
55. ASMAI 84, folder 250, internal note of the ministry, May 13, 1940.
56. The Armenian cemetery of Gulēlē. Registry of death of the Armenian church in Addis Abeba. Patapan (1930, p. 163). The dates that Bairu Tafla (1985) provides in this connection are no doubt incorrect.
57. All this information derives from Bairu Tafla (1985). The autobiographical manuscript is titled "The Unfinished Life of the Patriot in Khaki Breeches."
58. See also Patapan (1930, p. 215).
59. Bairu Tafla (1985).
60. Greenfield (1965, p. 229).
61. This was the name taken by the Armenian Nazaret Kherbekian when he decided to live as a hermit, in the costume of an Ethiopian monk, in the highlands of Entotto.
62. ASMAI 181/58, folder 287, "Armeno Semerdjibassian Iohannes," the governor of Italian East Africa to the minister, January 11, 1938. See also Avedis Terzian, Narrative 2, § 15 and Narrative 12, § 3. Terzian too was released from the camp at Quoram thanks to the intervention of the German representative, doubtless at his friend Semerjibashian's instigation.
63. According to Bairu Tafla, it was only because Rome's answer was delayed that, in the meantime, Hovhannes was released thanks to the intervention of the head of the German legation, Gustav Strohm.
64. ASMAI 181/58, folder 287, "Armeno Semerdjibassian Iohannes," January 11, 1938.
65. The others who took part in publishing and distributing this handwritten and mimeographed paper were Avedis Terzian and his cousin Mushegh Terzian, Haylä Täklä Arägay, Bäzunä Neway, and Dästa Alämmah. A dozen issues are supposed to have been distributed between late 1940 and spring 1941. Avedis Terzian, Narrative 8, § 36–7; Narrative 12, § 3–4, 9, and 13; Narrative 32, § 1.
66. This information is derived from Bairu Tafla, who points out that the same article had appeared in yä'Eretra Dems on December 6.
67. Avedis Terzian, Narrative 12, § 10–11; Bairu Tafla (1985, pp. 25–35).

Conclusion

1. Noiriel (2006, pp. 191–210, and 2007, pp. 525–6).
2. Anderson (1983, pp. 4–5).
3. Gellner (1983, p. 35).

Unpublished Materials

Oral Sources

Anna Marcerou, born Yazedjian in Addis Abeba in 1915: Nice, April 1996.
Avedis Terzian, born in Harar in 1904: Addis Abeba, August-September 1997, December 1999, and May–June 2000.
Elise, Louise, and Suzanne Boghossian, born in Addis Abeba in 1907, 1910, and 1914: Addis Abeba, August 1997.
Mardiros Vagharshagian, born in Van in 1908: Addis Abeba, August 1997.
Piuzant Nalbandian, born in Aleppo in 1924: Addis Abeba, September 1997.
George Israelian, born in Addis Abeba in 1927: Addis Abeba, August 2002.

Manuscripts

Nalbandian Nerses, Քափիդէն Գէորգ Նալպանտեանի կենսագրութիւնը [The biography of Captain Kevork Nalbandian], 1964, 6 ff.
Terzian Avedis, "The Armenian Community of Ethiopia," c. 1997, 16 ff.
Yazedjian Paylag, untitled memoirs, in Armenian, c. 1965, 80 ff.

Epigraphic Sources

Funerary inscriptions from the Armenian cemetery in Gulēlē (Addis Abeba).

Iconographic Sources

Album of Mushegh Terzian (Armenian Community in Ethiopia, Addis Abeba).
Collection of the Boghossian family (Addis Abeba).
Collection of the Marcerou family (Nice, Versailles).
Collection of the Nalbandian family (Addis Abeba).
Personal collection of Avedis Terzian (Addis Abeba).
Photographic collection of the AGBU Nubar Library (Paris).

Private Archives

Armenian Community in Ethiopia (Addis Abeba)

Registers of births and baptisms; engagements and marriages; deaths and funerals (Addis Abeba Armenian Church).
Register of the Armenian community in Dire Dawa.

Union générale arménienne de bienfaisance (UGAB, Paris)

Minutes of the AGBU Central Board.
General Correspondence of the AGBU.

Armenian Patriarchate of Jerusalem

General Correspondence, 1924.

Public Archives

Ministère des Affaires étrangères (MAE, France)

Nouvelle Série

Éthiopie 21: Agriculture. Industrie. Travaux publics. Dossier général, 1904–13.
Éthiopie 62: Questions judiciaires, 1900–14.
Éthiopie 64: Affaires commerciales. Dossier général II, 1906, July-December 1913.
Éthiopie 65: Affaires commerciales. Relations avec la France I, 1895–6 and 1902–7.
Éthiopie 71: Affaires commerciales. Relations avec la France, 1902–9, Missions commerciales françaises et étrangères, 1897–1906.
Éthiopie 72: Autorisations. Français en Éthiopie, 1897–1913, Missions scientifiques françaises, 1897–1914.

Afrique, Série K

Éthiopie 1, 79: Légation de France à Addis Abeba, June 1918–December 1929.
Éthiopie 1, 83/2: Protocole, May 1919–August 1929.
Éthiopie 122, 82: Conflit italo-éthiopien. Mise en défense de la légation de France et de Grande-Bretagne à Addis Abeba. Mesures d'évacuation et de protection des étrangers, 15 May–1st October 1935.
Éthiopie 21, 82/6: Protection des intérêts ottomans en Éthiopie, February 1920–November 1925.
Éthiopie 21, 82/7: Protection des intérêts étrangers en Éthiopie, March 1919–December 1929.
Éthiopie 155: Étrangers en Éthiopie, October 1930–September 1936.

Public Record Office, Foreign Office Archives (FO, United Kingdom)

Abyssinia 1896-1905

FO 1/32: Special Mission to King Menelik. Mr. J. Rennel Rodd Diplomatic, 1897.
FO 1/34: Mr. Harrington Diplomatic and Treaty, 1898.
FO 1/37: Col. Harrington, Vice-Consuls at Addis Ababa, Harrar, Duff, Gerolimato. Diplomatic, Consular Commercial Treaty, 1900.
FO 1/40: Col. Harrington, Mr Baird, Consul at Zaila, Keyser: Vice Consul at Harrar. Gerolimato. Various. Diplomatic, Consular, Commercial Treaty, 1902.

Political Departments: General Correspondence 1906-66

Abyssinia (1907-24): FO 371/190, 371/823, 371/2593, 371/3125, 371/3494, 371/9989.

Confidential print relating to Africa 1834-1957

Further Correspondence respecting the Red Sea and Somali Coast: FO 403/221 (January to June 1887), FO 403/239 (1895), FO 403/298 (1896).
Further Correspondence respecting Affairs in North-East Africa and the Soudan: FO 403/298 (1900).

Archivio Storico del Ministero dell'Africa Italiana (ASMAI, Italy)

Etiopia

ASMAI 34/4 (fasc. 41), 36/10 (fasc. 80-1): Relazioni col Negus e i Ras (1857-1907).
ASMAI 38/1 (fasc. 11), 38/3 (fasc. 28): Missione Ciccodicola (1897-1907).
ASMAI 39/1 (fasc. 9-10), 39/2 (fasc. 12), 39/5 (fasc. 23, 26, 30), 39/4 (fasc. 43): Azione Russa (1884-1905).

Ministero (1859-1945)

ASMAI 180/42 (fasc. 136), 180/44 (fasc. 154-6): Campagna 1939-45.

Africa Orientale Italiana (1928-40)

ASMAI 181/55 (fasc. 260-2), 181/56 (fasc. 269, 271), 181/58 (fasc. 287): Varie 1934-40.
ASMAI 181/66 (fasc. 334-6): Domande di lavoro 1936-8.

Affari Politici (1934-55)

ASMAI 7 (fasc. 53, 55), 73 (fasc. 190), 84 (fasc. 249-250), 91 (fasc. 287-288), 92 (fasc. 293-4), 95 (fasc. 344): Direzione Generale degli Affari Politici (1937-42).

Archivio centrale dello Stato (Italy)

Ministero dell'Africa Italiana

Archivio segreto della Direzione Generale Affari Politici (1906–44): Busta 22 (fasc. 11/9); 28 (fasc. 10).

Bibliography

Abbadie, Arnauld d'. (1868). *Douze ans dans la Haute-Éthiopie (Abyssinie)*. Paris: Librairie Hachette.
Adjemian, Boris. (1998). "Traditions et filiations des savoirs européens et orientaux dans une géographie arménienne: l'Éthiopie d'Agonc' en 1802." *Cahiers Du CRA*, no. 9: 147–70.
Adjemian, Boris. (2011a). "Immigrants arméniens, représentations de l'étranger et construction du national en Éthiopie (XIXe–XXe siècle): socio-histoire d'un espace interstitiel de sociabilités." Thèse de doctorat, École des hautes études en sciences sociales.
Adjemian, Boris. (2011b). "Une visite au cimetière arménien d'Addis Abeba. Éléments pour la connaissance d'une diaspora et de ses pratiques funéraires en Éthiopie." *Afriques. Débats, méthodes et terrains d'histoire*, no. 3.
Adjemian, Boris. (2013). *La fanfare du négus. Les Arméniens en Éthiopie (XIXe–XXe siècles)*. Paris: Éditions de l'EHESS.
Adjemian, Boris. (2020). *Les Petites Arménies de la vallée du Rhône: histoire et mémoires des immigrations arméniennes en France*. Lyons: Lieux dits éditions.
Adjemian, Boris. (2022). "Stateless Armenians in Ethiopia Under Fascist Occupation (1936–1941): Foreignness and Integration, From Local to Colonial Subject." In *Citizens and Subjects of the Italian Colonies: Legal Constructions and Social Practices, 1882–1943*, edited by Simona Berhe and Olindo De Napoli, 223–44. London: Routledge.
Aghavnuni, Mgrdich. (1929). Միաբանք եւ Այցելուք Հայ Երուսաղէմի *[Monks and Visitors to Armenian Jerusalem]*. Jerusalem: Armenian Patriarchate Printing Press.
Agonts, Sdepannos. (1802–8). Աշխարհագրութիւն չորից մասանց աշխարհի *[Geography of the four parts of the world]*. Venice: Mekhitarist Congregation of St. Lazare.
Alboyadjian, Archag. (1946). Հայ եպիսկոպոսի Մը Առաքելութիւն ի Հայեէշիստան ԺԷ Դարուն *[The Mission of an Armenian Bishop in 17th Century Ethiopia]*. Cairo: Nor Asdgh.
Alishan, Levon. (1896–7). "Un Viaggiatore Armeno Traverso l'Abissinia." *Atti del reale istituto veneto di scienze, lettere ed arti* 8: 1220–9.
Amselle, Jean-Loup. (1999). *Logiques métisses: anthropologie de l'identité en Afrique et ailleurs*. Paris: Payot.
Anderson, Benedict. (1983). *Imagined Communities: Reflections on the Origin and Spread of Nationalism*. London: Verso.
Annaratone, Carlo. (1914). *In Abissinia*. Rome: Enrico Voghera.
Antoniou, Panayota. (2007). "L'intégration des Arméniens en Grèce. La constitution passée et présente d'une partie de la diaspora arménienne." In *Arméniens et Grecs en diaspora: approches comparatives*, edited by Michel Bruneau, Ioannis Hassiotis, Claire Mouradian, and Martine Hovanessian, 385–96. Athens: École française d'Athènes.
Appleyard, David L., A. K. Irvine, and Richard Pankhurst. (1985). *Letters from Ethiopian Rulers (Early and Mid-Nineteenth Century)*. Oxford: Oxford University Press.

Armandy, André. (1930). *La désagréable partie de campagne: incursion en Abyssinie*. Paris: Librairie Alphonse Lemerre.
Arslanian, Kevork. (1930). Ուղևորութիւն Յ'Եթովպիա [Travel to Ethiopia]. Constantinople: Impr. Gutenberg.
Auberson, Jacques. (1936). "Étude sur le régime juridique des étrangers en Éthiopie." Annemasse: J. Rosnoblet.
Bahru Zewde. (1991). *A History of Modern Ethiopia: 1855–1974*. London: James Currey.
Bahru Zewde. (2002). *Pioneers of Change in Ethiopia: the Reformist Intellectuals of the Early Twentieth Century*. Oxford: James Currey.
Bairu Tafla, ed. (1977). *A Chronicle of Emperor Yohannes IV (1872–89)*. Wiesbaden: Steiner.
Bairu Tafla. (1985). "The Forgotten Patriot: The Life and Career of Johannes Semerdjibashian in Ethiopia." *Armenian Review* 38, no. 2: 13–39.
Bairu Tafla. (1994). *Ethiopia and Austria: A History of Their Relations*. Wiesbaden: Harrassowitz Verlag.
Bakalian, Anny P. (1993). *Armenian-Americans: From Being to Feeling Armenian*. New Brunswick: Transaction Publishers.
Bardey, Alfred. (1898). "Notes sur le Harar." Extrait du *Bulletin de géographie historique et descriptive*, no. 1.
Bardey, Alfred. (1981). *Barr-Adjam: souvenirs d'Afrique orientale, 1880–1887*. Edited by Joseph Tubiana and Centre national de la recherche scientifique. Paris: Éditions du CNRS.
Barthes, Roland. ([1980] 2010). *Camera lucida: Reflections on Photography*. New York: Hill and Wang.
Basset, René. (1882). *Études sur l'histoire d'Éthiopie*. Extrait du *Journal asiatique*. Paris: Impr. nationale.
Beckingham, Charles Fraser, and George Wynn Brereton Huntingford, eds. (1961). *The Prester John of the Indies: A True Relation of the Lands of the Prester John, Being the Narrative of the Portuguese Embassy to Ethiopia in 1520*, 2 vols. Cambridge: Hakluyt Society at the University Press.
Bensa, Alban. (2006). *La fin de l'exotisme: essais d'anthropologie critique*. Toulouse: Anacharsis.
Bensa, Alban, and Atéa Antoine Goromido. (2005). *Histoire d'une chefferie kanak (1740–1878): le pays de Koohnê-1 (Nouvelle-Calédonie)*. Paris: Karthala.
Berhanou Abebe. (2001). "Le coup d'État du 26 septembre 1916 ou le dénouement d'une décennie de crise." *Annales d'Éthiopie* 17, no. 1: 309–59.
Berhanou Abebe. (2003). "Montages et truquages photographiques dans l'Éthiopie moderne (1915–1955)." *Annales d'Éthiopie* 19, no. 1: 19–41.
Berhe, Simona, and Olindo De Napoli. (2022). *Citizens and Subjects of the Italian Colonies: Legal Constructions and Social Practices, 1882–1943*. London: Routledge.
Bezabeh, Samson A. (2015). *Subjects of Empires, Citizens of States: Yemenis in Djibouti and Ethiopia*. New York: The American University in Cairo Press.
Bloch, Marc. (1921). "Réflexions d'un historien sur les fausses nouvelles de la guerre." *Revue de synthèse historique* 33, no. 97–9: 13–35.
Bloch, Marc. ([1924] 1973). *The Royal Touch: Sacred Monarchy and crofula in England and France*. Translated by J. E. Anderson. London: Routledge & Kegan Paul, McGill-Queen's University Press.
Bonacci, Giulia. (2007). *Exodus ! L'histoire du retour des rastafariens en Éthiopie*. Paris: Scali.

Bonacich, Edna. (1973). "A Theory of Middleman Minorities." *American Sociological Review* 38, no. 5: 583–94.

Bordes-Benayoun, Chantal. (2002). "Revisiter les diasporas." *Diasporas. Histoire et sociétés*, no. 1: 11–21.

Borelli, Jules. (1890). *Éthiopie méridionale: Journal de mon voyage aux pays Amhara, Oromo et Sidama. Septembre 1885 à novembre 1888*. Paris: Ancienne Maison Quantin.

Borruso, Paolo. (2003). *L'Africa al confino: la deportazione etiopica in Italia, 1937–39*. Manduria: P. Lacaita.

Boudjikanian, Aïda. (2007). "La Grande Diaspora arménienne (xixe–xxie siècle)." In *Histoire du peuple arménien*, edited by Gérard Dédéyan, 819–903. Toulouse: Privat.

Braudel, Fernand. (1984). "La longue durée." In *Écrits sur l'histoire*, edited by Fernand Braudel, 41–83. Paris: Flammarion.

Braudel, Fernand. (1990). *La Méditerranée et le monde méditerranéen à l'époque de Philippe II*. Paris: Armand Colin.

Brayer, A. (1836). *Neuf années à Constantinople: observations sur la topographie de cette capitale, l'hygiène et les mœurs de ses habitants, l'islamisme et son influence*, 2 vols. Paris: Bellizard, Barthès, Dufour et Lowell.

Bruce, James. (1790). *Travels to Discover the Source of the Nile, in the Years 1768, 1769, 1770, 1771, 1772, and 1773*, 5 vols. Dublin: William Sleater.

Bureau, Jacques. (1987). *Éthiopie: un drame impérial et rouge*. Paris: Ramsay.

Burton, Richard Francis. (1856). *First Footsteps in East Africa or an Exploration of Harar*. London: Longman, Brown, Green, and Longmans.

Caix de Saint-Aymour, Amédée de. (1886). *La France en Éthiopie: Histoire des relations de la France avec l'Abyssinie chrétienne sous les règnes de Louis XIII et de Louis XIV (1634–1706)*. Paris: Challamel aîné.

Canard, Marius. (1983). "Le voyage de l'archevêque Hovhannès en Abyssinie." In *Guirlande pour Abba Jérôme*, edited by Joseph Tubiana, 179–95. Paris: Le Mois en Afrique.

Cannadine, David. ([1983] 2012). "The Context, Performance and Meaning of Ritual: The British Monarchy and the 'Invention of Tradition', c. 1820–1977." In *The Invention of Tradition*, edited by Eric Hobsbawm and Terence Ranger, 101–64. Cambridge: Cambridge University Press.

Castiglioni, Luca. (2022). "No More Greeks: Contrasting Identities in the Italian Dodecanese." In *Citizens and Subjects of the Italian Colonies: Legal Constructions and Social Practices, 1882–1943*, edited by Simona Berhe and Olindo De Napoli, 202–22. London: Routledge.

Cerroti, Ottavio. (1894). "Il secondo viaggio in Abissinia del Mashcov (1891–1892)." *Bollettino della Società Geografica italiana*, serie 3, vol. 7: 841–86.

Cerulli, Enrico. (1943–7). *Etiopi in Palestina: storia della comunità etiopica di Gerusalemme*, 2 vols. Rome: Libreria dello Stato.

Cerulli, Enrico. (1968). *Storia della letteratura etiopica*. Milan: Sansoni-Accademia.

Cini, Umberto. (2007). "La trajectoire de deux communautés marchandes à Livourne entre le xvie et le xxe siècle." In *Arméniens et Grecs en diaspora: approches comparatives*, edited by Michel Bruneau, Ioannis Hassiotis, Claire Mouradian, and Martine Hovanessian, 93–105. Athens: École française d'Athènes.

Cohen, Marcel. (1912). *Rapport sur une mission linguistique en Abyssinie (1910–1911)*. Paris: Impr. nationale.

Cohen, Marcel. (1924). "Couplets amhariques du Choa." Paris: Imprimerie Nationale.

Cohen, Robin. (1997). *Global Diasporas: An Introduction*. London: University College London Press.
Colin, Gérard. (2002). *La gloire des rois: épopée nationale de l'Éthiopie*. Geneva: P. Cramer.
Collat, Oreste. (1905a). "L'Abyssinie actuelle." *Renseignements coloniaux et documents publiés par le Comité de l'Afrique française et le Comité du Maroc. Supplément au Bulletin du Comité de l'Afrique française*, no. 11: 421–34.
Collat, Oreste. (1905b). "L'Abyssinie Actuelle." *Renseignements coloniaux et documents publiés par le Comité de l'Afrique française et le Comité du Maroc. Supplément au Bulletin du Comité de l'Afrique française*, no. 12: 491–502.
Combes, Edmond, and Maurice Tamisier. (1838). *Voyage en Abyssinie, dans le pays des Galla, de Choa et d'Ifat*. Paris: L. Desessart.
Conti Rossini, Carlo. (1916). "Vicende dell'Etiopia e delle missioni cattoliche ai tempi di Ras Ali, Deggiac Ubié e Re Teodoro secondo un documento abissino." *Rendiconti della reale Accademia dei Lincei*, no. 25: 425–550.
Conti Rossini, Carlo. (1935). *Italia ed Etiopia dal trattato d'Uccialli alla battaglia di Adua*. Rome: Istituto per l'Oriente.
Conti Rossini, Carlo. (1942). "Miniature Armene Del MS. Et. N. 50 Della Biblioteca Vaticana." *Rassegna Di Studi Etiopici*, no. 20: 191–7.
Conti Rossini, K., and Ignazio Guidi, eds. (1907). *Historia Regis Sarṣa Dengel (Malak Sagad)*, 2 vols. Paris, Leipzig: E Typographeo Reipublicae, O. Harrassowitz.
Conzelman, William Eliot. (1895). *Chronique de Galawdewos (Claudius), roi d'Éthiopie*. Paris: Émile Bouillon.
Coon, Carleton Stevens. (1936). *Measuring Ethiopia and Flight into Arabia*. London: J. Cape.
Crummey, Donald. (1972). *Priests and politicians: Protestant and Catholic missions in Orthodox Ethiopia, 1830–68*. Oxford: Clarendon Press.
Curtin, Philip D. ([1984] 2002). *Cross-Cultural Trade in World History*. Studies in Comparative World History. Cambridge, New York: Cambridge University Press.
Cust, Lionel G. A. (1980). *The Status Quo in the Holy Places*. Jerusalem: Ariel.
Dakhlia, Jocelyne. (1990). *L'Oubli de la cité: la mémoire collective à l'épreuve du lignage dans le Jérid tunisien*. Paris: La Découverte.
Darley, Henry. (1926). *Slaves and Ivory: A Record of Adventure and Exploration in the Unknown Sudan and Among the Abyssinian Slave-Raiders*. London: H.F. & G. Witherby.
De Castro, Lincoln. (1898). "De Zeilah au Harar." *Bulletin de la Société khédiviale de géographie* 5e série, no. 3: 133–61.
De Castro, Lincoln. (1909). "La città e il clima di Addis Abeba." *Bollettino della Società geografica italiana* 10, no. 4: 409–42.
De Castro, Lincoln. (1915). *Nella terra dei negus, pagine raccolte in Abissinia*, 2 vols. Milan: Fratelli Treves.
De Lorenzi, James. (2008). "Caught in the Storm of Progress: Timoteos Saprichian, Ethiopia, and the Modernity of Christianity." *Journal of World History* 19, no. 1: 89–114.
De Lorenzi, James. (2016). "A Cruel Destiny: The Armenian Stranger in Twentieth-Century Ethiopia." *The International Journal of African Historical Studies* 49, no. 3: 405–35.
Decaux, H. (no date [1907]). *Chasses en Abyssinie*. Paris: C. Delgrave.
Del Boca, Angelo. (1995). *Il Negus: vita e morte dell'ultimo re dei re*. Rome: Laterza.
Djerrahian, Elias. (1991). *Mémoires*. Montreal.

Dompnier, Nathalie. (1996). *Vichy à travers chants: pour une analyse politique du sens et de l'usage des hymnes sous Vichy*. Paris: Nathan.
Doughty, Charles Montagu. (2002). *Voyages dans l'Arabie déserte*. Paris: Karthala.
Douin, Georges. (1941). *Histoire du règne du khédive Ismaïl*, vol. 3. Cairo: Société royale de géographie d'Égypte.
Du Bourg de Bozas, Robert. (1906a). *Mission scientifique Du Bourg de Bozas: Communications adressées en cours de route à la Société de géographie*. Paris: F. R. de Rudeval.
Du Bourg de Bozas, Robert. (1906b). *Mission scientifique Du Bourg de Bozas: de la mer Rouge à l'Atlantique à travers l'Afrique tropicale (octobre 1900-mai 1903)*. Paris: F. R. de Rudeval, éditeur.
Duchesne-Fournet, Jean. (1909). *Mission en Éthiopie (1901-1903)*, 2 vols. Paris: Masson et Cie, éditeurs.
Dufoix, Stéphane. (2003). *Les diasporas*. Paris: Presses universitaires de France.
Dufton, Henry. (1867). *Narrative of a Journey through Abyssinia in 1862-3*. London: Chapman.
Durkheim, Émile. (1912). *Les formes élémentaires de la vie religieuse. Le système totémique en Australie*. Paris: Librairie Félix Alcan.
Eadie, John Inglis. (1924). *An Amharic Reader*. Cambridge: The University press.
Elias, Norbert. (1991). *Qu'est-ce que la sociologie ?* Paris: Éditions de l'Aube.
Erlich, Haggai. (2000). "Identity and Church: Ethiopian-Egyptian Dialogue, 1924-59." *International Journal of Middle East Studies* 32, no. 1: 23-46.
Escherich, Georg. (1921). *Im lande des Negus*. Berlin: G. Stilke.
Esme, Jean d'. (1928). *À travers l'empire de Ménélik*. Paris: Librairie Plon.
Espinoza, Filippo. (2022). "An Italian Nationality for the Levant: Citizenship in the Aegean from the Ottoman to the Fascist Empire (1912-1936)." In *Citizens and Subjects of the Italian Colonies: Legal Constructions and Social Practices, 1882-1943*, edited by Simona Berhe and Olindo De Napoli, 109-29. London: Routledge.
Esteves Pereira, Francesco Maria. (1901). "Vida de S. Gregorio Patriarcha Da Armenia." *Boletim Da Sociedade de Geographia de Lisboa*, no. 7-12: 853-90.
Faïtlovitch, Jacques. (1910). *Quer durch Abessinien: meine zweite Reise zu den Falaschas*. Berlin: M. Poppelauer.
Falceto, Francis. (2001). *Abyssinie Swing: A Pictorial History of Modern Ethiopian Music*. Addis Ababa: Shama Books.
Falceto, Francis. (2002). "Un siècle de musique moderne en Éthiopie." *Cahiers d'études africaines* 42, no. 168: 711-38.
Farago, Ladislas. (1935). *Abyssinia on the eve*. New York: G.P. Putnam's sons.
Ferret, Adolphe, and Joseph Germain Galinier. (1847). *Voyage en Abyssinie dans les provinces du Tigré, du Samen et de l'Amhara: dédié à S. A. R. Monseigneur le duc de Nemours*, 3 vols. Paris: Paulin.
Fiaccadori, Gianfrancesco. (1984-5). "Etiopia, Cipro e Armenia: La « vita » di 'Êwost'âtêwos, santo abissino del secolo XIV." *Felix Ravenna*, no. 127-130: 217-39.
Fiaccadori, Gianfrancesco. (1985). "Etiopia, Cipro e Armenia: La « vita » di 'Êwost'âtêwos, santo abissino del secolo XIV." In *XXXII Corso di cultura sull'arte ravennate e bizantina*, edited by Raffaela Farioli Campanati, 73-8. Ravenna: Edizione del Girasole.
Fikremariam Estifanos. (1986). "The Armenian Community in Addis Ababa." BA, Addis Ababa University.
Forbes, Rosita. (1925). *From Red Sea to Blue Nile: Abyssinian Adventures*. London.

Francfort, Didier. (2004). *Le chant des nations: musiques et cultures en Europe, 1870–1914*. Paris: Hachette Littératures.
Garcia, Afrânio. (1989). *Libres et assujettis: marché du travail et modes de domination au Nordeste*. Paris: Éd. de la Maison des sciences de l'homme.
Garretson, Peter. (1974). "A History of Addis Ababa from Its Foundation in 1886 to 1910." Ph.D, School of Oriental and African Studies.
Garretson, Peter. (2000). *A History of Addis Abäba from Its Foundation in 1886 to 1910*. Wiesbaden: Harrassowitz,
Gascon, Alain. (1995). *La grande Éthiopie, une utopie africaine: Éthiopie ou Oromie, l'intégration des hautes terres du Sud*. Paris: CNRS éditions.
Gebre-Igziabiher Elyas. (1994). *Prowess, Piety and Politics: The Chronicle of Abeto Iyasu and Empress Zewditu of Ethiopia (1909–1930)*. Translated by Reidulf Knut Molvaer. Köln: Rüdiger Köppe Verlag.
Geertz, Clifford. (May 1967). "Politics Past, Politics Present Some Notes on the Uses of Anthropology in Understanding the New States." *European Journal of Sociology* 8, no. 1: 1–14.
Geertz, Clifford. (1972). "Deep Play: Notes on the Balinese Cockfight." *Daedalus* 101, no. 1: 1–37.
Geertz, Clifford. (1973). *The Interpretation of Cultures: Selected Essays*. New York: Basic Books.
Geertz, Clifford. (1983). *Bali: interprétation d'une culture*. Translated by Denise Paulme and Louis Evrard. Paris: Gallimard.
Gellner, Ernest. (1983). *Nations and Nationalism*. Oxford: Basil Blackwell.
Getatchew Haile, Aasulv Lande, and Samuel Rubenson. (1998). *The Missionary Factor in Ethiopia: Papers from a Symposium on the Impact of European Missions on Ethiopian Society, Lund University, August 1996*. Frankfurt am Main: Peter Lang Verlag.
Ghanotakis, Anestis John. (1979). "The Greeks of Ethiopia, 1889–1970." Ph.D, Boston University Graduate School.
Ginzburg, Carlo. (May 1979). "Clues: Roots of a Scientific Paradigm." *Theory and Society* 7, no. 3: 273–88.
Gleichen, Count Edward. (1898). *With the Mission to Menelik, 1897*. London: Edward Arnold.
Gobat, Samuel. (1834). *Journal of a Three Years' Residence in Abyssinia, in Furtherance of the Objects of the Church Missionary Society*. London: Hatchard.
Green, Nancy L. (2002). *Repenser les migrations*. Paris: Presses universitaires de France.
Greenfield, Richard. (1965). *Ethiopia: A New Political History*. London: Pall Mall Press.
Gruntfest, Yann. (1984). "An Ethiopic-Armenian Phrase-Book from the 18th Century." In *Proceedings of the 7th International Conference of Ethiopian Studies*, edited by Sven Rubenson, 67–78. Addis Ababa: Institute of Ethiopian Studies.
Guèbrè Sellassié. (1930–1). *Chronique du règne de Ménélik II, roi des rois d'Éthiopie*. Edited by Maurice de Coppet, translated by Täsfa Sellasé. Paris: Maisonneuve frères.
Guida dell'Africa orientale italiana. Le Vie d'Italia. (1938). Milan: Consociazione turistica italiana.
Guidi, Ignazio, ed. (1903). *Annales Iohannis I, Iyāsu I, Bakāffā*. Corpus Scriptorum Christianorum Orientalium, Scriptores Aethiopici, Series altera 5. Paris: Charles Poussielgue.
Gulbenkian, Roberto. (1994–5). "L'habit arménien, laissez-passer oriental aux XVIe et XVIIe siècles." *Revue des études arméniennes* (Nouvelle série) 25: 369–88.

Haile Sellasie I. (1976). "*My Life and Ethiopia's Progress*," *1892-1937: The Autobiography of Emperor Haile Sellassie I*. Edited by Edward Ullendorff. London: Oxford University Press.

Halbwachs, Maurice. (1941). *La topographie légendaire des évangiles en Terre sainte: étude de mémoire collective*. Paris: Presses Universitaires de France.

Halbwachs, Maurice. ([1949] 1980). *The Collective Memory*. Edited by Mary Douglas, translated by Francis J. Ditter Jr. and Vida Yazdi Ditter. New York: Harper & Row, Publishers.

Halbwachs, Maurice. ([1941] 1992). *On Collective Memory*. Edited by Lewis A. Coser. Chicago: University of Chicago Press.

Hallé, Clifford. (1913). *To Menelek in a Moto-Car*. London: Hurst and Blackett.

Halls John James. (1831). *The Life and Adventures of Nathaniel Pearce written by himself during a residence in Abyssinia from the years 1810 to 1819, together with Mr Coffin's account of his visit to Gondar*. London: Henry Colburn and Richard Bentley.

Harre, Dominique. (2015). "The Indian Firm G. M. Mohamedally & Co in Ethiopia (1886-1937)." *Annales d'Éthiopie* 30, no. 1: 285-311.

Hassiotis, Ioannis. (February 2007). "La communauté arménienne de Thessalonique. Organisation, idéologie, intégration." *Hommes et migrations*, no. 1265: 70-81.

Haylä Sellasē. (1972). *Heywätēnna yältyopya Ermj* [My Life and Ethiopia's Progress]. Addis Abeba: Berhanenna Sälam.

Henin, Henri. (1907). "Éthiopie." In *Recueil consulaire contenant les rapports commerciaux des agents belges à l'étranger*, edited by Ministère des Affaires étrangères, 138:71-180. Brussels: Imprimerie Georges Piquart.

Hentze, Willy. (1908). *Am Hofe des Kaisers Menelik von Abessynien*. Leipzig: E.H. Mayer.

Herzbruch, Kurt. ([1907] 1925). *Abessinien: eine Reise zum Hofe Kaiser Meneliks II*. Munich: F. Seybold.

Hess, Robert L. (1970). *Ethiopia: The Modernization of Autocracy*. Ithaca: Cornell University Press.

Hintlian, George. (1989). *History of the Armenians in the Holy Land*. Jerusalem: Armenian Patriarchate Printing Press.

Hobsbawm, Eric John, and Osborn Ranger, Terence, eds. ([1983] 2012). *The Invention of Tradition*. Cambridge: Cambridge University Press.

Horowitz, Donald L. (1985). *Ethnic Groups in Conflict*. Berkeley: University of California Press.

Hovanessian, Martine (1992). *Le lien communautaire: trois générations d'Arméniens*. Paris: Armand Colin.

Hovanessian, Martine. (1995). *Les Arméniens et leurs territoires*. Paris: Éditions Autrement.

Hovanessian, Martine. (2005). "La notion de diaspora : les évolutions d'une conscience de la dispersion à travers l'exemple arménien." In *Les diasporas: 2000 ans d'histoire*, edited by Lisa Anteby-Yemini, William Berthomière, and Gabriel Sheffer, 65-78. Rennes: Presses universitaires de Rennes.

Hovanessian, Martine, ed. (2007a). "Diaspora arménienne et territorialités." Theme issue of *Hommes et migrations* 1265.

Hovanessian, Martine. (2007b). "Diasporas et identités collectives." *Hommes et Migrations* 1265, no. 1: 8-21.

Hovanessian, Martine. (2007c). "Lien communautaire et mémoire collective: figures de l'exil des Arméniens en France." In *Arméniens et Grecs en diaspora: approches *comparatives*, edited by Michel Bruneau, Ioannis Hassiotis, Claire Mouradian, and Martine Hovanessian, 447–54. Athens: École française d'Athènes.

Ihl, Olivier. (1996). *La fête républicaine*. Paris: Gallimard.

Institut du monde arabe. (2007). *L'Orient des photographes arméniens:* Edited by Mona Khazindar and Djamila Chakour. Paris: Institut du monde arab, Éditions Cercle d'art.

Isaac, Ephraïm. (1976). "Catalogue of the Ethiopic Manuscripts in the Manuscript Library of the Armenian Patriarchate of Jerusalem." *Le Muséon*, no. 89: 179–194.

Joutard, Philippe. (1977). *La légende des Camisards: une sensibilité au passé.* Paris: Gallimard.

Kazazian, Anne. (2007). "Les Arméniens au Caire dans la première moitié du XIXe siècle: L'implantation d'une communauté en diaspora." In *Arméniens et Grecs en diaspora: approches comparatives*, edited by Michel Bruneau, Ioannis Hassiotis, Claire Mouradian, and Martine Hovanessian, 133–49. Athens: École française d'Athènes.

Keller, Conrad. (1918). *Alfred Ilg, sein Leben und Werken als schweizerische Kulturbote in Abessinien*. Frauenfeld.

Kévorkian, Raymond Haroutiun, and Vahé Tachjian. (2006). *Un siècle d'histoire de l'Union Générale Arménienne de Bienfaisance*, vol. 1. Paris: Union Générale arménienne de bienfaisance.

Kouri, Nooaman. (1906). "Situation commerciale du Harrar En 1904." In *Rapports commerciaux des agents diplomatiques et consulaires de France*, edited by Ministère du Commerce et de l'Industrie, 512:4–40. Paris.

Kulmer, Friedrich. (1910). *Im Reiche Kaiser Meneliks: Tagebuch einer Abessinischen Reise*. Leipzig: Klinkhardt & Biermann.

Landor, Arnold Henry Savage. (1907). *Across Widest Africa: An Account of the Country and People of Eastern, Central and Western Africa as Seen during a Twelve Months' Journey from Djibuti to Cape Verde*, 2 vols. London: Hurst and Blackett.

Lang, David Marshall. (1988). *The Armenians. A People in Exile*. London: Unwin Paperbacks.

Le Gall-Kazazian, Anne. (2011). "Deux familles arméniennes dans l'Égypte du XIXe siècle: les Tcherakian et les Nubarian." *Cahiers de la Méditerranée*, no. 82: 341–58.

Le Roux, Hughes. (1901). *Ménélik et nous*. Paris: Librairie Nilsson, Per Lamm, Successeur.

Le Roux, Hugues. (1914). *Chez la reine de Saba: chronique éthiopienne*. Paris: Ernest Leroux.

Lefebvre, Théophile. (1845a). *Introduction à la relation d'un voyage en Abyssinie exécuté par ordre du roi pendant les années 1839, 1840, 1841, 1842, 1843*. Paris: Arthus Bertrand.

Lefebvre, Théophile. (1845b). *Voyage en abyssinie exécuté pendant les années 1839, 1840, 1841, 1842, 1843*. Paris: Arthus Bertrand.

Leiris, Michel. ([1934] 1988). *L'Afrique fantôme*. Paris: Gallimard.

Lépidis, Clément. (1973). *L'Arménien*. Paris: Seuil.

Leslau, Wolf. (1976). *Concise Amharic Dictionary*. Wiesbaden: Harrassowitz.

Levine, Donald Nathan. (1965). *Wax and Gold: Tradition and Innovation in Ethiopian Culture*. Chicago: University of Chicago Press.

Levine, Donald Nathan. ([1974] 2000). *Greater Ethiopia: The Evolution of a Multiethnic Society*. Chicago: University of Chicago Press.

Lewis, Oscar. (1961). *The Children of Sanchez: Autobiography of a Mexican Family*. Harmondsworth: Penguin Books.

Liano, Alejandro. (1929). *Éthiopie: empire des nègres blancs*. Paris: P. Roger.

Loti, Pierre. ([1921] 2006). *Suprêmes visions d'Orient*. Saint-Pourçain-sur-Sioule: Bleu autour.
Ludolf, Hiob. (1684). *A New History of Ethiopia: Being a Full and Accurate Description of the Kingdom of Abessinia*. London: Samuel Smith.
Lusini, Gianfrancesco. (1993). *Studi sul monachesimo eustaziano: secoli XIV–XV*. Naples: Istituto universitario orientale.
Ma Mung, Emmanuel. (1996). "Non-lieu et utopie: la diaspora chinoise et le territoire." In *Les réseaux des diasporas*, edited by Georges Prévélakis, 205–14. Paris, Nicosia: KYREM, L'Harmattan.
Marcus, Harold G. ([1975] 1995a). *The Life and Times of Menelik II: Ethiopia 1844–1913*. Lawrenceville, NJ: Red Sea Press.
Marcus, Harold G. ([1987] 1995b). *Haile Sellassie I: The Formative Years, 1892–1936*. Lawrenceville, NJ: Red Sea Press.
Markham, Clements Robert. (1869). *A History of Abyssinian Expedition*. London: Macmillan.
Martucci, Giuseppe. (1940). *La comunità armena d'Etiopia*. Rome: HIM.
Matteucci, Pellegrino. (1880). *In Abissinia, viaggio di Pellegrino Matteucci*. Milan: Trèves.
Mauco, Georges. (1932). *Les étrangers en France. Étude géographique sur leur rôle dans l'activité économique*. Paris: Armand Colin.
Maydon, H. C. (1925). *Simen, Its Heights and Abysses: A Record of Travel and Sport in Abyssinia with Some Account of the Sacred City of Aksum and the Ruins of Gondar*. London: H.F. & G. Witherby.
Mayo, Dermot Robert Wyndham Bourke. (1876). *Sport in Abyssinia, or the Mareb and Tackazzee*. London: J. Murray.
Mazade-Roussan, Simone. (1936). *Seule en Éthiopie*. Paris: Société d'Éditions Françaises.
McCabe, Ina Baghdiantz. (1999). *The Shah's Silk for Europe's Silver: The Eurasian Trade of the Julfa Armenians in Safavid Iran and India (1530–1750)*. Atlanta: University of Pennsylvania, Scholars Press.
McCabe, Ina Baghdiantz. (2007). "La diaspora marchande arménienne de la Nouvelle-Djoulfa et sa fonction dans l'État séfévide: un modèle théorique à revisiter." In *Arméniens et Grecs en diaspora: approches comparatives*, edited by Michel Bruneau, Ioannis Hassiotis, Claire Mouradian, and Martine Hovanessian, 77–84. Athens: École française d'Athènes.
Mérab, Étienne. (1920-9). *Impressions d'Éthiopie: (l'Abyssinie sous Ménélik II)*, 3 vols. Paris: H. Libert.
Merid Wolde Aregay. (1998). "The Legacy of Jesuit Missionary Activities in Ethiopia from 1555 to 1632." In *The Missionary Factor in Ethiopia: Papers from a Symposium on the Impact of European Missions on Ethiopian Society*, edited by Getatchew Haile, Aasulv Lande, and Samuel Rubenson, 31–56. Frankurt am Main: Peter Lang.
Michel, Charles. (1900). *Vers Fachoda: à la rencontre de la mission Marchand à travers l'Éthiopie*. Paris: Plon-Nourrit et Cie.
Mirak, Robert. (1983). *Torn between Two Lands: Armenians in America, 1890 to World War I*. Cambridge, MA: Harvard University Press.
Monfreid, Henry de. (1933). *Vers les terres hostiles de l'Éthiopie*. Paris: Grasset.
Monfreid, Henry de. (1954). *Ménélik tel qu'il fut*. Paris: Grasset.
Montandon, George. (1913). *Au pays Ghimirra: récit de mon voyage à travers le Massif éthiopien*. Neuchâtel: Impr. Attinger frères.
Montandon, George. (1916). "Alfred Ilg." *Le Globe* 54: 1–16.

Nalbandian, Vartkes. (2019). *"I Want to Die with a Flag." Ethiopia: My Delusions and Disillusionment*. (no place, Canada).
Natsoulas, Theodore. (1977). "The Hellenic Presence in Ethiopia: A Study of a European Minority in Africa (1740–1936)." *Abba Salama* 8: 5–218.
Nersessian, Vrej, and Richard Pankhurst. (1986). "The Visit to Eighteenth Century Ethiopia of the Armenian Jeweller Yovhannes T'ovmačean." In *Études arméniennes in memoriam Haïg Berbérian*, edited by Dickran Kouymdjian, 609–44. Lisbon: Fondation Calouste Gulbenkian.
Nesbitt, Lewis M. (1934). *Desert and Forest, the Exploration of Abyssinian Danakil*. London: Jonathan Cape.
Nicod, A. (1937). *Et in Etiopia Ego*. Avignon: Aubanel père.
Nicolopoulos, Demetre. (1923). *Addis Abeba ou Fleur nouvelle: souvenirs et contes d'Éthiopie*. Marseilles: impr. Ant. Ged.
Nizan, Paul. ([1931] 1990). *Aden Arabie*. Paris: Seuil, La Découverte.
Noiriel, Gérard. (2006). *Le creuset français: histoire de l'immigration, XIXe–XXe siècle*. Paris: Seuil.
Noiriel, Gérard. (2007). *Immigration, antisémitisme et racisme en France, XIXe–XXe siècle: discours publics, humiliations privées*. Paris: Fayard.
Norberg, Viveca Halldin. (1977). "Swedes in Haile Selassie's Ethiopia, 1924–1952: A Study in Early Development Co-operation." New York: Africiana, a division of Holmes & Meier.
Norden, Hermann. (1935). *En Abyssinie: Relation d'un voyage de la Mer Rouge au Soudan*. Paris: Payot.
Olderrodge Dimitri A. (1974). "L'Arménie et l'Éthiopie au IVe siècle (à propos des sources de l'alphabet arménien)." In *IV congresso internazionale di studi etiopici*, 195–203. Rome: Accademia Nazionale dei Lincei.
Orléans, Henri d'. (1898). *Une visite à l'empereur Ménélick: Notes et impressions de route*. Paris: E. Dentu.
Pankhurst, Richard. (1966). "The Role of Foreigners in Nineteenth-Century Ethiopia, Prior to the Rise of Menilek." In *Boston University Papers on Africa*, edited by Jeffrey Butler, 2:183–233. Boston: Boston University Press.
Pankhurst, Richard. (1967). "Menilek and the Utilisation of Foreign Skills in Ethiopia." *Journal of Ethiopian Studies* 5, no. 1: 29–86.
Pankhurst, Richard. (1968). *Economic History of Ethiopia, 1800–1935*. Addis Ababa: Haile Sellassie I University Press.
Pankhurst, Richard. (1977). "The History of Ethiopian-Armenian Relations (I)." *Revue des études arméniennes* (Nouvelle série) 12: 273–345.
Pankhurst, Richard. (1978-9). "The History of Ethiopian-Armenian Relations (II)." *Revue des études arméniennes* (Nouvelle série) 13: 259–312.
Pankhurst, Richard. (1981). "The History of Ethiopian-Armenian Relations (III)." *Revue des études arméniennes* (Nouvelle série) 15: 355–400.
Pankhurst, Richard. (1983). "Some Names for Foreigners in Menilek's Ethiopia: Färänj, Taleyan and 'Ali – and the Greek Who Became a Färänj." In *Ethiopian Studies Dedicated to Wolf Leslau on Occasion of His 75th Birthday*, edited by Stanislav Segert and Andras Bodrogligeti, 481–94. Wiesbaden: Harrassowitz.
Pankhurst, Richard. (2003). "Armenians." In *Encyclopaedia Aethiopica*, edited by Siegbert Uhlig, 1:344–7. Wiesbaden: Harrassowitz.
Pankhurst, Richard. (2005). "Färäng." In *Encyclopaedia Aethiopica*, edited by Siegbert Uhlig, 2:492–3. Wiesbaden: Harrassowitz.

Pariset, Dante. (1937). *Al Tiempo di Menelik*. Milan: V. Bompiani.

Parkyns, Mansfield. (1853). *Life in Abyssinia: Being Notes Collected during Three Years' Residence and Travels in that Country*, 2 vols. London: Murray.

Patapan, Hayg. (1930). Արդի Եթովպիա եւ Հայ Գաղութը [*Modern Ethiopia and the Armenian Colony*]. Venice: Mekhitarist Congregation of St. Lazare.

Pease, Alfred E. (1902). *Travel and Sport in Africa*. London: Arthur L. Humphreys.

Pennec, Hervé. (2003). *Des jésuites au royaume du prêtre Jean (Éthiopie): stratégies, rencontres et tentatives d'implantation, 1495–1633*. Paris: Centre culturel Calouste Gulbenkian.

Pinguet, Catherine. (2011). *Istanbul, photographes et sultans: 1840–1900*. Paris: CNRS éditions.

Portal, Gerald H. (1892). *My Mission to Abysinia*. London: Edward Arnold.

Powell-Cotton, Percy Horace Gordon. (1902). *A Sporting Trip Through Abyssinia: A Narrative of a Nine Months' Journey from the Plains of the Hawash to the Snows of Simien, with a Description of the Game, from Elephant to Ibex, and Notes on the Manners and Customs of the Natives*. London: R. Ward.

Prouty, Chris. (1986). *Empress Taytu and Menilek II: Ethiopia 1883–1910*. London: Ravens Educational and Development Services.

Prutky, Remedius. (1991). *Prutky's Travels in Ethiopia and Other Countries*. Edited by J. H. Arrowsmith-Brown and Richard Pankhurst. London: Hakluyt Society.

Puglisi, Giuseppe. (1952). *Chi è? dell Eritrea, 1952: Dizionario biografico, con una cronologia*. Asmara: Agenzia Regina.

Rassam, Hormuzd. (1869). *Narrative of the British Mission to Theodore, King of Abyssinia: With Notices of the Countries Traversed from Massowah, through the Soodân, the Amhâra, and Back to Annesley Bay, from Mágdala*. London: J. Murray.

Revel, Jacques, ed. (1996). *Jeux d'échelles: la micro-analyse à l'expérience*. Paris: Gallimard, Seuil.

Rey, Charles Fernand. (1923). *Unconquered Abyssinia as It Is To-day: An Account of a Little Known Country, Its Peoples & Their Customs, Considered from the Social, Economic & Geographic Points of View, Its Resources & Possibilities, & Its Extraordinary History as a Hitherto Unconquered Nation*. London: Seeley, Service.

Ricci, Lanfranco. (1955–8). "Le vite di Enbaqom e di Yohannes abbati di Dabra Libanos di Scioa." *Rassegna di Studi Etiopici* 14: 69–107.

Rimbaud, Arthur. (1995). *Correspondance: 1888–1891*. Edited by Jean Voellmy. Paris: Gallimard.

Rochet d'Héricourt, Charles Xavier. (1846). *Second voyage sur les deux rives de la mer Rouge: dans le pays des Adels, et le royaume de Choa*. Paris: Arthus Bertrand.

Rodd, James Rennell of. (1923). *Social and Diplomatic Memories 1884–1893*. London: Edward Arnold.

Rosen, Felix. (1907). *Eine deutsche Gesandtschaft in Abessinien*. Leipzig: Veit.

Rubenson, Sven. (1976). *The Survival of Ethiopian Independence*. London: Heinemann Educational Books.

Said, Edward Wadie. (1978). *Orientalism*. New York: Pantheon Books.

Salimbeni, Augusto. (1956). *Crispi e Menelich nel Diario inedito del conte Augusto Salimbeni. Con prefazione, introduzione, note e appendici a cura di Carlo Zaghi*. Edited by Carlo Zaghi and Istituto per la storia del Risorgimento italiano. Turin: Industria libraria tipografica editrice.

Sapritchian, Dimothéos Vartabet. (1871). *Deux ans de séjour en Abyssinie, ou Vie morale, politique et religieuse des Abyssiniens*. Jerusalem: Typogr. arménienne du couvent de Saint-Jacques.
Sarkissian, R. P. Miuron. (2005). Երվւպահայոց 40 Որբ Սաները «Արապա Լճոց», «Քառասուն Մանկունք» [Les 40 élèves orphelins arméniens en Éthiopie « Arba Ldjotch », « quarante enfants »]. Պատմութիւն Երվւպահայոց [Histoire des Arméniens d'Éthiopie] 1. Addis Abeba: Armenian Church Pastorate of Ethiopia.
Schnapper, Dominique. (2001). "De l'État-nation au monde transnational. Du sens et de l'utilité du concept de diaspora." *Revue européenne des migrations internationales* 17, no. 2: 9–36.
Scholler, Heinrich. (1985). *The Special Court of Ethiopia: 1920–1935*. Stuttgart: F. Steiner Verlag Wiesbaden.
Sergew Hable Selassie. (1974). "The Ge'ez Letters of Queen Eleni and Lebne Dingil to John, King of Portugal." In *IV Congresso Internazionale Di Studi Etiopici*, 554–8. Rome: Accademia Nazionale dei Lincei.
Shack, William Alfred. (1979). "Open Systems and Closed Boundaries: The Ritual Process of Stranger Relations in New African States." In *Strangers in African Societies*, edited by William A. Shack and Elliott Percival Skinner, 37–47. Berkeley: University of California Press.
Shack, William Alfred, and Elliott Percival Skinner, ed. (1979). *Strangers in African Societies*. Berkeley: University of California Press.
Skinner, Robert Peet. (1906). *Abyssinia of To-day: An Account of the First Mission Sent by the American Government to the Court of the King of Kings, 1903–1904*. London: E. Arnold.
Sohier, Estelle. (2007a). "Images Du Pouvoir." *Connaissance des Arts*, special issue no. 327: Les Boyadjian, photographes arméniens de la cour du négus, p. 32.
Sohier, Estelle. (2007b). "Politiques de l'image et pouvoir royal en Éthiopie de Menilek II à Haylä Sellasé (1880–1936)." Thèse de doctorat, Université Paris 1 Panthéon-Sorbonne.
Sohier, Estelle. (2012). *Le roi des rois et la photographie: politique de l'image et pouvoir royal en Éthiopie sous le règne de Ménélik II*. Paris: Publications de la Sorbonne.
Soleillet, Paul. (1886). *Voyages en Éthiopie, janvier 1882-octobre 1884: notes, lettres & documents divers*. Rouen: E. Cagniard.
Swayne, Harald George Carlos. (1900). *Seventeen Trips through Somaliland and a Visit to Abyssinia: A Record of Exploration and Big Game Shooting, 1885 to 1893; being the Narrative of Several Journeys in the Hinterland of the Somali Coast Protectorate, Dating from the Beginning of Its Administration by Great Britain Until the Present Time, with Descriptive Notes on the Wild Fauna of the Country*. London: Ward.
Taddesse Tamrat. (1972). *Church and State in Ethiopia 1270–1527*. Oxford: Clarendon Press.
Taddesse Tamrat. (1998). "Evangelizing the Evangelized: The Root Problem Between Missions and the Ethiopian Orthodox Church." In *The Missionary Factor in Ethiopia*, edited by Getatchew Haile, Aasulv Lande, and Samuel Rubenson, 17–30. Frankfurt am Main: Peter Lang Verlag.
Talai, Vered Amit. (1989). *Armenians in London: The Management of Social Boundaries*. Manchester: Manchester University Press.
Tedeschi, Salvatore. (1966). "Poncet et son voyage en Éthiopie." *Journal of Ethiopian Studies* 4, no. 2: 99–126.

Tedeschi, Salvatore. (1990). "Un prelato armeno nell'Etiopia del Seicento." *Africa*, 15, no. 1: 1–21.
Ter Minassian, Anahide. (1997). *Histoires Croisées: Diaspora, Arménie, Transcaucasie, 1880–1990*. Marseilles: Parenthèses.
Terzibashian, Avedis. (no date [1944]). Երկու Տարի Ադիս Աբեբայի Մէջ [Two Years in Addis Abeba]. Paris: Imp. A. Der Agopian.
Thesiger, Wilfred. (1987). *The Life of My Choice*. London: Collins.
Thévenot, Jean. (1665). *Relation d'un voyage fait au Levant*. Rouen: L. Billaine.
Thiesse, Anne-Marie. (1999). *La création des identités nationales: Europe XVIIIe–XXe siècle*. Paris: Seuil.
Thomas, William Isaac, and Florian Znaniecki. (1919). *The Polish Peasant in Europe and America*. Volume 3: *Life Record of an Immigrant*. Boston: R. Badger.
Tölölyan, Khachig. (2005). "Restoring the Logic of the Sedentary to Diaspora Studies." In *Les diasporas: 2000 ans d'histoire*, edited by Lisa Anteby-Yemini, William Berthomière, and Gabriel Sheffer, 137–48. Rennes: Presses universitaires de Rennes.
Topouzian, O. Kh. (1974). "Quelques aspects des villes éthiopiennes d'après les sources arméniennes des XVIIe et XIXe siècles." In *IV Congresso internazionale di studi etiopici*, 793–801. Rome: Accademia Nazionale dei Lincei.
Torkomian, Vahram H. (1928). "À propos de l'histoire de la plante kousso." *Revue des études arméniennes* 8, no. 1: 33–8.
Triulzi, Alessandro. (2002). "Battling with the Past: New Frameworks for Ethiopian Historiography." In *Remapping Ethiopia: Socialism and After*, edited by Wendy James, Donald Lewis Donham, Eisei Kurimoto, and Alessandro Triulzi, 276–88. Oxford: James Currey.
Ullendorff, Edward. ([1967] 2006). *Ethiopia and the Bible*. Oxford: Oxford University Press.
Valensi, Lucette. (1992). *Fables de la mémoire: la glorieuse bataille des trois rois*. Paris: Seuil.
Van der Laan, H. Laurens. (1975). *The Lebanese Traders in Sierra Leone*. The Hague: Mouton.
Van Donzel, Emeri J. (1974). "Two Ethiopian Letters of Job Ludolf." *Bibliotheca Orientalis* 31, no. 3/6: 226–38.
Van Donzel, Emeri J. (1979). *Foreign Relations of Ethiopia, 1642–1700: Documents Relating to the Journeys of Khodja Murād*. Istanbul: Nederlands historisch-archaeologisch Instituut.
Van Donzel, Emeri J. (2007). "L'Arménien Khodja Murad entre l'Éthiopie et les Indes néerlandaises: 1663–1699." In *Les Arméniens dans le commerce asiatique au début de l'ère moderne*, edited by Sushil Chaudhury and Kéram Kévonian, 113–17. Paris: Maison des Sciences de l'Homme.
Vanderlinden, Jacques. (1971). *Introduction au droit de l'Éthiopie moderne*. Paris: Librairie générale de droit et de jurisprudence.
Vanderheym, J.-Gaston. (1896). *Une expédition avec le négous Ménélik: vingt mois en Abyssinie*. Paris: Hachette et Cie.
Victor-Hummel, Ruth. (1995). "Culture and Image: Christians and the Beginnings of Local Photography in 19th Century Ottoman Palestine." In *The Christian Heritage in the Holy Land*, edited by Anthony O'Mahony, Göran Gunner, and Kevork Hintlian, 181–96. London: Scorpion Cavendish.

Vovelle, Michel. (1997). "La *Marseillaise*. La guerre ou la paix." In *Les lieux de mémoire*, 1, La République, edited by Pierre Nora, 85–136. Paris: Gallimard.
Wachtel, Nathan. ([1971] 1992). *La vision des vaincus: les Indiens du Pérou devant la conquête espagnole, 1530–1570*. Paris: Gallimard.
Waugh, Evelyn. ([1932] 1962). *Black Mischief*. London: Chapman & Hall.
Waugh, Evelyn. (1931). *Remote People, by Evelyn Waugh*. London: Duckworth.
Wellby, Montagu Sinclair. (1901). *Twixt Sirdar & Menelik. An Account of a Year's Expedition from Zeila to Cairo through Unknown Abyssinia*. London: Harper & Brothers.
Wolynsky, Decio. (1903a). "Dall'Harrar." *L'Esplorazione commerciale, viaggi e geografia commerciale. Bollettino della Società italiana di esplorazioni geografiche e commerciali*, no. 17–18: 281–2.
Wolynsky, Decio. (1903b). "Note Etiopiche." *L'Esplorazione commerciale, viaggi e geografia commerciale. Bollettino della Società italiana di esplorazioni geografiche e commerciali*, no. 24: 372–7.
Wolynsky, Decio. (1904). "Note Dall'Harrar." *L'Esplorazione commerciale, viaggi e geografia commerciale. Bollettino della Società italiana di esplorazioni geografiche e commerciali*, no. 4: 49–51.
Wylde, Augustus Blandy. (1888).*'83 to '87 in the Soudan*, 2 vols. London: Remington.
Ydlibi, May. (2006). *With Ethiopian Rulers: A Biography of Hasib Ydlibi*. Edited by Bahru Zewde. Addis Ababa: Addis Ababa University Press.
Zervos, Adrien. (1936). *L'empire d'Éthiopie: le miroir de l'Éthiopie moderne, 1906–1935*. Alexandria: Impr. de l'École professionnelle des frères.
Zewde Gabre-Sellassie. (1975). *Yohannes IV of Ethiopia: A Political Biography*. Oxford: Clarendon Press.

Index

Abäbä Arägay (*ras*) 211
Abbadie Antoine d' 200, 203
Abbadie Arnauld d' 38, 44, 203
Abdülaziz (sultan) 52
Abdülhamid II (sultan) 2, 51–2, 59, 79, 92, 100, 130, 135, 164, 228 n.9, 237 n.38, 238 n.18
Abdullahi (emir) 101, 230 n.34
Abdülmedjid (sultan) 25
Abruzzo (duke of) 17–18
abun, abunä 14, 29–31, 34, 37, 183
Abuseifian Piusant (photographer) 238 n.39
Abyssinia 2, 25, 28, 31, 33, 35, 38, 43, 48, 98, 113–14, 116–18, 159, 173, 181, 190, 192–3, 203–5
Adal (*ras*) 37
Adana 165, 237 n.38
Addi Ugri 176
Addis Abeba
    Armenian immigration 4, 6, 19, 45, 56–7, 65–6, 74, 79, 84, 87, 113, 115, 130, 135–6, 140, 142, 148, 156–7, 160, 165, 174–5, 183, 186–7, 191, 206, 209, 223 n.11 and 13, 242 n.60
    Armenian quarter and neighborhoods 2–3, 88, 144, 175–6, 233 n.26, 239 n.41
    baths *see* Fell Woha
    capital 76, 95
    cemeteries *see* Gulëlë
    ceremonies, parades 14, 16, 64, 193
    churches 61, 67, 87, 175, 183, 193, 238 n.19
    concessions 48, 112–13, 115, 238 n.31
    customs 56, 180
    foreigners 40–1, 43, 80, 85, 182, 201–2, 223 n.11 and 13
    foundation 75, 78–9, 81, 112, 123
    Italian occupation 194, 197, 209–11
    legations and diplomats 41, 98, 193, 205, 210, 212
    market and merchants 43–4, 178–9, 186, 202
    municipality 13, 56, 152, 180–1, 185, 204, 235 n.66
    official visitors 15, 17–18, 24, 240 n.16
    photo studios 180
    police 151–2, 163
    population 173–4, 223 n.10
    railway 41, 79, 82, 106–7, 140, 142
    roads 107–9, 204
Addis Aläm 81, 106, 129, 176
Aden 44, 47, 57, 174, 178
Adwa
    battle of 15, 19–20, 40, 48–9, 78, 98–9, 102, 150
    city of 2, 28, 37–8, 74, 94, 96
Afar, Afars 77, 102, 128, 151
Afdäm 176
Agonts Sdepannos (abbot) 35
Aksum 28, 96
Albania, Albanians 2, 38, 194
Aleppo 35–6, 52, 157, 165
Alexandria
    city of 2, 52, 140
    patriarch of 15, 17, 30, 34, 218 n.23, 227 n.103
Alvares Francisco (chaplain) 36
Amdä Berhan zä Ityopya (journal) 211–12
Amhara 84, 92, 95, 174
Amhareñña, Amharic 12–13, 18, 20, 35–6, 64–5, 78, 83, 87, 92, 99, 101, 105, 109, 116, 130, 134, 152, 155, 180–1, 187, 199, 200–1, 204–5, 210–11, 217 n.2
Angoläla 37–8
Ankobär 49, 75, 78, 91, 96, 102, 122
anthem *see* music
Antonelli Pietro (count) 47–8
Aqaqi 137–8, 176

Arabia, Arabs 35, 42, 44, 48, 173, 176, 185, 195–6, 201, 223 n.13, 243 n.5 and 12
Arabkir, *Arabkertsi* 75, 79–80, 100–2, 112, 119, 130, 142, 164–6, 168–9, 174, 204, 210
Arada (neighborhood) 2, 95
arada zäbäña (brass band) 13, 163–4
arba lejoch (brass band) 155–6, 160, 163, 166–9
Armandy André 17
Armenag (*lej*) *see* Armenag Baghdassarian
Armenia
country 24, 30, 34, 83, 98, 130, 165, 201
Republic of 126, 178, 191
Soviet 140, 157, 159
Armenian General Benevolent Union (AGBU) 155, 157, 159
Arslanian Kevork (archbishop) 65, 67, 227 n.93
Artin (Shopi Artin, farmer) 173
Artin Yakub 55
Asfa Wäsän 13
Asinara (camp) 208–10
Asmara 94, 239 n.49
Assab 19
Atamian Garabed 183
Atamian Yervant 194, 241 n.46 and 47
Awash 176
Aynajian Hayg (trader) 178
Ayntab, *Ayntabtsi* 165–6, 168–9, 236 n.35
Aznavorian Mardiros (liquor maker) 128, 137, 142

Babayan Berj (trader, employee) 197
Babitcheff (family) 208
Bägēmder 27
Baghdad 38, 52, 203
Baghdassarian
Anouchavan 57
Aramast 208–9, 242 n.54
Ardashes 209
Armenag (employee) 56, 208–9
Ghewont (jeweler) 56
Hagop (jeweler) 48, 55–7, 92, 129, 142, 182, 227 n.93
Hrant (jeweler) 56
Balcha (*Däjazmach*) 57–8, 66
Balē 179
Bardizag 100, 187, 210

Basmadjian Zareh (priest) 183
Bäzunä Neway 245 n.65
Bedushian (company) 176
Bedushian Berj 244 n.42
Behesnilian
company 137, 178, 180
Roupen (trader) 178
Samuel (trader, interpreter) 178, 181
Yeghia (trader) 178
Beirut 52, 157, 164
Belgium, Belgians 77, 82, 99, 116, 146, 178, 181
Berbera 178
Bergebedgian 206–7
Berhanou Abebe 101, 130, 132
Berru (*ras*) 94
Bethlehem (Armenian merchant) 37
Bethlehem (town) 166
Biyo Kaboba 46, 76, 101, 105–6
Bloch Marc (historian) 5, 148
Boghossian
Aghassi 57–8, 142
Charlotte 146
company 178
daughters (Elise, Louise, Suzanne) 62, 144, 234 n.36
Hampartsum 234 n.36
house 175
Khachig (senior official) 57, 142, 181
Khosrov or Khosroff (colonel) 57–8, 66, 68, 142, 208–10
Krikorios 62–4, 66, 124, 126–7, 129, 137–8, 142–4, 146, 151, 175
Sahag 234 n.36
Bombay 38
Boyadjian
Bedros (photographer) 53–4, 56, 60–2, 142, 149–50, 192
Dikranouhi, or Dicky (artist) 149
Haygaz (photographer) 52, 54, 56, 149
Torkom, or Tony (photographer) 52, 56, 64–5, 149
brass band (royal) *see also arba lejoch* 1, 5–6, 11–19, 21, 23, 31–2, 39–40, 51, 53, 64, 66, 83–4, 152, 154–60, 163–4, 167–8, 179, 183, 213
Braudel Fernand (historian) 32
Brémond Antoine (merchant) 44, 117–18

Bruce James 33–6
Budurian Garbiz 203–4, 209
Burē 176–7

Caesarea (Gesaria, Kayseri) 146
Cairo 2, 30, 33, 36–7, 52–3, 64, 96, 98–100, 128, 192, 202, 220 n.23
Castagna Sebastiano (engineer) 60
Catholicism, Catholics 15, 23–5, 32–3, 37, 65, 80, 174, 182, 197, 200, 221 n.44, 222 n.71
Chahbaz (studio) 238 n.39
Chakerian Suren (interpreter) 47, 181
Chalänqo (battle) 229 n.34
Chalgjian Krikor (goldsmith) 55
Chefneux Léon 95, 106, 108
Chelghadian Mgrdich (priest) 23, 53
Cherakian Artin 55
Chorbajian Krikor (tailor) 51
churches
    Entotto Maryam 79, 126
    Estifanos (Addis Abeba) 183
    Giyorgis (Addis Abeba) 176, 182–3
    Holy Savior (Jerusalem) 26, 160
    Holy Sepulcher (Jerusalem) 25, 34, 222 n.66
    Maryam (Addis Abeba) 183
    Maryam Tseyon (Aksum) 28
    Mikaēl (Addis Abeba) 183
    Saint George (Addis Abeba) see Giyorgis (church)
    Saint Minas (Armenian chapel, Dire Dawa) 126
    Saint Minas (Coptic church, Cairo) 220 n.23
    Sellasē (Addis Abeba) 64–5, 182–3
    Surp Asdvadzadzin (Armenian chapel, Addis Abeba) 166, 183
    Surp Kevork (Armenian church, Addis Abeba) 65, 67, 126
    Trinity see Sellasē (church)
Cilicia 165, 237 n.38
citizenship, citizens
    Aegean 197
    Ethiopian 60, 83, 130, 132, 134, 186–7, 190, 193, 240 n.17
    French 178, 191, 232 n.83
    Italian 196–7

collective memory 73, 87–8, 91, 101, 107, 114, 118, 135, 137, 141–2, 148, 152, 155, 160, 163, 165, 168–9, 213
Constantinople
    Armenian patriarchate 59, 192
    natives from 37, 55–6, 96, 187, 231 n.61, 233 n.10, 237 n.13
    trade, travels 38, 51, 96, 116
Coptic Church, Copts 15, 17, 23, 26, 28–30, 37–8, 94, 183, 203, 209, 218 n.23, 220 n.23, 228 n.7
Cosenza see Longobucco

Däbrä Libanos (monastery) 205, 207, 234 n.46
Däbrä Marqos 179
Damascus 52
Danakils, Dankali see Afar, Afars
Darakjian Stepan (tanner) 238 n.35
Därg (1974–1991) 6, 56, 189–90
Däsē 54, 177, 183
Dästa Alämmah 245 n.65
Dawenlē 176
Dayr al-Sultan (convent) 25–6, 228 n.7
Delsizian Garbis and Vahan (traders) 238 n.28, 239 n.49
Dembidollo 176–7
Demetrius (Greek architect) 37
Derballian Azniv 242 n.52
Derderian Artin 187
Derderian Yeghishe (patriarch) 26
Dimotheos see Sapritchian
Dire Dawa 41, 43–4, 75, 79, 82, 91, 106–8, 126, 140, 159, 174, 176, 178, 181–2, 186, 238 n.31, 239 n.51, 244 n.28
Djerrahian Elias and George (printers) 180, 239
Djibouti 41, 44, 47, 74–5, 77, 82, 91, 99, 101, 106–7, 110, 126–7, 140, 159, 174, 178, 187, 201, 209
Doresse Jean 18
drivers, chauffeurs 168, 179, 205–7
Durkheim Émile (sociologist) 147, 169

Ebeyan Arusiag 49, 142
Ebeyan Dikran (jeweler, trader) 48–51, 54–5, 74, 76–7, 79, 91, 94, 96–8, 100, 122–3, 126–9, 137, 139, 141–2, 165, 227 n.93, 237 n.15

Ebeyan Srpuhi (or Serpig) 77, 79–80, 122–6, 128–9, 142, 174, 237 n.15
Ebeyan Vartan (jeweler) 96
Egypt, Egyptians 2, 14–15, 23, 28–31, 37–8, 44, 47, 52, 55–6, 74–6, 83, 94, 96, 101–3, 105, 107, 160, 174, 181, 186, 188, 192–3, 210, 221 n.44, 228 n.3, 230 n.34, 238 n.30
Eleni (queen, c. 1508–22) 36
Elias (Armenian guide-interpreter) 33
Elias Norbert (sociologist) 4
Eliazarian Y. (grocer) 178
Entotto 45, 49, 74–6, 79, 102, 106, 112, 122–3, 128, 142, 237 n.15, 245 n.61
Eritrea, Eritreans 19, 24, 176, 194–6, 202, 236 n.34, 238 n.28, 239, 241 n.35, 242 n.50
Ewostatēwos (saint) : 24, 34

Färänj, Färänji 1, 107, 199–201, 205
Fasilädäs (emperor, 1632–67) 33, 36
Fayça Sarkis (Ethiopian servant) 143
Fell Woha 14, 112–13, 117, 146, 181, 204, 210
Finfinni 112–13
forty children *see arba lejoch*
France, French 13, 17, 19, 47, 84, 87, 112, 118, 126, 156–7, 178, 200–1, 204
 colonies 74–5, 77, 99
 consulate 41, 188, 196
 embassy *see* legation
 Franco-Ethiopian railway 50, 82, 107
 French immigrants in Ethiopia 41, 44, 47–8, 57, 80, 95, 106, 223 nn.11, 13
 French protégés 113–14, 178, 186, 188–92, 194, 197
 immigration to France 2, 85, 139–40, 203
 language 74, 87, 108, 152, 174, 180, 205–6, 210
 legation 43–4, 49, 83, 99, 118, 147, 165, 175, 177, 181, 190–3
 missionaries 174, 183, 218 n.26
 relations with Ethiopia 14, 19–20, 36, 45, 76, 78, 81
 travelers 30, 32–3, 36–8, 41, 51, 92, 117, 202–3

Galan Josef de (Yosēf Galan) 132, 187
Gälawdēwos (emperor, 1541–59) 33

Gambēla 176–7
Gännät 108, 112
Garabedian Vartan 187
Garabedian Yesayi (Armenian patriarch of Jerusalem, 1865–85) 24, 52, 220 n.20
Garikian Yesayi (farmer, tanner) 174
gebbi (palace) 47–8, 50–1, 54–7, 62, 121, 124, 126, 143, 149–50
Geertz Clifford (anthropologist) 5, 32, 64
Geldeissa *see* Gildessa
Gellner Ernest (sociologist) 59, 215
Gevherian Hovhannes (priest) 183
genocide 2, 4, 6, 82, 84, 137, 140, 157, 164–5, 168, 213
Germany, Germans 47, 178, 200, 204
 embassy *see* legation
 legation 47, 83, 111, 118, 181, 210–11, 239
 protection of Armenians 130, 147, 189–91
 relations with Ethiopia 81, 116, 133
 scholars 33–4, 36, 199
 travelers 38, 108–9
 weapons 77, 82, 99
Gerolimato Ioannis (British consul in Harar) 232 n.85, 239 n.51
Ghurlian Hapet 233 n.10, 235 n.64
Gildessa 76, 104–6
Goa 36
Goba 179
Gobat Samuel (Anglican bishop) 25
Gobäzé (*wagshum*) *see* Täklä Giyorgis (emperor, 1868–72)
Gojam 37, 94, 179, 201, 229 n.9
goldsmiths *see also* jewelry, jewelers 37–8, 49, 55–6, 74, 76, 78, 91–2, 96–8, 122–3, 126, 129, 137, 141, 163, 227 n.83
Gondär 27, 31, 33–6, 38
Gorē 176–7
Gorgoryos *see* Krikorios Boghossian
Gorguos (Armenian hat maker) 37
Grañ Ahmad (imam) 33, 220 n.10
Graziani Rodolfo (viceroy of Italian East Africa) 194, 208–9, 211
Great Britain, British
 colonies 57, 105, 181
 consulates 115, 222 n.66
 firms 48, 110, 114
 Greek and Armenian auxiliaries 239

legation 41, 44, 110, 181, 201, 210-1
occupation of Ethiopia (1941-3) 85-6,
  101, 181-2, 193, 212
protection of Greeks 191
relations with Ethiopia 20-1, 24-5,
  29, 37-8, 41, 47, 51, 81, 98-9, 191,
  219 n.46
Greece, Greeks
  Armenians in Greece 140
  Church, churches 3, 25, 66, 183
  diaspora 4, 6, 12
  employees 182, 212, 232 n.48, 239
  immigrants 41-5, 47-50, 62, 111, 113,
    147, 173-7, 179, 185-6, 207, 223 n.11
  and 13, 230 n.34, 238 n.29
  under Italian occupation 194-5, 197
  legation 181
  perceptions of 200-2
  protégés 191
  travelers 32-4, 37-8
Gregory the Illuminator (saint) 24
Gugiughian Garabed 187
Gugsa Wälē (ras) 14
Gulēlē (cemetery) 182-3

Habäsha 199, 201, 205
Habechlı Karapet (caravaneer) 38
Hachadurian (trader) 44
Hajji Abdullahi Ali Sadik 116-17
Hajji Kevork see Kevork Terzian
Hajitor (dragoman) see Hatchatoor
Hagopian (company) 178
Hagopian Yervant (trader) 178, 241 n.47
Haifa 52
Haile Selassie (Haylä Sellasē, emperor,
    1930-6 and 1941-74)
  and Armenian immigrants 1, 6, 50,
    52, 54-7, 64, 66, 81, 84, 123, 151-2,
    157, 169, 187, 202-4, 210-11, 227
    n.88 and 93
  and Armenian Church 24, 83, 190
  coronation 151, 181, 205, 210
  and Ethiopian aristocracy 59
  and Ethiopian Church 30, 156
  exile 211
  and foreigners 46, 48
  and foreign powers 11, 21, 50, 85-6
  and music 12, 236 n.35
  relatives 14, 64, 76, 118, 176

restoration 142, 212
Hakalmazian Garabed (musician) 13, 18,
  163-4, 183
Halbwachs Maurice (sociologist) 7, 89, 101,
  118, 148, 155, 166
Hamasēn 203
Harar, Harari
  Armenian settlement 2, 43, 74-6, 79,
    94, 100-3, 118, 129, 135-6, 140, 142,
    164-5, 173-6, 178, 183, 206, 210
  British consulate 115, 210, 232 n.51
  city 81-2, 112, 115-17, 149, 194,
    197, 200
  foreigners 41, 43-7, 51, 174-6, 182, 202
  occupied by the Egyptians 75, 94, 101
  occupied by Menelik 75-6, 91, 98, 102-
    3, 105-6, 132, 163
  Turkish consulate 147, 191
  see also Täfäri and Mäkonnen
Harärgē 176
Harrington John (British ambassador) 111
Hatchatoor (dragoman) 38
Hatzakordzian Helen (midwife) 52
Haylä Giyorgis (nägädras) 137-8
Haylä Täklä Arägay 245 n.65
Haylu (ras) 201
Hazarian Dikran 227 n.93
Hazarian Mihran (upholsterer) 51, 137,
  234 n.37, 241 n.36
Hintlian Kevork 26, 220 n.23
Holy Land, holy places see Jerusalem
Hovanessian Martine (anthropologist)
  139
Hovhanessian Vahan (priest, from Venice)
  197
Hovhannes (priest, from Isfahan) 31
Hovhannes Smiurnatsi (Armenian
  patriarch of Jerusalem, 1850-60) 27
Hovhannes, or Hajji Hovhannes
  (goldsmith and gunsmith) 37-8
Howyan Krikor (engineer, astronomer)
  111, 137, 141, 166, 231 n.61, 241 n.36
Hripsime (saint) 24
Hurso (camp), see Sarkama
Hussissian Yervant (trader) 241 n.36

Ilg Alfred (trader, state counselor) 43, 47,
  95, 106, 108, 132-3
Illubabor 176

India, Indians 3–4, 6, 23, 39, 41–4, 83, 173, 176, 182, 196, 200–2, 207, 223 n.11 and 13, 235 n.60, 238 n.29
interpreters 34–5, 37–8, 47, 55, 66, 83, 132, 181, 196, 203, 206, 210–11, 239 n.49
Iran, Iranians 2, 34, 39–40, 52, 186, 189, 221 n.33
Isfahan *see also* New Julfa 31, 40
Islam, Muslims 2, 30, 32–3, 36, 54, 59, 75–6, 102–3, 115–16, 148–51, 207
Ismail (khedive) 38, 52, 55, 94, 96, 98, 101
Israelian
    company 178
    George 231 n.70, 243 n.74
    Kegham 176
    Ohan 176
Istanbul
    archbishop 65, 67, 227 n.93
    emigrants 165
    merchants 83
    photographers 52
    studies 94, 100
    travels 228 n.8
    see also Constantinople
Italy, Italians
    diplomats 17–19, 45–6, 48–50, 81, 105–6
    expansionism 19–20, 40, 45–50, 75–8, 98–9, 116–18, 123, 150, 179, 188, 205
    Fascist 13, 19, 166, 185, 194–7, 203
    Italian East Africa (Africa Orientale Italiana) 186–7, 194–6, 208–11
    occupation of Ethiopia (1936–1941) 12–13, 15, 26, 56, 59, 66, 84, 100–1, 143, 166, 168, 175, 181, 185, 188–9, 191, 193–8, 204, 208, 211–12
    settlers 19, 41, 60, 176, 194, 200, 223 n.11 and 13, 226 n.71, 230 n.34, 242 n.50
    subjects 186–7, 195, 209
    travelers and traders 42, 44
Iyasu (*lej*) 53–4, 57, 81, 113, 117, 146–52, 157, 169, 204, 211, 227 n.93
Iyasu I (emperor, 1682–1706) 36, 202
Iyoas (emperor, 1755–69) 35

Jacobis Justin de 32, 38
Jamaica, Jamaicans 240 n.16
Janhoy-Mēda (esplanade) 212
Japan 18, 31

Jarosseau André 23, 218 n.26
Java 37
Jeddah 220 n.20
Jerusalem 2, 12, 21, 23–9, 31, 34, 52, 79, 83, 89, 96, 118, 155–63, 187, 200, 222 n.66
Jesuits *see* missionaries
jewelry, jewelers *see also* goldsmiths 35, 50, 98, 179, 220 n.24, 226–7 n.83
Jidedjian Nigoghos (jeweler) 55
Jijiga 168, 176
Jimma 176, 178–9
João (king of Portugal) 36

Käbäna 111, 233 n.26
Kaloustian Vahan (administrator) 174, 181
Karabian Astrig (restaurant owner) 177
Karamanian Matheos (joiner) 144–6, 234 n.37
Karaseferian Ardashes (goldsmith) 56
Karaseferian Hrant (goldsmith) 56
Kasa (*däjazmach*) 28–30, 38, 94, 220 n.24, 229 n.9 *see also* Yohannes IV
Kasabian family 174
Kassabian Maksud (trader) 178
Kassala 38
Kaymakian Mihran (veterinarian) 180
Kazanjian Simon 183
Kehiayan Kevork (tanner) 238 n.35
Kenajian Avedis 242 n.52
Kenajian Sarkis (grocer) 178
Kevorkian (company) 176
Kevorkian Shemavon 241 n.36
Kevorkian Vazken (photographer) 238 n.39
Kevorkoff
    company 44, 178
    Matig (trader) 126, 178, 191, 197, 227 n.93, 238 n.31, 241 n.42, 242 n.56
    school 64, 126, 175, 197
Kharibian Vahram (embroiderer) 51
Kharpert (Harput) 24, 165
Khartum 149, 178, 238 n.30
Kherbeguian Mina *see* Minas Kherbekian
Kherbekian
    family 174
    Karekin 174
    Minas (engineer) 111–12, 142, 174, 180, 204–5, 242 n.54
    Nazaret (hermit) 245 n.61
    Pilibbos (mason) 112, 129, 141–2, 164

Klobukowski Antony 188–9
Koeurhadjian
　Abraham 56, 168, 181, 187, 204, 208–10, 244 n.29
　family 208–10
Krikorian Garabed (photographer, Jerusalem) 52

La Guibourgère marquis de 19
Lagarde Léonce 77, 99
Läqämtē 177, 183
Lausanne (Treaty of) 192
Lawrence T. E. (colonel) 149
Le Roux Hugues (journalist) 82, 106–8
Lebanon, Lebanese 2, 6, 39, 52, 165, 167, 186, 189–90, 195
Lebnä Dengel (emperor) 36
Lenoir du Roule (ambassador) 33, 37
Levine Donald (sociologist) 32
Liège 47, 77, 99
London 4, 20, 47, 85, 116, 205
Longobucco (camp) 208–10
Ludolf Job 34, 36, 199

Mad Mullah 149
Mahdi 75, 98
Maillet Benoist de (consul) 33, 36–7, 202
Mäkonnen (*däjazmach,* then *ras*)
　and Armenians 3, 50–1, 57, 109, 141, 169, 174–5
　in Harar 45, 76, 105, 230 n.38, 234 n.46
　relatives 81, 150–1
　and Sarkis Terzian, 46–7, 91, 105–6, 116, 118, 132
Mamo (Ethiopian servant) 143
Mampre Sirunian (archbishop) 64
Mänän (empress) 13, 50, 52, 55, 57, 64, 126, 156, 162–3, 235 n.65
Mängestu Haylä Maryam 95
Manoel (king of Portugal) 36
Manuelian Goriun (priest) 184
Manugian Hagop (musician) 236 n.34
Mäqälē 2, 74, 95
Mäqdäla 20
Marcerou Anna (née Yazedjian) 57, 79, 81, 83, 85, 87, 130, 152, 228 n.10, 235 n.65
Margos (Armenian traveler, Massawa) 222 n.66

Markar Mirza (trader) 238 n.31
Markarian Boghos (merchant)
　and Armenian community 92–4, 98
　envoy to Egypt 38, 47, 94, 126
　relatives 57, 244 n.50
　serving Menelik 78, 92, 94–6, 142
　serving Yohannes IV 74, 91, 94, 96
Marseilles 77, 87, 99, 117, 135, 181, 204
Mäshäsha Wärqē (*däjazmach*) 51, 228 n.8
Mäsqäl 16, 158
Massawa 2, 28, 37–8, 74, 94, 96, 222 n.66
Mätämma 38, 98, 229 n.13
Matēwos (*abunä*) 23, 60–1, 151, 175–6, 227 n.103
Matēwos (envoy) *see* Matthew the Armenian
Matikian M. (grocer) 178
Matthew the Armenian 36
mechanics 43, 179–80 and *see* drivers, chauffeurs
Mgrdichian (company) 99
Mehmed IV (sultan) 26
Mehmet Ali (khedive) 37–8, 55
Mekhjian Jirayr (photographer) 238 n.39
Mekhitarists (congregation) 197
Menelik (emperor, 1889–1913)
　and Armenians 37, 39, 44–7, 49–57, 59–63, 66, 77–80, 91–2, 95–9, 101–3, 105, 121–6, 128–33, 137, 140–3, 164, 166–9, 174–6, 187, 191, 208
　concessions and monopolies 46, 114–15, 178
　conquests 12, 59, 75–6, 95, 98, 102–3, 105
　court and *gebbi* (palace) 23, 48–9, 51, 55, 57
　crown 20, 50, 53, 98
　death 53, 81, 143–4, 146–8, 152
　and foreigners 6, 40–1, 46–8
　illness 55, 62, 141, 147, 190
　imperial reign 2, 5, 11, 76, 78, 92, 175, 177, 200
　and modernity 14, 20–1, 106–13
　negus of Shäwa 30, 74, 76, 94, 96, 188
　railway 82, 106–11
　relations with foreign powers 19, 21, 38, 41, 43, 45, 46–7, 49–50, 80–1, 94, 106, 116–17, 188
　succession 53–4, 146, 148, 150–1

and Sultan Abdülhamid II 79, 92, 130, 135
war with Italy 15, 78
Menelik I (son of Solomon and the Queen of Sheba) 29
Mentewwab (empress) 35
Metemma *see* Mätämma
Mikaēl (*ras,* then *negus*) 53–4, 57, 94, 148, 150–2, 228 n.13, 234 n.52
Mikayel the Abyssinian (monk, Jerusalem) 28
Minassian
 company 178
 Hrant (trader) 126, 178, 238 n.31
Missakian Hovhannes 183
Mnatseganian Giragos (Armenian patriarch of Jerusalem) : 26, 220 n.23
Mody J. G. (Indian photographer) 235 n.60
Mohamed Abdhalla (officer) 105
Missions, missionaries 32–3, 37–8, 46, 80–1, 174, 183, 221 n.44, 222 n.71
Mohamed Ali (from Wällo) *see* Mikaēl (*ras,* then *negus*)
Mojo 176
Monfreid Henry de 173, 204–5
Monophysites, monophysitic 23, 83, 183
Moscopoulos (Greek intelligence officer) 211
Muradian Kevork (trader) 178, 238 n.30
Muradian Mihran (trader) 178
Muhettin Pacha (Turkish representative) 18
Murad (Khodja Murad's nephew) 36, 202
Murad (Khodja) 34–6, 38, 202
music
 Armenian revolutionary march 18
 Ethiopian anthem 6, 12–13, 163, 168
 Funeral March (Chopin's) 17–18
 March Täfäri 12, 14, 84, 168
 Marseillaise 13–14, 16, 18
 Military marches 12–15, 156
 national anthems 12–14, 16–17
 Turkish anthem, *Turkish March* 168
Muslim *see* Islam
Mussolini Benito 15, 18, 185, 194, 241 n.42, 242 n.62, 243 n.75

Nalbandian Hagop (musician) 236 n.34
Nalbandian Kevork (musician) 6, 12–14, 66, 84, 156, 159, 163, 167–8, 194, 227 n.93

Nalbandian Nerses (musician) 163, 236 n.35
Nalbandian Piuzant (jeweler) 236 n.34
Nationality *see* Citizenship
New Julfa 34, 39–40
Nicosia 4
Norarevian Yervant 241 n.47

Obock 47, 74–5, 77, 99
Occupied Enemy Territory Administration (OETA) 181, 193
Ogaden 105, 132, 224 n.40
Ohanessian Melidos 241 n.47
Orphanage 155–9
Orphanides (architect) 62
Ottoman Empire 25, 35, 38, 52, 55–6, 59, 79, 86, 96, 99–100, 149, 167, 181, 188, 191
Ottoman subjects 34, 43, 130, 147, 189–92

Paez Pedro 221 n.44
Paghtasarian Avedik (monk, traveler) 221 n.49
Pankhurst Richard 40
Papazian (company) 176
Papazian Alice 242 n.65
Papazian Antranig (interpreter) 181
Papazian Hrant 241 n.36
Papazian Khachig (engineer) 176, 180
Papazian Stepan (architect, designer) 181
Pariset Dante 117–18
Parunagian Missak 241 n.35
Persia *see* Iran, Iranians
Peshdilmaji Ardashes (interpreter) 181, 239 n.50
photography, photographers
 and Armenian community 40, 57, 117, 179–80, 238 n.39
 and Ethiopian grandees 21, 52–4, 56, 60–4, 66, 123–4, 140, 142, 148–51, 192, 211
 and memory 3, 76, 89, 91–2, 103–5, 110–11, 126–7, 135, 137, 144, 152, 163, 167
 in the Ottoman Empire and the Middle East 52
Piazza, 2, 95, 175
Poladian Terenig (bishop) 227 n.100
Poncet Charles Jacques 33, 36, 202

Port Said 159
Portugal, Portuguese 33, 36
Protestants 26, 32, 65, 200
Prutky Remedius 33

Qērelos VI (*abunä*) 15, 227 n.103
Quoram (camp) 194, 245 n.62

railway *see* France, French
Rastafarians 156, 240 n.16
Red Sea 2, 27, 34, 77, 176
Rimbaud Arthur 2, 44, 47, 106, 230 n.44
Robert College 100
Rome 33, 116, 211
Roosevelt Franklin Delano 85
Roosevelt Theodore 116
Russia, Russians 2, 19, 31, 45, 76, 84, 189–92, 196–7, 200–1, 208

Sägälē 152, 228 n.14
Sahak Kharpertsi (archbishop) 24, 27–31, 34, 38
Sahak Mesrop (school) 166
Sahlä Dengel (emperor) 26
Sahlä Sellasē (*negus*) 31–2, 37–8
Sahlä Tsedalu 235 n.65
Saint James (monastery) 28, 157, 161–2
Säla Denga 95, 229 n.12
Sälama (*abunä*) 31–2, 37–8, 222 n.71
Salaydinga *see* Säla Denga
Salimbeni Augusto (Italian envoy) 49–50, 105
Salvadei 19
Sapritchian Dimotheos (*vartabed*) 24–5, 27–31, 34, 38
Sarafian Hagop (mechanic) 245 n.52
Sarkama 194
Sarkis Al-Armanī Al-Habašī 26
Sarkis babur 82, 106–13
Seʼelä Krestos 221 n.44
Sebastia *see* Sivas
Seferian (company) 176–7, 180, 197
Seferian Krikor 238 n.30
Seferian Papken 237 n.45
Segulian Hagop (interpreter) 239 n.49
Sehin (*wäyzäro*) 14, 57
Selim Tabet (company) 176
Semerjibashian
  Avedis 210

family 174
Hovhannes or Johannes (interpreter) 66, 181, 210–2, 227 n.93, 239 n.51, 245 n.62
Vahakn-Aklilu 211
Sennar 33, 37
Sevadjian Avedis (tanner) 178, 238 n.35
Sevadjian Bedros (jeweler) 56
Sèvres (Treaty of) 178, 240 n.29
Shabin Karahissar 174
Shahbazian Aram (photographer) *see* Chahbaz (studio)
Shant (photographer) 238 n.39
Shäwa Rägga 229 n.10, 234 n.52
Shäwa 30–2, 37, 47, 54, 74–6, 94–6, 98–9, 102, 188, 195, 197
shoemakers, shoes 78, 178–9
Shola 135–7
Sidamo 177, 179
Sinoda (*abunä*) 34
Sivas 9, 174
Sivrissarian Agop 185–6, 242 n.51
Smyrna 27, 55, 165, 186
Solingen 77, 99
Somalia, Somalis, Somaliland 19, 74, 76–7, 99, 101–2, 105, 115, 132, 149–50, 179, 196, 242 n.51
Sukiasian Amasia (surveyor) 180
Suakin 220 n.20
Sudan, Sudanese 2, 27, 33, 38, 75–6, 98, 105, 126, 176–8
Suez 2, 200
Surat 36
Surp Hagop (cemetery) *see* Gulēlē
Susenyos (emperor, 1607–1632) 33
Sweden, Swedes, Swedish 46, 49, 183, 188, 210
Swiss 13, 19, 38, 43, 47–8, 86, 95, 106, 114, 133, 189, 200, 231 n.73
Syria, Syrians 2, 37–8, 40–5, 52, 165, 167, 173, 176, 186, 189–90, 195, 225 n.48
Syriacs, Jacobite Church 23, 25–6, 29, 83, 183, 222 n.61

Tablets of the Law 14, 29
Tabriz 52
Tadjoura 74, 77, 96, 99, 123, 128
Täfäri Mäkonnen (*däjazmach, ras, negus*)

and Armenians 1, 32, 53, 55–7, 59, 64, 65–6, 124, 150–2, 155–60, 168–9, 187–8, 204, 227 n.88 and 93
and Church 15, 23, 30, 53, 65
coronation, crown (*negus*) 50, 55, 227 n.93
crown prince and regent (1916–30) 1, 6, 11, 81, 150
and foreign policy 11, 15–21
and the forty orphans (*Arba lejoch*) 156–60, 167, 183, 187, 213
in Harar 218 n.26
in Jerusalem 12, 21, 23, 83, 156–9
and *Lej* Iyasu 146–8, 150–1, 211
lycée 13, 179
and modernization 11–15, 51–3, 124, 188
Täfäri Benti 56
Täfärra Wärq Kidanä Wäld 211
Täklä Giyorgis (emperor, 1868–72) 28, 31, 229 n.9
Täklä Haymanot 146
Tamzara 174
Tarpinian Vache (grocer) 178
Täsämma (*ras*) 234 n.46
Täsämma Eshätē 117
Taytu (empress) 41, 49–52, 55, 96, 107, 112–13, 124, 126, 146, 150, 231 n.61, 234 n.52, 237 n.15
Teheran 52
Terzian Abraham 99, 110–12, 128–9
Terzian Antranig 237 n.13
Terzian Avedis
  childhood 74, 100, 115, 136, 142–3, 237 n.13
  interpreter 87, 180–1
  under Italian occupation 100–1, 245 n.62
  member of Armenian community council 83, 85, 88
  narratives 55, 62, 73–92, 95, 98–103, 105, 107–8, 112–15, 117, 123–5, 128–30, 132–3, 135, 137, 146–7, 151–2, 157, 160, 164–5, 168–9, 180, 183, 204–5, 213–14
  Oriental secretary 85, 100–1, 181
  studies and youth 94, 100, 128–9, 141–3
Terzian Brothers (company) 44, 46, 110, 229 n.19

Terzian Emmanuel (dentist) 237 n.13
Terzian Garabed 141, 182
Terzian Kevork (baker) 75, 94, 101
Terzian Mamas 118, 141
Terzian Mushegh 89, 91, 110–11, 135, 144, 183, 237 n.14, 245 n.65
Terzian Nartuhi 237 n.14
Terzian Ohannes (trader) 46, 110–11, 141, 229 n.19, 237 n.14
Terzian Ovsanna 237 n.13
Terzian Sarkis
  arms smuggling 46, 77–8, 98–9, 106, 125, 168
  citizenship 80, 113, 130–3, 187, 191
  concessionaire 48, 112–16
  counterfeiter of the imperial seal 116–17
  death 118, 141, 182, 191
  in Harar 91, 100–5, 115, 117, 163, 174
  importer 81–2, 125, 106–12
  with Menelik 46, 60–2, 64, 77, 79–80, 100, 105, 112–14, 119, 128–33, 142–3, 187, 227 n.93
  in Ogaden 76, 103–6, 132
  with *Ras* Mäkonnen 46, 118, 169
  Tellik Sarkis 92, 105, 108, 116, 118
  travels abroad 47, 98, 106–7, 116, 125, 127
Terzian Vahram (accountant) 128, 174, 180, 242 n.51
Terzian Vartuhi 122, 136, 174, 182
Terzian Yervant 136, 182, 237 n.13
Terzibashian Avedis 200
Teso Gobäzé (rebel) 27, 31
Tewodros II (emperor, 1855–1868) 20–1, 24–5, 27–8, 30–2, 38, 220 n.20, 222 n.66, 229 n.9
Thovmajian Hovhannes (jeweler, traveler) 35, 220 n.24
Tiflis 37
Tigré (Tegray) 28–30, 32, 37–8, 54, 59, 74–5, 84–5, 92, 94–5, 177, 234 n.37
Tiridates (king of Armenia) 24
Topalian Vahan (priest) 183
Tulumbajian Hayg (grocer) 178, 241 n.36
Tourian Yeghishe (Armenian patriarch of Jerusalem, 1921–9) 23, 156–7, 159–60, 162
Trebizond 117

Turkey 100, 115, 117, 129, 141, 143, 190, 210
  anthem *see* music
  origins of Armenian immigrants 92, 141, 146, 164, 166, 174, 186–7, 209
  refugees from 79–80, 82, 140, 164, 203, 226 n.77
  relations with Ethiopia 188
  Republic of 18, 52, 100
  Young Turk Revolution 78, 193
Turkish, Turks 25, 28, 34–6, 38, 41–2, 46, 48
Tutunji Hovhannes (bishop) 33–5

Ucciali (Treaty of) *see* Wetchalē

Vagharshagian Mardiros 159, 218 n.20, 235 n.7
Vartanian Panos (goldsmith) 55
Vazken I (catholicos) 190
Venice 35, 197, 243 n.74
Vienna 47, 116
Vitalien (doctor) 63
Vorperian Rupen (employee, poet) 177

Wälamo 49
Wäldä Giyorgis (*ras*) 54, 109
Wäldu (*däjazmach*) 38
Wällägga 177
Wällo 53–4, 94, 148, 150, 177, 228 n.13, 234 n.52
Wararanian Hrant (photographer) 238 n.39
Wäräyulu 37, 94
Wärqē Karapet (caravaneer, envoy) 38
Waugh Evelyn 147, 202, 205–7
Washington 47, 116, 132
Webē (*däjazmach*) 32, 37–8
Webē Atnaf Sägäd (*ras*) 125
Wechalē (Treaty of) 20, 47, 50, 76, 98, 123, 188, 219 n.43

Ya'eqob (emperor) 221 n.44

Yamalian Avedis (cook, gardener) 51
Yazedjian (family) 150–2, 174
Yazedjian Anna *see* Anna Marcerou
Yazedjian Araxi (carpet maker) 52, 56–7, 125–6, 135, 142, 150, 162–3
Yazedjian Levon (painter, photographer) 53–4, 56–7, 81, 126, 130, 140, 142, 148, 150–4, 164, 169, 181, 227 n.93, 235 n.68
Yazedjian Mardiros (lawyer) 235 n.68
Yazedjian Paylag (senior civil servant) 56, 81, 102–3, 105, 117, 181, 235 n.66
Yazedjian Robert (carpet maker) 56
Yazedjian Stepan (employee) 174, 181
Ydlibi Hasib 225 n.48
Yemen, Yemenis 36, 196, 210
Yerzingatsian (family) 174
Yerzingatsian (company) 180
Yirga Aläm 177, 179
Yohannes I (emperor, 1667–82) 33–4, 36
Yohannes IV (emperor, 1872–1889) 30, 32, 38, 74–6, 91–2, 94–6, 98, 126, 129, 148, 229 n.9
Yosēf Galan *see* Galan (Joseph de)
Yosēf Negusē 132
Youkoumian Krikor 202, 244 n.29
Yusufian Boghos 55

Zä Dengel (emperor) 221 n.44
Zamanian Armenag 174
Zamanian Menagar 174
Zamanian Satenig 237 n.14
Zaphiro or Zaphiropoulos Photios (interpreter) 239 n.51
Zäwditu (empress, 1916–30) 14–5, 20–1, 23, 50, 53–6, 65–7, 81, 125–6, 146–8, 150–1, 156, 159–60, 168, 228 n.16
Zäwdu 201
Zeila 46–7, 75–6, 91, 105–6, 178
Zeqwala 95
Zervos Yakobos (doctor, Greek consul) 49
Zeytun 187

www.ingramcontent.com/pod-product-compliance
Lightning Source LLC
Chambersburg PA
CBHW071809300426
44116CB00009B/1249